利尻島
り しり とう

オホーツク海
かい

北海道
ほっかい どう

国後島
くなしりとう

択捉島
えとろふとう。

札幌
さっぽろ

北海道
ほっかい どう

歯舞諸島
はぼまいしょとう

色丹島
しこたんとう

津軽海峡
つ がる かいきょう

青森
あおもり

青森
あおもり

秋田
あき た

盛岡
もり おか

秋田
あき た

岩手
いわ て

東北
とうほく

山形
やまがた

宮城
みや ぎ

山形
やまがた

仙台
せん だい

福島
ふくしま

福島
ふくしま

栃木
とち ぎ

都宮
つのみや

茨城
いばらき

水戸
と

関東
かんとう

千葉
ば

太平洋
たい へい よう

0　40　80　120　160　200km

JAPANESE FOR BUSY PEOPLE

II

JAPANESE FOR BUSY PEOPLE

Revised Edition

BUSY PEOPLE

II

Association for Japanese-Language Teaching

KODANSHA INTERNATIONAL
Tokyo • New York • London

This is the revised edition of Part I of *Japanese for Busy People II*, published in 1990.

Distributed in the United States by Kodansha America, Inc., 114 Fifth Avenue, New York, N.Y. 10011, and in the United Kingdom and continental Europe by Kodansha Europe Ltd., 95 Aldwych, London WC2B 4JF.

CONTENTS

Introduction to the Revised Edition — 7

Introducing the Characters — 12

Lesson 1: Rush Hour — 17

Lesson 2: Lost and Found — 25

Lesson 3: The Health Club — 35

Lesson 4: A Business Trip — 45

Lesson 5: A New Word Processor — 53

Lesson 6: A Pale Face — 64

Lesson 7: Mr. Johnson's Arrival — 73

Lesson 8: The O-Bon Festival — 83

Lesson 9: Prep School — 93

Lesson 10: Letter from Kyushu — 102

Lesson 11: Job Interview — 107

Lesson 12: Hotel Reservations — 116

Lesson 13: A Gift of Chocolate — 127

Lesson 14: The Referee's Role — 137

Lesson 15: A Forgotten Umbrella — 148

Lesson 16: The New Showroom Design — 157

Lesson 17: Brown's Diary — 167

Lesson 18: Birthday Flowers — 177

Lesson 19: The Public Library — 186

Lesson 20: Cherry Blossoms — 195

Appendices   201

    A. Plain Forms and Connective Patterns   201

    B. Verb Conjugations   202

    C. Grammatical Patterns and Common Constructions   205

Japanese–English Glossary   207

English–Japanese Glossary   216

Index   222

Supplement   225

    Quiz Answers   227

    Romanized Text   231

    Full Text with Kanji   271

INTRODUCTION TO THE REVISED EDITION

This text carries on from where *Japanese for Busy People I* leaves off, and, as in the previous work, the main focus is on having adult students acquire a working knowledge of everyday spoken Japanese. This revised edition contains some fundamental changes to the earlier Book II published in 1990, which has been expanded and divided into this book and Book III. This has allowed a larger typeface to be used, making it easier to read, and various other modifications have been introduced to render the transition from Book I smoother, as well as to make new grammatical elements easier to understand and to present more natural practice dialogues and exercises. In addition, the *kanji*, or Sino-Japanese characters, relevant to each lesson are introduced at the end of that lesson, rather than at the end of the book as in the earlier Book II. Aside from minor changes, the format remains the same as in Book I. The twenty lessons in this volume require approximately 120 hours of classroom time.

A key factor in the development of these texts has been a thorough evaluation of existing teaching materials and a reassessment of the ability and objectives of students. It has generally been assumed that businessmen, diplomats, technicians or scholars for whom Japanese is a second language can only use it in their work after having reached an advanced level. However, both the spoken and written languages encountered in science or business, being specialized and adapted to a particular field, are more explicit than the language found in literature or even informal conversation. Moreover, having professional knowledge of a subject area contributes to comprehension, which is understandably more difficult if one is on unfamiliar ground. Consequently, it is possible for motivated learners to go on to specialized programs of their choice after finishing the basic level—the level reached at the end of Book III—by expanding their vocabulary with *kanji* and *kanji* compounds dealing with their particular field.

As in Book I, the vocabulary and situations introduce the daily language and life of adult Japanese. Some lessons deal with aspects of business life, others with practical daily occurrences such as losing things or making hotel reservations, or introduce some facets of Japanese culture, with comments by both Japanese and foreigners. These will interest not only business people but students who would like to visit or live in Japan but have no chance to. Our objective is to stimulate adult students' interest in Japan.

Compared with Book I, where the intent is survival, the conversations in Book II are more natural and include abbreviated expressions and suitable responses. Thus Book II is a stepping stone to Book III, which presents further speech levels and styles. As a whole, the *Japanese for Busy People* series emphasizes Japanese as a means of communication when explaining, requesting, persuading or making assertions to other people. This is significantly different from many other beginner textbooks, which concentrate on teaching the student as many *kanji* as possible in preparation for examinations.

To the Reader

This text presupposes familiarity with the grammar and vocabulary in Book I; any student who has difficulty with the first lessons in this book should review that text before proceeding to this more advanced material.

Mastery of *hiragana* and *katakana* was recommended in the introduction to Book I, since reliance on romanized Japanese tends to have a negative effect on pronunciation. Another reason for learning the Japanese writing systems as early as possible is that romanized Japanese has only very limited applications, the only publications printed in this script being basic texts for Japanese as a second language.

In Book II, romanized Japanese only appears in the vocabularies and the appendices. With the exceptions of the Reading Reviews in Lesson 10 and Lesson 20, each lesson contains the following elements.

Opening Dialogues

Whether these are practical in content, such as reserving hotel rooms, or are discussions of specific topics, they are kept as natural as possible. It is extremely important to learn expressions in context, so listen to the tapes repeatedly to comprehend the contextual situation fully. Some unusual terms, such as *sakura zensen* or *dohyō*, or expressions customarily used by shop assistants, for example, need not be memorized, but they should be familiar enough to be recognized when they occur. A new feature of this volume is the gradual introduction of *kanji*. On its first occurrence in a lesson, a kanji is accompanied by *furigana* (the contextual reading of the character in *hiragana*, placed below the *kanji*).

The English Translations

Instead of being word-for-word translations, these are the equivalent in natural English. Sometimes a literal translation is also included for the sake of understanding the nuances of the Japanese.

Vocabularies

The vocabulary lists have been compiled in a similar way, with the contextual meanings of words given first, and if the literal meaning is different, that is given, too. When a term has other common additional meanings, these are also given as far as possible. This should help the student to avoid forming the habit of thinking a word is always translated into English in exactly the same way, whereas in fact a great many words require a certain amount of flexibility.

Grammar and Lesson Objectives

In this section, new sentence patterns and elements in the lesson are explained. This is not always done comprehensively at one time, however, since the same constructions may appear both at earlier and advanced levels, so the grammatical explanations may be to some extent repeated. When appropriate, explanations include related constructions or patterns.

Although English grammar terms are employed in the explanations of Japanese grammar, these should be regarded as expedients only, since Japanese and English belong to quite different language families and the terms are not exactly parallel in both languages. For example, words indicating conditions, size, or mood are termed adjectives in English and are not conjugated, whereas in Japanese they are. Some books call these adjectivals or use various other neologisms, but we have avoided such unfamiliar terms.

Key Sentences

The most important sentence patterns introduced in the Opening Dialogue are shown here in as simple form as possible. All the basic sentence patterns usually learned in primary courses are included in the Key Sentences presented in these three volumes.

Exercises

These provide oral practice in the grammar and expressions introduced in the lesson, and they are arranged in order from simple to more complicated patterns. Many of the exercises take the form of dialogues that have practical applications, and systematic practice in these will ensure fluency.

Short Dialogues

Since it is not easy to memorize the Opening Dialogues in their entirety, the Short Dialogues offer a simpler alternative, together with variations to make them applicable in a variety of situations. They consist of the following:
1. Idiomatic expressions with various functions such as making requests, expressing gratitude, excusing oneself or paying compliments, and the appropriate responses.
2. Related expressions that are useful, for example, in starting conversations or in maintaining smooth personal relationships.
3. Some informal expressions included for recognition purposes.

Quizzes

These may be used for study either in class or at home, and they provide additional oral practice. To ensure accurate understanding, it is advisable that the answers also be written down.

The Supplement with the Texts Written Vertically

Here all the Opening Dialogues are presented in the vertical form that is the standard Japanese written style. Students already able to read them should treat them as their main text, or a least use them for reference. Other students will find this section valuable both for studying *kanji* and for getting used to the conventions of Japanese writing. After a lesson has been studied, the text in the Supplement can be compared with the Opening Dialogue or reading passage.

The Kanji in Books II and III

Modern Japanese is written primarily with three types of characters: *kanji*, *hiragana* and *katakana*. Arabic numerals and the English alphabet (*rōmaji*) are also used when needed. Japanese is typically written as a mixture of *kanji* and *hiragana*, although the number of words written in *katakana* is increasing. *Katakana* is used for words borrowed from other languages, the names of foreign people and places, the names of plants and animals, and so on.

The Opening Dialogues in Book I are written only in *hiragana*. A few *kanji* are introduced in an appendix to Book I, but from Lesson I of Book II they are introduced systematically. While *hiragana* is a phonemic writing system in that each symbol represents a specific sound, *kanji* are ideographic, that is, the characters represent ideas. Each one has its own meaning, and a glance at the *kanji* in a printed text will often reveal the content of the piece. Learning *kanji* is an essential element in learning the Japanese language.

In total, there are over 50,000 *kanji*, but the number used in daily life is between about 2,500 and 3,000. Many newspapers, magazines and textbooks restrict themselves to the 1,945 *kanji* (called *jōyō kanji*) designated by the Japanese government in 1981 for writing Japanese. According to a study conducted by the National Language Research Institute, 500 of these *jōyō kanji* account for about 80 percent of the *kanji* that appear in contemporary newspapers, magazines, and suchlike. A mixture of *kanji* and *kana* is used in all the Opening Dialogues in this textbook, beginning with Lesson 1, and the *kanji* were chosen from those the above-mentioned study found occur most frequently.

In this text, the student's load has been lightened by introducing only a round six new *kanji* per lesson. In the Opening Dialogues, *furigana* (the readings in the phonetic *hiragana*) are appended to all new *kanji* that appear for the first time, to all *kanji* with new readings, and to all *kanji* that have already been studied. When a *kanji* appears later in the same lesson, the *furigana* are omitted. When a *kanji* reappears in a later lesson, it is coupled with the *furigana* to remind the student how to read it. In text running horizontally, *furigana* is normally printed above the character. However, in this textbook we have put the *furigana* below the *kanji* so that the student can cover them with a piece of paper as he/she tries to learn the readings.

Japanese *kanji* have two types of readings: the *on* and the *kun*. *On* readings are the Japanese versions of the Chinese pronunciations that were introduced into Japan from China together with the characters themselves. The original Chinese pronunciations varied depending on the era and the region they originated from, so some *kanji* have two or three *on* readings. In most cases, though, only one *on* reading is used. *Kun* readings are Japanese words with meanings similar or identical to those of their associated *kanji*. Some *kanji* have several *kun* readings, while others have none. There are also a few *kanji* called *kokuji* that were created in Japan, and some of these lack *on* readings. In ordinary *kanji* dictionaries, when *furigana* are attached to *kanji*, the *on* readings are generally written in *katakana* and the *kun* readings in *hiragana*. Combinations of *kanji*, called *jukugo*, usually consist of only *on* readings or only *kun* readings. Some *jukugo*, however, include mixtures of *on* and *kun* readings.

The new *kanji* that appear at the end of each lesson are presented in the following form:

1. 電話

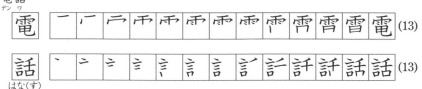

Both 電, *den*, and 話, *wa*, are the *on* readings, so the *furigana* are written in *katakana* as デンワ. Since 電 has no *kun* reading, no *furigana* are given next to the boxes showing the stroke order. The *kanji* 話 also has the *kun* reading *hanasu*, which is given under the *kanji* in *hiragana*. Since *hanasu* is a verb, the verbal suffix appears in parentheses.

In Book II, the complete stroke order for every *kanji* is shown progressively in the boxes, with the total number of strokes appearing in parentheses to the right. In Book III, the stroke order is often omitted for *kanji* with components that have already been studied. The stroke order is important both for writing and in order to know the number of strokes in a *kanji*. When looking up a word in a dictionary, even if you don't know the reading or the meaning of a *kanji*, you can find it in the index listing characters by the number of strokes.

When a *kanji* appears in the Opening Dialogue with a reading that is different from that in a previous lesson, the entry for readings shows both the previous and new readings. The *kanji* given "for recognition" are those frequently encountered in proper names and suchlike, and the student need not remember how to write them, only to read them. The *kanji* given in "related *kanji*" are important ones that do not appear in the Opening Dialogue but are related to those that do. For example, if only 東, "east," 西, "west," and 南, "south," appear in the Opening Dialogue, 北, "north," is included in this section. Similarly, when only one *kanji* of a pair with opposite meanings appears in the Opening Dialogue, then its counterpart is shown, with a double arrow (↔). The English meanings of all "related *kanji*" are given.

As a reference for the student, a list of the *kanji* used in this series is given in the order of their appearance on the endpapers of Book II and Book III. The Supplement includes the texts of the Opening Dialogues written vertically, and here *kanji* are used whenever they would normally appear, without any *furigana*. All the *kanji* used in this textbook are included in the *jōyō kanji* list.

ACKNOWLEDGMENTS

Four AJALT teachers have written this textbook. They are Ms. Miyako Iwami, Ms. Shigeko Miyazaki, Ms. Masako Nagai and Ms. Kimiko Yamamato. They were assisted by two other teachers, Ms. Kumiko Endo and Ms. Chikako Ogura.

For background information, many sources were consulted. The authors would particularly like to thank the Japan Sumo Association for making it possible to write Lesson 14, and the Meteorological Agency for material included in Lesson 20. They also wish to express their appreciation to the editors at Kodansha International for assistance with translating and rewriting, as well as the usual editorial tasks.

ACKNOWLEDGMENTS FOR THE REVISED EDITION

We would like to express our gratitude to the following people for preparing the new editions of Book II and Book III: Ms. Miyako Iwami, Ms. Shigeko Miyazaki, Ms. Masako Nagai and Ms. Kimiko Yamamato. They were assisted by Ms. Mikiko Ochiai.

ABBREVIATIONS

aff.	affirmative	*ex.*	example
neg.	negative	-**i** adj.	-**i** adjective
Aa:	answer, affirmative	-**na** adj.	-**na** adjective
An:	answer, negative		

† Indicates a word or expression that is not found in contemporary Japanese.

INTRODUCING THE CHARACTERS

スミス（43さい）
スミスふじん（41さい）
　　スミスさんは　ABCの　べんごしです。3ねんまえに　おくさんと
にほんに　きました。ふたりは　でんとうてきな　にほんの
ぶんかに　きょうみが　あります。

ブラウン（35さい）
ブラウンふじん（36さい）
　　ブラウンさんは　2ねんまえに　にほんに　きました。ブラウンさ
んも　ABCの　べんごしです。ブラウンふじんは　にほんのれきし
に　きょうみが　あります。ブラウンさんは　うきよえが　すき
です。ブラウンさんは　ときどき　にほんごで　てがみを　かき
ます。

はやし（45さい）
はやしふじん（38さい）
　　はやしさんは　ABCの　ぶちょうです。ときどき　ジョギングを
します。たまに　やまに　のぼります。はやしふじんは　りょう
りが　じょうずです。そして、かんきょうもんだいに　ねっしん
です。

かとう（37さい）
かとうふじん（36さい）
　　かとうさんは　ABCの　かちょうです。しごとは　とても　いそが
しいです。かとうさんは　まえに　ほっかいどうに　すんでいま
した。

チャン（おとこ　28さい）
　　チャンさんも　ABCに　つとめています。せんげつ　ホンコンしし
ゃから　きました。チャンさんは　えいごと　ちゅうごくごが
できます。おんがくが　すきです。

すずき（25さい）
すずきふじん（25さい）
　　すずきさんも　ABCの　しゃいんです。2ねんまえに　けっこんし
ました。すずきさんは　おもしろい　ひとですが、ときどき
しっぱいします。

ジョンソン（おとこ　26さい）
　　ジョンソンさんは　ABCの　ロンドンじむしょに　つとめていまし
た。ことし　とうきょうほんしゃに　てんきんしました。ジョン
ソンさんは　あかるい　ひとです。とうきょうの　せいかつを
たのしんでいます。

なかむら（おんな　26さい）
　　なかむらさんは　おととし　だいがくを　そつぎょうして、しょ
うしゃに　つとめていました。しかし、せんもんの　しごとが
できませんでしたから　やめました。そして　ABCに　はいりまし
た。

ほかに、わたなべさん（おんな）、きむらさん（おとこ）、さとうさん
（おとこ）などが　ABCで　はたらいています。

たなか（51さい）
たなかふじん（47さい）
　　たなかさんは　とうきょうでんきの　ぶちょうです。とうきょう
でんきは　ABCの　とりひきさきです。たなかさんの　かぞくは
スミスさんや　ブラウンさんの　かぞくと　とても　したしいです。

たなか　けいこ（おんな　18さい）
　　けいこさんは　たなかさんの　むすめです。ことし　こうこうを
そつぎょうしました。けいこさんと　ジョンソンさんは　ともだ
ちです。

だいすけ（おとこ　19さい）
　　だいすけさんは　チャンさんの　ともだちです。だいがくせいで
す。チャンさんの　うちの　ちかくに　すんでいます。

ほかに、スミスふじんの　ともだちの　リンダさん（おんな）や　Mせ
っけいじむしょの　やまかわさん（おとこ）も　とうじょうします。

Mr. Smith (43 years old)
Mrs. Smith (41 years old)
　　Mr. Smith is a lawyer at ABC. He came to Japan with his wife three years ago.
They are both interested in traditional Japanese culture.

Mr. Brown (35 years old)
Mrs. Brown (36 years old)
　　The Browns came to Japan two years ago. Mr. Brown is also a lawyer at ABC.
Mrs. Brown is interested in the history of Japan. Mr. Brown likes Japanese *ukiyo-e* woodblock prints. He sometimes writes letters in Japanese.

Mr. Hayashi (45 years old)
Mrs. Hayashi (38 years old)

Mr. Hayashi is a division chief at ABC. He sometimes goes jogging. Occasionally he goes mountain climbing. Mrs. Hayashi is good at cooking. She is concerned with environmental issues.

Mr. Katō (37 years old)
Mrs. Katō (36 years old)

Mr. Katō is a section chief at ABC. He is very busy at work. He used to live in Hokkaido.

Mr. Chang (28 years old)

Mr. Chang also works for ABC. He came to Japan last month from the Hong Kong branch office. He can speak English and Chinese. He likes music.

Mr. Suzuki (25 years old)
Mrs. Suzuki (25 years old)

Mr. Suzuki is also an employee of ABC. He got married two years ago. He often makes jokes, but sometimes makes mistakes in his work.

Mr. Johnson (26 years old)

Mr. Johnson used to work at the London office of ABC. He was transferred to the Tokyo head office this year. He is a cheerful person. He's enjoying life in Tokyo.

Ms. Nakamura (26 years old)

Ms. Nakamura graduated from university the year before last and worked for a trading company. However, she left that company because her work was not related to her specialty. Then she joined ABC.

Ms. Watanabe, Mr. Kimura and Mr. Satō are other staff members of ABC.

Mr. Tanaka (51 years old)
Mrs. Tanaka (47 years old)

Mr. Tanaka is a division chief at Tokyo Electric. Tokyo Electric is a client of ABC. The Tanakas are good friends of the Smiths and the Browns.

Keiko Tanaka (18 years old)

Keiko is the daughter of Mr. and Mrs. Tanaka. She graduated from high school this year. Keiko is a friend of Mr. Johnson.

Daisuke (19 years old)

Daisuke is a friend of Mr. Chang. He is a university student. He lives near Mr. Chang.

Other characters appearing in this book are Linda, who is a friend of Mrs. Smith, and Mr. Yamakawa of the M Design Office.

ふじん	**fujin**	Mrs., woman
まえに	**mae ni**	before
でんとうてき（な）	**dentōteki(na)**	traditional
～に きょうみが あります	**ni kyōmi ga arimasu**	be interested in
うきよえ	**ukiyo-e**	woodblock prints, "floating-world pictures"
ぶちょう	**buchō**	division chief, department head
たまに	**tama ni**	occasionally
のぼります	**noborimasu**	climb
かんきょう	**kankyō**	environment
もんだい	**mondai**	problem, issue
ねっしん（な）	**nesshin(na)**	keen, devoted, enthusiastic
かちょう	**kachō**	section chief
しゃいん	**shain**	company employee
しっぱいします	**shippai shimasu**	fail, make a mistake
ほんしゃ	**honsha**	head office
てんきんします	**tenkin shimasu**	transfer, be transferred
せいかつ	**seikatsu**	life, living
たのしみます	**tanoshimimasu**	enjoy
だいがく	**daigaku**	university
そつぎょうします	**sotsugyō shimasu**	graduate
しょうしゃ	**shōsha**	trading company
しかし	**shikashi**	however, but
せんもん	**semmon**	specialty
やめます	**yamemasu**	leave, quit
ほかに	**hoka ni**	besides, other
はたらきます	**hatarakimasu**	work
とりひきさき	**torihikisaki**	client, business contact
したしい	**shitashii**	friendly with, close
こうこう	**kōkō**	high school
だいがくせい	**daigakusei**	university student
とうじょうします	**tōjō shimasu**	appear

LESSON **1** RUSH HOUR

Mr. Chang tells Mr. Smith about taking a rush hour train for the first time.

チャン：けさ　はじめて　でんしゃで　会社に　来ました。とて
　　　　も　こんでいました。すごかったですよ。

スミス：でも　でんしゃの　ほうが　くるまより　はやいですよ。
　　　　みちが　こんでいますから。

チャン：スミスさんは　まいにち　なんで　会社に　来ますか。

スミス：わたしは　行きも　かえりも　ちかてつです。とうきょ
　　　　うの　こうつうきかんの　中で　ちかてつが　いちばん
　　　　べんりですよ。

チャン：ちかてつは　あさも　ゆうがたも　こんでいますか。

スミス：ええ。でも　あさの　ほうが　ゆうがたより　こんでい
　　　　ます。
　　　　あさの　8時はんごろが　ピークですから、わたしは
　　　　まいあさ　7時に　うちを　でます。

チャン：その　じかんは　すいていますか。

スミス：ええ、7時ごろは　8時ごろより　すいています。わたし
　　　　は　まいあさ　ちかてつの　中で　日本語を　べんきょ
　　　　うしています。

チャン：そうですか。

Chang: This morning I came to work by train for the first time. It was awfully crowded. It was terrible.

Smith: Trains are faster than cars, though. Because the roads are crowded.

Chang: How do you come to the office every day?

Smith: I come and go back by subway. The subway is the most convenient of all transportation systems in Tokyo.

Chang: Is the subway crowded mornings and evenings?

Smith: Yes. But mornings are more crowded than evenings. Around 8:30 (A.M.) is the peak of the rush hour, so every morning I leave home at seven.

Chang: Is it less crowded at that time?

Smith: Oh, yes. Around 7 o'clock is less crowded than around 8 o'clock. I study Japanese on the subway every morning.

Chang: Really?

Vocabulary

チャン	**Chan**	Chang
けさ	**kesa**	this morning
はじめて	**hajimete**	for the first time
すごい	**sugoi**	terrible, wonderful
でも	**demo**	though
～の　ほうが	**no hō ga**	= -er/more/less
ほう	**hō**	more (*lit.* "side")
～より	**yori**	than
はやい	**hayai**	fast
みち	**michi**	road, street, way
いき	**iki**	going
かえり	**kaeri**	coming back, returning
～も～も	**mo . . . mo**	both . . . and
こうつう	**kōtsū**	transportation
きかん	**kikan**	system
～の　なかで	**no naka de**	of all, among
いちばん	**ichiban**	most, number one
ピーク	**pīku**	peak
その　じかん	**sono jikan**	that time
すいています	**suite imasu**	be empty
すきます（すく）	**sukimasu (suku)**	be/become empty/uncrowded
べんきょうしています	**benkyō shite imasu**	study/am studying
べんきょうします	**benkyō shimasu**	study
（べんきょうする）	**(benkyō suru)**	

GRAMMAR & LESSON OBJECTIVES

• Comparisons

. . . no hō ga . . . yori

Densha no hō ga kuruma yori hayai desu. The word order can be reversed:
Kuruma yori densha no hō ga hayai desu.

Things that are superior (or more . . .) precede **no hō ga**, and inferior things are followed by **yori**.

To compare two things the question pattern is: . . . **to** . . . **to dochira/dotchi ga** . . . **desu/-masu ka.**

ex. **Yokohama to Tōkyō to dochira ga ōkii desu ka.** "Which is bigger, Yokohama or Tokyo?"

The response, "Tokyo is bigger than Yokohama," can be as follows:

Tōkyō no hō ga Yokohama yori ōkii desu. Or simply, **Tōkyō no hō ga ōkii desu.**

Tōkyō wa Yokohama yori ōkii desu is a statement with Tokyo as the topic and has the same meaning. The dialogue sentence **7-ji goro wa 8-ji goro yori suite imasu** is of this type.

. . . no naka de . . . ichiban

Tōkyō no kōtsū kikan no naka de chikatetsu ga ichiban benri desu.

Ichiban, "number one," "the first," before adjectives expresses the superlative degree of comparison—**ichiban suki,** "most likeable," "best liked," **ichiban kirei,** "prettiest," and so on.

Note how the subject marker **ga** discriminates the subject exclusively from other possibilities. The example above implies that neither taxis nor buses nor trains but subways are the most convenient.

ex. 1. **Nihon no toshi no naka de Tōkyō ga ichiban ōkii desu.** "Among Japanese cities, Tokyo is the biggest."
2. **Kudamono no naka de ringo ga ichiban suki desu.** "Of all fruits, (I) like apples best."

To compare three or more things, the question pattern is: . . . **no naka de nani/ dore/dare/itsu/doko ga ichiban . . . desu/-masu ka.**

ex. **Nihon no toshi no naka de doko ga ichiban ōkii desu ka.** "Which among Japanese cities is the biggest?"

NOTES

1. **Watashi wa iki mo kaeri mo chikatetsu desu.**

   Chikatetsu wa asa mo yūgata mo konde imasu.

   Mo, repeated to mean "both . . . and . . . ," is also used in negative sentences to express "neither . . . nor . . ." Words like **iki** and **kaeri** (the -**masu** stems of the verbs **iki-masu** and **kaerimasu**) are at times employed in a way similar to English gerunds (here *coming* and *going back*).

2. **sono jikan**

   Chang is referring to Smith's preceding sentence, "I leave home at seven." **Ko-, so-, a-, do-** words are not limited to things immediately at hand. They may, like *this* and *that*, refer to intangibles, abstractions or previous phrases or statements. (See Book I, Appendix F.)

3. **Nihon-go o benkyō shite imasu**

   Both **benkyō o shimasu** and **benkyō shimasu** are correct, but when, as here, there is a direct object followed by **o**, **benkyō shimasu** is the inevitable choice. Similar phrases are:

   ex. **Denwa (o) shimasu.** "I'll telephone."
   Sōdan (o) shimasu. "I'll consult (her)."

PRACTICE

KEY SENTENCES

1. とうきょうと　おおさかと　どちらが　おおきいですか。
   とうきょうの　ほうが　［おおさかより］　おおきいです。
2. ［わたしは］　スポーツの　なかで　テニスが　いちばん　すき
   です。
3. とうきょうは　おおさかより　おおきいです。

1. Which is bigger, Tokyo or Osaka?
   Tokyo is bigger (than Osaka).
2. I like tennis best of all sports.
3. Tokyo is bigger than Osaka.

Vocabulary

〜と〜と	**to . . . to**	(particle for comparisons)
どちら	**dochira**	which
スポーツ	**supōtsu**	sports

EXERCISES

I　Make dialogues by changing the underlined parts as in the examples given.

A. *ex.* **Q:** <u>とりにく</u>と　<u>ぎゅうにく</u>と　どちら/どっち　が　<u>やすい</u>
   ですか。

   A: <u>とりにく</u>の　ほうが　<u>やすいです</u>。

   1. ファックス、てがみ、べんりです
   2. あさ、ゆうがた、こんでいます
   3. かとうさん、すずきさん、たくさん　（お）さけを
      のみます

B. *ex.* **Q:** のみものは　<u>コーヒー</u>と　<u>こうちゃ</u>と　どちら/どっち
   が　いいですか。

   A: <u>コーヒー</u>の　ほうが　いいです。

   1. りょうり、てんぷら、しゃぶしゃぶ
   2. じかん、ごぜん、ごご
   3. デザート、アイスクリーム、くだもの
   4. パーティー、きんようび、どようび

C. *ex.* **Q:** スポーツの　なかで　なにが　いちばん　すきですか。

A: テニスが　いちばん　すきです。

1. ししゃ、どこ、おおきいです、ニューヨーク
2. この　みっつの　え、どれ、すき、まんなかの　え
3. いちにち、いつ、こんでいます、あさ　8じごろ
4. かいしゃ、だれ、よく　はたらきます、しゃちょう

II　Practice the following pattern by changing the underlined parts as in the example given.

ex. ちきゅうは　つきより　おおきいです。

1. ひこうき、しんかんせん、はやいです
2. アメリカ、にほん、ひろいです
3. さっぽろ、とうきょう、きたに　あります
4. チャンさん、ジョンソンさん、よく　べんきょうします

| Vocabulary |

どっち	dotchi	which
ファックス	fakkusu	facsimile
てんぷら	tempura	tempura
ニューヨーク	Nyū Yōku	New York
まんなか	mannaka	middle
いちにち	ichinichi	(in) a day
よく	yoku	much, a great deal
はたらきます（はたらく）	hatarakimasu (hataraku)	work
しゃちょう	shachō	president of a company
ちきゅう	chikyū	earth, globe
つき	tsuki	moon
ひろい	hiroi	spacious, wide
さっぽろ	Sapporo	Sapporo (city)
きた	kita	north
ジョンソン	Jonson	Johnson

SHORT DIALOGUE

A: コーヒーと　こうちゃと　どちらが　すきですか。

B: どちらも　すきです。

A: Which do you like more, coffee or tea?
B: I like both.

どちらも　　　　　　　　　　　**dochira mo**　　　　both

QUIZ

I　Read this lesson's Opening Dialogue and answer the following questions.

1. ちかてつは　あさと　ゆうがたと　どちらが　こんでいますか。
2. どうして　でんしゃの　ほうが　くるまより　はやいですか。
3. スミスさんは　まいあさ　なんじに　うちを　でて、なんで　かいしゃに　いきますか。
4. ちかてつは　あさの　なんじごろが　いちばん　こんでいますか。
5. スミスさんは　ちかてつの　なかで　にほんごを　べんきょうしていますか。

II　Put the appropriate particles or inflections in the parentheses.

1. しんかんせんは　くるま（　　　）はやいです。
2. けさ　7じ（　　　）うち（　　　）でて、ちかてつ（　　　）かいしゃ（　　　）きました。
3. でんしゃは　あさも　ゆうがた（　　　）こんでいます。
4. こちらの　ほう（　　　）しずかですから、ここ（　　　）はなしを　しましょう。
5. かいしゃ（　　　）なか（　　　）だれが　いちばん　よく　はたらきますか。

III　Complete the questions so that they fit the answers.

1. ちかてつと　バスと（　　　）が　べんりですか。
   ちかてつの　ほうが　べんりです。
2. ちかてつは（　　　）が　いちばん　こんでいますか。
   あさが　いちばん　こんでいます。
3. （　　　）が　いちばん　テニスが　じょうずですか。
   リンダさんが　いちばん　じょうずです。
4. くだものの　なかで（　　　）が　いちばん　すきですか。
   みかんが　いちばん　すきです。
5. のみものは　コーヒーと　こうちゃと　（　　　）が　いいですか。
   コーヒーを　おねがいします。

IV Complete the sentences with the appropriate form of the verbs indicated.

1. その　レストランは（　　　）いますか。（すきます）
2. くるまで（　　　）ないでください。（きます）
3. ちちは　いま　ニューヨークで（　　　）います。（はたらき
ます）
4. みちが（　　　）いますから、タクシーを（　　　）、（　　　）
ましょう。（こみます、おります、あるきます）
5. この　くるまを（　　　）も　いいですか。（つかいます）
わたしが（　　　）ますから、（　　　）ないでください。
（つかいます、つかいます）

V Answer the following questions.

1. あなたは　スポーツの　なかで　なにが　いちばん　すきで
すか。
2. ごかぞくの　なかで　どなたが　いちばん　よく　はたらき
ますか。
3. すしと　すきやきと　どちらが　すきですか。
4. あなたの　まちの　こうつうきかんの　なかで　なにが
いちばん　べんりですか。

NEW KANJI

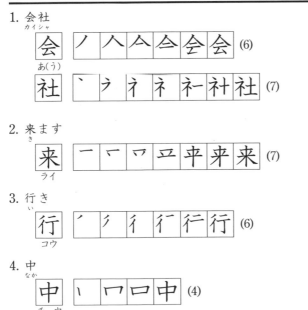

1. 会社
カイシャ
会｜ノ｜ハ｜人｜今｜会｜会｜(6)
あ(う)
社｜ヽ｜ラ｜ネ｜ネ｜ネ｜礻｜社｜(7)

2. 来ます
き
来｜一｜ﾷ｜ｦ｜ﾖ｜平｜来｜来｜(7)
ライ

3. 行き
い
行｜ノ｜ﾉ｜彳｜行｜行｜行｜(6)
コウ

4. 中
なか
中｜ﾄ｜冂｜口｜中｜(4)
チュウ

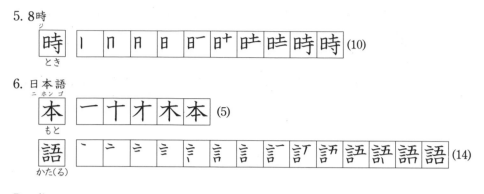

5. 8時

時 _{とき} ／ 冂 日 日 旷 旷 旷 旷 時 時 (10)

6. 日本語

本 _{もと} 一 十 才 木 本 (5)

語 _{かた(る)} 丶 亠 亠 言 言 言 言 訂 訂 語 語 語 語 語 (14)

Readings:

日：　日よう日，日本語

LESSON 2 LOST AND FOUND

Mr. Chang realizes he left something on the train and tells a station employee about it.

チャン ： すみません。

えきいん ： はい、なんでしょうか。

チャン ： わすれものを しました。

えきいん ： どの 電車ですか。

チャン ： 20分ぐらい 前の 電車で、うしろから 二ばんめの しゃりょうです。

えきいん ： なにを わすれましたか。

チャン ： くろくて 大きい かみの ふくろです。

えきいん ： なかみは なんですか。くわしく せつめいしてください。

チャン ： マフラーと セーターです。マフラーは ウールで、くろと しろの しまの もようです。セーターは あかくて、むねに うまの もようが あります。

えきいん ： いま 東京駅に 電話を かけて ききますから、ちょっと まってください。

チャン ： すみません。

After calling Tokyo Station, the man comes back to Mr. Chang.

えきいん ： ありました。東京駅の じむしつに とどいています から、きょうじゅうに とりに 行ってください。

Chang: Excuse me.
Station
Employee: Yes. May I help you?
Chang: I forgot something (in the train).
Employee: Which train (was it)?
Chang: It was the train (which left) about twenty minutes ago, second car from the back.
Employee: What did you forget?
Chang: It's a big black paper bag.
Employee: What're the contents? Please describe (them) in detail.
Chang: (There's) a scarf and a sweater. The scarf is wool and has a pattern of black and white

stripes. The sweater is red with a horse design on the chest.

Employee: I'll call Tokyo Station now and ask. Please wait a moment.

Chang: Thank you.

Employee: (Your bag) is there. It went to the clerks' office in Tokyo Station. (So) Please go pick them up today.

Vocabulary

えきいん	ekiin	station employee
でしょうか	deshō ka	(softer than desu ka)
わすれもの	wasuremono	forgotten or lost article
まえ	mae	before
うしろ	ushiro	back
～ばんめ	-bamme	counter for ordinal numbers
しゃりょう	sharyō	car, vehicle
わすれます（わすれる）	wasuremasu (wasureru)	forget
かみ	kami	paper
ふくろ	fukuro	bag
なかみ	nakami	contents
くわしく	kuwashiku	in detail
くわしい	kuwashii	detailed
せつめいします	setsumei shimasu	explain
（せつめいする）	(setsumei suru)	
せつめい	setsumei	explanation
マフラー	mafurā	scarf, muffler
ウール	ūru	wool
くろ	kuro	black(ness)
しろ	shiro	white(ness)
しま	shima	stripe
もよう	moyō	pattern, design
むね	mune	chest
うま	uma	horse
でんわを　かけて	denwa o kakete	telephone
かけます（かける）	kakemasu (kakeru)	call
じむしつ	jimu-shitsu	clerks' office
とどいています	todoite imasu	has arrived
とどきます（とどく）	todokimasu (todoku)	arrive, reach
きょうじゅうに	kyō-jū ni	(within) today
～じゅう／ちゅうに	-jū/-chū ni	within
とりに　いきます	tori ni ikimasu	go to pick up
とります（とる）	torimasu (toru)	pick up, get, take, pass

GRAMMAR & LESSON OBJECTIVES

- **De**, connective form of **desu**
  20-pun gurai mae no densha de, ushiro kara 2-bamme no sharyō desu.
  Mafurā wa ūru de, kuro to shiro no shima no moyō desu.

De, for **desu**, is the equivalent of the -**te** form of verbs. Each of these sentences has the same meaning as two independent sentences, each ending in **desu**.

- **-te/-de** form of adjectives as a connective
Kurokute ōkii kami no fukuro desu.
Sētā wa akakute, mune ni uma no moyō ga arimasu.
The -**te/-de** form of adjectives can be a connective, just as the -**te** form of verbs is used to combine two phrases, clauses or sentences.

-**i** adj.: **hiroi** → **hirokute; ōkii** → **ōkikute; yasui** → **yasukute**
ex. **Ano kōen wa hiroi desu. Shizuka desu.** → **Ano kōen wa hirokute shizuka desu.** "That park is spacious and quiet."

-**na** adj.: **benrina** → **benri de; kireina** → **kirei de; shizukana** → **shizuka de**
ex. **Chikatetsu wa benri desu. Hayakute yasui desu.** → **Chikatetsu wa benri de hayakute yasui desu.** "Subways are convenient, fast and cheap."

Two or more adjectives can be connected using this pattern only when these adjectives have the same inclination—positive value with positive, and vice versa. Thus, **Kono kōen was kitanakute hiroi desu,** "This park is dirty and spacious," is awkward. In such cases, **. . . kitanai desu ga hiroi desu,** ". . . dirty but spacious," is the right pattern.

- **-ku/-ni** form of adjectives as adverbial use
Kuwashiku setsumei shite kudasai.
The -**ku/-ni** form of adjectives is used to modify verbs.

-**i** adj.: **hayai** → **hayaku; hiroi** → **hiroku; ii/yoi** → **yoku**
ex. **Hayaku okimashita.** "(I) got up early."

-**na** adj.: **kireina** → **kirei ni; genkina** → **genki ni**
ex. **Kirei ni kaite kudasai.** "Please write it neatly."

Both -**i** and -**na** adjectives have various forms and functions. The form of -**i** adjectives found in dictionaries can be used as it is as a noun modifier or predicatively. For -**na** adjectives, bilingual dictionaries generally give the stem, so it is necessary to add -**na** when modifying nouns. It is better to think of -**na** adjectives in the same way as -**i** adjectives, words composed of a stem, which can be used independently as a noun, to which are added inflections. In romanized Japanese, the space put between **shizuka** and **de** or **ni** is only to make it easier to read and does not mean it is a grammatical segment. In Japanese, words are written without spaces between them, as seen in the Supplement.

Adjectives: Stem and Inflections

		Connective form	Adverbial form	Stem
-i adj.	kuroi	kurokute	kuroku	kuro
	ōkii	ōkikute	ōkiku	ōki
	hayai	hayakute	hayaku	haya
-na adj.	shizukana	shizuka de	shizuka ni	shizuka
	benrina	benri de	benri ni	benri

● . . . ni iku

Tori ni itte kudasai.

The **-masu** stem of a verb followed by **ni ikimasu/kimasu/kaerimasu** is a pattern for expressing the objective of "coming/going/returning." (For other verbs, other patterns are necessary.)

ex. 1. **Kinō Kamakura ni oyogi ni ikimashita.** "(I) went to Kamakura yesterday to swim."

    2. **Sukiyaki o tabe ni ikimasen ka.** "Wouldn't you like to go and have sukiyaki?"

NOTES

1. **Nan deshō ka.** (*lit.*) "What might it be (that you want)?"
This sounds softer than **Nan desu ka**, which may also be heard in the appropriate situation.

2. **Wasuremono**
This belongs to a category of nouns formed by adding **mono**, "thing," to the **-masu** stem of a verb. Another example previously encountered was **nomimono** (in Book I). Other everyday words not in this text but worth remembering are **tabemono**, "food"; **yomimono**, "reading material," especially light reading; and **kowaremono** (**ko-wareru**, "break," "be broken"), a "breakable thing."

3. **Dono densha desu ka.**
Note that the Japanese is the equivalent of "Which train is (it)?" whereas the English would normally be "Which train was it?" There were similar cases of differences in verb form or tense in the first volume and more will be encountered later on.

4. **Nakami wa nan desu ka. Kuwashiku setsumei shite kudasai.**
Being in charge of the platform, the station employee straightforwardly ascertains the contents, as well as the appearance, of the lost bag so as to be able to identify them, know whether anything is missing, and see that the bag is returned to the right person. A policeman or any person in charge of lost articles would do the same.

5. **Arimashita.**
The translation of the dialogue is fairly literal. Since this word is heard when a person finds something he has been looking for, a free translation would be "(It's been) found!" Similar expressions are **Basu ga kimashita**, "(Ah) here comes the bus," and **Omoidashimashita**, "(I've just) recalled (it)."

6. **Kyō-jū ni**
This **-jū ni** indicates the time within which something is expected to happen. **Jū** is a phonetic variation of **chū**. Other examples: **kotoshi-jū ni**, "(within) this year"; **raishū-chū ni**, "(within) next week," "sometime next week."

7. **Tōkyō eki no jimu-shitsu ni todoite imasu kara, . . .**
This literally means "(It) has reached the clerks' office in Tokyo Station and is still there," a usage of the **-te imasu** form explained in Book I (p. 168).

PRACTICE

1. はやしさんは　にほんじんで、ABCの　ぶちょうです。
2. ここは　ひろくて　しずかな　こうえんです。
3. かんじを　きれいに　かいてください。
4. レストランに　ひるごはんを　たべに　いきました。

1. Mr. Hayashi is a Japanese and is a department head at ABC.
2. This is a quiet, spacious park.
3. Please write the *kanji* neatly.
4. (I) went to a restaurant to eat lunch.

Vocabulary

ぶちょう	**buchō**	department head, division chief
ぶ	**bu**	department, division

EXERCISES

Make dialogues by changing the underlined parts as in the examples given.

A. *ex.* **Q**: どんな　ところですか。
A-1: ひろくて　しずかな　ところです。
A-2: しずかで　きれいな　ところです。

1. ところ、とおい、ふべんな　ところ
2. ところ、にぎやか、おもしろい　ところ
3. もんだい、やさしい、おもしろい　もんだい
4. もんだい、ふくざつ、むずかしい　もんだい

B. *ex.* **Q**: やまださんは　どんな　ひとですか。
A-1: わかくて　げんきな　ひとです。
A-2: まじめで　あかるい　ひとです。

1. あかるい、せが　たかい
2. あたまが　いい、しんせつ
3. テニスが　じょうず、げんき
4. しずか、かみが　ながい

C. *ex.* Q: すずきさんは　みちを　せつめいしましたか。
　　A-1: ええ、くわしく　せつめいしました。
　　A-2: ええ、しんせつに　せつめいしました。

　　1. もう　おきました、あさ　はやい
　　2. つきました、ゆうべ　おそい
　　3. しごとを　しています、しずか
　　4. ちずを　かきました、じょうず

D. *ex.* A: どこに　いきますか。
　　B: ぎんざに　いきます。
　　A: なにを　しに　いきますか。
　　B: えいがを　みに　いきます。

　　1. きょうと、ふるい　おてらを　みます
　　2. デパート、くつを　かいます
　　3. かとうさんの　へや、てがみを　とどけます
　　4. こうえん、しゃしんを　とります

E. *ex.* Q: らいしゅう　なにを　しますか。
　　A: デパートに　かぐを　かいに　いきます。

　　1. きょうと、さくらを　みます、いきます
　　2. だいがく、いとうきょうじゅに　あいます、いきます
　　3. りょうしんの　うち、やすみます、かえります
　　4. また　ここ、はなしを　します、きます

Vocabulary

ふべん（な）	**fuben(na)**	inconvenient
もんだい	**mondai**	problem
ふくざつ（な）	**fukuzatsu(na)**	complicated
わかい	**wakai**	young
まじめ（な）	**majime(na)**	serious, diligent
あかるい	**akarui**	cheerful
せが　たかい	**se ga takai**	tall
せ	**se**	back
たかい	**takai**	tall, high
あたまが　いい	**atama ga ii**	bright, clever
かみが　ながい	**kami ga nagai**	long-haired
かみ	**kami**	hair
ながい	**nagai**	long

みちを　せつめいします	**michi o setsumei shimasu**	give directions (*lit.* "explain the way")
おきます（おきる）	**okimasu (okiru)**	get up, wake up
はやい	**hayai**	early
ゆうべ	**yūbe**	last night/evening
ぎんざ	**Ginza**	Ginza (area of Tokyo)
さくら	**sakura**	cherry blossom
だいがく	**daigaku**	university
いとう	**Itō**	Japanese surname
きょうじゅ	**kyōju**	professor
やすみます（やすむ）	**yasumimasu (yasumu)**	rest

SHORT DIALOGUES

1. ホワイト：おかねを　ひろいました。
   けいかん：どこに　おちていましたか。
   ホワイト：スーパーの　まえの　みちに　おちていました。
   けいかん：なんじごろ　ひろいましたか。
   ホワイト：15ふんぐらい　まえです。

White:　　　I found (this) money.
Policeman: Where was (it)? (*lit.* "Where had (it) been dropped?")
White:　　　It was on the street in front of the supermarket.
Policeman: Around what time did you pick it up?
White:　　　About fifteen minutes ago.

2. すずき：　　さいふを　おとしました。
   けいかん：どんな　さいふですか。
   すずき：　　おおきい　かわの　さいふです。
   けいかん：なかに　なにが　はいっていますか。
   すずき：　　げんきんが　3まんえんぐらいと　めいしです。

Suzuki: I've lost my wallet.
Policeman: What kind of wallet is it?
Suzuki: It's a big leather wallet.
Policeman: Is there something (contained) in it?
Suzuki: Cash, about ¥30, 000, and business cards.

Vocabulary

ひろいます（ひろう）	**hiroimasu (hirou)**	find, pick up
おちます（おちる）	**ochimasu (ochiru)**	drop, fall
さいふ	**saifu**	wallet, purse
おとします（おとす）	**otoshimasu (otosu)**	lose, drop
かわ	**kawa**	leather
はいります（はいる）	**hairimasu (hairu)**	contain, include
げんきん	**genkin**	cash

QUIZ

I Read this lesson's Opening Dialogue and answer the following questions.

1. チャンさんは　どんな　ふくろを　わすれましたか。
2. うしろから　なんばんめの　しゃりょうに　わすれましたか。
3. あかい　セーターは　むねに　うまの　もようが　ありますか。
4. えきいんは　チャンさんの　せつめいを　きいて、なにを
   しましたか。
5. チャンさんは　わすれものを　どこに　とりに　いきますか。

II Put the appropriate particles in the parentheses.

1. チャンさんは　ウール（　　）マフラー（　　）あかい
   セーター（　　）わすれました。
2. まえ（　　）3ばんめ（　　）しゃりょうです。
3. くろ（　　）しろ（　　）しまの　セーターで、むね（　　）
   ちいさい　かさの　もよう（　　）あります。
4. じむしつ（　　）　とどいています（　　）、きょうじゅう
   （　　）　とり（　　）きてください。

III Complete the questions so that they fit the answers.

1. さいふを　おとしました。
   （　　）さいふですか。
   くろい　かわの　さいふです。
2. （　　）で　おとしましたか。
   こうえんで　おとしました。

3. なかに （　　　）が　はいっていますか。
　　おかねと　めいしが　はいっています。
4. （　　　）に　マフラーを　かいに　いきますか。
　　デパートに　かいに　いきます。

IV　Complete the sentences with the appropriate form of the words in parentheses.

1. ブラウンさんは（　　　）かんじを　かきます。（じょうず）
2. （　　　）せつめい　してください。（くわしい）
3. きょうは（　　　）かいしゃに　いきます。（はやい）
4. あたまが（　　　）、ねつが　あります。（いたい）
5. こどもは（　　　）ほんを　よんでいます。（しずか）
6. れきしが（　　　）、（　　　）まちです。（ふるい、ゆうめい）
7. かんじを（　　　）かいてください。（おおきい）

V　Connect the sentences using the appropriate verb or adjective form.

1. この　でんしゃに　のります。とうきょうえきで　おりてください。
2. あの　レストランは　ひろいです。あかるいです。
3. この　みせは　あたらしいです。きれいです。すいています。
4. それは　あおい　セーターです。はなの　もようが　あります。
5. わたなべさんは　あたまが　いいです。しんせつです。
6. チャンさんは　まじめです。よく　はたらきます。
7. じむしつに　でんわを　かけます。ききます。

VI　Answer the following questions.

1. あなたの　おとうさんは　どんな　ひとですか。(Use . . . -te/-de . . . -te/-de.)
2. あなたの　まちは　どんな　ところですか。(Use . . . -te/-de . . . -te/-de.)
3. こうえんに　なにを　しに　いきますか。
4. あなたは　あした　どこに　いきますか。
　　なにを　しに　いきますか。

NEW KANJI

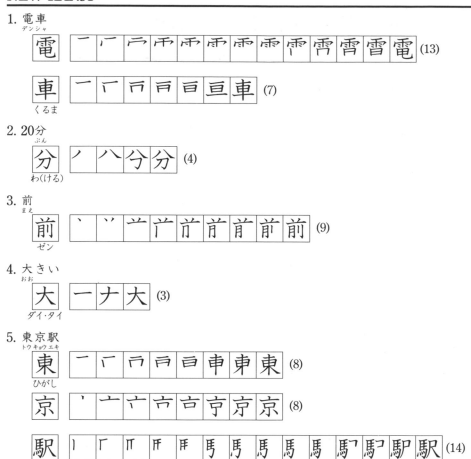

1. 電車
   デンシャ

   電　一 雨 雨 雨 雨 雨 雨 雨 雷 雷 雷 電 (13)

   車　一 ㄷ ㄸ 戸 百 亘 車 (7)
   くるま

2. 20分
   ぶん

   分　ノ 八 分 分 (4)
   わ(ける)

3. 前
   まえ

   前　丶 丷 丷 广 广 广 肖 肖 前 前 (9)
   ゼン

4. 大きい
   おお

   大　一 ナ 大 (3)
   ダイ・タイ

5. 東京駅
   トウキョウエキ

   東　一 ㄷ ㄸ 戸 亘 車 束 東 (8)
   ひがし

   京　丶 亠 古 古 古 古 京 京 (8)

   駅　l ㄷ 「 ㄝ 厗 馬 馬 馬 馬 馬 馬 駅 駅 駅 駅 (14)

6. 電話
   デン ワ

   話　丶 亠 亖 亖 言 言 言 訂 訐 評 評 話 話 (13)
   はな(す)

LESSON **3**   THE HEALTH CLUB

Mr. Brown visits a health club.

ブラウン：　あのう、ちょっと　おねがいします。こちらの　ス
　　　　　　ポーツクラブに　もうしこみを　する　前に、中を
　　　　　　見る　ことが　できますか。

クラブの人：はい。しつれいですが、どちらさまでしょうか。

ブラウン：　ブラウンです。

クラブの人：ブラウンさまですか。では、ごあんないしましょう。

The clerk invites Mr. Brown in and shows him around.

ブラウン：　とても　ひろくて　きれいな　ところですね。

クラブの人：こちらの　テニスコートには　コーチが　いますか
　　　　　　ら、コーチに　ならう　ことも　できます。こちら
　　　　　　は　おんすいプールで、一年中　およぐ　ことが
　　　　　　できます。

ブラウン：　こちらでは　みんな　いろいろな　マシーンを
　　　　　　つかっていますね。

クラブの人：ええ。どれでも　おすきな　ものを　つかう　こと
　　　　　　が　できますが、はじめる　前に　インストラクタ
　　　　　　ーに　ごそうだんください。

ブラウン：　ええ、そう　します。

クラブの人：いかがでしたか。
ブラウン：　とても　気に　入りました。もうしこみしょが
　　　　　　ありますか。
クラブの人：はい。こちらに　お名前と　ご住所を　おかきくだ
　　　　　　さい。

Brown:　Er, can you help me? May I look around inside before applying to join this health club?
Clerk:　Yes. Excuse me, but may I have your name?
Brown:　It's Brown.
Clerk:　Mr. Brown, is it? Let me show you around.

Brown:　It's a very spacious and nice place, isn't it?
Clerk:　Since there's a coach at our tennis court, you can learn from the coach. Here we have a heated swimming pool. You can swim all year round.
Brown:　Everyone here uses machines of various kinds, I see.
Clerk:　Yes, you can use anything you like, but please consult the instructor before starting.
Brown:　All right, I'll do that.

Clerk:　How do you like it?
Brown:　It's very satisfactory. Have you an application form?
Clerk:　Certainly. Would you write your name and address here, please?

Vocabulary

あのう	anō	er
スポーツクラブ	supōtsu kurabu	health club
もうしこみ	mōshikomi	application
ことが　できます（できる）	koto ga dekimasu (dekiru)	can
クラブの　ひと	kurabu no hito	sports club staff
どちらさま	dochira-sama	who
ごあんないします（あんないする）	go-annai shimasu (annai suru)	show around
あんない	annai	guidance
テニスコート	tenisu kōto	tennis court
コーチ	kōchi	coach
ならいます（ならう）	naraimasu (narau)	learn
おんすいプール	onsui pūru	heated (swimming) pool.
おんすい	onsui	warm water
プール	pūru	pool
いちねんじゅう	ichi-nen-jū	all year round
〜じゅう	-jū	throughout
およぎます（およぐ）	oyogimasu (oyogu)	swim
マシーン	mashīn	machine
どれでも	dore demo	any(thing)
でも	demo	any (particle)
おすきな　もの	o-sukina mono	thing(s) you like
もの	mono	thing, goods, wear

はじめます（はじめる）	**hajimemasu (hajimeru)**	begin, start
インストラクター	**insutorakutā**	instructor
ごそうだん	**go-sōdan**	consultation
きに いりました	**ki ni irimashita**	was/is satisfactory
き	**ki**	feeling
もうしこみしょ	**mōshikomi-sho**	application form
〜しょ	**-sho**	*lit.* "book, document, note"

GRAMMAR & LESSON OBJECTIVES

• Dictionary form of verbs

The basic verb form introduced in this lesson is known as the *dictionary form* because it is the one under which verbs are listed in dictionaries.

Without exception the final vowel is always **u**. (See Book I, p. 54.)

The three conjugations—Regular I, Regular II and Irregular (**shimasu** and **kimasu** only)—are introduced in Book I (pp. 130–31). You have already learned some of the seven forms and the rest will be introduced in the following lessons.

Regular I: Five-vowel conjugation

	-nai stem	-masu stem	dictionary	conditional	volitional	-te	-ta
use	**tsukawa-**	**tsukai-**	**tsukau**	**tsukaeba**	**tsukaō**	**tsukatte**	**tsukatta**
swim	**oyoga-**	**oyogi-**	**oyogu**	**oyogeba**	**oyogō**	**oyoide**	**oyoida**
go	**ika-**	**iki-**	**iku**	**ikeba**	**ikō**	**itte**	**itta**

The penultimate vowel of all Regular II verbs is either **i** or **e** and the dictionary form (if written in *rōmaji*) ends in **-iru** or **-eru**. (It should be noted that verbs having these endings are not invariably Regular II. A small number are Regular I. Common examples are **kaeru**, "return"—**kaeranai, kaerimasu; hairu**, "enter"—**hairanai, hairimasu;** and **kiru**, "cut"—**kiranai, kirimasu.**)

To tell whether a verb is Regular I or Regular II, look at the **-nai** stem. For Regular I verbs, this stem has the final vowel **a**.

Regular II: Single-vowel conjugation

	-nai stem	-masu stem	dictionary	conditional	volitional	-te	-ta
be	**i-**	**i-**	**iru**	**ireba**	**iyō**	**ite**	**ita**
begin	**hajime-**	**hajime-**	**hajimeru**	**hajimereba**	**hajimeyō**	**hajimete**	**hajimeta**
eat	**tabe-**	**tabe-**	**taberu**	**tabereba**	**tabeyō**	**tabete**	**tabeta**

Irregular

	-nai stem	-masu stem	dictionary	conditional	volitional	-te	-ta
come	**ko-**	**ki-**	**kuru**	**kureba**	**koyō**	**kite**	**kita**
do	**shi-**	**shi-**	**suru**	**sureba**	**shiyō**	**shite**	**shita**

- Plain forms of verbs

    The dictionary form is also referred to as the *plain present form*. Other plain forms are the **-nai** plain negative and the **-ta** plain past forms. A fourth one, the plain past negative made with the verb/adjective inflection **-nakatta** (past form of **-nai**), is introduced in Lesson 8. As noted in Book I, a sentence ending in a plain form is less polite than one ending in the **-masu** form. Within a sentence plain forms do not affect the politeness level, and, as in this lesson's dialogue, certain phrase and sentence patterns are commonly formed with plain forms.

- **. . . koto ga dekimasu**

    Naka o miru koto ga dekimasu ka.

    Ichi-nen-jū oyogu koto ga dekimasu.

    The pattern consisting of the dictionary form and **koto ga dekiru** indicates possibility or capability. An even more common way of expressing the same thing (using verb inflections) is given in Lesson 19.

- **. . . mae ni**

    Mōshikomi o suru mae ni, . . .

    Hajimeru mae ni, . . .

    The verb coming before **mae ni** is always in the dictionary form.

    ex. **Nihon ni kuru mae ni kanji o naraimashita.** "(I) learned Sino-Japanese characters before coming to Japan."

NOTES

1. **Anō.**

    Anō is an informal expression used at the beginning of a sentence and indicates hesitation or deference. Here it keeps the sentence from sounding brusque.

2. **Dochira-sama deshō ka.**

    Dochira-sama is a very polite alternative for **donata**. Literally, this sentence is "Who might (you) be?"

3. **Kochira no tenisu kōto niwa . . .**

    Kochira dewa . . .

    The use of **(ni)wa** and **(de)wa** serves to emphasize the topics of the sentences.

4. **Kōchi ni narau**

    With the verb **narau**, "to learn," the particle **ni** is used after the person, as in the case of the verb **morau**, "to receive," in **"Tanaka-san wa Kurāku-san ni kabin o moraimashita."** (Book I, p. 108). **Ni** is similarly used with **kariru**, "to borrow," and the particle **kara** can replace it in such cases.

5. **Dore demo**, anything

    This is formed with the interrogative **dore**, "which (one)," plus the particle **demo**. Other terms of this type include **nan demo**, "anything," **doko demo**, "anywhere,"

Other terms of this type include **nan demo**, "anything," **doko demo**, "anywhere," **dare demo**, "anyone," and **itsu demo**, "anytime."
ex. **Itsu demo ii desu.** "Anytime will do."

6. **go-annai, o-sukina mono, go-sōdan, o-namae, go-jūsho**
These words are examples of the usage given in Book I (p. 88) to show respect to the person spoken to or persons or things connected with him or her. There are a few cases where usage is determined not by the addressee but by the subject matter, e.g., **o-kane**, "money," **o-satō**, "sugar," **o-cha**, "tea." Whether **o-** or **go-** is added is simply a matter of usage; these honorifics are more commonly used by women.

7. **Go-sōdan kudasai**
Rather than **sōdan shite kudasai**, **o-/go-** with a noun and **kudasai** may be used.
ex. **O-denwa kudasai,** "Please call (me)."
   Go-kinyū kudasai, "Please fill in (the form)."
Still polite, but slightly more businesslike, is the pattern **o-** with the **-masu** stem followed by **kudasai.**
ex. **O-machi kudasai** (instead of **Matte kudasai**), "Please wait."
   O-tsukai kudasai (instead of **Tsukatte kudasai**). "Please use (it)."

PRACTICE

KEY SENTENCES

1. この プールでは いちねんじゅう およぐ ことが できます。
2. まいあさ かいしゃに いく まえに、しんぶんを よみます。

1. As for this pool, it can be swum in all year round.
2. (I) read the newspaper every morning before going to work.

EXERCISES

I Verbs: Study the examples, convert into the dictionary form, and memorize.

A. Regular I
   ex. いきます→いく　　あそびます→あそぶ　　いいます→いう
   のみます→のむ　　はなします→はなす　　あります→ある
   しにます→しぬ　　まちます→まつ

   1. あいます　　6. はいります　　11. なおします　　16. とります
   2. おとします　7. いそぎます　　12. もちます　　　17. すきます
   3. うります　　8. よびます　　　13. わかります　　18. こみます
   4. ききます　　9. もらいます　　14. ぬぎます　　　19. おくります
   5. すいます　　10. とどきます　　15. かいます　　　20. はたらきます

B. Regular II

ex. たべます→たべる　　みます→みる

1. みせます　　　　　4. あげます　　　7. います
2. おきます (get up)　5. かんがえます　8. とめます
3. おります　　　　　6. おちます　　　9. しめます

C. Irregular

ex. きます→くる　　します→する

1. けっこんします　　3. あんないします
2. もってきます　　　4. せつめいします

II Make dialogues by changing the underlined parts as in the examples given.

A. *ex.* **Q:** この　プールで　いま　およぐ　ことが　できますか。
　　Aa: はい、できます。
　　An: いいえ、できません。

1. この　へやを　つかいます
2. きょうじゅうに　とどけます
3. とうきょうえきに　とりに　いきます
4. おたくの　ちかくに　くるまを　とめます

B. *ex.* **Q:** ［あなたは］にほんごを　はなす　ことが　できますか。
　　A: ええ、できますが、あまり　じょうずでは　ありません。

1. にほんの　うたを　うたいます
2. かんじを　かきます
3. くるまを　うんてんします
4. にほんりょうりを　つくります

C. *ex.* **Q:** いつ　はを　みがきますか。
　　A: ねる　まえに　はを　みがきます。

1. さけを　のみます、ねます
2. てを　あらいます、しょくじを　します
3. シャワーを　あびます、でかけます
4. かえります、みちが　こみます

D. *ex.* **Q:** <u>もうしこみを　する　まえに</u> <u>なかを　みる</u> ことが
できますか。

A: ええ、できますよ。

1. はじめます、インストラクターに　そうだんします
2. おおさかに　いきます、はやしさんに　あいます
3. しんかんせんに　のります、おべんとうを　かいます

| Vocabulary |

しぬ	**shinu**	die
あそぶ	**asobu**	play
はなす	**hanasu**	talk, speak, tell
いそぐ	**isogu**	hurry
よぶ	**yobu**	call, invite
なおす	**naosu**	correct, improve, repair
もつ	**motsu**	have, hold
ぬぐ	**nugu**	take off
かんがえる	**kangaeru**	think, consider
うた	**uta**	song
うたう	**utau**	sing
うんてんする	**unten suru**	drive
うんてん	**unten**	driving
つくる	**tsukuru**	cook, prepare
みがく	**migaku**	brush, polish
ねる	**neru**	sleep, go to bed
て	**te**	hand, arm
あらう	**arau**	wash
シャワーを　あびる	**shawā o abiru**	take a shower
シャワー	**shawā**	shower
あびる	**abiru**	bathe, pour
でかける	**dekakeru**	go out
（お）べんとう	**(o-)bentō**	box lunch

NB: From here on the verb form in the vocabulary lists is the dictionary form.

SHORT DIALOGUE ————————————————————————

ホワイト：いけばなの　クラスを　みに　いっても　いいでしょ
うか。

なかむら：ええ。こんど　いっしょに　いきましょう。

ホワイト：いつ　クラスが　ありますか。

なかむら：1しゅうかんに　2かい、か、もくに　あります。

White:　　May I go to see the flower-arranging class?
Nakamura:　Yes. Let's go together next time.

White: When are the classes?
Nakamura: Twice a week. Tuesdays and Thursdays.

Vocabulary

いけばな	**ikebana**	flower arranging
クラス	**kurasu**	class
こんど	**kondo**	next (time)
〜かい	**-kai**	time(s) (counter)
か	**ka**	Tuesday
もく	**moku**	Thursday

QUIZ

I   Read this lesson's Opening Dialogue and answer the following questions.

1. ブラウンさんは スポーツクラブに なにを しに いきましたか。

2. だれが ブラウンさんを あんないしましたか。

3. この スポーツクラブでは いちねんじゅう プールで およぐ ことが できますか。

4. ブラウンさんは スポーツクラブの なかを みる まえに、もうしこみを しましたか。

II   Put the appropriate particles in the parentheses.

1. わたしは アメリカ（　　　）にほんじんの せんせい（　　　）にほんご（　　　）ならいました。

2. どれ（　　　）おすきなもの（　　　）つかうこと（　　　）できます（　　　）、はじめる まえ（　　　）インストラクター（　　　）ごそうだんください。

3. この かみ（　　　）おなまえ（　　　）ごじゅうしょ（　　　）おかきください。

4. 1かげつ（　　　）1かい おおさか（　　　）いきます。

III   Convert the following verbs into the dictionary form.

1. いきます	6. みます	11. きます
2. あいます	7. あります	12. たべます
3. あんないします	8. けします	13. べんきょうします
4. おしえます	9. とめます	14. でんわを かけます
5. わすれます	10. まがります	15. もってきます

IV Complete the sentences with the appropriate form of the verbs indicated.

1. ここで　スライドを　（　　　）ことが　できますか。（みます）
2. ひるごはんを　（　　　）に　（　　　）も　いいでしょうか。
（たべます、いきます）
3. （　　　）まえに　でんわを　（　　　）ください。（きます、
かけます）
4. あした　たなかさんに　（　　　）に　（　　　）ことが　できます
か。（あいます、いきます）
5. （　　　）まえに　シャワーを　あびます。（でかけます）
6. ここに　くるまを　（　　　）ことが　できますか。（とめます）
いいえ、ここは　ちゅうしゃきんしですから、くるまを
（　　　）でください。（とめます）

V Answer the following questions.

1. あなたは　およぐ　ことが　できますか。
2. あなたは　かんじを　よむ　ことが　できますか。
3. あなたは　まいにち　ねる　まえに　はを　みがきますか。
4. あなたは　あさごはんを　たべる　まえに　なにを　しますか。
5. 1しゅうかんに　なんかい　にほんごの　じゅぎょうが　あ
りますか。

NEW KANJI

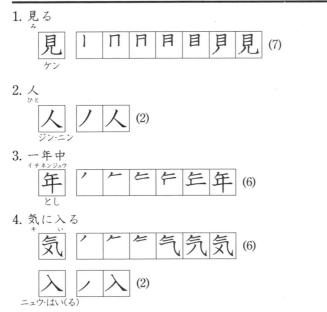

1. 見る
み
見　｜　冂　冃　月　目　貝　見　(7)
ケン

2. 人
ひと
人　ノ　人　(2)
ジン・ニン

3. 一年中
イチネンジュウ
年　ノ　ゲ　ヒ　仁　玍　年　(6)
とし

4. 気に入る
キ
気　ノ　ゲ　ヒ　气　気　気　(6)
入　ノ　入　(2)
ニュウ・はい（る）

5. 名前
<ruby>名<rt>な</rt></ruby> <ruby>前<rt>まえ</rt></ruby>

名　ノ　ク　タ　タ　名　名　(6)
メイ

6. 住所
<ruby>住<rt>ジュウ</rt></ruby> <ruby>所<rt>ショ</rt></ruby>

住　ノ　イ　イ　仁　仹　住　住　(7)
す(む)

所　一　ラ　ヨ　戸　戸　所　所　所　(8)
ところ

Readings:

中：　中，　一年中
　　　なか　　イチネンジュウ

LESSON 4 A BUSINESS TRIP

Mr. Kimura and Mr. Brown chat about Brown's upcoming business trip to the Sapporo branch office.

きむら：　ブラウンさん、しゅっちょうですか。

ブラウン：ええ、あしたから　さっぽろ支店に　しゅっちょうです。
　　　　　きむらさんは　ほっかいどうに　行った　ことが
　　　　　ありますか。

きむら：　ええ、がくせいの　ころ　いちど　ほっかいどうへ
　　　　　りょこうに　行った　ことが　あります。車で　ほっ
　　　　　かいどうを　まわりました。

ブラウン：さっぽろは　どんな　ところですか。

きむら：　さっぽろの　町は　にぎやかで、なかなか　おもしろ
　　　　　いですよ。ブラウンさんは　はじめてですか。

ブラウン：ええ、しゃしんを　見た　ことは　ありますが、行っ
　　　　　た　ことは　ありません。

きむら：　ひとりで　しゅっちょうですか。

ブラウン：かとうさんも　いっしょです。ふたりで　さっぽろ市
　　　　　内の　とりひきさきを　まわったり、銀行に　あいさ
　　　　　つに　行ったり　します。

きむら：　かとうさんは　住んでいた　ことが　ありますから、
　　　　　さっぽろを　よく　知っていますよ。

ブラウン：そうですか。あんしんしました。

Kimura: Mr. Brown, is it a business trip you're going on?

Brown: Yes. From tomorrow, to the Sapporo branch office. Have you ever been to Hokkaido?

Kimura: Yes, at the time I was a (college) student, (we) once made a trip to Hokkaido. We toured Hokkaido by car.

Brown: What kind of place is Sapporo?

Kimura: The city of Sapporo is a really bustling (place) and quite interesting. Is this (your) first time?

Brown: Yes. I've seen pictures, but I've never been there.

Kimura: Are you making (this) trip alone?

Brown: (No,) with Mr. Katō. The two of us will go around to (our) business contacts within Sapporo and pay our respects at the banks (and so on).

Kimura: Mr. Katō has lived in Sapporo, so he knows (it) well.
Brown: Is that right? I'm relieved.

| Vocabulary |

きむら	**Kimura**	Japanese surname
しゅっちょう	**shutchō**	business/official trip
してん	**shiten**	branch (office/store)
ほっかいどう	**Hokkaidō**	Hokkaido (prefecture)
ことが　ある	**koto ga aru**	had the experience of
ころ	**koro**	time
まわる	**mawaru**	tour, go round
なかなか	**nakanaka**	quite, very
しない	**shinai**	within a city
とりひきさき	**torihikisaki**	business contact
あいさつ	**aisatsu**	greeting, address
〜たり〜たり　する	**-tari . . . -tari suru**	do X, Y, etc.
あんしんする	**anshin suru**	be relieved/relaxed
あんしん	**anshin**	peace of mind

GRAMMAR & LESSON OBJECTIVES

- **-ta koto ga arimasu**
  Hokkaidō ni itta koto ga arimasu ka.
  As can be seen in the dialogue, the **-ta** form of a verb plus **koto ga aru** expresses the fact that a person has experienced a particular thing.
  ex. **Sapporo ni sunde ita koto ga arimasu.** "(He) has lived in Sapporo."

- **-te** and **-ta** forms from **-masu** form
  Certain **-te** forms were given and used in Book I. Now let's see how they can be made from the **-masu** form.
  With Regular II and the two Irregular verbs it is only necessary to replace **-masu** with **-te** or **-ta**.
  Regular II: **tabe(masu)** → **tabete/tabeta**; **mi(masu)** → **mite/mita**
  Irregular: **ki(masu)** → **kite/kita**; **shi(masu)** → **shite/shita**

  Regular I verbs

	-masu form → -te/-ta form	Other similar verbs
Type 1 -ite/-ita -ide/-ida	**kakimasu** → **kaite/kaita** **oyogimasu** → **oyoide/oyoida**	**kikimasu, arukimasu, nugimasu, isogimasu**
Type 2 -tte/-tta	**kaimasu** → **katte/katta** **mochimasu** → **motte/motta** **kaerimasu** → **kaette/kaetta**	**iimasu, moraimasu, machimasu, tachimasu, urimasu, norimasu**

	-masu form → -te/-ta form	Other similar verbs
Type 3	asobimasu → asonde/asonda	yobimasu, erabimasu,
-nde/-nda	nomimasu → nonde/nonda	sumimasu, yomimasu
	shinimasu → shinde/shinda	*

* There are no other verbs belonging to this category.

Note that no euphonic change occurs when the syllable is **shi**, e.g., **hanashi(masu)** → **hanashite/hanashita**, **naoshi(masu)** → **naoshite/naoshita**, and for **ikimasu** the transformation is **iki(masu)** → **itte/itta**.

- **. . . -tari . . . -tari shimasu**
  Sapporo shinai no torihikisaki o mawattari, ginkō ni aisatsu ni ittari shimasu.
  In the dialogue this pattern implies doing X, Y and other things, which is also the implication when only one verb is used. In other cases, the pattern means that two or more actions are done alternately or repeatedly.
  The **-tari** form is made by adding **ri** to the **-ta** form.
  ex. 1. **Nichi-yōbi ni wa hon o yondari, ongaku o kiitari shimasu.** "On Sundays I read books, listen to music (and so on)."
     2. **Doa o aketari shimetari shinaide kudasai. Urusai desu.** "Please don't (keep on) opening and closing the door. It's (too) noisy."

NOTES

1. **Kuruma de Hokkaidō o mawarimashita.**
   The particle **o** as used here is the same as **shingō o migi ni magatte** (Book I, p. 141). Some other verbs of motion taking the particle **o** when the action is through, along or from a certain place, are **tōru**, "pass along/through," **aruku**, "walk," **tobu**, "fly," and **deru**, "go out, leave."
   ex. 1. **Watashi wa Ginza-dōri o arukimashita.** "I walked along the (main) Ginza street."
      2. **Hikōki ga sora o tonde imasu.** "The plane is flying through the air."

2. **Sapporo no machi wa nigiyaka de, nakanaka omoshiroi desu yo.**
   Dictionaries equate **nakanaka** with "quite," "very," "considerably," "exceedingly," reflecting the good impression or high evaluation of whatever the speaker is commenting on.

3. **Shashin o mita koto wa arimasu ga, itta koto wa arimasen.**
   Besides being a topic marker, the particle **wa** is used for contrast or to particularize or emphasize the subject. Particles such as **ni**, **de** and **kara** can be combined with **wa**, but not **ga** and **o**. These are replaced by **wa**.
   ex. 1. **Minna kara henji o moraimashita ka.** "Did you get answers from everybody?"
      Iie, mada desu. Kimura-san to Tanaka-san kara wa moraimashita. "No, not yet. (I) got (them only) from Kimura and Tanaka."

2. **Koko kara mae no seki dewa tabako o suwanaide kudasai.** "Please, no smoking in the seats ahead of these."

3. **Maitoshi Kurisumasu kādo o kakimasu ka.** "Do (you) send (*lit.* write) Christmas cards every year?"

   Kurisumasu kādo wa kakimasen ga, nenga-jō wa maitoshi kakimasu. "(I) don't (always) send Christmas cards, but (I) send New Year's cards every year."

4. **Hokkaidō ni/e. . .**

   Either **ni** or **e** can occur with such verbs as **iku**. On the interchangeability of these particles, see Book I, p. 53.

PRACTICE

KEY SENTENCES

1. わたなべさんは　ホンコンに　いった　ことが　あります。
2. にちようびは　ほんを　よんだり、おんがくを　きいたり　します。

1. Ms. Watanabe has been to Hong Kong.
2. Sundays, (I) read books, listen to music (and so on).

Vocabulary

わたなべ	**Watanabe**	Japanese surname

EXERCISES

I Verbs: Study the examples, convert into -**te** and -**ta** forms, and memorize.

A. Reg. I

ex. かきます→　　かく→　　　かいて→　　　かいた
　　よみます→　　よむ→　　　よんで→　　　よんだ
　　あいます→　　あう→　　　あって→　　　あった
　　おわります→　おわる→　　おわって→　　おわった

1. ならいます	6. のぼります	11. ぬぎます	16. はなします
2. およぎます	7. おきます (put)	12. おとします	17. すわります
3. しにます	8. みがきます	13. はたらきます	18. なおします
4. あそびます	9. もちます	14. かいます	19. あるきます
5. たちます	10. とびます	15. いきます	20. やすみます

B. Reg. II and Irreg.

ex. Reg. II　つけます→　　　　つける→　つけて→　つけた
　　　　　おきます (get up)→　おきる→　おきて→　おきた

Irreg.　　きます→　　　くる→　　　きて→　　　きた
　　　　　します→　　　する→　　　して→　　　した

1. きます (wear)　　6. わすれます　　　11. れんしゅうします
2. かんがえます　　7. みせます　　　　12. うっています
3. おちます　　　　8. でかけます　　　13. でます
4. ねます　　　　　9. もってきます　　14. はじめます
5. あんしんします　10. すんでいます　　15. おります

II　Make dialogues by changing the underlined parts as in the examples given.

A. *ex.* **Q:** スミスさんは　まえに　<u>きゅうしゅうに　いった</u>　こと
　　　　が　ありますか。
　　A: はい、いちど　<u>いった</u>　ことが　あります。

　　1. はやしさんの　おくさんに　あいました
　　2. ふじさんに　のぼりました
　　3. しんかんせんに　のりました
　　4. ヨーロッパを　まわりました

B. *ex.* **Q:** スミスさんは　<u>ユーフォー(UFO)を　みた</u>　ことが
　　　ありますか。
　　A: いいえ、ざんねんですが、<u>みた</u>　ことが　ありません。

　　1. アフリカへ　いきました
　　2. じゅうどうを　ならいました
　　3. だいとうりょうに　あいました

C. *ex.* **Q:** <u>さっぽろの　まち</u>を　しっていますか。
　　A: <u>しゃしんを　みた</u>　ことは　ありますが、<u>いった</u>　こと
　　は　ありません。

　　1. ジョンソンさん、なまえを　ききました、あいました
　　2. とうふ、スーパーで　みました、たべました
　　3. シェークスピアの　ハムレット、えいがを　みました、
　　　ほんを　よみました

D. *ex.* **Q:** しゅうまつに　なにを　しましたか。
　　A: <u>かいものに　いっ</u>たり、<u>ともだちに　あっ</u>たりしました。

　　1. テニスを　する、さんぽを　する

2. ビデオを　みる、こどもと　あそぶ

3. てがみを　かく、ざっしを　よむ

4. ともだちと　はなす、レコードを　きく

5. うみで　およぐ、つりを　する

Vocabulary

のぼる	**noboru**	climb
おく	**oku**	put, set up
とぶ	**tobu**	fly
すわる	**suwaru**	sit, take a seat
きる	**kiru**	wear, put on
れんしゅうする	**renshū suru**	practice
れんしゅう	**renshū**	practice
きゅうしゅう	**Kyūshū**	Kyushu (place name)
ふじさん	**Fuji-san**	Mount Fuji
〜さん	**-san**	Mount (with names)
ユーフォー	**yūfō**	UFO (unidentified flying object)
ざんねん（な）	**zannen(na)**	disappointing
アフリカ	**Afurika**	Africa
じゅうどう	**jūdō**	judo
だいとうりょう	**daitōryō**	president
とうふ	**tōfu**	tofu
シェークスピア	**Shēkusupia**	Shakespeare
ハムレット	**Hamuretto**	Hamlet
ビデオ	**bideo**	video
つりを　する	**tsuri o suru**	fish
つり	**tsuri**	fishing

SHORT DIALOGUES

1. A: きょうとに　いった　ことが　ありますか。

   B: はい、あります。

   A: いつ　いきましたか。

   B: きょねんの　8がつに　いきました。

   A: Have (you) ever been to Kyoto?
   B: Yes, I have.
   A: When did (you) go?
   B: (I) went last August.

2. たなか：よく　おおさかに　しゅっちょうしますね。

   かとう：ええ。1かげつに　5かいぐらい　とうきょうと　おおさ
   かを　いったり　きたり　しています。

   Tanaka: You often make business trips to Osaka, don't you?
   Katō: Yes. I come and go (between) Tokyo and Osaka about five times a month.

I Read this lesson's Opening Dialogue and answer the following questions.

1. ブラウンさんは　だれと　ほっかいどうに　いきますか。
2. ブラウンさんは　ほっかいどうに　いった　ことが　ありますか。
3. きむらさんも　いっしょに　さっぽろしてんに　いきますか。
4. ブラウンさんは　さっぽろへ　いって　なにを　しますか。

II Put the appropriate particles in the parentheses.

1. ヨーロッパ（　　）りょこう（　　）いった　ことが　あります。
2. くるま（　　）ほっかいどう（　　）まわりました。
3. すしを　たべた　こと（　　）あります（　　）、つくった　こと（　　）ありません。
4. スミスさんは　ひとり（　　）こうえん（　　）あるいています。

III Convert the following verbs into the **-ta** form.

1. のぼります　　6. おとします　　11. まわります
2. あいます　　　7. よみます　　　12. せつめいします
3. たべます　　　8. わすれます　　13. およぎます
4. ききます　　　9. みます　　　　14. ならいます
5. います　　　10. あそびます　　15. でかけます

IV Complete the sentences with the appropriate form of the verbs indicated.

1. ふじさんに（　　）ことが　ありますか。（のぼります）
2. パーティーで　いちど　スミスさんの　おくさんに（　　）ことが　あります。（あいます）
3. この　ラジオで　がいこくの　ニュースを（　　）ことが　できますか。（ききます）
4. きのうの　ばん　ほんを（　　）だり、てがみを（　　）たり　しました。（よみます、かきます）
5. しゅうまつに　えいがを（　　）たり、ともだちに（　　）たり　します。（みます、あいます）

V   Answer the following questions.

1. あなたは　かぶきを　みた　ことが　ありますか。
2. あなたは　ちゅうごくに　いった　ことが　ありますか。
3. あなたは　しんかんせんに　のった　ことが　ありますか。
4. あなたは　にちようびに　なにを　しますか。
   (Use . . . **tari** . . . **tari shimasu.**)
5. あなたは　きょねんの　なつやすみに　なにを　しましたか。
   (Use . . . **tari** . . . **tari shimashita.**)

NEW KANJI

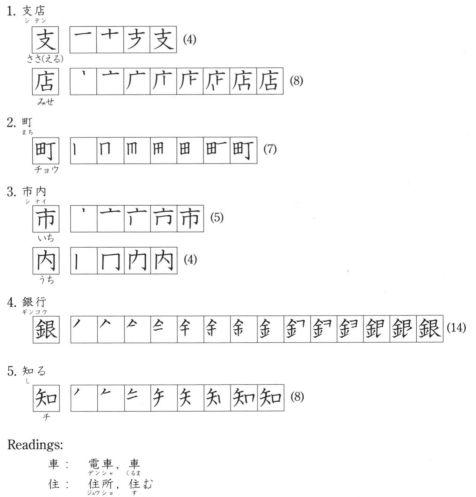

1. 支店
   シ テン

   支　一 十 キ 支 (4)
   ささ(える)

   店　丶 一 广 庁 庄 庄 店 店 (8)
   みせ

2. 町
   まち

   町　丨 冂 冂 田 田 町 町 (7)
   チョウ

3. 市内
   シ ナイ

   市　丶 一 广 方 市 (5)
   いち

   内　丨 冂 内 内 (4)
   うち

4. 銀行
   ギンコウ

   銀　ノ 𠂉 𠂉 𠂉 牟 牟 金 金 釘 釘 釘 鈤 銀 銀 (14)

5. 知る
   し

   知　ノ 𠂉 𠂉 チ 矢 知 知 知 (8)
   チ

Readings:
車：　電車，車
　　　デンシャ　くるま
住：　住所，住む
　　　ジュウショ　す
行：　行き，銀行
　　　い　　ギンコウ

LESSON **5**   A NEW WORD PROCESSOR

Mr. Hayashi gives Mr. Chang some advice about work procedures.

はやし ： ワープロの　カタログが　たくさん　ありますね。

チャン ： ええ、きのう　セールスの　人が　くれました。
うちの　課の　ワープロが　古く　なりましたから、新しいのに　かえたいです。

はやし ： ほう、どれに　しますか。

チャン ： A 社の　45S が　安く　なりましたが、まだ　きめていません。

はやし ： ところで、システム部の　おがわさんに　話しましたか。

チャン ： いいえ、まだ　話していません。

はやし ： ちょっと　まずいですねえ。まず　おがわさんと　そうだんしてから　きめてください。

チャン ： わかりました。

One month later.

すずき ： あ、新しい　ワープロが　来ましたね。

チャン ： ええ。これは　つかいかたが　かんたんですし、がめんも　大きいですし、いいですよ。

すずき ： ぼくも　こんな　ワープロが　ほしいなあ。

Hayashi: (You) have a lot of word processor catalogues, I see.
Chang:　Yes, a salesman gave (them to me) yesterday. Our section's word processor is old, so I want to change it for a new one.
Hayashi: Oh, which type have (you) decided on?
Chang:　A Company's 45S has become cheaper, but we still haven't decided yet.
Hayashi: By the way, have you talked to Mr. Ogawa in the Systems Department?
Chang:　No, I haven't spoken (to him) yet.
Hayashi: (That makes things) a little awkward. Before you do anything else, consult Mr. Ogawa and then please decide.
Chang:　I understand.

Suzuki:　Ah, the new word processor has arrived, hasn't it?
Chang:　Yes. This (model) is both simple to use and it has a large screen, so it's (a) good (one).
Suzuki:　I wish I had a word processor like this.

ワープロ	**wāpuro**	word processor
セールスの　ひと	**sērusu no hito**	salesperson
セールス	**sērusu**	sales
くれる	**kureru**	give
うちの	**uchi no**	our
か	**ka**	section
かえる	**kaeru**	change
ほう	**hō**	oh
〜に　する	**ni suru**	decide
Aしゃ	**A-sha**	A Company
なる	**naru**	become
きめる	**kimeru**	decide
ところで	**tokorode**	by the way
システムぶ	**shisutemu-bu**	systems department
システム	**shisutemu**	system
おがわ	**Ogawa**	Japanese surname
まずい	**mazui**	awkward, unsavory
まず	**mazu**	before anything (else)
そうだんする	**sōdan suru**	consult
〜てから	**-te kara**	after
つかいかた	**tsukai-kata**	way of using
〜かた	**-kata**	way, how to
かんたん（な）	**kantan(na)**	simple, easy
〜し	**shi**	and, moreover
がめん	**gamen**	screen
ぼく	**boku**	I (informal men's speech)
こんな	**konna**	like this, this sort of
ほしい	**hoshii**	want, desire
〜なあ	**nā**	(particle indicating emphasis; informal)

GRAMMAR & LESSON OBJECTIVES

- **-ku/ni narimasu**
  A-sha no 45S ga yasuku narimashita.
  When they come before **naru** (or other verbs), the **i** of **-i** adjectives is changed to **-ku**, as in **ōkiku narimasu**, "become big," and **akaku narimasu**, "get red."
  With **-na** adjectives and nouns, **ni** is used.
  ex. **shizukana** → **Shizuka ni narimasu.** "It'll get quiet."
  　　Arashi ni narimashita. "It got stormy."
  　　Kōchi ni naritai desu. "(I) want to become a coach."
  Narimasu can also follow **nai**, which changes the same as an **-i** adjective, and negative verbs can be used in the same way.
  ex. **Ōsaka niwa ikanaku narimashita**, "The plan was changed to not going to Osaka."

- Noun **ni shimasu,** a pattern to express the speaker's intention or conscious decision.
  Dore ni shimasu ka.
  This sentence is used to ask the second person's choice, just as **Kore ni shimasu,** meaning, "I choose this one," expresses the speaker's decision.
  ex. **Doko de o-cha o nomimashō ka.** "Where shall we have tea?"
      Ano kissaten ni shimashō. "Let's make it that coffee shop."

- **-te kara**
  Ogawa-san to sōdan shite kara kimete kudasai.
  The **-te** form plus **kara** means "after -ing." It should not be confused with **kara** meaning "because."
  ex. **Watashi no setsumei o kiite kara shitsumon shite kudasai.** "After listening to my explanation, please ask questions."

- **-te imasen**
  Mada kimete imasen.
  Ogawa-san ni hanashimashita ka. Iie, mada hanashite imasen.
  One meaning of **-te imasen** is to indicate that something has not occurred or been achieved; it conveys a feeling of unfinishedness. The answer above could not be **hanashimasen deshita,** as that would imply Chang does not intend to consult Ogawa. Compare this with the following examples.
  ex. 1. **Kyō no shimbun o yomimashita ka.** "Did you read today's newspaper?"
      Iie, mada yonde imasen. "No, not yet."
      2. **Kodomo no toki, shimbun o yomimashita ka.** "Did you read newspapers when (you were) a child?"
      Iie, yomimasen deshita. "No, (I) didn't read (them)."

- Connective particle **shi**
  Kore wa tsukai-kata mo kantan desu shi, gamen mo ōkii desu shi, ii desu yo.
  The particle **shi** joins clauses, which are usually explanations, excuses or reasons, with the main clause. Past and negative forms of verbs and adjectives can also be used before **shi,** and a single **shi** clause or several of them may be used.
  ex. 1. **Kinō wa ame deshita shi, doko ni mo dekakemasen deshita.** "It was raining yesterday, and I did not go out anywhere."
      2. **Kono taipuraitā wa yoku koshō shimasu shi, omoi desu shi, atarashii no o kaimashō.** "This typewriter goes wrong often and it's heavy, so let's buy a new one."

NOTES

1. **Sērusu no hito ga kuremashita.**
   As pointed out in Book I (p. 109), **kureru** is used in this case because the receiver is the speaker and his group.

2. **Atarashii no ni kaetai desu.**
   Atarashii no here means **atarashii wāpuro.** The particle **no** can be used to stand for a noun provided what it denotes is mutually understood.
   ex. **Gurasu o karite mo ii desu ka?** "May I borrow a glass?"

Dōzo. Soko ni kireina no ga arimasu kara, sukina no o tsukatte kudasai.
"Please do. There are some clean ones over there. Please use any one you like."

3. **Chotto mazui desu nē.**

Hayashi adds **chotto** to make his negative comment sound softer. This word is sometimes used in requests and refusals with the same purpose.

4. **Tsukai-kata**

-**kata** added to the -**masu** stem of a verb is a common way to indicate "how" or "way (of doing)."

ex. **kanji no yomi-kata,** "how to read kanji"

hashi no tsukai-kata, "the way to use chopsticks"

kōshū denwa no kake-kata, "how to make a call from a public telephone"

5. **Boku**

This word is sometimes heard in familiar conversation instead of **watashi,** as is **kimi** in place of **anata.** Both are men's words and neither is appropriate when talking to older people.

6. Noun **ga hoshii**

Boku mo konna wāpuro ga hoshii nā.

Hoshii, which means "want," conjugates in the same way as -**i** adjectives. Note that the particle **ga** should be used before **hoshii,** just like the pattern . . . **ga suki desu. Banana ga suki desu,** "I like bananas." **Nā** is a particle indicating emphasis and is informal. Since **hoshii** sounds too direct, it cannot be used freely when addressing other people. Here Suzuki is speaking to himself. Note that the phrase -**ga hoshii n desu ga** . . . is the conventional way of requesting something at stores or hotels. (See, Lesson 11, Short Dialogue No. 1.)

PRACTICE

KEY SENTENCES ———————————————————————

1. ふゆものの　コートや　セーターが　やすく　なりました。
2. たんじょうびの　プレゼントは　セーターに　します。
3. てを　あらってから　サンドイッチを　たべましょう。
4. もう　きめましたか。
　いいえ、まだ　きめていません。
5. おいしいですし、きれいですし、あの　レストランは　いいですよ。

1. Winter clothes like coats and sweaters have become cheap.
2. (I) have decided on a sweater as (his) birthday present.
3. Let's eat the sandwiches after washing our hands.
4. Did you decide?
　No, I haven't decided yet.
5. That restaurant is good, you know, because the food's delicious and the decor is attractive.

Vocabulary

ふゆもの	**fuyu-mono**	winter clothes/goods
ふゆ	**fuyu**	winter
コート	**kōto**	coat

EXERCISES

I　Make dialogues by changing the underlined parts as in the examples given.

A. *ex.* **Q**: どう　なりましたか。

　　A: <u>よく</u>　なりました。／<u>げんきに</u>　なりました。

1. おおきい
2. にぎやか
3. つまらない
4. くらい
5. あかるい
6. しずか
7. ふくざつ
8. べんり
9. じょうず
10. かんたん
11. つよい
12. きれい

B. *ex. 1.* **Q**: <u>くらいです</u>。<u>でんきを　つけました</u>。どう　なりました
か。

　　A: <u>あかるく</u>　なりました。

ex. 2. **Q**: <u>へやが　きたないです</u>。<u>そうじを　しました</u>。どう
なりましたか。

　　A: <u>きれいに</u>　なりました。

1. さむいです、ヒーターを　つけました、あたたかい
2. かぜを　ひきました、くすりを　のみました、いい
3. パーティーが　おわりました、しずか
4. にほんごを　いっしょうけんめい　べんきょうしまし
た、じょうず

II　Practice the following pattern by changing the underlined parts as in the example given.

ex. わたしは　<u>ピアニストに</u>　なりたいです。

1. ゆうめい、なりたい
2. あたまが　いい、なりたい
3. うちゅうひこうし、なりたかった
4. びょうき、なりたくない
5. びんぼう、なりたくなかった

III Make dialogues by changing the underlined parts as in the examples given.

A. *ex.* **Q:** <u>なにを</u>　<u>たべ</u>ましょうか。
　　　A: <u>てんぷらに</u>　しましょう。

　　　1. どこで、おちゃを　のみます、あの　きっさてん
　　　2. なんで、いきます、タクシー
　　　3. なにを、つくります、とうふの　みそしる
　　　4. どこで、スライドを　みます、2かいの　かいぎしつ
　　　5. だれに、あげます、ハンサムな　ひと

B. *ex.* **Q:** いつから　<u>にほんごの　べんきょうを</u>　はじめましたか。
　　　A: <u>にほんに　きて</u>から　はじめました。

　　　1. ゴルフ、けっこんする
　　　2. テニス、スポーツクラブに　はいる
　　　3. この　しごと、だいがくを　でる
　　　4. うんてん、30さいに　なる

C. *ex.* **Q:** いつも　<u>そうだんして</u>から　<u>きめ</u>ますか。
　　　A: はい、たいてい　<u>そうだんして</u>から　<u>きめ</u>ます。

　　　1. カタログを　みる、かう
　　　2. コーヒーを　のむ、しごとを　はじめる
　　　3. よやくを　する、レストランに　いく
　　　4. でんわを　かける、ともだちを　たずねる

D. *ex.* **Q:** もう　<u>この　ほんを　よみ</u>ましたか。
　　　A: いいえ、まだ　<u>よんでいません</u>。

　　　1. きっぷを　かう
　　　2. でんわを　かける
　　　3. にもつが　とどく
　　　4. てがみを　だす

E. *ex.* **Q:** <u>あたらしい　うちは</u>　どうですか。
　　　A: <u>ひろい</u>ですし、<u>きれい</u>ですし、<u>すばらしい</u>です。

　　　1. あたらしい　カメラ、かるい、べんり、きに　いって
　　　　います。

2. いまの　しごと、いそがしい、ざんぎょうが　ありま
   す、たいへんです。
3. いまの　アパート、せまい、うるさい、ひっこしたい
   です。

F. *ex.* スミス：　　たなかさんは　かとうさんに　なにを　あげま
　　　　　　　　したか。
　　わたなべ：ネクタイを　あげました。
　　スミス：　あなたには？
　　わたなべ：わたしには　かびんを　くれました。

1. きょうとの　おかし、きょうとの　やきもの
2. しまの　シャツ、きぬの　スカーフ
3. えいがの　きっぷ、かぶきの　きっぷ
4. ウイスキー、はなたば

Vocabulary

どうなりましたか	**Dō narimashita ka**	(*lit.*) "How have (things) become?" (See Book III, Lesson 11, Note 1.)
あかるい	**akarui**	bright
つよい	**tsuyoi**	strong
きたない	**kitanai**	dirty
そうじを　する	**sōji o suru**	clean
そうじ	**sōji**	cleaning
ヒーター	**hītā**	heater
あたたかい	**atatakai**	warm
かぜを　ひく	**kaze o hiku**	catch a cold
かぜ	**kaze**	a cold
ひく	**hiku**	catch
いっしょうけんめい	**isshōkemmei**	as hard as one can
ピアニスト	**pianisuto**	pianist
うちゅうひこうし	**uchū hikōshi**	astronaut
うちゅう	**uchū**	universe
ひこうし	**hikōshi**	aviator
びょうき	**byōki**	sickness
びんぼう（な）	**bimbō(na)**	poor
みそしる	**misoshiru**	miso soup
みそ	**miso**	soybean paste
しる	**shiru**	soup
ハンサム（な）	**hansamu(na)**	handsome
でる	**deru**	graduate, leave
たいてい	**taitei**	usually, most of the time
たずねる	**tazuneru**	visit
にもつ	**nimotsu**	baggage, cargo

だす	**dasu**	mail
かるい	**karui**	light
ざんぎょう	**zangyō**	overtime
たいへん（な）	**taihen(na)**	hard, difficult
アパート	**apāto**	apartment
せまい	**semai**	small, narrow
ひっこす	**hikkosu**	move (house)
やきもの	**yakimono**	pottery
シャツ	**shatsu**	shirt
きぬ	**kinu**	silk
スカーフ	**sukāfu**	scarf
ウイスキー	**uisukī**	whiskey
はなたば	**hanataba**	bouquet

SHORT DIALOGUES

1. A: なんに　しますか。

B: ぼくは　コーヒーに　します。

C: そうですねえ。わたしは　ジュースが　いいです。

D: わたしは　アイスクリームです。

A: What'll you have?
B: I'll have coffee.
C: Let's see . . . I'll have juice.
D: Ice cream for me.

2. A: この　しょるいは　どう　しましょうか。

B: コピーしてから　すぐ　おくってください。

A: What should we do with this document?
B: Please send it immediately after making a copy (of it).

3. A: こんばん　えいがに　いきませんか。

B: あした　しけんが　ありますし、ざんねんですが . . .。

A: Would you like to go to a movie with me tonight?
B: I have an examination tomorrow, so although I'd like to . . .

4. A: おこさんは　おいくつですか。

B: らいげつ　やっつに　なります。

A: How old is you child?
B: He/She will be eight next month.

Vocabulary		
しょるい	**shorui**	document
すぐ	**sugu**	immediately

しけん	**shiken**	examination
おこさん	**okosan**	(someone else's) child(ren)
（お）いくつ	**(o-)ikutsu**	how old (for a person)
やっつ	**yattsu**	eight years old

QUIZ

I Read this lesson's Opening Dialogue and answer the following questions.

1. チャンさんは　だれに　ワープロの　カタログを　もらいましたか。
2. Aしゃの　ワープロの　45Sは　たかく　なりましたか、やすく　なりましたか。
3. おがわさんは　なにぶの　ひとですか。
4. あたらしい　ワープロは　つかいかたが　かんたんですか。

II Put the appropriate particles in the parentheses.

1. ともだちが　わたし（　　）しま（　　）シャツ（　　）くれました。
2. デザートは　アイスクリーム（　　）しましょう。
3. きょう　あたらしい　ワープロ（　　）きました。つかいかた（　　）かんたんです（　　）、とても　べんりです。
4. とりひきさき（　　）じゅうしょは　わたしより　ひしょ（　　）ほう（　　）よく　しっています。
5. ひるごはん（　　）たべてから、こうえん（　　）さんぽしましょう。
6. わたしは　こども（　　）ころ　ピアニスト（　　）なりたかったです。
7. みちが　こんでいます（　　）、ひとが　おおいです（　　）、いきたくないです。
8. テレビ（　　）ふるく　なりましたから、あたらしいの（　　）かえます。
9. あたらしい　カメラ（　　）ほしいなあ。

III Complete the questions so that they fit the answers.

1. （　　）ワープロを　かいますか。
   45S に　します。
2. （　　）でんわを　かけますか。
   うちに　かえってから　かけます。

3. （　　）に　そうだんしましたか。
システムぶの　おがわさんに　そうだんしました。

IV Complete the sentences with the appropriate form of the verbs indicated.

1. みそしるの（　　）かたを（　　）ください。（つくる、
おしえる）

2. わすれものは　まだ　じむしつに（　　）いません。（とど
く）

3. まいにち　うちに（　　）から、1じかんぐらい　にほんごを
べんきょうします。（かえる）

4. よく（　　）から（　　）ください。（かんがえる、きめる）

5. こどもに（　　）まえに、かないと　よく　そうだんします。
（はなす）

6. にほんの　うたを（　　）ことが　できますか。（うたう）

V Answer the following questions.

1. あなたは　にほんごが　じょうずに　なりましたか。

2. あなたは　もう　けさの　しんぶんを　よみましたか。

3. あさ　しょくじを　する　まえに　はを　みがきますか、
しょくじを　してから　はを　みがきますか。

4. あなたの　すきな　りょうりの　つくりかたを　かんたんに
せつめいしてください。（Use . . . **te kara**, . . . **mae ni.**）

NEW KANJI

1. 課 _カ

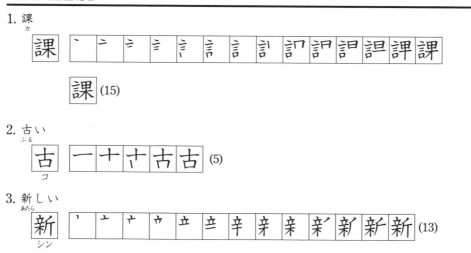

課 ` ｀ ｀ ｚ ｚ ｚ 言 言 訁 訂 評 評 課 課
課 (15)

2. 古い _{ふる}

古 一 十 十 古 古 (5)
_コ

3. 新しい _{あたら}

新 ` ｀ ㇒ ㇒ 立 立 辛 辛 亲 亲 新 新 新 (13)
_{シン}

4. 安(やす)い

安 (アン) 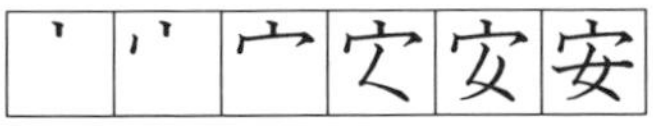 (6)

5. システム部(ブ)

部 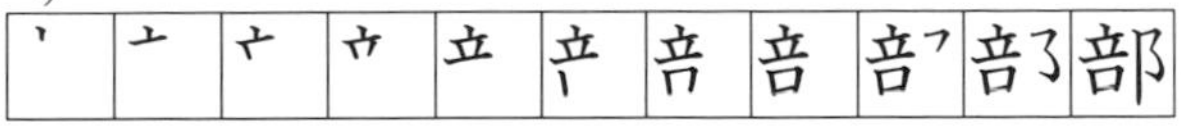 (11)

Readings:

話：　電話(デンワ)，話(はな)す

LESSON **6**   A PALE FACE

After meeting Mr. Chang in the elevator Mr. Katō advises him to take the rest of the day off.

かとう： かおいろが よく ありませんね。かぜですか。

チャン： ええ、おととい いしゃに 行って 薬を もらってき ましたが、なかなか よく なりません。けさは ねつ が 38度 ありました。

かとう： それじゃ、早く うちに かえって 休んだ ほうが いいですよ。

チャン： でも、この プロジェクトが はじまったばかりですか ら・・・。

かとう： むりを しない ほうが いいですよ。来しゅうは も っと いそがしく なりますから、いまの うちに なおした ほうが いいですよ。

チャン： それでは もうしわけありませんが、すずきくんか き むらくんに 後を よく たのんでから、かえります。

かとう： すずきくんには さっき べつの 用事を たのみまし たから、きむらくんの ほうが いいですよ。

チャン： わかりました。では、おさきに しつれいします。

かとう： お大事に。

Katō: (Your) complexion isn't good. Caught cold?

Chang: Eh, I went to the doctor the day before yesterday and got medicine, but it's not getting any better. My temperature this morning was 38 degrees.

Katō: In that case it's better to go home early and get some rest.

Chang: Actually, since this project has just started—

Katō: It's better not to overdo it. Next week'll be (even) busier. It'd be better if you got well right away.

Chang: Well then, I'm sorry but I'll leave after asking Suzuki or Kimura (to look after) the rest (of my work).

Katō: I just asked Suzuki (to do) some other work. It'll have to be Kimura.

Chang: I see. Good-bye, then.

Katō: Take care of yourself.

かおいろ	kaoiro	complexion
かお	kao	face
いろ	iro	color
〜てくる	-te kuru	(*lit.*) "go, do something and return"
なかなか〜ない	nakanaka . . . nai	not any/at all
それじゃ	soreja	in that case
〜た ほうが いい	-ta hō ga ii	it's better to . . ./ (you) had better . . .
プロジェクト	purojekuto	project
はじまる	hajimaru	start
〜たばかり	-ta bakari	(have) just
むりを する	muri o suru	overdo
むり	muri	impossible
〜ない ほうが いい	-nai hō ga ii	it's better not to . . .
もっと	motto	more
いまの うちに	ima no uchi ni	right away, before it's too late
それでは	sore dewa	well then
もうしわけありません	mōshiwake arimasen	I'm sorry (*lit.* "There's no excuse")
もうしわけ	mōshiwake	excuse, apology
〜くん	-kun	Mr., Master (informal men's speech)
か	ka	or (particle)
あと	ato	rest
たのむ	tanomu	request
さっき	sakki	a short time ago
べつの	betsu no	some other (thing)
ようじ	yōji	work, business
おさきにしつれいします	o-saki ni shitsurei shimasu	good-bye
さき	saki	ahead, before, beyond
おだいじに	o-daiji ni	Take care of yourself. (Said to sick people.)

GRAMMAR & LESSON OBJECTIVES

- **. . . hō ga ii desu**
  Uchi ni kaette yasunda hō ga ii desu yo.
  Muri o shinai hō ga ii desu yo.
  Ima no uchi ni naoshita hō ga ii desu yo.
  Kimura-kun no hō ga ii desu yo.
  As in these sentences, which are suggestions, the **-ta** form is more common before **hō ga ii desu**, although recently the dictionary form has also come to be used. For negatives, whether verbs or adjectives, always use the plain **-nai** form. For either type of adjective, use the ordinary form, such as **ōkii hō ga ii desu** or **benrina hō ga ii desu**. After nouns add the particle **no**.

NOTES

1. **Yoku arimasen.**
   This is the same as **yokunai desu** (Book I, p. 97).
   ex. 1. **Ōkiku arimasen/nai desu.**
   　　2. **Takaku arimasen/nai desu.**
   Similarly with **-na** adjectives: **Shizuka dewa/ja arimasen** or **Benri dewa/ja arimasen** (introduced in Book I, p. 99) can be **Shizuka dewa/ja nai desu** or **Benri dewa/ja nai desu**. These alternative patterns are interchangeable in meaning.

2. **Isha ni itte kusuri o moratte kimashita.**
   This **-te kuru** pattern sometimes has its literal meaning of "go, do something and return." (See Book III, Lesson 7 for a fuller discussion of this pattern.) The sentence can be translated, "I went to the doctor, got (some) medicine, and came back."
   ex. **Pan o katte kimasu.** "I'll buy bread (and come back)."

3. **Nakanaka yoku narimasen.**
   Nakanaka plus a negative implies that, contrary to expectations, something does not exist or has not happened or a favorable outcome is lacking despite a person's efforts or expectations.
   ex. 1. **Eigo ga nakanaka jōzu ni narimasen.** "(I) still haven't become good at English."
   　　2. **Tanaka-san kara tegami ga nakanaka todokimasen.** "The letter (I've been waiting for) from Tanaka hasn't arrived."

4. **Kono purojekuto ga hajimatta bakari desu kara.**
   The pattern **-ta bakari** indicates something has just happened.
   ex. 1. **Watashi wa ima kita bakari desu.** "I just now arrived."
   　　2. **Sono nyūsu o shitta bakari desu.** "I just learned that news."

5. **Suzuki-kun ka Kimura-kun ni . . .**
   -kun is less polite than **-san**. Typically heard when younger boys or men are being spoken to, it is never used between women or when addressing elders.

6. **O-saki ni shitsurei shimasu.**
   The sense of this is that by leaving before others, one is doing something one should excuse oneself for. It is a very common expression, often shortened to either **o-saki ni** or **shitsurei shimasu**. (See Book I, p. 61.) **O-saki ni** may also be said when proceeding others through a door or into a car and so on.

PRACTICE

KEY SENTENCES

1. すぐ けいさつに でんわした ほうが いいです。
2. あの みせへ いって、たばこを かってきます。

1. You'd better telephone the police immediately.
2. I'm going to that shop to buy tobacco.

けいさつ　　　　　　　　**keisatsu**　　　　　police

EXERCISES ——————————————————————

I　Review: Study the examples again and convert the verbs into the **-nai** form.

　A. Reg. I

　　ex.　いく →　　いかない　　　はなす→ はなさない
　　　　　いそぐ→ いそがない　　　まつ→　　またない
　　　　　のむ→　　のまない　　　ならう→ ならわない
　　　　　しぬ→　　しなない　　　なおる→ なおらない
　　　　　あそぶ→ あそばない　　　ある→　　ない

　　　　1. およぐ　　　4. もらう　　　7. すむ　　　10. ひろう
　　　　2. つくる　　　5. おとす　　　8. かかる　　　11. けす
　　　　3. みがく　　　6. もつ　　　　9. よぶ　　　12. つかう

　B. Reg. II and Irreg.

　　ex.　しめる→ しめない　　　くる→ こない
　　　　　おりる→ おりない　　　する→ しない

　　　　1. はじめる　　3. いる　　　5. もってくる　　　7. でんわする
　　　　2. できる　　　4. きめる　　6. せつめいする　　8. わすれる

II　Make dialogues by changing the underlined parts as in the examples given.

　A. *ex.* **A:** <u>タクシーで　いき</u>ましょうか。
　　　　B: いいえ、<u>ちかてつで　いった</u>　ほうが　いいですよ。

　　　　1. すずきさんに　きく、かとうさんに
　　　　2. ごご　でんわする、ごぜんちゅうに
　　　　3. あした　しょるいを　おくる、いま　すぐ

　B. *ex.* **Q:** <u>いく　まえに　でんわした</u>　ほうが　いいですか。
　　　　A: ええ、その　ほうが　いいですよ。

　　　　1. ねる　まえに　くすりを　のむ
　　　　2. ふなびんで　おくる
　　　　3. ストーブを　けす
　　　　4. たなかさんに　しらせる

C. *ex.* **Q:** どう　しましょうか。

　　　A: <u>はやしさんに　はなした</u>　ほうが　いいです。

　　　　1. まどを　しめる　　　　4. バスで　いく
　　　　2. たなかさんに　いう　　5. はやしさんに　そうだんする
　　　　3. すぐ　でかける　　　　6. （お）さけを　もってくる

D. *ex.* **Q:** いま　でんわしても　いいですか。

　　　A: <u>もう　おそいです</u>から、<u>し</u>ない　ほうが　いいですよ。

　　　　1. たばこを　すう、けんこうに　よくないです
　　　　2. ここに　くるまを　とめる、こうさてんに　ちかいで
　　　　　す
　　　　3. さけを　のむ、まだ　びょうきが　なおっていません
　　　　4. もう　はっぴょうする、まだ　ぶちょうに　はなして
　　　　　いません

E. *ex.* **Q:** <u>だれ</u>が　いいですか。

　　　A: <u>すずきくんか　きむらくん</u>が　いいです。

　　　　1. なに、ちゅうかりょうり、フランスりょうり
　　　　2. いつ、げつよう、かよう
　　　　3. どこ、ぎんざ、しんじゅく
　　　　4. いくらの、1,500えん、2,000えんの

F. *ex.* **Q:** どちらへ？

　　　A: <u>いしゃに　いって</u>、<u>くすりを　もらって</u>きます。

　　　　1. ほんやに　いく、しゅうかんしを　かう
　　　　2. しょくどうへ　いく、しょくじを　する
　　　　3. うちへ　かえる、ひるごはんを　たべる
　　　　4. ぎんこうに　いく、おかねを　はらう
　　　　5. ゆうびんきょくへ　いく、てがみを　だす

Vocabulary

なおる	**naoru**	get well, be fixed
ストーブ	**sutōbu**	(heating) stove
しらせる	**shiraseru**	inform
けんこう	**kenkō**	health

はっぴょうする	**happyō suru**	announce, publicize
はっぴょう	**happyō**	announcement
ちゅうかりょうり	**Chūka ryōri**	Chinese cooking
げつよう	**getsuyō**	Monday
かよう	**kayō**	Tuesday
しんじゅく	**Shinjuku**	Shinjuku (area in Tokyo)
しゅうかんし	**shūkan-shi**	weekly magazine
はらう	**harau**	pay

SHORT DIALOGUES

1. A: おかぜですか。

   B: ええ。たいした　ことは　ありませんが、せきが　とまりません。

   A: それは　いけませんね。

   A: (Do you have) a cold?
   B: Yes. It's nothing serious, but the coughing doesn't stop.
   A: That's too bad. (*lit.* "It doesn't go [well], does it?")

2. A: おかぜは　いかがですか。

   B: おかげさまで　だいぶ　よくなりました。

   A: それは　よかったですね。

   A: How's your cold?
   B: Thank you (for asking). It's considerably better.
   A: That's good.

3. すずき: もしもし、すずきです。これから　びょういんに　よってから、かいしゃに　いきます。すみませんが、すこし　おそく　なります。

   かとう: どうか　しましたか。

   すずき: ええ、ちょっと　あしに　けがを　しました。

   Suzuki: Hello. This is Suzuki. I'm going to stop by the hospital, and I'll come to the office after that. So I'll be a little late.
   Katō: What's the matter? (*lit.* "Has something happened . . . ?")
   Suzuki: Well, I've hurt my leg.

Vocabulary		
たいした	**taishita**	serious, important
せき	**seki**	coughing, cough
とまる	**tomaru**	stop
おかげさまで	**o-kage-sama de**	Thank you (*lit.* "Thanks to [you]")
だいぶ	**daibu**	considerably, greatly
これから	**korekara**	from now (on)

よる		**yoru**	stop by, drop in
どうか　する		**dōka suru**	something is wrong
あし		**ashi**	leg, foot
けがを　する		**kega o suru**	(be) hurt
	けが	**kega**	injury, wound

QUIZ

I Read this lesson's Opening Dialogue and answer the following questions.

1. チャンさんは　だれに　くすりを　もらいましたか。
2. チャンさんは　けさ　なんど　ねつが　ありましたか。
3. いしゃに　いってから、チャンさんの　かぜは　すぐ　よく
　なりましたか。
4. チャンさんは　きょう　はやく　うちに　かえりますか。

II Put the appropriate particles in the parentheses.

1. いまの　うち（　　）なおした　ほう（　　）いいですよ。
2. かとうさんは　げつようび（　　）かようび（　　）にほ
　んに　かえります。
3. ［わたしは］　さっき　すずきくん（　　）べつ（　　）よう
　じを　たのみました。
4. かぜ（　　）なおりません。もうしわけありません（　　）、
　うち（　　）かえっても　いいですか。
5. では、おさき（　　）しつれいします。

III Complete the sentences with the appropriate form of the verbs indicated.

1. じかんが　ありませんから、（　　）ほうが　いいですよ。
　（いそぐ）
2. この　さかなは　ふるいですから、（　　）ほうが　いいで
　すよ。（たべる）
3. まだ　かぜが（　　）いませんから、うちで（　　）も
　いいですか。（なおる、やすむ）
4. はやく　かぞくに（　　）ほうが　いいですよ。（しらせる）
5. わたなべさんの　へやに（　　）、タイプを（　　）きます。
　（いく、たのむ）
6. きょうは　みちが（　　）いますから、くるまで（　　）
　ほうが　いいですよ。（こむ、いく）

IV Circle the correct words in the parentheses.

1. わたしは （あまり、たいてい） でんしゃの なかで しんぶんを よみます。

2. タクシーを まっていますが、（なかなか、ゆっくり） きません。

3. （はじめて、まず） はやしさんに しらせて、（それでは、それから） みんなに しらせてください。

4. すずきくんは （さっき、もうすぐ） きました。

V Choose a sentence to make a suggestion appropriate to the situation described.

A. Your friend is embarrassed about having left his bag on the train.

1. でんしゃを おりて、えきいんに はなしてきます。

2. えきの じむしつに いって、えきいんに はなした ほうが いいです。

3. でんしゃに のって、えきいんに はなした ことが あります。

B. Your friend, despite having a fever, is drinking sake.

1. おさけを たくさん のんだ ほうが いいですよ。

2. はやく ねた ほうが いいですよ。

3. すこし おさけが のみたいです。

NEW KANJI

1. 薬
(くすり)

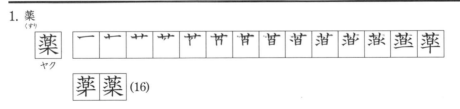

ヤク

薬 一 十 艹 艹 艹 甘 甘 甘 甘 莒 莒 莒 薬 薬

薬 薬 (16)

2. 38度
(ド)

度 ` 亠 广 广 庐 庐 庐 庐 度 (9)

たび

3. 早く
(はや)

早 丨 口 日 日 旦 早 (6)

ソウ

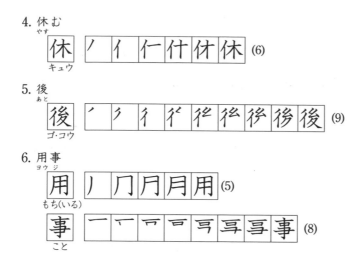

4. 休む
やす
休 ノ イ 仁 什 休 休 (6)
キュウ

5. 後
あと
後 ノ ク 彳 彳 彳 彳 彳 後 (9)
ゴ・コウ

6. 用事
ヨウ ジ
用 ノ 刀 月 月 用 (5)
もち(いる)

事 一 一 一 一 写 写 写 事 (8)
こと

Readings:

　来： 来ました，来しゅう
　　　　　　　　　　ライ
　大： 大きい，お大事に
　　　　おお　　　　ダイ ジ

LESSON 7 MR. JOHNSON'S ARRIVAL

Mr. Katō and Mr. Suzuki are talking about Mr. Johnson's arrival tomorrow.

かとう： あしたは ジョンソンさんが 日本に 来る 日です ね。

すずき： ええ、そうです。

かとう： だれか 成田空港まで むかえに 行ってくれません か。

すずき： 私が 行きます。時間が ありますから。

かとう： けさ たのんだ 仕事は きょうじゅうに おわります か。

すずき： はい、できます。

かとう： じゃ、おねがいします。ところで、ジョンソンさんを 知っていますか。

すずき： ロンドンの じむしょに いた 人ですね。

かとう： ええ。

すずき： しゃしんで 見た ことが あります。

かとう： 成田空港に 着く 時間は 14時50分です。ひこうきは 早く 着く ことも ありますから、早めに ちゅう しょくを すませて 出発してください。

すずき： はい。ジョンソンさんの とまる ホテルは どこです か。

かとう： わたなべさんが 知っていますから、わたなべさんに きいてください。

すずき： はい。

Katō: Tomorrow is the day Mr. Johnson comes to Japan, isn't it?
Suzuki: Yes, that's right.
Katō: Won't someone be going to meet (him) at Narita Airport?
Suzuki: I'll go. I have time.
Katō: Will the work (I) asked (you to do) this morning be finished today?
Suzuki: Yes, I can (do it).
Katō: All right, please meet him. By the way, do you know Mr. Johnson?

Suzuki: He's (one of the) people in the London Office, I believe.

Katō: Right.

Suzuki: (I've) seen (his) picture.

Katō: His arrival time at Narita Airport is 14: 50. Since planes sometimes arrive early, please finish lunch earlier and leave.

Suzuki: Yes, sir. Where's the hotel Mr. Johnson's staying at?

Katō: Ms. Watanabe knows. Please ask her.

Suzuki: I see.

Vocabulary

だれか	**dare ka**	someone, anyone
むかえに　いく	**mukae ni iku**	go to meet
むかえる	**mukaeru**	meet, greet
ロンドン	**Rondon**	London
じむしょ	**jimusho**	office
はやめに	**hayame ni**	early
ちゅうしょく	**chūshoku**	lunch
すませる	**sumaseru**	finish
しゅっぱつする	**shuppatsu suru**	leave
しゅっぱつ	**shuppatsu**	departure
とまる	**tomaru**	stay, stop at

GRAMMAR & LESSON OBJECTIVES

• Modifying nouns

A pattern corresponding to the relative clause in English is made by placing the modifiers before the noun. A verb appearing in the middle of the sentence is in a plain form, as noted earlier (p. 38).

present	aff.	**ashita kuru hitotachi**, "people (who are) coming tomorrow"
	neg.	**ashita konai hitotachi**, "people (who are) not coming tomorrow"
past	aff.	**kinō kita hitotachi**, "people (who) came yesterday"
	neg.	**kinō konakatta hitotachi**, "people (who) didn't come yesterday"

The following show how a sentence is converted into a modifying clause.

ex. 1. **Watashi wa hon o kaimashita.** → **Watashi ga/no katta hon**, "the book (that) I bought"

   2. **Watashi wa kinō Ginza de hon o kaimashita.** → **Watashi ga kinō Ginza de katta hon**, "the book (which) I bought in the Ginza yesterday"

Note the changes in word order, the verb forms and the particles. Particle **wa** is replaced by **ga**, or when a clause is very short, it often becomes **no**.

ex. 1. **tenisu no jōzuna hito**, "a person (who is) good at tennis"

   2. **ashi no nagai otoko**, "a man who has/having long legs." Alternatively, "a man with long legs" or "a long-legged man."

Clauses ending -i and -na adjectives and noun plus **desu** in the plain form, either past or negative, can modify nouns. (See Appendix A for the patterns.)

These plain forms, shown in the following three examples, are also discussed in the next lesson. (See the table, p. 85.)

ex. 1. **takakatta hon**, "a book which was expensive"

    2. **suki datta hito**, "a person (I) once liked"

    3. **kyonen no natsu made byōin datta tatemono**, "the building which was a hospital until last summer"

Take careful note of five sentences in the dialogue in which this type of modification pattern occurs.

1. **Ashita wa Jonson-san ga Nihon ni kuru hi desu ne.**
2. **Kesa tanonda shigoto wa kyō-jū ni owarimasu ka.**
3. **Rondon no jimusho ni ita hito desu ne.**
4. **Narita Kūkō ni tsuku jikan wa 14-ji 50-pun desu.**
5. **Jonson-san no tomaru hoteru wa doko desu ka.**

NOTES

1. **Dare ka kūkō made mukae ni itte kuremasen ka.**

   -te kuremasen ka is a form of request, but it would not be used when speaking to a superior. The meaning is "do (something) for (me/us)."

   ex. **Kite kuremasen ka.** "Won't you please come?"

   Some other interrogatives of the same type as **dare ka** are **nani ka**, "something," **itsu ka**, "sometime," and **doko ka**, "somewhere."

   ex. 1. **Dare ka mite imashita ka.** "Was anyone watching?"

       2. **Kyōto ni itsu ka ikitai desu.** "(I) want to go to Kyoto sometime."

       3. **Nani ka tsumetai nomimono o kudasai.** "Give me (any kind of) cold drink."

2. **Hikōki wa hayaku tsuku koto mo arimasu.**

   In addition to the information given in Lesson 4, you should observe that **koto** is a noun meaning "thing," "happening," "experience" and the pattern **koto mo arimasu** conveys the idea "it sometimes happens that . . . ," "there are/have been cases of . . ."

   ex. 1. **Ōsaka e wa taitei Shinkansen de ikimasu ga, hikōki de iku koto mo arimasu.** "(I) usually go to Osaka on the Shinkansen, but sometimes (I) go by plane."

       2. **Do-yōbi wa shigoto wa yasumi desu ga, kaigi o suru koto mo arimasu.** "Saturday is a day off, but sometimes meetings are held."

       3. **Nihon no chūgakkō de wa seito ni Eigo o oshiemasu ga, Furansu-go o oshieru gakkō mo arimasu.** "Japanese middle schools teach English to (their) students, but there are some schools which teach French."

PRACTICE

KEY SENTENCES

1. スミスさんは　ABCで　はたらいている　べんごしです。
2. きゅうしゅうは　あたたかい　ところですが、ふゆは　ゆきが ふる　ことも　あります。

1. Mr. Smith is a lawyer who works for ABC.
2. Kyushu is a warm region, but in winter sometimes it snows.

Vocabulary

ゆきが　ふる	**yuki ga furu**	it snows (*lit.* "snow falls")
ゆき	**yuki**	snow
ふる	**furu**	fall

EXERCISES

I　Noun-modifying patterns: Memorize the following sentences.

A. 1. これは　<u>あした　おくる</u>　にもつです。
2. たなかさんは　<u>あそこで　ほんを　よんでいる</u>　ひとです。
3. これは　<u>ははが　かいた</u>　えです。
4. <u>らいしゅう　ならう</u>　レッスンは　8かです。
5. <u>きのう　きた</u>　ひとは　やまださんです。
6. <u>わたしが　とまった</u>　ホテルは　すばらしかったです。

B. 1. <u>ぎんこうに　いく</u>　じかんが　ありません。
2. <u>しらない</u>　ひとが　たずねて　きました。
3. <u>きってを　うっている</u>　ところを　しっていますか
4. <u>ロンドンから　きた</u>　ともだちに　あいました。
5. <u>きのう　こなかった</u>　ひとは　てを　あげてください。

C. 1. かれは　<u>あたまが　いい</u>　ひとです。
2. あれは　<u>ちちが　すきな</u>　えです。
3. <u>かみが　ながい</u>　ひとは　ホワイトさんです。
4. <u>フランスごが　じょうずな</u>　ひとを　しっていますか。

II　Make dialogues by changing the underlined parts as in the examples given.

A. *ex.* Q: これは　なんですか。
　　A: <u>えを　かく</u>　どうぐです。

　　1. ゆでたまごを　きります
　　2. トイレを　そうじします

3. おもい　にもつを　はこびます
4. ケーキを　やきます

B. *ex.* Q: すみません、とうきょうへ　いく　バスは　どれですか。
   A: あの　えきの　まえに　とまっている　バスです。

   1. 10じに　でます
   2. ぎんざを　とおります
   3. おおさかから　きました
   4. おおさかを　10じに　しゅっぱつしました

C. *ex.* Q: しんぶんを　うっている　ところを　しっていますか。
   A: さあ、ちょっと　わかりません。

   1. テニスが　できます
   2. たなかさんが　つとめています
   3. やすくて　おいしいです
   4. おいしくて　あまり　たかくないです

D. *ex.* Q: まいにち　いそがしいですか。
   A: ええ、てがみを　かく　じかんも　ありません。

   1. しんぶんを　よみます
   2. こどもと　あそびます
   3. ともだちと　おしゃべりします
   4. ふうふげんかを　します

E. *ex.* Q: パーティーに　きた　ひとは　だれですか。
   A: きむらさんです。

   1. きょねん　けっこんしました
   2. かさを　わすれました
   3. まだ　きていません
   4. まだ　もうしこんでいません
   5. かいぎに　しゅっせきしませんでした

F. *ex.* A: あの　ひとは　だれですか。
   B: どの　ひとですか。
   A: めがねを　かけている　ひとです。

B: ああ、あの　めがねを　かけている　ひとですか。
あれは　ホワイトさんです。

   1. せきを　しています
   2. いま　たちました
   3. おおきい　こえで　わらっています
   4. かみが　みじかいです
   5. せが　たかいです

III　Practice the following pattern by changing the underlined parts as in the example given.

ex. だれか　きましたか。

   1. なに、いってください
   2. どこ、いきたいですね
   3. いつ、あそびに　きてください
   4. だれ、よびましょうか

IV　Make dialogues by changing the underlined parts as in the example given.

ex. **Q**: いつも　ひこうきで　いきますか。
   A: ええ、たいてい　ひこうきで　いきますが、しんかんせん
で　いく　ことも　あります。

   1. じぶんで　ネクタイを　えらびます、つまが　えらび
ます
   2. あさごはんを　たべます、たべません
   3. やくそくの　じかんを　まもります、たまに　おそく
なります

| Vocabulary |

レッスン	**ressun**	lesson
〜か	**-ka**	lesson (counter)
しらない　ひと	**shiranai hito**	stranger
あげる	**ageru**	raise
かれ	**kare**	he
どうぐ	**dōgu**	implement, machine, appliance, tool
ゆでたまご	**yude tamago**	boiled egg
きる	**kiru**	cut
トイレ	**toire**	toilet
おもい	**omoi**	heavy
はこぶ	**hakobu**	carry, transport

やく	**yaku**	bake, grill, roast
とおる	**tōru**	go through/past
も	**mo**	even (emphasis)
おしゃべりする	**o-shaberi suru**	chat
ふうふげんか	**fūfu-genka**	marital disagreement
ふうふ	**fūfu**	husband and wife
けんか	**kenka**	quarrel, fight
もうしこむ	**mōshikomu**	apply, propose
しゅっせきする	**shusseki suru**	attend
しゅっせき	**shusseki**	attendance
かける	**kakeru**	wear, put on (glasses)
せきを する	**seki o suru**	cough
たつ	**tatsu**	stand up
こえ	**koe**	voice
わらう	**warau**	laugh, smile
みじかい	**mijikai**	short
じぶんで	**jibun de**	by oneself
じぶん	**jibun**	oneself
えらぶ	**erabu**	choose
つま	**tsuma**	(one's own) wife
やくそく	**yakusoku**	promise, appointment
まもる	**mamoru**	keep, obey
たまに	**tama ni**	once in a while

SHORT DIALOGUES

1. かちょう： だれか ちょっと てを かしてください。
   わたなべ： なんでしょうか。
   かちょう： この しりょうを かたづけてくれませんか。
   わたなべ： はい、わかりました。

Section Chief: Won't someone lend me a hand for a moment?
Watanabe: What is it (you want)?
Section Chief: Do me the favor of putting away these papers.
Watanabe: Yes, certainly.

2. A: スーパーに いきますが、なにか かってきましょうか。
   B: ジュースを かってきてください。
   A: どんな ジュースが いいですか。
   B: あまり あまくないのを おねがいします。

A: I'm going to the supermarket. Can I get you anything?
B: Please get me some juice.
A: What kind of juice do you want.
B: The one that's not too sweet.

か ちょう	**kachō**	section chief
て を　かして	**te o kashite**	lend a hand
かす	**kasu**	lend
しりょう	**shiryō**	papers, documents
かたづける	**katazukeru**	put away, tidy up

QUIZ

I　Read this lesson's Opening Dialogue and answer the following questions.

1. だれが　ジョンソンさんを　くうこうまで　むかえに　いきますか。
2. ジョンソンさんは　どこの　じむしょに　いた　ひとですか。
3. かとうさんは　ジョンソンさんの　とまる　ホテルを　しっていますか。
4. すずきさんは　ジョンソンさんに　あった　ことが　ありますか。

II　Put the appropriate particles in the parentheses.

1. これは　わたし（　　）かいた　えです。
2. えき（　　）つく　じかんは　なんじですか。
3. わたしは　ジョンソンさん（　　）あった　ことは　ありませんが、しゃしん（　　）みた　ことは　あります。
4. はやく　しごと（　　）すませて、うちに　かえります。
5. くうこうまで　くるま（　　）むかえ（　　）いきます。
6. たいてい　ひとり（　　）りょこうしますが、ともだち（　　）いっしょに　いく　こと（　　）あります。

III　Complete the sentences with the appropriate form of the verbs indicated.

1. スペインごが（　　）ひとは　だれですか。（できます）
2. 〔あなたが〕　やまださんに（　　）ひは　いつですか。（あいます）
3. きのう　スライドを（　　）ひとは　きょう　みてください。（みませんでした）
4. えいごが（　　）ひとには　にほんごで　せつめいしましょう。（わかりません）

5. きのう（　　）ひとに　この　てがみを　おくってください。
（きませんでした）

6. きょう（　　）ものの　なかで　これが　いちばん　たかかったです。（かいました）

7. ジョンソンさんが（　　）ホテルを　しっていますか。
（とまっています）

8. これは　パンを（　　）どうぐです。（やきます）

9. きょう　おかねを（　　）ひとは　こちらで（　　）ください。（はらいます、はらいます）

10. これは　つまが（　　）ネクタイです。（えらびました）

VI Look at the picture and answer the questions.

1. いすに　すわっている　ひとは　だれですか。
2. めがねを　かけている　ひとは　だれですか。
3. セーターを　きている　ひとは　だれですか。
4. かさを　もっている　ひとは　だれですか。
5. たっている　ひとは　だれですか。

スミスさん　　スミスさんの　おくさん　　たなかさん

V Answer the following questions.

1. あなたが　すんでいる　ところは　どこですか。
そこは　どんな　まちですか。
2. あなたの　すきな　りょうりは　なんですか。
3. あなたが　みた　えいがの　なかで　なにが　いちばん　おもしろかったですか。
4. いままで　りょこうに　いった　ところの　なかで　どこが　いちばん　すばらしかったですか。

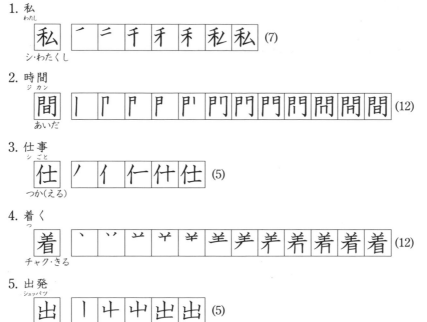

1. 私
   わたし
   私 — シ・わたくし (7)

2. 時間
   ジカン
   間 — あいだ (12)

3. 仕事
   シ ごと
   仕 — つか(える) (5)

4. 着く
   っ
   着 — チャク・きる (12)

5. 出発
   シュッパツ
   出 — で(る) (5)
   発 — ハツ・た(つ) (9)

Readings:

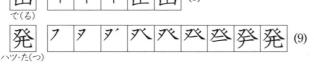

来 ： 来ます，来しゅう，来る
　　　 き　　　 ライ　　　　 く
日 ： 日よう日，日本語，来る日
　　　 ニチ　　 び　 ニ ホン ゴ　　 く　 ひ
事 ： 用事，仕事
　　　 ヨウ ジ　　 シ ごと

Kanji for recognition:　成田空港
　　　　　　　　　　　 なり た クウコウ

LESSON 8 THE O-BON FESTIVAL

Mr. Chang, who's thinking about a trip to Kyoto, asks Mr. Katō for advice.

チャン： 8月の 10日ごろ 京都へ あそびに 行きたいと 思いますが、しんかんせんと ひこうきと どちらが べんりですか。

かとう： しんかんせんの ほうが べんりだと 思いますよ。でも しんかんせんの していけんは もう ないと 思います。ひこうきの きっぷも たぶん うりきれでしょう。

チャン： どうしてですか。

かとう： 8月の 中ごろは おぼんで、くにへ かえる 人が おおぜい います。10日ごろから、この きせいラッシュが はじまりますから、りょこうは やめた ほうが いいですよ。

チャン： すずきくんも 10日に 京都の 家に かえると 聞きましたが・・・。

かとう： ええ、かれは 1か月 前に きっぷを かったと 言っていました。

チャン： そうですか。じゃ、京都まで 車で どのぐらい かかりますか。

かとう： 10時間 いじょう かかると 思いますよ。すずきくんは きょ年は 車で 行きましたが、すごい じゅうたいだったと 言っていました。

チャン： 日本は 人も 車も おおいですからね。ラッシュの ない ところへ 行きたいですねえ。

かとう： ラッシュの ない ところが ありますよ。

チャン： どこですか。

かとう： どこだと 思いますか。おぼんの ころの 東京ですよ。

チャン： なるほど。

Chang: Around August 10, I think I'd like to take a (pleasure) trip to Kyoto. Which is more convenient, the Shinkansen or a plane?

Katō: I reckon the Shinkansen is more convenient. But then I'm afraid there aren't any more Shinkansen reserved tickets. Plane tickets are probably sold out, too.

Chang: Why is that?

Katō: The O-Bon Festival is around the middle of August. There are hordes of people returning to their home towns. This homecoming rush begins around the tenth. It'd be best to give up your trip.

Chang: I heard Suzuki's going back to his home in Kyoto on the tenth, too.

Katō: Um. He said he bought a ticket a month early.

Chang: Is that so? How long does it take to Kyoto by car?

Katō: I guess it'd take more than ten hours. Suzuki went by car last year and he said the congestion was terrible.

Chang: It's because Japan has a lot of people and cars, wouldn't you say? I'd like to go some place where it's not crowded.

Katō: There is a place without crowds.

Chang: Where's that?

Katō: Where do you think it is? It's Tokyo around O-Bon.

Chang: I see.

Vocabulary		
おもう	**omou**	think
していけん	**shitei-ken**	reserved ticket
してい	**shitei**	appointment, designation, specification
けん	**ken**	ticket
もう〜ない	**mō . . . nai**	any/no more, any/no longer
うりきれ	**urikire**	sold out
なかごろ	**naka-goro**	around the middle
おぼん	**O-Bon**	O-Bon (midsummer festival)
くに	**kuni**	home town, birthplace, country
おおぜい	**ōzei**	hordes/lots of people
きせい	**kisei**	homecoming
ラッシュ	**rasshu**	rush
やめる	**yameru**	give up, stop
いえ	**ie**	house, home
いじょう	**ijō**	more than
じゅうたい	**jūtai**	congestion, traffic jam
おおい	**ōi**	many, much
なるほど	**naruhodo**	I see, it's reasonable

GRAMMAR & LESSON OBJECTIVES

• **to omou, to kiku, to iu**
  Kyōto e asobi ni ikitai to omoimasu. (I think)
  Shinkansen no hō ga benri da to omoimasu yo. (I reckon)
  Shinkansen no shitei-ken wa mō nai to omoimasu. (I'm afraid)
  Suzuki-san mo 10-ka ni Kyōto no ie e kaeru to kikimashita ga. (I heard)

Kare wa 1-kagetsu mae ni kippu o katta to itte imashita. (He said)
Suzuki-san wa kyonen wa kuruma de ikimashita ga, sugoi jūtai datta to itte imashita. (He said)

. . . to iu obviously signals quoted material. It should be noted that when a third person's statement is cited, the verb is **. . . to itte imashita** or **. . . to itte imasu.**

ex. **Hayashi-san wa Kyōto ni ikitai to itte imashita.** "Hayashi said that he wanted to go to Kyoto."

If the emphasis is on the action of saying, the verb **iu** is used in the same way as other verbs, e.g., **Suzuki-san wa dare ni iimashita ka.** "Whom did Mr. Suzuki say (it) to?"

cf. **Suzuki-san wa dare ni aimashita ka** "Whom did Mr. Suzuki meet?" Note that **to iimashita** is found in story-telling style, written or verbal. See Book III, Lesson 12.

A verb tense form in quoted material has no relation to the tense form of the verb ending the sentence, so it may be the same or it may be different. It is also quite common for negation to be expressed in the first, rather than the main verb, and this sometimes contrasts with the pattern in English, as in **Sumisu-san wa ashita konai to omoimasu,** if this is translated, "I don't think Smith is coming tomorrow."

When the subject is the speaker or the listener in interrogative sentences, **. . . to omou** is the recommended form to use. If the subject is a third person, **. . . to omotte iru** is used exclusively.

As in the examples above, verbs, adjectives and **desu** after nouns coming at the end of quoted material are in plain forms, as shown in the chart below.

Plain forms which precede **to omoimasu/to iimasu.**
Verbs

	Present		Past	
	aff.	neg.	aff.	neg.
Reg. I	tsukau	tsukawanai	tsukatta	tsukawanakatta
Reg. II	iru	inai	ita	inakatta
Irr.	kuru suru	konai shinai	kita shita	konakatta shinakatta

Adjectives, Noun + **desu**

	Present		Past	
	aff.	neg.	aff.	neg.
-i adj.	akai	akaku nai	akakatta	akaku nakatta
-na adj.	shizuka da	shizuka dewa/ja nai	shizuka datta	shizuka dewa/ja nakatta
N + **desu**	N da	N dewa/ja nai	N datta	N dewa/ja nakatta

• **deshō**
Hikōki no kippu mo tabun urikire deshō.

Deshō, seen in Lessons 2 and 3 as a way to soften a direct question, may indicate conjecture or probability, or what the speaker believes to be true. Words coming before **deshō** are in a plain form and in the case of **-na** adjectives, **deshō** comes directly after the stem, just as it directly follows nouns.

ex. 1. **Ano kōen wa shizuka desu.** → **Ano kōen wa shizuka deshō.** "That park is probably quiet."
2. **Kare wa bengoshi desu.** → **Kare wa bengoshi deshō.** "He's a lawyer, I suppose."
3. **Chan-san wa mada Ogawa-san ni hanashite inai deshō.** "Chang probably hasn't told Ogawa yet."

For fuller connective patterns, see Appendix A.

Since it implies tentativeness, **deshō** would sound awkward or irresponsible if it referred to the speaker's own action.

ex. **Sumisu-san wa ashita Ōsaka ni iku deshō.**

However, **Watashi mo ashita Ōsaka ni iku deshō** is awkward.

NOTES

1. The **O-Bon** Festival

For this festival on August 13–15 (there are a few local variations on the dates), many companies close down and millions of people desert the big cities. Originating in Buddhist beliefs fused with folk traditions, it celebrates the return of ancestral spirits to their birthplaces for a three-day visit and is, together with the New Year's holidays, a major event among the literally hundreds of annual festivals. Secularized to some extent in recent times, **O-Bon** is an occasion for family reunions, and the highlights are the **Bon Odori**, "Bon Dance," **O-haka-mairi**, "visits to (ancestral) graves," and the lighting of fires and lanterns to welcome and send off the spirits of the dead.

2. **Shitei-ken wa mō nai to omoimasu.**

The usage of **mō**, "already," **mō nai**, "not any more/longer," and **mada**, "yet, still," need not be confusing. Study the following examples.

ex. 1. Q: **Mada kippu wa arimasu ka.** "Do (you) still have tickets?"
A*a*: **Hai, mada arimasu.** "Yes, there are still (some available)."
A*n*: **Iie, mō arimasen.** "No, there aren't any more."
2. Q: **Kare wa mō dekakemashita ka.** "Has he gone out already?"
A*a*: **Hai, mō dekakemashita.** "Yes, he's already gone out."
A*n*: **Iie, mada dekakete imasen. Mada ie ni imasu.** "No, he hasn't left yet. He's still at home."

As shown in Book I (p. 95), **mō** can also mean simply "more," i.e., **Mō 1-mai kippu o kudasai,** "Give me one more ticket, please."

3. **Doko da to omoimasu ka.**

Expressions similar to this one are:
1. **Naze da to omoimasu ka.** "Why is it, do you think?"
2. **Dare ga sō itta to omoimasu ka.** "(Can) you guess who said so?"

PRACTICE

KEY SENTENCES

1. あしたは　ストですから、でんしゃも　バスも　うごかないと
おもいます。

2. きむらさんは　さっぽろを　しっていると　いっていました。

3. あしたは　たぶん　あめでしょう。

1. There's a strike tomorrow, so I expect trains and buses won't be running.
2. Kimura said he knows Sapporo.
3. Tomorrow will probably be rain(y).

Vocabulary

スト	**suto**	strike
うごく	**ugoku**	run, move, operate
たぶん	**tabun**	probably, perhaps
あめ	**ame**	rain

EXERCISES

Make dialogues by changing the underlined parts as in the examples given.

A. *ex.* **Q**: あたらしい　プロジェクトを　どう　おもいますか。

   A: <u>たいへんだ</u>と　おもいます。

    1. むずかしいです　　4. たいくつです
    2. おもしろいです　　5. リサーチが　ひつようです
    3. つまらないです　　6. むずかしい　しごとです

B. *ex.* **Q**: <u>たなかさんは　きます</u>か。

   Aa: はい、<u>くる</u>と　おもいます。

   An: いいえ、<u>こない</u>と　おもいます。

    1. この　しごとは　あしたまでに　できます
    2. にもつは　きょうじゅうに　つきます
    3. しゅしょうは　この　ニュースを　もう　しっています
    4. たなかさんは　こどもが　あります

C. *ex.* **Q**: <u>たなかさんは　もう　かえりました</u>か。

   Aa: ええ、もう　<u>かえった</u>と　おもいます。

   An: いいえ、まだ　<u>かえっていない</u>と　おもいます。

    1. しゅうかいは　もう　はじまりました
    2. だいじんは　この　ニュースを　もう　ききました
    3. たなかさんは　おきゃくさんに　もう　あいました
    4. けんきゅうしりょうは　もう　まとまりました

D. *ex.* Q: なつやすみに　なにを　しますか。
A: <u>ほっかいどうへ　あそびに　いきたいと</u>　おもいます。

1. ほんを　たくさん　よむ
2. すいえいを　ならう
3. にわの　ていれを　する
4. きゅうしゅうの　ともだちを　たずねる

E. *ex.* Q: あの　ひとの　<u>じむしょの　ある　ところを</u>　しってい
ますか。
A: <u>けいさつの　となりだと</u>　おもいます。

1. おくに、あたたかい　ところです
2. そつぎょうした　だいがく、にほんの　だいがくでは
ありません
3. しけんの　けっか、あまり　よくありませんでした
4. わかい　ころの　しごと、かんごふさんでした

F. *ex.* Q: すずきさんは　なんと　いっていましたか。
A: すずきさんは　<u>きのうは　どこにも　いかなかったと</u>
いっていました。

1. リンダ、さくらは　とても　きれいでした
2. ブラウン、あの　ミュージカルは　あまり　おもしろ
くありませんでした
3. スミス、あした　かいぎに　でたくないです
4. やまだ、あまり　スポーツを　する　じかんが　あり
ません

G. *ex.* Q: あしたの　てんきは　どうでしょうか。
A: たぶん　<u>あめ</u>でしょうね。

1. あの　みせ、たかいです
2. あの　しばい、おもしろくないです
3. にちようびの　こうえん、にぎやかです
4. これ、てきとうじゃ　ないです
5. あしたの　てんき、ゆきが　ふります
6. たなかさん、くる　ことが　できません
7. チャンさんの　かぜ、よく　なりました

Vocabulary

たいくつ（な）	**taikutsu(na)**	boring
リサーチ	**risāchi**	research
ひつよう（な）	**hitsuyō(na)**	necessary
しゅしょう	**shushō**	prime minister
しゅうかい	**shūkai**	gathering, assembly
だいじん	**daijin**	minister (of state)
おきゃくさん	**o-kyaku-san**	client, guest, visitor
けんきゅう	**kenkyū**	research, study
まとまる	**matomaru**	be brought together, be in order
すいえい	**suiei**	swimming
ていれ	**teire**	care, trimming, mending
となり	**tonari**	next, neighboring
そつぎょうする	**sotsugyō suru**	graduate
そつぎょう	**sotsugyō**	graduation
けっか	**kekka**	result
かんごふ（さん）	**kangofu(-san)**	nurse
ミュージカル	**myūjikaru**	musical
でる	**deru**	attend
しばい	**shibai**	play
てきとう（な）	**tekitō(na)**	suitable, appropriate

SHORT DIALOGUES

1. ブラウン： しんかんせんの　ざせきしていけんは　どこで
   うっていますか。

   つうこうにん：あそこの　みどりの　まどぐちで　うっていま
   す。

   ブラウン： きょうとまで　おとな　2まい　こども　1まい
   おねがいします。

Brown:　　Where are Shinkansen reserved seat tickets sold?
Passerby: (They're) sold at the Green (Ticket) Window over there.

Brown:　　I'd like two adult tickets and one child's to Kyoto.

Midori no Madoguchi

2. A: 10じ30ぷんはつ　ながのいきの　とっきゅうは　なんばんせん
　　　から　でますか。

　B: 8ばんせんです。

A: What (number) track does the 10:30 express going to Nagano depart from?
B: It's track number eight.

Vocabulary		
ざせき	**zaseki**	seat
つうこうにん	**tsūkōnin**	passerby
みどりの	**Midori no**	Green (Ticket) Window (for reserved
まどぐち	**Madoguchi**	seat and express tickets)
みどり	**midori**	green
まどぐち	**madoguchi**	window, clerk
おとな	**otona**	adult
〜はつ	**-hatsu**	departure
ながの	**Nagano**	Nagano (city)
〜いき	**-iki**	bound for
とっきゅう	**tokkyū**	special/limited express
〜ばんせん	**-bansen**	(counter for tracks)

QUIZ

I　Read this lesson's Opening Dialogue and answer the following questions.

　1. チャンさんは　8がつの　10かごろ　どこへ　あそびに　いき
　　　たいと　おもっていますか。

　2. おぼんの　ころは　どうして　はやく　ひこうきや　しんか
　　　んせんの　きっぷが　うりきれに　なりますか。

　3. すずきさんは　きょねん　くるまで　くにへ　かえりました
　　　か、しんかんせんで　かえりましたか。

　4. おぼんの　ころの　とうきょうには　ラッシュが　ないと
　　　だれが　いいましたか。

　5. あなたは　チャンさんが　8がつ10かに　きょうとへ　いくと
　　　おもいますか、いかないと　おもいますか。

II　Put the appropriate particles in the parentheses.

　1. 8ばんの　バスは　ぎんざ　（　　）とおる　（　　）おもいま
　　　す。

　2. スミスさんは　その　しごと　（　　）おがわさん　（　　）た
　　　のんだ　（　　）いっていました。

3. ねつが　あります（　　　）、のども　いたいです（　　　）、か
ぜだ（　　　）おもいます。

4. かれも　8がつ　10か（　　　）おおさか（　　　）うち（　　　）
かえる（　　　）いっていました。

III　Complete the questions so that they fit the answers. (Use a question word.)

1. すずきくんと　きむらくんと（　　　）が　わかいですか。
きむらくんの　ほうが　わかいと　おもいます。

2. リンダさんは（　　　）にほんに　くるでしょうか。
たぶん　らいねん　くるでしょう。

3. かれは（　　　）と　いっていましたか。
あしたは　つごうが　わるいと　いっていました。

4. この　えを（　　　）おもいますか。
なかなか　すばらしいと　おもいます。

5. あなたは（　　　）いきませんか。
あついですし、ひとが　おおいですし、いきたく　ありま
せん。

IV　Complete the sentences with the appropriate form of the verbs indicated.

1. かれは　きのう　たいしかんへ（　　　）と　おもいます。
（いきませんでした）

2. すずきさんは　あした（　　　）と　いっていました。（きま
せん）

3. かとうさんは（　　　）と　だれが　いっていましたか。（げ
んきでした）

4. かれは　ジョンソンさんに　あった　ことが（　　　）と　い
っていました。（ありません）

5. きのうの　えいがは（　　　）と　みんな　いっていました。
（おもしろくなかったです）

6. あの　ひとは　ブラウンさんの（　　　）と　おもいます。
（おくさんでは　ありません）

7. あしたは　たぶん　あめが（　　　）でしょう。（ふりません）

8. かいぎは　まだ（　　　）と　おもいます。（おわっていませ
ん）

V   Answer the following questions.

1. あしたは　いい　てんきでしょうか。
2. あなたは　いつから　にほんごを　ならっていますか。
3. にほんごの　べんきょうは　おもしろいと　おもいますか。
4. あなたは　なつやすみに　どこか　りょこうに　いきますか。

NEW KANJI

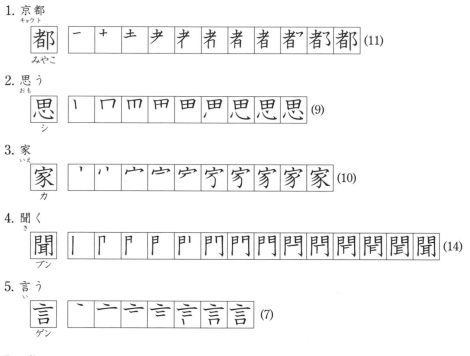

1. 京都
ょゥト
都
みゃこ
一 十 土 耂 耂 者 者 者 者 者 都 (11)

2. 思う
おも
思
シ
ノ 口 冖 田 田 田 思 思 思 (9)

3. 家
いえ
家
カ
丶 宀 宀 宀 宀 宀 宀 家 家 家 (10)

4. 聞く
き
聞
ブン
ｌ 門 門 門 門 門 門 門 門 門 門 門 聞 聞 (14)

5. 言う
い
言
ゲン
丶 一 二 言 言 言 言 (7)

Readings:

月：　月よう日，8月
　　ゲツ　　び　　ガツ

日：　日よう日，日本語，来る日，10日
　　ニチ　　び　ニ ホン ゴ　く ひ　とおか

LESSON **9** PREP SCHOOL

When going to the Tanakas' house, Mr. Johnson meets their daughter, Keiko, on her way out.

けい子： あら、ジョンソンさん。

ジョンソン： あ、けい子さん、お出かけですか。

けい子： ええ、これから 出かけなければ なりません。

ジョンソン： 今 すぐですか。

けい子： ごめんなさい。今日中に よび校の 申し込みを しなければ なりませんから。

ジョンソン： よび校？

けい子： ええ。いちばん 入りたかった 大学に ごうかくできませんでしたから、来年 また しけんを うけます。

ジョンソン： そうですか。じゃ、行ってらっしゃい。

けい子： 行ってまいります。

At the prep school.

けい子： 申し込みの しょるいは これで いいですか。これ、入学金と 3か月分の じゅぎょうりょうです。
それから サマーコースも 申し込みたいと 思いますが、後で ゆうびんで 申し込んでは いけませんか。

まどぐちの人： ゆうびんでも いいですよ。しはらいも わざわざ ここまで 来なくても いいですよ。銀行に ふりこんでください。

けい子： げんきんかきとめでも いいですか。

まどぐちの人： はい、どちらでも けっこうです。

Keiko:　　Oh, Mr. Johnson.

Johnson:　Ah, Keiko, are you going out?

Keiko:　　Yes, I have to (go out).

Johnson: (Do you have to leave) right now?

Keiko: Sorry, (yes). I have to register at a prep school today.

Johnson: Prep school?

Keiko: Yes. I didn't pass the exam for the university I wanted to attend, so I'll take the exams again next year.

Johnson: Well, well. Good-bye.

Keiko: Bye-bye.

Keiko: Are (my) application papers all right (like) this? This is the entrance fee and (here's) three months' tuition. I think I'd like to register for the summer course, too. Can't I register later by mail?

Clerk: Yes, mail is OK. As for payment, you don't have to go to the trouble of coming (all the way) here. Please transfer (it) to our bank.

Keiko: Is sending it by registered-cash mail all right?

Clerk: Yes, either will be fine.

Vocabulary

けいこ	**Keiko**	female given name
あら	**ara**	Oh! (women's speech)
〜なければ ならない	**-nakereba naranai**	must
ごめんなさい	**gomen-nasai**	I'm sorry, Excuse me
よびこう	**yobikō**	preparatory school
ごうかくする	**gōkaku suru**	pass (an examination), succeed
ごうかく	**gōkaku**	success, eligibility
うける	**ukeru**	take (an examination), receive, undergo, have
いってらっしゃい	**itte rasshai**	good-bye
いってまいります	**itte mairimasu**	good-bye
にゅうがくきん	**nyūgaku-kin**	entrance/matriculation fee
にゅうがく	**nyūgaku**	matriculation
さんかげつぶん	**san-kagetsu-bun**	3 months' (worth)
〜ぶん	**-bun**	portion, share
じゅぎょうりょう	**jugyō-ryō**	tuition
じゅぎょう	**jugyō**	instruction, lesson
〜りょう	**-ryō**	fee, charge
サマーコース	**samā kōsu**	summer course
あとで	**atode**	later, afterward
ゆうびん	**yūbin**	mail
〜ては いけない	**-te wa ikenai**	must not
でも いい	**demo ii**	is all right
しはらい	**shiharai**	payment
わざわざ〜する	**wazawaza (suru)**	go to the trouble of
わざわざ	**wazawaza**	especially
〜なくても いい	**-nakute mo ii**	don't have to
ふりこむ	**furikomu**	transfer
げんきんかきとめ	**genkin kakitome**	registered mail (for cash)
かきとめ	**kakitome**	registered mail

| どちらでも | dochira demo | either |
| けっこう（な） | kekkō(na) | fine |

GRAMMAR & LESSON OBJECTIVES

• Obligations, orders, prohibitions and permission

Kore kara dekakenakereba narimasen.

Kyō-jū ni mōshikomi o shinakereba narimasen.

-**nakereba** (made from the -**nai** form) **narimasen**, basically a pattern expressing obligation, may be used in making excuses, as here. As an order—"you must"—it sounds harsh and willful (not the kind of thing heard in polite circles). On the other hand, the tone is fairly neutral if it reflects conditions beyond the speaker's or listener's control.

ex. **Kyō wa basu mo chikatetsu mo suto desu kara, kuruma de ikanakereba narimasen yo.** "Since both buses and subways are on strike today, (you'll) have to go by car."

Sentences ending with -**te wa ikemasen**, "must not," have an imperative tone.

ex. **Ima dete wa ikemasen.** "You mustn't leave now."

Ato de yūbin de mōshikonde wa ikemasen ka.

This pattern and -**nakereba narimasen ka** (with the particle **ka** at the end) are freely used in asking questions. With almost the same meaning as -**te mo ii desu ka** (Book I, p. 149), -**te wa ikemasen ka** can be a way of asking permission. The pattern -**nakereba narimasen ka** means "Must you . . . ?" or "Must I . . . ?"

Yūbin demo ii desu.

Genkin kakitome demo ii desu ka.

Noun plus **demo ii desu** or **demo ii desu ka** is similarly used to give or ask permission. One meaning of **demo** being "even," the sense of **demo ii desu** is that it's all right even if X happens or a certain condition exists.

Koko made konakute mo ii desu.

By using this negative verb form, this pattern says it is OK not to do something.

NOTES

1. **O-dekake desu ka.**

This common expression is formed with **o-** plus the -**masu** stem and **desu**. It is used in its literal sense here but may occur simply as a greeting not particularly requiring an answer.

2. **Itte rasshai, itte mairimasu**

 Tadaima, okaeri nasai

 Itte rasshai is said to a person who will return to the place he or she is leaving, so it may be heard in offices and other places as well as homes. The person who leaves generally replies with **itte mairimasu/itte kimasu**. The expressions used when the person returns are **tadaima** and **okaeri nasai**, as given in the Short Dialogues in this lesson and on p. 15 of Book I.

3. **Yobikō**

Students attend **yobikō**, "prep schools," to prepare for college entrance examinations. The ratio of applicants to openings, especially at the top schools, is quite high and aspirants may take entrance exams for two or more years before meeting with success. Good prep schools may also have more applicants than openings, which explains why Keiko wants to apply early for the summer course.

4. **Kore, nyūgaku-kin to san-kagetsu-bun no jugyō-ryō desu.**

Note the absence of a particle after **kore**. This actually draws attention to the subject and here is like saying, "Here is the money for . . ."

5. **Kore de ii desu ka.**

After a noun or pronoun, asking permission or confirmation is done with **de ii desu ka,** and giving it with **de ii desu.** (See also Lesson 14.)

. . . **de yoku nai desu** cannot be used for refusals, the style of which is apt to vary with the situation.

ex. **Superu wa kore de ii desu ka.** "Is this spelling right?"

Hai, sore de ii desu. "Yes, that's right."

6. **Wazawaza koko made konakute mo ii desu yo.**

An adverb meaning "go to the trouble of," **wazawaza** may express appreciation or reluctance.

ex. 1. **Wazawaza kite kudasatte, arigatō gozaimasu.** "Thank you for coming (all this way to see us)."

2. **Parēdo o mi ni ikimasen ka.** "Wouldn't you like to watch the parade?"

Nichi-yōbi ni wazawaza Ginza made? "All the way to the Ginza? On Sunday?" (implying, "No thanks.")

7. **Dochira demo kekkō desu.**

Compared with **dochira demo ii desu**, this is a little politer.

In questions, **dochira demo/kore de ii desu ka** can be used, but **dochira demo/kore de kekkō desu ka** cannot.

PRACTICES

KEY SENTENCES

1. すぐ でかけなければ なりません。
2. あした がっこうに いかなくても いいです。
3. ゆうびんで おくっては いけませんか。
4. もうしこみは ゆうびんでも いいです。

1. I must go out now.
2. You don't have to go to school tomorrow.
3. Can't I send it by mail?
4. You can send your application form by mail.

EXERCISES

I Verbs: Review the examples and convert the verbs into the plain negative form.

ex. Reg. I　　はじまる→はじまらない
　　Reg. II　　いる→いない
　　Irreg.　　くる→こない
　　　　　　する→しない

1. まとまる	10. たずねる	19. わらう
2. かえる (change)	11. しゅっぱつする	20. かたづける
3. たのむ	12. ふる	21. えらぶ
4. しらせる	13. きる (cut)	22. まもる
5. はらう	14. むかえる	23. そつぎょうする
6. だす	15. やく	24. かわる
7. とまる	16. そうじする	25. いる (need)
8. よぶ	17. やめる	26. かす
9. でる	18. かってくる	27. もらってくる

II Practice the following pattern by changing the underlined parts as in the example given.

ex. あのう、ちょっと　たいしかんに　いかなければ　なりませんから　おさきに　しつれいします。

1. びょういんへ　いく
2. 6じの　とっきゅうに　のる
3. ビザを　もらいに　いく
4. ぎんこうで　おかねを　おろす

III Make dialogues by changing the underlined parts as in the examples given.

A. *ex.* **Q**: いま　おかねを　はらわなければ　なりませんか。
　A*a*: はい、おねがいします。
　A*n*: いいえ、いま　はらわなくても　いいです。

1. わたしも　くる
2. あしたまでに　する
3. いま　もうしこむ
4. パスポートを　みせる
5. きょうじゅうに　しらせる

B. *ex.* **Q**: <u>なまえを　かかなく</u>ても　いいですか。

   A*a*: はい、<u>かかなくても</u>　いいです。

   A*n*: すみませんが、<u>かいて</u>ください。

     1. スミスさんを　むかえに　いく
     2. みなさんに　せつめいする
     3. ひしょに　しらせる
     4. コピーを　たのむ

C. *ex.* <u>びょういんで　たばこを　すっては</u>　いけません。

     1. クラスに　おくれる
     2. みちに　ごみを　すてる
     3. こうさてんに　くるまを　とめる

D. *ex.* **Q**: <u>この　へやを　つかっては</u>　いけませんか。

   A*a*: どうぞ、<u>つかっても</u>　いいですよ。

   A*n*: すみませんが、<u>つかわ</u>ないでください。

     1. ここで　たばこを　すう
     2. なまえを　はっぴょうする
     3. クーラーを　つける
     4. くるまで　くる
     5. にわで　しゃしんを　とる

E. *ex.* **Q**: いま　<u>はんこ</u>が　ありません。<u>サイン</u>でも　いいですか。

   A: はい、<u>サイン</u>でも　けっこうです。

     1. ペン、えんぴつ
     2. じかん、あと
     3. ひま、にちようび
     4. げんきん、カード

Vocabulary

かわる	**kawaru**	change
いる	**iru**	need
ビザ	**biza**	visa
おろす	**orosu**	withdraw
パスポート	**pasupōto**	passport
おくれる	**okureru**	be late
ごみ	**gomi**	rubbish

すてる	**suteru**	throw away
クーラー	**kūrā**	air conditioner
はんこ	**hanko**	seal
サイン	**sain**	signature
えんぴつ	**empitsu**	pencil
カード	**kādo**	(credit) card

SHORT DIALOGUES

1. おとこの　ひと：かんごふさん、おさけを　すこし　のんでは
　　　　　　　　　　いけませんか。

　かんごふ：　　　まだ　だめですよ。もう　すこし　がまんし
　　　　　　　　　てください。

Man:　May I drink a little sake, Nurse?
Nurse:　No, (you) can't yet. Bear it a little longer.

2. やまだ：　　ただいま。

　わたなべ：おかえりなさい。なかやまさんは　いましたか。

　やまだ：　ええ、あって　しょるいを　わたしてきました。

Yamada:　　I'm back!
Watanabe:　Oh, good. Was Ms. Nakayama (there)?
Yamada:　　Yes, I saw her and handed her the documents.

Vocabulary

だめ（な）	**dame(na)**	not good
がまんする	**gaman suru**	bear, endure, be patient
ただいま	**tadaima**	I'm back!, I'm home!
おかえりなさい	**okaeri nasai**	Welcome home!
なかやま	**Nakayama**	Japanese surname
わたす	**watasu**	hand (over)

QUIZ

I　Read this lesson's Opening Dialogue and answer the following questions.

1. けいこさんは　いちばん　はいりたかった　だいがくに
ごうかくしましたか。

2. けいこさんは　どこに　いかなければ　なりませんか。

3. けいこさんは　サマーコースの　もうしこみに　また　よび
こうまで　いかなければ　なりませんか。

4. サマーコースの　しはらいは　げんきんかきとめでも　いい
ですか。

5. けいこさんは　サマーコースの　しはらいを　ぎんこうに
ふりこむでしょうか、げんきんかきとめで　おくるでしょう
か。

II　Put the appropriate particles in the parentheses.

1. とうふを　ちいさく　きりましたが、これ（　　　）いいです
か。
2. うち（　　　）むすこは　ことし　だいがく（　　　）ごうかく
しました。
3. えんぴつ（　　　）かいては　いけませんか。
ペン（　　　）おねがいします。
4. よく　かんがえて（　　　）、きめます。
5. じゅぎょうりょうを　ぎんこう（　　　）ふりこみます。

III　Complete the questions so that they fit the answers.

1. （　　　）までに　もうしこまなければ　なりませんか。
らいしゅうちゅうに　もうしこんでください。
2. （　　　）はらわなければ　なりませんか。
5,000えんです。
3. （　　　）たいしかんへ　いかなければ　なりませんか。
パスポートが　ひつようですから。
4. コーヒーと　こうちゃと（　　　）が　いいですか。
どちらでも　けっこうです。
5. （　　　）ぶんの　じゅぎょうりょうですか。
6かげつぶんです。

VI　Complete the sentences with the appropriate form of the verbs indicated.

1. あしたの　あさ　5じに（　　　）なければ　なりません。
（おきる）
2. しょるいを（　　　）は　いけませんよ。（わすれる）
3. この　ほんを　きょうじゅうに（　　　）なければ　なりませ
ん。（よむ）
4. かんじで（　　　）なければ　なりませんか。（かく）
5. いつまでに　おかねを（　　　）なければ　なりませんか。
（はらう）

6. ここを （　　　） も いいですか。（かたづける）

   まだ つかいますから、（　　　） なくても いいです。（かた

   づける）

7. ここは ちゅうしゃきんしですから、くるまを （　　　） は

   いけません。（とめる）

V   Answer the following questions.

1. にほんに いる がいこくの ひとは みんな にほんごを

   べんきょうしなければ なりませんか。

2. こうさてんに くるまを とめても いいですか。

3. デパートでは げんきんで はらわなくても いいですか。

4. あなたは あした なにを しなければ なりませんか。

NEW KANJI

1. けい子

   子（シ、こ）　マ　了　子　(3)

2. 今

   今（コン、いま）　ノ　入　今　今　(4)

3. よび校

   校（コウ）　一　十　オ　木　杧　杧　杧　杧　杧　校　(10)

4. 申し込み

   申（シン、もう）　丨　口　日　日　申　(5)

   込（こ）　ノ　入　入　込　込　(5)

5. 大学

   学（ダイガク、まな（ぶ））　丶　丷　ツ　ツ　ツ　学　学　学　(8)

Readings:

出： 出発，出かける
   シュッパツ　で

大： 大きい，大学
   おお　ダイガク

分： 20分，3か月分，
   ブン　ゲッブン

今： 今，今日中
   いま　きょう ジュウ

入： 気に入る，入る，入学金
   キ　い　はい　ニュウガクキン

来： 来ます，来年，来る，来ない
   き　ライネン　く　こ

LESSON 10 LETTER FROM KYUSHU

田中一郎　様

　ごぶさたしていますが、おげんきですか。

　私は　今　かぞくと　いっしょに　きゅうしゅうに　来ています。きのう、前から　行きたかった　あそ山に　行きました。すばらしい　ながめでした。

　私たちが　とまっている　りょかんの　にわで　ゆうべ　ほたるを　見ました。前に　東京の　りょうていで　かごの　中の　ほたるを　見た　ことは　ありますが、しぜんの　ほたるは　はじめてです。ほたるを　見ながら　りょかんの　主人と　話しました。　主人は　のうやくの　しようを　やめてから、川が　きれいに　なって、ほたるが　ふえたと　言っていました。

　あさって、私たちは　ここを　出て、くまもと市内を　けんぶつした　後、ながさきへ　行きます。ながさきは　えど時代の　日本の　たった　一つの　ぼうえきこうで、その　ころは　日本の　中で　一番　こくさいてきな　町だったと　ざっしで　よんだ　ことが　あります。家内は　日本の　れきしに　きょうみが　ありますから、とても　たのしみに　しています。

　みなみきゅうしゅうにも　行きたいと　思いますが、来しゅう木よう日に　アメリカ本社から　社長が　来ますから、それまでに　東京に　かえらなければ　なりません。

　おくさまにも　どうぞ　よろしく　おつたえください。

7月30日

　　　　　　　　　　　　　　　　　　ジョン・ブラウン

Dear Mr. (Ichirō) Tanaka,

It has been a long while since I last wrote you. I hope you are well.

I've come to Kyushu with my family. Yesterday we went to Mt. Aso, where we've wanted to go from quite some time ago. The view was splendid.

Last evening, in the garden of the inn we're staying at, we saw fireflies. I once saw fireflies in a cage at a Japanese restaurant in Tokyo, but this was the first time (for me) to see fireflies in their natural setting. While we were watching the fireflies, we chatted to the proprietor of the inn. He told us that after they stopped using agricultural chemicals, the rivers became cleaner and the fireflies proliferated.

The day after tomorrow we leave here, and after sightseeing in Kumamoto (City), we go to Nagasaki. I once read in a magazine that in the Edo period Nagasaki was Japan's only trading port and at that time it was the most international city in Japan. My wife is interested in Japanese history, so she's looking forward (to going there).

I'd like to go to southern Kyushu, too, but our president's coming from the U.S. head office Thursday of next week, so I have to get back to Tokyo by then.

Please give my best regards to your wife.

John Brown

Vocabulary

ごぶさたしています	**go-busata shiteimasu**	I have been remiss in not writing to you
ごぶさた	**go-busata**	remiss (in not writing, not visiting, etc.)
あそさん	**Aso-san**	Mt. Aso
ながめ	**nagame**	view
りょかん	**ryokan**	inn
ほたる	**hotaru**	firefly
りょうてい	**ryōtei**	Japanese restaurant, teahouse
かご	**kago**	cage, basket
しぜん	**shizen**	nature
～ながら	**-nagara**	while . . . -ing, at the same time
しゅじん	**shujin**	proprietor
のうやく	**nōyaku**	agricultural chemicals
しよう	**shiyō**	using, use, application
やめる	**yameru**	stop
かわ	**kawa**	river, creek, stream
ふえる	**fueru**	proliferate, increase
くまもと	**Kumamoto**	Kumamoto (city and prefecture)
けんぶつする	**kembutsu suru**	sightsee
けんぶつ	**kembutsu**	sightseeing, visit
ながさき	**Nagasaki**	Nagasaki (city and prefecture)
えどじだい	**Edo jidai**	Edo period
えど	**Edo**	Edo (former name of Tokyo)
たった ひとつ	**tatta hitotsu**	one only
たった	**tatta**	only
ぼうえき	**bōeki**	trading
～こう	**-kō**	port

こくさいてき（な）	**kokusai-teki(na)**	international
〜てき	**-teki**	like, resembling (suffix)
〜に きょうみが ある	**ni kyōmi ga aru**	be interested in
きょうみ	**kyōmi**	interest
みなみ	**minami**	south
ほんしゃ	**honsha**	head office, main company
おくさま	**oku-sama**	(someone else's) wife (polite)
つたえる	**tsutaeru**	give, convey, impart

NOTES

1. Ryōtei

Ryōtei are restaurants so exclusive that they accept reservations only from regular customers or through referrals by established patrons. They are typically buildings preserving a traditional, residential style of architecture with gardens, and the waitresses dress in kimono. Decor and atmosphere, traditional and varying with the season, may include such touches as displaying fireflies to heighten the feeling of a summer evening.

2. Hotaru o minagara ryokan no shujin to hanashimashita.

This is made with the stem of the **-masu** form and **-nagara**, and then the main clause is added. It is used when the subject of the sentence, always animate, is doing two things at the same time. The primary activity is designated in the main clause.

3. Ryokan no shujin to hanashimashita.

Remember the sentence, **Ogawa-san ni hanashimashita ka** in Lesson 5. (Person) **to hanasu** can be translated as "to talk with," whereas (person) **ni hanasu** means "to tell." The nuances of **to** and **ni** differ in that **to** suggests mutuality and interactiveness, while with the particle **ni** the feeling is more of one-sidedness.

4. Kumamoto-shinai o kembutsu shita ato, Nagasaki e ikimasu.

Ato means "after (doing . . .)" and the preceding verb is always in the **-ta** form, regardless of the tense of the verb in the main clause.

5. Edo jidai

Having ended over a century of civil unrest in 1600, Ieyasu, the first of the Tokugawa shoguns, then established (in 1603) the military government that stabilized the country and maintained peace until the Meiji Restoration in 1868.

6. kokusai-tekina

Adding the suffix **-teki** to nouns makes them **-na** adjectives. Other examples: **josei**, "woman, female," **josei-tekina**, "womanly, effeminate"; **dentō**, "tradition," **dentō-tekina**, "traditional."

7. Nagasaki wa Edo jidai no . . . ichiban kokusai-tekina machi datta to zasshi de yonda koto ga arimasu.

The particle **to** here shows the content of what Mr. Brown read in the magazine. It has the same function with such verbs as **hanasu**, "to speak," **renraku suru**, "to notify," **setsumei suru**, "to explain," and **narau**, "to learn."

8. **Dōzo yoroshiku o-tsutae kudasai.**

This sentence, conventionally included at the end of personal letters, is politer than **Dōzo yoroshiku.**

PRACTICE

EXERCISES

Make dialogues by changing the underlined parts as in the example given.

ex. **Q:** かとうさんは　なにを　していますか。

　　A: <u>ラジオを　ききながら</u>　<u>しんぶんを　よんでいます</u>。

　　1. コーヒーを　のみます、しごとを　します
　　2. たばこを　すいます、てがみを　かきます
　　3. はなしを　します、バスを　まちます
　　4. イヤホーンで　おんがくを　ききます、べんきょうします

QUIZ

Read this lesson's letter and answer the following questions.

1. ブラウンさんは　だれに　てがみを　だしましたか。
2. ブラウンさんは　ひとりで　りょこうを　していますか。
3. ブラウンさんが　まえから　いきたかった　ところは　どこで
　すか。
4. ブラウンさんは　あその　りょかんで　はじめて　ほたるを
　みましたか。
5. りょかんの　しゅじんは　どうして　ほたるが　ふえたと
　いっていましたか。
6. ブラウンさんは　どこを　けんぶつしてから　とうきょうに
　かえりますか。
7. えどじだいの　ながさきは　どんな　まちでしたか。
8. にほんの　れきしに　きょうみが　ある　ひとは　だれですか。
9. ブラウンさんは　どうして　らいしゅう　もくようびまでに
　とうきょうに　かえらなければ　なりませんか。
10. ブラウンさんは　みなみきゅうしゅうにも　いくと　おもいま
　すか。

NEW KANJI

1. あそ山
　　<ruby>山<rt>サン</rt></ruby>　｜　山　山　(3)
　　<ruby>山<rt>やま</rt></ruby>

2. 主人
　　<ruby>主<rt>シュジン</rt></ruby>　丶　二　干　主　主　(5)
　　おも(に)

3. 川
　　<ruby>川<rt>かわ</rt></ruby>　ノ　川　川　(3)
　　<ruby>川<rt>セン</rt></ruby>

4. 時代
　　<ruby>代<rt>ジダイ</rt></ruby>　ノ　イ　仁　代　代　(5)
　　か(わる)

5. 一番
　　<ruby>番<rt>イチバン</rt></ruby>　一　二　平　平　采　采　番　番　番　番　(12)

6. 社長
　　<ruby>長<rt>シャチョウ</rt></ruby>　｜　厂　厂　FF　巨　長　長　長　(8)
　　なが(い)

Readings:

人：　　人，　主人
　　　　ひと　シュジン
家：　　家，　家内
　　　　いえ　カナイ

LESSON 11 JOB INTERVIEW

Mr. Hayashi looks over Ms. Nakamura's resume while interviewing her.

はやし： 中村さんは おととし 大学を そつぎょうしたんです
か。

中村： はい。そつぎょうしてから 商社に つとめていました。

はやし： なぜ やめたんですか。

中村： 私の せんもんの 仕事が できませんでしたから、
おもしろくなかったんです。

はやし： どうして この 会社を えらんだんですか。

中村： こちらでは コンピューターを つかう 仕事が 多い
と 聞いたからです。私は 大学で コンピューターサ
イエンスを べんきょうしていました。この 会社では
私の 好きな 仕事が できると 思ったんです。

はやし： 会社に 入ってから 1か月 けんしゅうしなければ
ならない ことを 知っていますか。

中村： ええ、知っています。

はやし： それに 外国に しゅっちょうする ことも 多いです
よ。

中村： はい、だいじょうぶです。

はやし： そうですか。では けっかは 後で れんらくします。

Hayashi:	You graduated from college the year before last?
Nakamura:	Yes. After graduating, I worked for a trading company.
Hayashi:	Why did you quit?
Nakamura:	(I) couldn't work at my specialty, so it wasn't satisfactory.
Hayashi:	Why did you pick this company?
Nakamura:	Because I heard that here there's a lot of work using computers. I studied computer science in college. In this company I feel I'd be able to do the kind of work I like.
Hayashi:	Are you aware that after joining the company you have to do a one-month training (program)?
Nakamura:	Yes, I know (that).
Hayashi:	And overseas business trips are frequent.
Nakamura:	That's (quite) all right.
Hayashi:	Is it? Well, then, (we'll) contact you later regarding the outcome.

おととし	ototoshi	year before last
〜んです(か)	n desu ka	(*lit.*) "Is it the case that . . . ?"
しょうしゃ	shōsha	trading company
なぜ	naze	why
やめる	yameru	quit
せんもん	semmon	specialty
コンピューター	kompyūtā	computer
サイエンス	saiensu	science
けんしゅうする	kenshū suru	study, train
けんしゅう	kenshū	training (program)
こと	koto	matter, fact
それに	sore ni	moreover
しゅっちょうする	shutchō suru	take a business trip
れんらくする	renraku suru	contact
れんらく	renraku	contact, communication, connection

GRAMMAR & LESSON OBJECTIVES

• n desu

To understand the usage of . . . **n desu**, it is best to look at the situation. Since Hayashi has Nakamura's resume in front of him, it is hardly necessary to ask when she finished college. Instead of **sotsugyō shimashita ka**, he evokes confirmation and supplemental information with this pattern. Although the sentence ending **n desu** occurs freely after the plain forms of adjectives and verbs, remember the patterns for nouns and -**na** adjectives are, for example, **kaigi na n desu** and **shizukana n desu**. (See Appendix A.) In writing or more formal speech, **no desu** is the pattern used. (See p. 198.)

The difference between -**masu** and **n desu** is very subtle, and word-for-word translation of the latter can be difficult. All the following examples have an explanatory or confirmatory function.

ex. 1. (On seeing a coworker in the office with a big suitcase) **Doko ni iku n desu ka.** "Well, well, where are you off to?"

2. (On seeing snake meat in a grocery store showcase) **Hebi o taberu n desu ka.** "Is that snake meat sold for food?"
Ee. "Um."
Hontō ni taberu n desu ka. "You mean to say you actually eat it?"

3. **Kaihi o haratte kudasai.** "Would you mind paying the membership fee now, please?"
Ashita demo ii desu ka. Ima o-kane ga nai n desu. "Wouldn't tomorrow be all right? I don't have the money (with me) now."

4. (To a roommate putting on pajamas early in the evening) **Mō neru n desu ka.** "You're going to bed already?"
Ee. Ashita wa 4-ji ni okiru n desu. "Yes, 4: 00 A.M. is the time I have to get up tomorrow."

Compare this with the situation of simply asking a person what he intends to do:

Ashita nan-ji ni okimasu ka. "What time are you getting up tomorrow?"
6-ji ni okimasu. "I'll get up at 6 o'clock."

NOTES

1. **Daigaku o sotsugyō shita n desu ka.**
   Note that the particle is **o**, although what comes before **o** is not strictly speaking a direct object. (See p. 47.) Some other verbs in this category, which are alike in that a place or thing is being left, are **deru**, **shuppatsu suru** and **oriru**.
2. **1-kagetsu kenshū shinakereba naranai koto o shitte imasu ka.**
   In this case as well, plain forms come before the noun **koto**. Refer to Lesson 7 regarding noun-modifying patterns.
   ex. **Kare ga kinō kono hon o motte kita koto wa himitsu desu.** "That he brought this book yesterday is a secret."

PRACTICE

KEY SENTENCES

1. あした　かいぎが　ありますから、いま　しりょうを　コピー
   しているんです。
2. ブラウンさんが　きゅうしゅうへ　りょこうに　いった　ことを
   しっていますか。

1. Since there's a meeting tomorrow, I'm copying the material now.
2. Do you know the Browns took a trip to Kyushu?

EXERCISES

I   Practice the following patterns.

A. *ex.* いきます →　　いくんです　　　　いかないんです
　　　　　　　　　　いったんです　　　　いかなかったんです

1. およぎます	6. あいます	11. すんでいます
2. よみます	7. いいます	12. あげます
3. あそびます	8. できます	13. みます
4. けします	9. あります	14. きます
5. まちます	10. います	15. そうだんします

B. *ex.* やすいです →　やすいんです　　　やすくないんです
　　　　　　　　　やすかったんです　　やすくなかったんです

1. おいしいです	4. たかいです
2. あぶないです	5. つめたいです
3. むずかしいです	6. あたまがいいです

7. つごうが　わるいです　　9. やすみたいです

8. みずが　ほしいです

C. *ex.* すきです→　すきなんです　　　すきでは　ないんです
　　　　　　　　すきだったんです　すきでは　なかったんです

1. じょうずです　　　　5. かいぎです

2. ひまです　　　　　　6. しごとです

3. べんりです　　　　　7. びょうきです

4. あんぜんです　　　　8. けんしゅうです

II　Make dialogues by changing the underlined parts as in the examples given.

A. *ex.* **Q:** あした　ゴルフに　いきませんか。

A: ざんねんですが、ちょっと　あしたは　いそがしいんで
す。

1. かいぎが　あります

2. びょういんに　いかなければ　なりません

3. ともだちと　あう　やくそくを　しました

4. くにから　ははが　きています

5. あしたから　しゅっちょうです

6. かないが　びょうきです

7. ゴルフは　あまり　すきでは　ありません

8. ちょっと　からだの　ぐあいが　よくないです

B. *ex.* **Q:** きのう　パーティーに　きませんでしたね。

A: ええ、いそがしかったんです。

1. ちょっと　ようじが　ありました

2. しょうたいじょうを　もらいませんでした

3. きゅうに　つごうが　わるく　なりました

4. パーティーが　ある　ことを　しりませんでした

5. こどもが　びょうきでした

C. *ex.* **Q:** あした　ストライキが　ある　ことを　しっていますか。

A: そうですか。しりませんでした。

1. なかむらさんが　こんやくしました

2. あした　こなくても　いいです

3. ジョーンズさんが　こちらに　きています
4. すずきさんの　おかあさまが　なくなりました

D. *ex.* A: いつから　<u>ジョギング</u>を　はじめましたか。
B: <u>けっこんして</u>から　はじめました。
A: どうして　やめたんですか。
B: <u>けがを　</u>したからです。

1. ピアノ、しょうがっこうに　はいります、きょうみが
なくなりました
2. えいかいわ、だいがくを　そつぎょうします、いそが
しく　なりました
3. やまのぼり、かいしゃに　はいります、こどもが
うまれました

Vocabulary

あぶない	**abunai**	dangerous
つめたい	**tsumetai**	cold, cool, chilled
あんぜん（な）	**anzen(na)**	safe
からだの　ぐあい	**karada no guai**	health (*lit.* "body condition")
からだ	**karada**	body, health
ぐあい	**guai**	condition
しょうたいじょう	**shōtai-jō**	invitation card/letter
しょうたい	**shōtai**	invitation
〜じょう	**-jō**	letter (suffix)
きゅうに	**kyū ni**	suddenly
ストライキ	**sutoraiki**	strike
こんやくする	**kon'yaku suru**	become engaged
こんやく	**kon'yaku**	engagement
ジョーンズ	**Jōnzu**	Jones
おかあさま	**okā-sama**	(someone else's) mother (polite)
なくなる	**nakunaru**	pass away, be lost/missing, disappear
ピアノ	**piano**	piano
しょうがっこう	**shōgakkō**	elementary school
えいかいわ	**eikaiwa**	spoken English (*lit.* "English conversation")
かいわ	**kaiwa**	conversation
やまのぼり	**yamanobori**	mountain climbing
うまれる	**umareru**	be born

SHORT DIALOGUES

1. スミス：　　　　この　ちかくの　ちずが　ほしいんですが、
　　　　　　　　　　ありますか。
　ホテルの　ひと：はい、どうぞ。
　スミス：　　　　どうも。

Smith:　　　　I'd like a map of this area. Do you have one?
Hotel Clerk:　Here you are.
Smith:　　　　Thank you.

2. きゃく：　とけいを　かいたいんですが　なんかいですか。
　てんいん：とけいうりばは　6かいでございます。

Customer:　　I'd like to buy a watch. What floor is it?
Store Clerk:　The watch counter is (on) the sixth floor.

3. スミス：　　おおきい　バッグですね。
　ブラウン：ええ、テニスの　どうぐが　はいっているんです。
　　　　　　　テニスを　はじめたんですよ。
　スミス：　　そうですか。スポーツは　からだに　いいですね。

Smith:　What a big bag you have!
Brown:　Yes, my tennis racquet and other things are in it. I've taken up tennis.
Smith:　Really? Sports are good for the health, wouldn't you say?

4. すずき：あした　うちで　バーベキューパーティーを　やるん
　　　　　です が、きませんか。
　きむら：ざんねんですが、あしたは　ちょっと　やくそくが
　　　　　あるんです。
　すずき：そうですか。じゃ　つぎの　きかいには　ぜひ。

Suzuki:　Tomorrow I'm having a barbecue party at my house. Won't you come?
Kimura:　I'm sorry, but I have another appointment tomorrow.
Suzuki:　I see. Well, please come next time, then.

Vocabulary

～でございます	**de gozaimasu**	(polite for **desu**)
からだに　いい	**karada ni ii**	good for the health
バーベキュー	**bābekyū**	barbecue
やる	**yaru**	do, give (more colloquial than **suru**, **ageru**), play
きかい	**kikai**	opportunity, occasion
ぜひ	**zehi**	please

I   Read the lesson's Opening Dialogue and answer the following questions.

    1. なかむらさんは　いつ　だいがくを　そつぎょうしました
      か。

    2. なかむらさんは　なぜ　まえに　つとめていた　しょうしゃ
      を　やめましたか。

    3. なかむらさんの　せんもんは　なんですか。

    4. なかむらさんは　ABCでは　すきな　しごとが　できると
      おもっていますか。

    5. 1かげつ　けんしゅうしなければ　ならない　ことを　なか
      むらさんは　しっていましたか。

II   Put the appropriate particles in the parentheses.

    1. なかむらさんは　しょうしゃ（　　　）つとめていました。

    2. かれは　1965ねん（　　　）だいがく（　　　）そつぎょうしま
      した。

    3. かれが　べんごし（　　　）なった　こと（　　　）しっていま
      すか。

    4. けっかは　あと（　　　）れんらくします。

    5. どうして　この　かいしゃ（　　　）えらんだんですか。
      こちらでは　にほんごを　つかう　しごと（　　　）おおい
     （　　　）きいた（　　　）です。

III   Complete the questions so that they fit the answers.

    1. （　　　）パーティーに　こなかったんですか。
      あたまが　いたかったんです。

    2. （　　　）したんですか。
      てに　けがを　したんです。

    3. この　コンピューターは（　　　）つかうんですか。
      ちょっと　ふくざつですから、わたなべさんに　きいてくだ
      さい。

    4. （　　　）を　みているんですか。
      きょうとで　とった　しゃしんを　みているんです。

IV   Complete the sentences with the appropriate form of the verbs indicated.

1. すずきさんは　いませんか。もう　うちに（　　）んです
   か。
   ええ、30ぷんぐらい　まえに　かえりましたよ。(かえりま
   した)

2. おがわさんに（　　）んですか。
   ええ、おがわさんは　きのう（　　）んです。(しらせませ
   んでした、やすみでした)

3. どこに（　　）んですか。でんわが　ありましたよ。
   どうも　すみません。ちょっと　コーヒーを　のみに　いっ
   ていました。(いっていました)

4. なにも（　　）んですか。
   ええ、（　　）んです。(たべません、たべたくないです)

5. タクシーで（　　）んですか。
   ええ、じかんが　あまり（　　）んです。(でかけます、あ
   りません)

6. すずきさんは　やすみですか。
   ええ、（　　）んです。(びょうきです)

7. きのう　あなたが（　　）ことを　かれにも（　　）くださ
   い。(いいました、はなします)

8. かんじを（　　）ことは　むずかしくないです。(おぼえま
   す)

V   Choose a statement appropriate to the situation described.

A. You hear a friend has quit his job and you ask him about it.

1. いつ　かいしゃを　やめるんですか。
2. かいしゃを　やめては　いけませんか。
3. ほんとうに　かいしゃを　やめたんですか。

B. You see a friend doing something ridiculous.

1. なにを　しているんですか。
2. なにを　しなければ　なりませんか。
3. かれは　なんと　いっていますか。

C. You tell a friend that you didn't go to her party because of a headache.

1. とても　あたまが　いたいんです。

2. きゅうに あたまが いたく なったんです。

3. あたまが いたかったと おもいます。

NEW KANJI

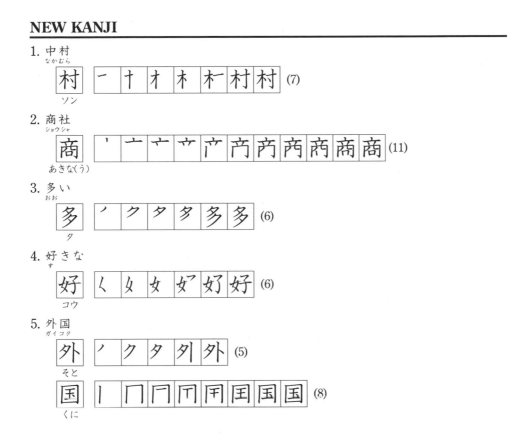

1. 中村
   なかむら
   村 一 十 才 木 村 村 村 (7)
   ソン

2. 商社
   ショウシャ
   商 ` 亠 テ 产 产 芍 芍 芍 商 商 商 (11)
   あきな(う)

3. 多い
   おお
   多 ノ ク タ タ 多 多 (6)
   タ

4. 好きな
   す
   好 く タ 女 女' 好 好 (6)
   コウ

5. 外国
   ガイコク
   外 ノ ク タ 外 外 (5)
   そと
   国 丨 冂 冂 用 用 国 国 国 (8)
   くに

LESSON **12**   HOTEL RESERVATIONS

Mr. Smith makes a reservation at an inn in Kyoto by phone.

よやくがかり： みやこりょかんでございます。

スミス： もしもし、来月の　4日と　5日に　よやくを　お
ねがいしたいんですが、部屋は　あいていますか。

よやくがかり： はい、ございます。何名さまですか。

スミス： ふたりです。いくらですか。

よやくがかり： 1ぱく2しょくつきで、おひとり　18,000円でござい
ます。ぜい金と　サービスりょうは　べつでござ
います。

スミス： はい、じゃ、それで　おねがいします。

よやくがかり： お名前と　お電話番号を　どうぞ。

スミス： スミスと　言います。電話番号は　東京03-3405-
3636です。そちらは　京都の　駅から　近いですか。

よやくがかり： 駅から　車で　10分ぐらいです。駅まで　おむか
えに　行きますが・・・。

スミス： じゃ、駅に　ついた　時、電話を　しますから、
よろしく　おねがいします。

よやくがかり： はい、かしこまりました。ご到着は　何時ごろで
　　　　　　　すか。

スミス：　　　　4時ごろです。

よやくがかり： はい、わかりました。8時より　おそく　なる　ば
　　　　　　　あいは、かならず　ごれんらくください。

スミス：　　　　はい。それで、りょう金は　いつ　払いましょう
　　　　　　　か。

よやくがかり： おそれいりますが、内金として　18,000円　おおく
　　　　　　　りください。

スミス：　　　　わかりました。

Reservation

Clerk:　(This is the) Miyako Inn.

Smith:　Hello, I'd like to make a reservation for the fourth and fifth of next month. Are rooms available (*lit.* "vacant")?

Clerk:　Yes, sir. (For) how many people?

Smith:　Two. How much is it?

Clerk:　Per day, with two meals, is ¥18, 000 per person. Tax and service charge are extra.

Smith:　I see. Will you do me the favor, then (of making the reservation)?

Clerk:　Your name and phone number, please.

Smith:　My name is Smith. The telephone number is Tokyo 03-3405-3636. Are you near Kyoto Station?

Clerk:　It's about ten minutes by car from the station. We can come to the station to meet you . . . (if you wish).

Smith:　Well, when (we) arrive at the station, I'll call you, so I'd appreciate it if you could.

Clerk:　Certainly, sir. Your arrival will be about what time?

Smith:　Around four o'clock.

Clerk:　I see. In case (it's) later than eight o'clock, be sure to call us.

Smith:　All right. When should I pay the (room) charge?

Clerk:　Excuse (my asking) but could you please send ¥18, 000 by mail as a deposit?

Smith:　Yes, of course.

Vocabulary

よやく がかり	**yoyaku-gakari**	reservation clerk
かかり／〜がかり	**kakari/-gakari**	person in charge
あく	**aku**	be empty, be vacant, (be) open
ございます	**gozaimasu**	(polite for **arimasu**)
〜めい（さま）	**-mei (-sama)**	(counter for people; polite)
〜はく／ぱく	**-haku/-paku**	night (counter)
〜しょく	**-shoku**	meal (counter)
〜つき	**-tsuki**	included, attached
ぜいきん	**zeikin**	tax
サービスりょう	**sābisu-ryō**	service charge
べつ（な／の）	**betsu(na/no)**	extra, distinctive

とき	toki	when, while
かしこまりました	kashikomarimashita	certainly
（ご）とうちゃく	(go-) tōchaku	arrival
ばあい	baai	(in) case, occasion, circumstance
かならず	kanarazu	be sure to, certainly
それで	sorede	and then
りょうきん	ryōkin	charge, fee
おそれいります	osoreirimasu	excuse me, be sorry (polite for **sumimasen**)
うちきん	uchikin	deposit, partial payment
～として	to shite	as, in the capacity of

GRAMMAR & LESSON OBJECTIVES

• Verb tense

In the second grammar section in Book I (p. 54), it was pointed out that the two verb tense forms in Japanese are present and past, and with the present form expressing habitual or future action and the past being sometimes past and sometimes present perfect, there is a basis for correspondence with English verb tenses. In complex sentences, however, non-final verbs do not necessarily have the same relation to the main verbs as English verbs do. In translating, preservation of the Japanese tense may require some adjustment in the sentence. Look again at the translation of the dialogue sentence **Eki ni tsuita toki, denwa o shimasu kara, yoroshiku onegaishimasu**, translated as "Once we('ve) arrive(d) at the station, I'll call, so . . ." Think of the underlying meaning as being "Once arrival at the station has become an accomplished fact, a telephone call will be made, so . . ."

Compare the following sentences which differ from each other only in the verb forms in the first clause.

ex. 1. **Nihon ni kuru toki kūkō de kaimashita.** "While coming to Japan I bought (it) at the airport." (Implicitly meaning an airport outside of Japan.)
   2. **Nihon ni kita toki kūkō de kaimashita.** "When I came (i.e., having come) to Japan (I) bought (it) at the airport." (Meaning an airport in Japan.)

• **Toki** and **baai**

Basically **toki** is "time" and **baai** is "case," but these nouns are interchangeable at certain times while at other times this is not the case. Keep in mind that (1) if something has actually occurred, **baai** cannot be used; **-ta baai** is used to express a supposed situation, meaning, "Suppose/If . . . has happened . . ." And (2) clues to the intended meaning lie in thinking of *time* and *circumstances* or *situation* in a contrastive way. Some examples:

1. **Kesa watashi ga okita toki**, "When I got up this morning, . . ."
2. **Denwa de renraku suru toki/baai**, "When contacts are made by phone, . . ."
3. **Muzukashii toki/baai**, "If it's difficult, . . ."
4. **Fubenna toki/baai**, "If it's inconvenient, . . ."
5. **Shigoto ga yasumi no toki/baai**, "When (there's) time off (from) work, . . ."
6. **Kodomo no toki**, "during childhood"
7. **Kodomo no baai**, "in the case of children"

NOTES

1. **yoyaku-gakari**

   Like many other words, **kakari** undergoes a phonetic change when compounded with other terms. Other examples: **hako** becomes **hon-bako**, "bookcase"; **hi** becomes **nichi-yōbi**; **hanashi**, becomes **otogi-banashi**, "fairy tale"; **kuchi**, "mouth" or "door," becomes **iri-guchi**.

2. **shitai n desu ga**

   -tai n desu is more frequently heard than **-tai desu**.

3. **Nan-mei-sama desu ka.**

   Only such people as restaurant and hotel employees commonly use **nan-mei-sama** as a polite alternative for **nan-nin**, but **nan-mei**, which is more formal than **nan-nin**, is widely used.

4. **1-paku 2-shoku (ippaku ni-shoku)**

   One night per person with supper and breakfast is the most conspicuous formula for **ryokan** charges. It is not common in Western-style hotels, which are more apt to quote room charge only or room charge plus, optionally, breakfast. There is no general pattern for asking or not asking for a deposit or including or not including tax and service charge in the quoted room rate.

5. **O-namae to o-denwa-bangō o dōzo.**

   Sentences like this, ending with **dōzo** instead of **-te kudasai**, may be used when the situation is clear; they suggest the action to be taken. Similarly, **Kono denwa o dōzo** can mean "Please use this phone."

6. **Sumisu to iimasu.**

   The literal translation is "I'm called/I call myself Smith." **To mōshimasu** means the same but is more humble, hence politer. The pattern is like others introduced previously, **to omou, to kiku** and so on, as in **Kore wa Nihon-go de nan to iimasu/iu n desu ka.** "What is this called in Japanese."

7. **Kashikomarimashita**

   More formal than **wakarimashita**, this expression, "I understand and will do it," is a standard one often said by servants, clerks and others when receiving requests, orders or instructions. It is not appropriate in a classroom or among friends or family members.

8 **Uchikin to shite**

   To shite is used as follows:

   ex. 1. **Kanojo wa hisho to shite kono ka de hataraite imasu.** "She works in this section as a secretary."
   2. **Kitte-dai to shite 200-en haratte kudasai.** "Please pay ¥200 for the postage." (**dai**, "charge, price")

PRACTICE

KEY SENTENCES

1. スミスさんは　ほんを　よむ　とき、めがねを　かけます。

2. えきに ついた とき、でんわを します。

3. おそく なる ばあいは れんらくします。

4. わたしは スミスと いいます。

1. Smith wears glasses when he reads (books).
2. When I get to the station I'll phone.
3. If it's late I'll contact you.
4. My name is Smith.

EXERCISES

I　Make dialogues by changing the underlined parts as in the examples given.

A. *ex.* **Q**: よく さんぽしますか。

　　A: ええ、あさ すずしい とき、さんぽします。

　　　1. この くすりを のむ、あたまが いたい
　　　2. ジョギングを する、てんきが よくて さむくない
　　　3. クーラーを つかう、とても あつい
　　　4. えいがを みる、ひまな

B. *ex.* **Q**: こどもの とき、どこに すんでいましたか。

　　A: おおさかに すんでいました。

　　　1. かいぎ、どの へやを つかいますか、この へやを
　　　2. がくせい、どこを りょこうしましたか、ヨーロッパを
　　　3. しけん、なにを もっていきますか、えんぴつと けしゴムを

C. *ex.* **Q**: しょくじを はじめる とき、なんと いいますか。

　　A: 「いただきます」と いいます。

　　　1. しょくじが おわりました、ごちそうさまでした
　　　2. うちを でます、いってまいります
　　　3. うちに かえりました、ただいま
　　　4. はじめて ひとに あいました、はじめまして
　　　5. ひとと わかれます、さようなら
　　　6. さきに かえります、おさきに しつれいします
　　　7. ひとに なにか たのみます、おねがいします
　　　8. プレゼントを もらいました、ありがとうございます

II   Practice the following pattern by changing the underlined parts as in the examples given.

A. *ex.* しんぶんを　よむ　とき、めがねを　かけます。

1. くにに　かえる、おみやげを　かいます
2. かいしゃに　いく、ちかてつを　つかいます
3. みちが　わからない、けいかんに　ききます
4. だいがくを　そつぎょうする、ろんぶんを　かきます

B. *ex.* えきに　ついた　とき、でんわします。

1. つかれた、モーツアルトを　ききます
2. そちらに　いった、くわしく　せつめいします
3. もくようびに　あった、いっしょに　しょくじを　しましょう
4. ねむく　なった、コーヒーを　のみます

C. *ex.* ドイツに　すんでいた　とき、けっこんしました。

1. きのう　しょくじを　していた、じしんが　ありました
2. せんそうが　おわった、とうきょうに　いませんでした
3. しゃちょうが　しんだ、（お）そうしきに　おおぜい　ひとが　きました

III   Make dialogues by changing the underlined parts as in the examples given.

A. *ex.* **Q:** しゅうまつの　りょこうは　どう　しましょうか。
    A: あめの　ばあいは　やめましょう。

1. でんしゃが　ストです
2. たなかさんの　つごうが　わるいです
3. てんきが　よくないです

B *ex.* **Q:** おそく　なる　ばあいは　れんらくしてください。
    A: はい、そうします。

1. おくれます
2. きません
3. おかねが　たりません

4. よていが　かわりました

5. びょうきに　なりました

C *ex.* **Q**: Roseは　にほんごで　なんと　いうんですか。

　　A: ばらと　いいます。

　　1. ball-point pen、ボールペン

　　2. pants、ズボン

　　3. contract、けいやく

Vocabulary		
すずしい	**suzushii**	cool
もっていく	**motte iku**	take (things)
けしゴム	**keshigomu**	eraser
いただきます	**itadakimasu**	(phrase used before eating)
ごちそうさまでした	**go-chisōsama deshita**	(phrase used after eating)
わかれる	**wakareru**	part, split up
さようなら	**sayōnara**	good-bye
ろんぶん	**rombun**	thesis
（お）みやげ	**o-miyage**	souvenir
つかれる	**tsukareru**	get tired
モーツアルト	**Mōtsuaruto**	Mozart
ねむい	**nemui**	sleepy
じしん	**jishin**	earthquake
せんそう	**sensō**	war
（お）そうしき	**o-sōshiki**	funeral
たりる	**tariru**	be enough
よてい	**yotei**	plan, schedule
ばら	**bara**	rose
ボールペン	**bōru-pen**	ball-point pen
ズボン	**zubon**	trousers
けいやく	**keiyaku**	contract

SHORT DIALOGUES

1. A: ひまな　ときは　なにを　しますか。

　B: ひまな　ときですか。そうですねえ、おんがくを　きいたり
　　しています。

A: What do you do in your free time?
B: In my free time? Well, I listen to music and things like that.

2. わたなべ：　にほんの　せいかつに　なれましたか。

　ジョンソン：ええ、すこしずつ。

　わたなべ：　こまった　ときは　いつでも　いってください。

Watanabe: Are (you) getting used to living in Japan?
Johnson: Well, little by little.
Watanabe: If (you're at all) inconvenienced, please tell me about it anytime.

3. きむら ： あしたの　スポーツたいかいの　ことなんですが、
　　　　　　あめが　ふった　ときは　どう　しますか。
　 すずき ： あさ　6じまでに　やまない　ばあいは　ちゅうしで
　　　　　　す。
　 きむら ： よく　わからない　ときは　どう　しますか。
　 すずき ： その　ばあいは　ここに　でんわを　して　たしかめ
　　　　　　てください。

Kimura: About tomorrow's athletic meeting,what happens if it rains?
Suzuki: If it doesn't stop by six in the morning, it'll be called off.
Kimura: If it's not clear (*lit.* "not understandable"), what should I do?
Suzuki: In that case, please make sure by phoning here.

Vocabulary

せいかつ	**seikatsu**	living, life
なれる	**nareru**	get used to
すこしずつ	**sukoshi-zutsu**	little by little
〜ずつ	**-zutsu**	(suffix)
こまる	**komaru**	be inconvenienced/troubled/embarrassed
いつでも	**itsu demo**	any-/sometime
たいかい	**taikai**	(big) meeting, conference, tournament
やむ	**yamu**	stop
ちゅうし	**chūshi**	discontinuance, interruption
たしかめる	**tashikameru**	make sure

QUIZ

I Read this lesson's Opening Dialogue and answer the following questions.

1. スミスさんは　どこに　でんわを　しましたか。
2. りょかんの　ひとは　へやが　あいていると　いいました
  か。
3. みやこりょかんは　えきから　くるまで　なんぷんぐらい
  かかりますか。
4. スミスさんは　1ぱく2しょくの　りょうきんと　なにを
  はらわなければ　なりませんか。
5. みやこりょかんの　ばあいは　とまる　まえに　うちきんを
  はらわなければ　なりませんか。

II Put the appropriate particles in the parentheses.

1. りょうきんは　おひとり　10,000えん（　　　）ございます。
2. わたしは　スミス（　　　）いいます。
3. えき（　　　）ついた　とき、でんわを　します。えき（　　　）
   むかえ（　　　）きてくれませんか。
4. 6じ（　　　）おそく　なる　ばあいは、かならず　れんらく
   してください。
5. 1ぱく2しょくつき（　　　）ひとり　15,000えん　かかります
   が、いいですか。
6. かれは　とうきょうだいがくの　きょうじゅ（　　　）して、
   にほんに　きています。
7. かいぎ（　　　）とき、おちゃを　もってきてください。

III Complete the questions so that they fit the answers.

1. リンダさんは（　　　）きたんですか。
   7じの　ニュースを　きいている　とき　きました。
2. これは　にほんごで（　　　）と　いうんですか。
   けしゴムと　いいます。
3. （　　　）りょかんに　おそく　なると　れんらくしなかった
   んですか。
   でんわを　する　じかんが　なかったんです。

IV Complete the sentences with the appropriate form of the words indicated.

1. きょねん　きょうとに（　　　）とき、きれいな　かみの
   かさを　かいました。（いきました）
2. うけつけの　ひとが（　　　）ばあいは　でんわを　してくだ
   さい。（いません）
3. あさ（　　　）とき、あめが（　　　）いました。（おきました、
   ふります）
4. あしたまでに（　　　）ばあいは、きょうじゅうに　れんらく
   を（　　　）ください。（できません、します）
5. むすめが（　　　）とき、スミスさんから　スプーンを
   もらいました。（うまれました）
6. らいしゅう　こちらに（　　　）ばあいは　かならず（　　　）
   ください。（きます、しらせます）

7. きのう　ひるごはんを　（　　　）とき、きゅうに　おなかが
（　　　）なりました。（たべていました、いたい）

8. じかんが　（　　　）とき、サンドイッチを　たべます。（あり
ません）

9. （　　　）とき、イギリスを　（　　　）ことが　あります。
（わかい、りょこうします）

10. （　　　）とき、ほんを　（　　　）だり、こどもと　（　　　）だり
しています。（ひま、よみます、あそびます）

V　Choose the most polite statement appropriate to the situation described.

A. You're at work and you answer the phone.

1. ABCでございます。
2. ABCと　いいます。
3. ABCです。

B. You tell a client you will show him around when it's convenient for him.

1. ごつごうの　いい　とき、ごあんないください。
2. じかんが　ある　とき、あんないしますよ。
3. ごつごうの　いい　とき、ごあんないします。

C. You call Kato's house and ask if he's at home.

1. かとうさんに　ごれんらくください。
2. かとうさんは　いらっしゃいますか。
3. かとうさんは　いますか。

NEW KANJI

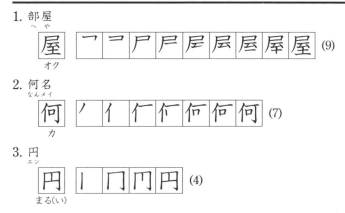

1. 部屋
へや
屋　コ　ヨ　尸　尸　尼　尾　屋　屋　屋　(9)
オク

2. 何名
なんメイ
何　ノ　イ　仁　仁　何　何　何　(7)
カ

3. 円
エン
円　丨　冂　冂　円　(4)
まる(い)

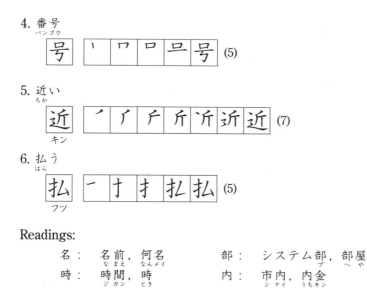

4. 番号
   バンゴウ

号　｜　ロ　ロ　ロ　号 (5)

5. 近い
   ちか

近　ノ　ア　斤　斤　斤　近　近 (7)
   キン

6. 払う
   はら

払　一　寸　扌　払　払 (5)
   フツ

Readings:

名 ： 名前, 何名 部 ： システム部, 部屋
　　　 なまえ なんメイ 　　　 ブ へや
時 ： 時間, 時 内 ： 市内, 内金
　　　 ジカン とき 　　　 シナイ うちキン

Kanji for recognition:　到着
　　　　　　　　　　　トウチャク

LESSON 13　A GIFT OF CHOCOLATE

Mr. Chang hands Mr. Johnson a small box with a card.

チャン：　　　ジョンソンさん、これ、わたなべさんから　ジョンソンさんへの　プレゼントですよ。きのう　ジョンソンさんが　いなかったので、ぼくが　あずかりました。カードも　ありますよ。

ジョンソン：どうも　ありがとう。わたなべさんからの　おくりもの、うれしいですね。

チャン：　　　なかみは　チョコレートでしょう。

ジョンソン：開けたんですか。

チャン：　　　カードは　ラブレターかもしれませんよ。

ジョンソン：えっ、よんだんですか。

チャン：　　　はははは・・・。じつは　ぼくも　同じ　ものを　もらったんです。すずきくんも　もらっただろうと　思いますよ。

ジョンソン：えっ？　みんな　もらったんですか。

チャン：　　　ギリチョコですよ、ギリチョコ。

ジョンソン：ギリチョコって　何ですか。

チャン：　　　ぎりの　チョコレートです。日本の　バレンタインデーの　しゅうかんです。しょくばでも　よく　女性から　男性の　じょうしや　どうりょうに　チョコレートを　プレゼントします。

ジョンソン：「いつも　おせわに　なっています。これからも　よろしく。まゆみ」やっぱり　ギリチョコでした。

チャン：　　　ざんねんでした。

ジョンソン：でも、ギリチョコを　たくさん　もらった　人は　どう　するんでしょうか。

チャン：　　　たぶん　おくさんや　ガールフレンドが　食べるんでしょう。

ジョンソン：じゃ、よろこぶ　人は　女性と　かしやですね。

Chang: Mr. Johnson, here's a present for you from Ms. Watanabe. Since you weren't (here) yesterday, I took care of it. There's a card, too.

Johnson: Thank you. A present from Ms. Watanabe, how delightful!

Chang: Chocolates inside, I suppose.

Johnson: You opened it?

Chang: Maybe the card is a love letter.

Johnson: Huh! You read it?

Chang: Ha, ha! As a matter of fact, I got the same thing. I think Suzuki got (one) too.

Johnson: Eh? Did everyone get one?

Chang: Well, it's *giri-choko.*

Johnson: *Giri-choko?* What do you mean?

Chang: Chocolate (given) out of a sense of obligation. It's a Japanese Valentine's Day custom. It's a common gift from women to male superiors or coworkers.

Johnson: "Thank you for your helpfulness and kindness. Please continue to treat me with favor. (From) Mayumi." Just as you said, *giri-choko.*

Chang: Disappointing, isn't it?

Johnson: Um. What does a man who gets a lot of *giri-choko* do?

Chang: Probably his wife or girl friend (get to) eat it.

Johnson: Well then, the happy people are most likely the women and the confectioners.

Vocabulary

プレゼント	**purezento**	present
ので	**node**	since, because
あずかる	**azukaru**	take care of, keep
カード	**kādo**	(greeting) card
おくりもの	**okurimono**	gift
うれしい	**ureshii**	delighted, happy
チョコレート	**chokorēto**	chocolate
ラブレター	**raburetā**	love letter
かもしれません	**kamo shiremasen**	may be
えっ	**e**	Oh, dear! (exclamation of surprise)
ははは	**hahaha**	Ha, ha!
じつは	**jitsu wa**	as a matter of fact, in fact, actually
おなじ	**onaji**	same
だろう	**darō**	(plain form of **deshō**)
ギリチョコ	**giri-choko**	*giri* chocolate
ぎり	**giri**	(sense of) obligation
～って なんですか	**tte nan desu ka**	What do you/does it mean?
～って	**tte**	= **to iu no wa** (informal)
バレンタインデー	**Barentain dē**	Valentine's Day
しゅうかん	**shūkan**	custom, habit
しょくば	**shokuba**	workplace
じょせい	**josei**	woman, female
だんせい	**dansei**	man, male
じょうし	**jōshi**	superior
どうりょう	**dōryō**	coworker
おせわに なる	**o-sewa ni naru**	be under the care of, be indebted to
せわ	**sewa**	help, kindness, care

まゆみ	**Mayumi**	female given name
やっぱり	**yappari**	(just) as we/you expected
ガールフレンド	**gāru furendo**	girl friend
よろこぶ	**yorokobu**	be happy, be pleased
かしや	**kashi-ya**	confectioner, confectionery

GRAMMAR & LESSON OBJECTIVES

• **kamo shiremasen, darō to omoimasu**, expressing uncertainty
  Kādo wa rabu retā kamo shiremasen.
  Suzuki-san mo moratta darō to omoimasu.
  Darō is a plain form of **deshō**, expressing uncertainty, and **kamo shiremasen** shows even more uncertainty than either of them.
  These patterns follow nouns and the stem of **-na** adjectives.
  ex. **benri deshō/darō to omoimasu/kamo shiremasen.**
  They also follow plain past and negative forms. (See Appendix A.) Unlike the other two, **kamo shiremasen** can be used in referring to one's own actions.
  ex. **Watashi mo Ōsaka e iku kamo shiremasen.** "I may go to Osaka (myself)."

• **node** expressing reason
  Kinō Jonson-san ga inakatta node, boku ga azukarimashita.
  Like **kara**, **node** indicates reason or cause but it sounds a bit softer. It follows plain forms. For nouns and **-na** adjectives, **na** is used, as in **benrina node, ame na node.** (See Appendix A.) Recently, **node** has come to be used after **desu** and the **-masu** form as well.

NOTES

1. **Jonson-san e no purezento**
   Dōryō ni/e chokorēto o purezento shimasu.
   As seen in these examples, a distinction is made between cases of combining **e** or **ni** with **no**. When a noun is being modified, only **e no** occurs. Besides **ni**, the particles **wa, ga** and **o** never come before **no**. (See also Book I, p. 55.)
   Other examples of particles combined with **no**:
   ex. 1. **Tōkyō de no kaigi,** "a meeting in Tokyo"
       2. **Ōsaka made no kippu,** "a ticket to Osaka"
       3. **Tanaka-san kara no moraimono,** "a present from Tanaka"

2. **Giri-choko**
   This term combines, rather humorously, a traditional social relationship and the shortened form of the word **chokorēto.** Having **giri,** "(a sense of) obligation," to one's seniors goes back many centuries. **Giri-choko** is, needless to say, a custom of modern times.

3. **Giri-choko tte nan desu ka.**
   The function of **tte** is to draw attention to the meaning. It is the informal equivalent of **to iu no wa,** which is found in Book III, Lesson 8. Johnson's utterance could be translated more directly as, "What's *giri* chocolate?"

4.「いつも　おせわに　なっています。これからも　よろしく。まゆみ」

The half brackets in this passage signify the beginning (「) and end (」) of a direct quotation.

5. **Yappari**

This word, the more formal form of which is **yahari**, sometimes expresses a feeling akin to déjà-vu and may be translated as "after all," "as I expected" or "as is usually the case."

ex. **Yappari Tōkyō no rasshu awā wa sugoi desu ne.** "As might be expected, rush hours in Tokyo are awful."

6. **Zannen deshita.**

Chang is teasing, of course, using a common expression said when there is cause for regret or one finds things not to one's liking.

PRACTICE

KEY SENTENCES

1. ゆきが　たくさん　ふっているから、ひこうきは　とばないかもしれません。
2. すずきさんは　リンダさんを　しらないだろうと　おもいます。
3. ひこうきが　とばないので、りょこうに　いく　ことが　できません。

1. It's snowing hard so planes probably aren't flying.
2. I don't think Suzuki knows Linda.
3. Since planes aren't flying, I can't go on (my) trip.

EXERCISES

I   Make dialogues by changing the underlined parts as in the examples given.

A. *ex.* A: くるまが　たくさん　とまっていますね。
B: そうですね。じこかもしれませんね。

1. となりの　うちは　にぎやかです、パーティーです
2. たなかさんが　きていません、やすみです
3. さむく　なりました、あしたは　ゆきです
4. みちが　こんでいます、くるまより　ちかてつの　ほうが　はやいです

B. *ex.* A: たなかさんは　じかんが　あるかもしれませんよ。
B: そうですか。
A: きょうは　ひまだと　いっていましたから。

1. れきしに　きょうみが　あります、ならや　きょうと
が　すきです
2. りょこうに　いきました、こんしゅうは　やすみです
3. きょう　かいしゃに　きません、おくさんが　びょう
きです
4. みんなと　カラオケに　いきませんでした、カラオケ
は　きらいです

C. *ex.* **A**: <u>かいぎは　いつですか。</u>
　　B: <u>あしたの　ごぜんちゅう</u>だろうと　おもいますよ。

1. たなかさん、どこ、3かいの　かいぎしつ
2. たんとうしゃ、だれ、すずきさんか　さとうさん
3. しけん、なんかから　なんかまで、1かから　10かまで
4. Bしゃの　あたらしい　パソコン、いくらぐらい、18ま
んえんぐらい

D. *ex.* **A**: <u>ほっかいどうは　いま　さむい</u>でしょうか。
　　B: ええ、<u>さむい</u>だろうと　おもいますよ。

1. この　きかいの　ほうが　べんりです
2. やまださんは　かいしゃを　やめます
3. ちかてつは　もう　すいています
4. たなかさんは　もう　かえりました

E. *ex.* **Q**: たなかさんは　くるでしょうか。
　　Aa: ええ、たぶん　<u>くる</u>だろうと　おもいます。
　　An: たぶん、<u>こない</u>だろうと　おもいます。

1. あたらしい　ひしょは　スペインごが　わかります
2. スミスさんは　わたしを　しっています
3. えきの　ちかくの　スーパーで　（お）さけを　うって
います
4. スミスさんは　わたなべさんから　ギリチョコを
もらいました

II Practice the following pattern by changing the underlined parts as in the example given.

ex. <u>さいふを　わすれた</u>ので　<u>ともだちに　（お）かねを　かり</u>
<u>ました</u>。

  1. いそがしいです、デートを　ことわりました
  2. やせたいです、スポーツクラブに　はいりました
  3. べんりです、ちかてつで　かいしゃに　いきます
  4. きのうは　やすみでした、みんなで　ハイキングに
    いきました
  5. らいげつ　りょこうします、ホテルの　よやくを
    しました
  6. バスも　タクシーも　きませんでした、えきまで
    あるきました
  7. むりを　しました、びょうきに　なりました

III Make dialogues by changing the underlined parts as in the example given.

ex. **A:** <u>くるまで　いきます</u>か。
  B: いいえ、<u>みちが　こんでいる</u>ので・・・。

  1. ざんぎょうします、デートが　あります
  2. ケーキを　たべます、いま　おなかが　いっぱいです
  3. ゴルフを　しますか、すきじゃ　ないです
  4. あたらしい　ワープロを　かいました、たかかったです

IV Practice the following dialogues.

A. **Q:** これは　わたなべさん<u>から</u>　<u>もらった</u>　おくりものですか。
  A: はい、わたなべさん<u>からの</u>　おくりものです。

B. **Q:** これは　たなかさん<u>に</u>　<u>だす</u>　てがみですか。
  A: はい、たなかさん<u>への</u>　てがみです。

C. **Q:** これは　どこ<u>で</u>　<u>おきた</u>　もんだいですか。
  A: おおさかししゃ<u>での</u>　もんだいです。

D. **Q:** これは　どの　かいしゃ<u>と</u>　<u>した</u>　けいやくですか。
  A: ABC<u>との</u>　けいやくです。

Vocabulary

じこ	**jiko**	accident
カラオケ	**karaoke**	karaoke
きらい（な）	**kirai(na)**	dislike
たんとうしゃ	**tantō-sha**	person in charge
〜しゃ	**-sha**	person (suffix)
パソコン	**pasokon**	personal computer
きかい	**kikai**	machine, equipment
スペインご	**Supein-go**	Spanish
かりる	**kariru**	borrow, rent
デート	**dēto**	date
ことわる	**kotowaru**	decline, reject
やせる	**yaseru**	lose weight, become thin
はいる	**hairu**	join, become a member
いっぱい（の／な）	**ippai (no/na)**	full
おきる	**okiru**	happen, occur

SHORT DIALOGUES

1. たなか：あのう、これ、つまらない ものですが・・・。
   かとう：やあ、どうも。えんりょなく いただきます。

   Tanaka: Er . . . this is a trifling thing (really, but . . .).
   Katō: Ah, thank you very much. (*lit.* "I accept (it) without hesitation.")

2. A: みそしるって なんですか。
   B: にほんじんが よく のむ スープです。

   A: What's *miso shiru*?
   B: It's a soup. Japanese often have it.

3. きむら：とうきょうでんきの たなかさんと やくそくが
          ありますので、これで しつれいします。
   かとう：それじゃ、たなかさんに よろしく いってください。

   Kimura: I have an appointment with Mr. Tanaka of Tokyo Electric, so I have to go now.
   Katō: OK. Please say hello for me.

Vocabulary

つまらない	**tsumaranai**	trifling, worthless
やあ	**yā**	ah, oh, my (men's speech)
えんりょなく	**enryo naku**	without hesitation/reserve
えんりょ	**enryo**	reserve, restraint, diffidence
いただく	**itadaku**	accept, receive (politer than **morau**)

I   Read this lesson's Opening Dialogue and answer the following questions.

1. ジョンソンさんが　もらった　チョコレートは　だれからの
   プレゼントですか。

2. チャンさんも　チョコレートと　カードを　もらいましたか。

3. チャンさんが　ジョンソンさんへの　プレゼントを　あずか
   った　ひは　なんの　ひですか。

4. ギリチョコを　たくさん　もらった　だんせいは　ひとりで
   ぜんぶ　たべるだろうと　チャンさんは　いいましたか。

II   Put the appropriate words in the parentheses.

1. ガールフレンド（　　）の　プレゼントを　かいに　いきま
   した。

2. とうきょう（　　）の　せいかつは　ほんとうに　たのしか
   ったです。

3. ロンドン（　　）の　にもつが　とどきました。

4. いつも　おせわ（　　）なっています。これ（　　）も
   どうぞ　よろしく。

5. よびこうっ（　　）なんですか。

III   Complete the questions so that they fit the answers.

1. きのう（　　）こなかったんですか。
   いそがしかったので、しつれいしました。

2. （　　）を　しているんですか。
   べんごしが　こないので、まっているんです。

3. あたらしい　ぶちょうは（　　）ひとでしょうか。
   あたまが　よくて　まじめな　ひとだろうと　おもいます
   よ。

4. みそしるって（　　）ですか。
   みその　スープですよ。

IV   Complete the sentences with the appropriate form of the words indicated.

1. かれが（　　）ので、あんしんしました。（げんきです）

2. これは（　　）だろうと　おもいます。（スミスさんの
   ものでは　ありません）

3. たなかさんは（　　）かもしれませんよ。（びょうきです）

4. きのうは（　　　）ので（　　　）だろうと　おもいますよ。
（まつりでした、にぎやかでした）
5. しゅじんは　たぶん　かさを（　　　）だろうと　おもいます。
（もっていきませんでした）
6. この　ちかてつは　ぎんざを（　　　）だろうと　おもいます。
（とおりません）
7. しんぶんは　いすの　うえに（　　　）かもしれません。
（おきました）
8. すぐ　あたらしい　せいかつに（　　　）でしょう。（なれます）
9. でんしゃが（　　　）ので、バスで　きました。（うごきませんでした）
10. チョコレートを　もらった　だんせいは（　　　）だろうと　おもいます。（よろこびます）

V Choose a statement appropriate to the situation described.

A. You tell your section chief you have to go to the hospital to see your father.

　　1. ちちが　びょうきなので、びょういんへ　いくかもしれません。
　　2. おとうさんが　びょうきなので、びょういんへ　いっては　いけませんか。
　　3. ちちが　びょうきなので、びょういんへ　いかなければ　ならないんですが・・・。

B. You want to know the meaning of the acronym UFO.

　　1. ユーフォーって　なんですか。
　　2. ユーフォーと　いいます。
　　3. ユーフォーは　なんと　いいますか。

C. You finish working and go out of the office, leaving your section chief behind.

　　1. ごめんなさい、かえります。
　　2. えんりょなく、さようなら。
　　3. おさきに　しつれいします。

NEW KANJI

1. 開ける
   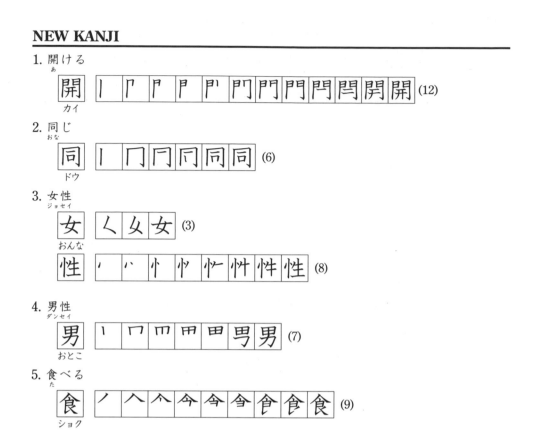

2. 同じ

3. 女性

4. 男性

5. 食べる

LESSON 14 THE REFEREE'S ROLE

On entering the *sumō* arena, Mr. Smith and Mr. Tanaka first look around for Linda and Mr. Smith's wife.

スミス： わあ、すごい 人ですね。

たなか： すもうの しょ日は いつも まんいんです。人が た
くさん いて、リンダさんや おくさんが よく 見え
ませんね。

スミス： あ、あそこに いました。ほら、すもうを 見ながら
やきとりを 食べているのが 見えますよ。

たなか： さあ、私たちも あそこへ 行って、ビールでも 飲み
ながら すわって 見ましょう。

スミス： ええ、でも この とりくみが 終わるまで ここで
いいです。うるさくて アナウンスが よく 聞こえま
せんが、どひょうの 上に いるのは？

たなか： ふじのみねと さくらりゅうです。

スミス： はでな きものを 着て、どひょうの 上で 動きまわ
っているのは どういう 人ですか。

たなか： あれは ぎょうじです。

スミス： ああ、ジャッジですね。

たなか： ええ、でも 黒い きものを 着て、どひょうの まわ
りに すわっているのが ほんとうの ジャッジです。
あの 人たちは りきしの OBで、えらいんですよ。

スミス： じゃ、ぎょうじは　ジャッジでは　ないんですか。

たなか： ええ、じつは　けっていけんは　ないんです。

スミス： そうですか。ちょっと　なっとくできませんね。

たなか： でも　発言けんは　ありますよ。
　　　　　　　　はつげん

スミス： それを　聞いて　安心しました。
　　　　　　　　　　　　あんしん

Smith: Wow! An awful lot of people, aren't there?

Tanaka: It's always full on the first day of a *sumō* tournament. With so many people we aren't
          going to find Linda and your wife (easily).

Smith: Oh, they're over there. Look! (I see) they're watching the *sumō* and eating *yakitori*.

Tanaka: Well, let's go over there ourselves and while drinking (some) beer (or something), sit
          down and watch (the bouts).

Smith: Umm, it's just as well (to stay) here until this bout is over. It's noisy and (I) can't hear
          the announcements very well. (The ones) on the ring are . . . ?

Tanaka: Fujinomine and Sakuraryū.

Smith: (And the one) wearing the gay kimono, moving around the ring, what's his role?

Tanaka: That's the *gyōji*.

Smith: Ah, he's the referee.

Tanaka: Yes. The ones sitting around the ring wearing black kimono are the real judges. They're
          OBs among the wrestlers; they're quite important men.

Smith: So the referee isn't a judge?

Tanaka: To tell the truth, he doesn't have any power of decision.

Smith: Is that so? That (makes it) a little hard to understand, doesn't it?

Tanaka: He has a right to say (his) views, though.

Smith: That's a relief! (i.e., "Hearing that I feel relieved.")

Vocabulary

わあ	**wā**	wow, oh
すもう	**sumō**	*sumō* wrestling
しょにち	**shonichi**	first/opening day
いつも	**itsumo**	always
まんいん	**man'in**	full (of people)
まん〜	**man-**	full (prefix)
みえる	**mieru**	can see, be visible
ほら	**hora**	Look!, There!
やきとり	**yakitori**	grilled chicken
さあ	**sā**	come now
〜でも	**demo**	let's say, for example
とりくみ	**torikumi**	bout
アナウンス	**anaunsu**	announcement
きこえる	**kikoeru**	can hear, be audible
どひょう	**dohyō**	(*sumō*) ring
ふじのみね	**Fujinomine**	ring name of a *sumō* wrestler
さくらりゅう	**Sakuraryū**	ring name of a *sumō* wrestler
はで（な）	**hade(na)**	flashy, gorgeous
きもの	**kimono**	kimono

うごきまわる	**ugokimawaru***	move around
どういう	**dō iu**	what kind of
ぎょうじ	**gyōji**	referee
ジャッジ	**jajji**	judge
〜の　まわりに	**no mawari ni**	around
ほんとう（の）	**hontō (no)**	real
りきし	**rikishi**	*sumō* wrestler
OB	**ōbī**	OB (old boy), alumnus/i
えらい	**erai**	important, illustrious, eminent
けっていけん	**kettei-ken**	decisive say, authority
けってい	**kettei**	decision, conclusion
〜けん	**-ken**	power, authority, right
なっとく	**nattoku**	understanding, consent
はつげんけん	**hatsugen-ken**	right to say one's views
はつげん	**hatsugen**	view, observation, utterance

* Compound words like this (**ugoku** plus **mawaru**) are very common.

GRAMMAR & LESSON OBJECTIVES

- **-te/-de** form indicating reason or condition
  Hito ga takusan ite, Rinda-san ya okusan ga yoku miemasen.
  Urusakute anaunsu ga yoku kikoemasen.
  Sore o kiite anshin shimashita.
  In these sentences the words and clauses ending with **-te** give the reason for making the concluding statement. Similarly, as seen in the Exercises in this lesson, **-na** adjectives are used in this way, too.
  ex. **Kimura-san wa kuruma ga kirai de, taitei kaisha made arukimasu.**
  "Kimura doesn't like cars so he usually walks to the office."

  Suwatte mimashō.
  Hadena kimono o kite, dohyō no ue de ugokimawatte iru no wa . . . ?
  In these cases the **-te** form specifies the condition or manner in which an action or activity takes place. As here, the clause refers to the subject of the sentence, whether or not the subject is explicitly stated.

- **no** in noun clauses
  Yakitori o tabete iru no ga miemasu yo.
  Dohyō no ue de ugokimawatte iru no wa dō iu hito desu ka.
  Kuroi kimono o kite, dohyō no mawari ni suwatte iru no ga hontō no jajji desu.
  The pattern of clause followed by **no** plus a particle—**wa, ga** or **o**—identifies that segment of the sentence as the topic or subject or object of the sentence as a whole. It is called a noun clause and, as in these examples, frequently pinpoints a situation, a person or a thing. Comparable to this is putting **no** after an adjective for a similar purpose.
  ex. **ōkii no**, "a big one"; **kantanna no**, "a simple one"
  Sometimes **no** is used to represent certain things happening, as in **Tonari no heya**

de Yamada-san ga Ei-go o hanashite iru no ga kikoemasu. "I can hear Ms. Yamada speaking English in the next room."

- **mieru** and **kikoeru**
Rinda-san ya okusan ga miemasen ne.
Anaunsu ga yoku kikoemasen.
The real meanings of these two verbs is that something is within sight or something emits sound. Strictly translated, these sentences would be "Linda and your wife can't be seen." and "The announcements can't be heard well." Note the particle is **ga** (not **o**).

NOTES

1. **Sumō** is a traditional Japanese sport that is still popular in Japan. Two fighters, or **rik-ishi**, wrestle in a circle, or **dohyō**, and the one who throws down his opponent, or pushes or carries him outside the ring, wins. The wrestler who wins the most bouts during the fifteen-day series is the champion of that tournament. The apparel, setting and procedures of **sumō** are imbued with tradition.

2. **Sā, watashi-tachi mo . . . suwatte mimashō.**
Sā at the beginning of a sentence is an attention-getter and suggests and invites action.

3. **Bīru demo nominagara . . .**
Bīru o nomimasen ka often sounds brusque. With **demo** added, the sense is "drink (something), even (if it's only) beer."

4. **Kono torikumi ga owaru made koko de ii desu.**
The sense of **de ii** is "will do," "is satisfactory," "is OK."
   ex. 1. **Tegami o taipu shimashita ga, kore de ii desu ka.** "I typed the letter. Is it all right?"
   2. **Sumimasen. Kōhī mo jūsu mo arimasen.** "Sorry. We have neither coffee nor juice."
   Mizu de ii desu. "Water's fine."
   cf. **Nani ka nomimasu ka. Kōhī. O-cha.** "What'll you have to drink? Coffee? Tea?"
   Mizu ga ii desu. "I'd prefer water."

5. **Kono torikumi ga owaru made . . .**
Made, "until," follows not only time expressions but also the dictionary form of verbs.
   ex. **Kinō watashi-tachi wa kuraku naru made tenisu o shimashita.** "Yesterday we played tennis until it got dark."

6. **Fujinomine, Sakuraryū**
These names mean "Summit of (Mount) Fuji" and "Cherry Dragon." One genre of *sumō* wrestlers' names evokes things beautiful, noble, fierce, everlasting, or variations on these themes. Other names are taken from rivers, seas or mountains in or near the wrestlers' birthplaces. Still others, wholly or in part, give the wrestler a bond with an admired predecessor.

7. **Dō iu hito desu ka.**
Although both **dō iu** and **donna** are translated as "what kind of," **dō iu** implies expectation of an answer going beyond simple appearances or obvious qualities.

8. **Gyōji wa jajji dewa nai n desu ka.**
   Ee, jitsu wa kettei-ken wa nai n desu.
   This is an example of answering a negative question with **ee** signifying agreement
   ("Yes, that's right."), whereas the English would be "no." (See Book I, p. 20.)

9. **Chotto nattoku dekimasen ne.**
   Think of the meaning of **nattoku** as "consent, agree." A freer translation would be
   "I'm not convinced," that is, "I can't agree with what you say," here implying "That's
   strange."

PRACTICE

KEY SENTENCES

1. その はなしを きいて、あんしんしました。
2. きむらさんは あるいて かいしゃに いきます。
3. ジョンソンさんを なりたくうこうまで むかえに いったの
   は すずきさんです。
4. ホテルの まどから ふじさんが みえます。

1. When I heard that, I felt relieved.
2. Kimura goes to the company on foot.
3. It was Suzuki who went all the way to Narita Airport to meet Johnson.
4. You can see Mount Fuji from the hotel window.

EXERCISES

I   Make dialogues by changing the underlined parts as in the example given.

   ex. **Q**. どう したんですか。
      A: <u>あつくて のむ</u> ことが できないんです。

      1. おもい、ひとりで もちます
      2. くらい、よみます
      3. ふくざつ、せつめいします
      4. こんでいます、はいります
      5. はやしさんが いません、そうだんします

II   Practice the following pattern by changing the underlined parts as in the examples given.

   A. *ex.* ニュースを <u>きいて</u> <u>あんしんしました</u>。

      1. ははから てがみを もらいました、あんしんしました
      2. よなかに でんわが ありました、おどろきました
      3. へんじが きません、こまっているんです
      4. しけんに おちました、がっかりしました

B. *ex.* はしって　いしゃを　よびに　いきました。

   1. すわる、はなしましょう

   2. いそぐ、しりょうを　あつめてください

   3. でんわを　する、ききます

   4. ちずを　かく、せつめいしました

III Make dialogues by changing the underlined parts as in the examples given.

A. *ex.* **Q:** まいにち　べんきょうしていますか。
   A: ええ、まいにち　べんきょうするのは　たいへんです。

   1. よる　おそくまで　しごとを　します、たいへん

   2. こどもと　あそびます、たのしい

   3. しょくじを　つくります、めんどう

   4. あさ　5じに　おきます、むずかしい

B. *ex.* **Q:** よく、えを　かきますね。
   A: ええ、えを　かくのが　すきなんです。

   1. やまを　あるきます

   2. じょうだんを　いいます

   3. りょこうを　します

   4. えいがを　みます

C. *ex.* **Q:** なにを　わすれたんですか。
   A: しゅくだいを　もってくるのを　わすれたんです。

   1. でんわします

   2. おかねを　はらいます

   3. せっけんを　かいます

   4. たなかさんに　れんらくします

D. *ex.* **Q:** きょう　くるのは　だれですか。
   A: ええと、きょう　くるのは　たなかさんです。

   1. ともだちに　あいます、いつ、どようび

   2. パーティーに　きません、だれ、スミスさん

   3. きのう　じこが　ありました、どこ、とうきょうホテ
     ルの　ちかく

4. スペインごが　じょうずです、だれ、はやしさんの
   あたらしい　ひしょ

E. *ex.* **Q:** おたくから　<u>ふじさん</u>が　みえますか。
   A: てんきが　いい　ときは　よく　みえます。

1. うみ
2. とうきょうタワー
3. とおくの　やま

IV Practice the following pattern by changing the underlined parts as in the example given.

ex. <u>こうえん</u>で　<u>こどもたちが　あそんでいる</u>のが　<u>みえます</u>。

1. プール、たなかさんが　およいでいます、みえます
2. スーパーの　まえ、すずきさんが　タクシーを　まっ
   ています、みえます
3. どこか、ピアノを　ひいています、きこえます
4. となりの　へや、こどもが　うたを　うたっています、
   きこえます

V Make dialogues by changing the underlined parts as in the examples given.

A. *ex.* **Q:** <u>ひるごはんを</u>　<u>たべ</u>ないんですか。
   A*a*: ええ、<u>たべません</u>。
   A*n*: いいえ、<u>たべます</u>よ。

1. じかんが　ありません。
2. けさの　しんぶんを　よみませんでした。
3. わすれものを　とりに　いきませんでした。

B. *ex.* **Q:** きのう　いつまで　まっていたんですか。
   A: <u>かいぎが　おわる</u>まで　まっていました。

1. くらく　なります。
2. へんじが　きます。
3. しりょうが　とどきます。

Vocabulary

よなか	**yonaka**	middle of the night, midnight
おどろく	**odoroku**	be surprised
へんじ	**henji**	reply, answer

おちる	**ochiru**	fail
がっかりする	**gakkari suru**	be disappointed
はしる	**hashiru**	run
あつめる	**atsumeru**	gather, collect, assemble
めんどう（な）	**mendō(na)**	troublesome, annoying, a nuisance
じょうだんを　いう	**jōdan o iu**	crack a joke
じょうだん	**jōdan**	joke
しゅくだい	**shukudai**	homework
せっけん	**sekken**	soap
ええと	**ēto**	let me see
タワー	**tawā**	tower
とおく	**tōku**	long distance
ひく	**hiku**	play (a musical instrument)

SHORT DIALOGUES

1. すずき：　もしもし、もしもし、きこえますか。

やまかわ：もしもし、おでんわが　とおいんですが、もう　す
　　　　　こし　おおきい　こえで　おねがいします。

すずき：　こちらは　すずきですが、きこえますか。

やまかわ：あ、きこえました。すずきさんですね。

Suzuki:　　Hello, hello—can you hear me?
Yamakawa:　Hello. I can't hear (you). Speak a little louder, please.
Suzuki:　　This is Suzuki. Can you hear (now)?
Yamakawa:　Ah, I can hear now. It's Mr. Suzuki, isn't it?

2. A: しつれいですが、たなかさんじゃ　ありませんか。

B: はい、たなかですが・・・。

A:　Excuse me, but aren't you Mr. Tanaka?
B:　Yes, I'm Tanaka.

Vocabulary

| でんわが　とおい | **denwa ga tōi** | I can't hear (you) (*lit.* "[Your voice over] the phone seems far away.") |

QUIZ

I　Read this lesson's Opening Dialogue and answer the following questions.

1. リンダさんと　スミスさんの　おくさんは　すもうを　みな
がら　なにを　していますか。

2. うるさくて　アナウンスが　よく　きこえないと　いったの
は　だれですか。

3. はでな　きものを　きて　どひょうの　うえで　うごきまわ
っているのは　だれですか。
4. ほんとうの　ジャッジは　どこに　いますか。

II　Put the appropriate particles in the parentheses.

1. てんき（　　）いい　とき、ふじさん（　　）みえます。
2. わたしは　てがみ（　　）とどく（　　）を　まっていまし
た。
3. よる　おそく　くるま（　　）おと（　　）きこえました。
4. くろい　きもの（　　）きている（　　）は　たなかさんの
おくさんです。
5. これは　ほんとう（　　）はなしです。じょうだんでは
ありません。

III　Complete the questions so that they fit the answers.

1. あの　ひとは（　　）ひとですか。
だいとうりょうの　むすこで、ゆうめいな　ピアニストで
す。
2. （　　）まで　ここで　まつんですか。
かいぎが　おわるまで　まっていてください。
3. （　　）を　みているんですか。
ケーキを　つくっているのを　みているんです。
4. 3がつ　3かは（　　）ひですか。
おんなの　この　おまつりの　ひで、ともだちを　よんで
パーティーを　したり　する　ひです。

IV　Complete the sentences with the appropriate form of the words indicated.

1. ニュースを（　　）、おどろきました。（ききます）
2. ちかてつの　なかで　テープを（　　）ながら、にほんごを
べんきょうしています。（ききます）
3. あそこで（　　）のが　みえますか。
（　　）て　よく　みえません。（つりを　しています、とお
いです）
4. てがみを（　　）のを　わすれました。（だします）
5. じかんが（　　）て　いく　ことが　できません。（ありま
せん）

6. しょくじが（　　　）まで　テレビでも　みましょう。（でき
　　ます）

7. はなしが（　　　）で　よく　わかりません。（ふくざつです）

8. でんわを（　　　）ながら　（　　　）のは　あぶないです。
　　（します、うんてんします）

V　Circle the correct words in the parentheses.

1. あついですね。ビール（や、でも、ごろ）のみませんか。
　　いいですね。

2. 6じまでに（かならず、わざわざ、たいてい）れんらくして
　　ください。

3. ごうかくするのは　むずかしいと　おもっていましたが、
　　（かならず、やっぱり、たぶん）だめでした。

4. あなたは　しらなかったんですか。
　　ええ、（ぜひ、それに、じつは）しらなかったんです。

VI　Answer the following questions.

1. あなたは　すもうを　みた　ことが　ありますか。

2. あなたの　へやから　なにが　みえますか。

3. よる　あなたの　へやに　いる　とき、くるまの　おとが
　　きこえますか。

4. あなたは　やまに　のぼるのが　すきですか。

5. しょくじを　はじめる　とき、にほんごで　なんと　いいま
　　すか。

NEW KANJI

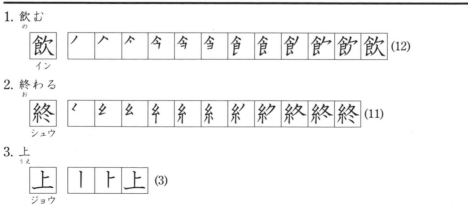

1. 飲む
　の
　飲　ノ　ハ　⺈　今　今　今　食　食　食　飮　飮　飲　(12)
　イン

2. 終わる
　お
　終　く　⺥　幺　糸　糸　糸　糸　終　終　終　終　(11)
　シュウ

3. 上
　うえ
　上　｜　ト　上　(3)
　ジョウ

4. 動く
   うご

動　一　二　三　三　自　自　重　重　動　動 (11)
ドウ

5. 黒い
   くろ

黒　丶　口　日　日　甲　甲　里　里　黒　黒　黒 (11)
コク

6. 安心
   アンシン

心　丶　心　心　心 (4)
こころ

Readings:

著 ：　著く，著る　　　　　言 ：　言う，発言
　　　つ　　　き　　　　　　　　　　い　　　ハツゲン

発 ：　出発，発言　　　　　安 ：　安い，安心
　　　シュッパツ　ハツゲン　　　　　　　やす　　アンシン

Related words:　上 ⟷ 下
　　　　　　　　　うえ　　した
　　　　　　　　　黒い ― 青い ― 赤い ― 白い
　　　　　　　　　くろ　　あお　　あか　　しろ

LESSON **15** A FORGOTTEN UMBRELLA

Mr. Brown takes care of Mr. Yamamoto's umbrella.

ブラウン： きのう スポーツクラブに 行ったら 山本さんに 会いました。

わたなべ： 山本さん？ おととい ここに 来た 山本さんです か。

ブラウン： ええ、かれも そこの 会員だと 言っていました。

わたなべ： あっ そうそう、山本さんが かさを わすれて 帰 りましたが、どうしましょうか。

ブラウン： 私が その かさを あずかりましょう。また 会う かもしれませんから。今度 スポーツクラブへ 行く 時、持っていきます。

わたなべ： じゃ これ、おねがいします。

ブラウン： 山本さんに 会ったら わたします。もし 会わなか ったら 受付に あずけます。

At the health club.

受付： おはようございます。

ブラウン： おはようございます。山本たろうさんは 今日 来ま すか。

受付： 会員の 山本さまですね。今日は 山本さまは ゆう がた 6時に いらっしゃいます。

ブラウン： そうですか。これ、山本さんの かさなんですが、6時 に 来るなら 今 あずけても いいですか。

受付： はい、どうぞ。

ブラウン： じゃ、かれが 来たら わたしてください。

受付： はい、たしかに。

Brown: When I went to the health club yesterday, I ran into Mr. Yamamoto.
Watanabe: Mr. Yamamoto? The Mr. Yamamoto who came here the day before yesterday?
Brown: Um. He said he is a member of that club.
Watanabe: Oh, by the way, he left and forgot his umbrella. What shall (I) do with it?

148

Brown:	I'll take care of the umbrella. I'll probably meet him again. When I next go to the health club, I'll take it with me.
Watanabe:	Oh, then please take it.
Brown:	If I see Mr. Yamamoto I'll give it to him. If I don't, I'll leave it at the reception desk.

Receptionist:	Good morning.
Brown:	Good morning. Is Mr. Taro Yamamoto coming here today?
Receptionist:	You mean the Mr. Yamamoto who's a member here? He's coming today at six in the evening.
Brown:	Is he? This is his umbrella. If he's coming at six, may (I) leave it here now?
Receptionist:	Yes, of course.
Brown:	When he comes, please give it to him.
Receptionist:	Yes, certainly.

Vocabulary

〜たら	-tara	= when, if (for completed action or supposition)
やまもと	**Yamamoto**	Japanese surname
かいいん	**kaiin**	club/society member
そうそう	**sōsō**	by the way
もし	**moshi**	if
あずける	**azukeru**	deposit, entrust
たろう	**Tarō**	male given name
〜さま	**-sama**	= -san (polite)
いらっしゃいます	**irasshaimasu**	(polite form of **kuru**)
〜なら	**nara**	if
たしかに	**tashika ni**	certainly

GRAMMAR & LESSON OBJECTIVES

• **-tara**

Kinō supōtsu kurabu ni ittara Yamamoto-san ni aimashita.

A . . . -**tara** basically expresses completed action. -**tara** (-**kattara, dattara**) is combined with verbs, adjectives and nouns and means A has been done and B happened. Since B (-**mashita**) is unexpected, -**tara** is used here. In sentences like **Kinō Tanaka-san ga kita toki, kare ni hanashimashita**, "When Tanaka came yesterday, I told him (about it)," **toki** (not a -**tara** pattern) occurs because the speaker's action of telling Mr. Tanaka something is not an accidental happening. The difference between -**te** and -**tara** should be noted. If Brown had said **Kinō supōtsu kurabu ni itte Yamamoto-san ni aimashita** ("I went to the health club yesterday and saw Yamamoto"), it would have meant that he had intended to see Yamamoto at the health club. The neutral version, **Kinō supōtsu kurabu ni itta toki Yamamoto-san ni aimashita**, is used to answer the question, **Itsu Yamamoto-san ni aimashita ka.**

Yamamoto-san ni attara watashimasu. Moshi awanakattara uketsuke ni azukemasu.

If the time is the future (A . . . -**tara** B . . . -**masu**/-**mashō**/-**te kudasai**), this pattern expresses supposition, for nothing in the future is absolutely certain, and thus it can be translated as "if." If the situation is expected to actually happen, "when" is used in translation.

ex. 1. **Ashita ame ga futtara, pikunikku wa yamemasu.** "If it rains tomorrow, the picnic will be cancelled."

2. **Kuraku nattara, hanabi o hajimemashō.** "We'll begin the fireworks when it gets dark."

Verbs, adjectives and nouns are combined as follows:

	aff.	neg.
iku miru	ittara mitara	ikanakattara minakattara
takai	takakattara	takaku nakattara
shizukana	shizuka dattara	shizuka de/ja nakattara
ame	ame dattara	ame de/ja nakattara

- **nara**

6-ji ni kuru nara, ima azukete mo ii desu ka

Although **nara** is also used when there its uncertainty, it may be different from **-tara** in some aspects. In this example, Brown has definitely decided to leave the umbrella, assuming Yamamoto is coming to the club. At times either **-tara** or **nara** is used to mean the same thing. The following two sentences, however, are different.

ex. 1. **Katō-san ga kitara kaerimasu.** "I'll leave after Katō comes."

2. **Katō-san ga kuru nara kaerimasu.** "If Katō's coming, I'll leave (now)."

Remember the time accordance of the A . . . **-tara** B pattern. The main clause, B, always happens after A has been completed. Other examples where **-nara** and **-tara** are not interchangeable are:

ex. 1. **Kono hon, yomu nara motte itte ii desu yo.** "If you are really going to read this book, you can take it home."

2. **Yondara kaeshite kudasai.** "After you have read it, please return it to me."

Nara can come after adjectives—**yasui nara**, **benri nara**—or nouns, as in **Ame nara kasa o motte ikimashō.** "If it's going to rain, (I'll) take (my) umbrella."

Nara implies some assumption of the speaker and cannot be used to relate things that are obvious. **Konban kuraku naru nara . . . ,**"If it gets dark this evening . . . ," is awkward.

NOTES

Watashi ga sono kasa o azukarimashō.

Kore, Yamamoto-san no kasa na n desu ga, 6-ji ni kuru nara, ima azukete mo ii desu ka.

As can be seen, both **azukaru** (Regular I), "to be entrusted and keep for some period," and **azukeru** (Regular II), "to entrust something," take the same object and the same particle. Be careful not to confuse verbs like these.

Compare: 1. **Buraun-san wa Watanabe-san kara kasa o azukarimashita.** (*lit.*) "Brown was entrusted with an umbrella by Watanabe."

2. **Buraun-san wa uketsuke ni kasa o azukemashita.** "Brown had the receptionist take care of the umbrella."

3. **Uketsuke no hito wa Buraun-san kara kasa o azukarimashita.**
"The receptionist (was given) an umbrella to take care of by Brown."

PRACTICE

KEY SENTENCES

1. きょうとまで くるまで いったら 10じかん かかりました。
2. もし よていが かわったら しらせます。
3. ひこうきで いくなら はやく きっぷを かった ほうが いいですよ。

1. When we went to Kyoto by car, it took ten hours.
2. If my schedule changes, I'll let you know.
3. If you're going by plane, it's better to buy (your) tickets early.

EXERCISES

I Practice the following patterns by changing the underlined parts as in the example given.

ex. スポーツクラブに いったら、むかしの ともだちに あいました

1. かどを まがりました、うみが みえました
2. たんじょうびの プレゼントを あけました、かわいい いぬが でてきました
3. うんどうしました、せなかが いたく なりました
4. あさ おきました、ゆきが ふって いました
5. うちに かえりました、てがみが きていました

II Make dialogues by changing the underlined parts as in the examples given.

A. *ex.* **Q:** かいぎは いつ はじめますか。
   A: 10じに なったら すぐ はじめます。

1. しゃちょうが きます
2. ぜんいんが そろいます
3. ちゅうしょくが すみます
4. しりょうの コピーが できます

B. *ex.* **Q:** ひまが あったら どう しますか。
   A: ひまが あったら にほんじゅう りょこうしたいです。

1. おかね、おおきい うちを かいます

2. たくさん　おかね、はんぶん　きふします
3. くるま、ほっかいどうを　まわります
4. おかねと　じかん、せかいじゅうの　ともだちを　たずねます

C. *ex.* **Q:** みちが　わからないかもしれませんよ。
   A: もし　わからなかったら　こうばんで　ききます。

1. おかねが　たりません、ともだちに　かります
2. きょうは　かいぎが　ありません、ほかの　しごとを　します
3. バスが　はしっていません、タクシーで　かえりましょう

III Practice the following pattern by changing the underlined parts as in the example given.

ex. あつかったら　まどを　あけてください。

1. さむい、ヒーターを　つけても　いいです
2. たかい、かわないでください
3. つごうが　わるい、ほかの　ひに　しましょう
4. きぶんが　よくない、やすんだ　ほうが　いいですよ
5. つまらない、よまなくても　いいです

IV Make dialogues by changing the underlined parts as in the examples given.

A. *ex.* **Q:** あめだったら　どうしますか。
   A: あめなら　よていを　かえます。

1. スト、いきません
2. たなかさんが　るす、また　あとで　でんわします
3. けっかが　だめ、もういちど　やります
4. つかいかたが　ふくざつ、かうのを　やめます

B. *ex.* **A:** ひるごはんを　たべたいんですが。
   B: ひるごはんを　たべるなら　あの　レストランが　いいですよ。

1. スポーツクラブに　はいります、いい　クラブを　しょうかいしましょう
2. うみに　いきます、わたしの　くるまを　つかっても　いいですよ

3. テープレコーダーを　かいます、ちいさい　ほうが
   べんりだと　おもいます
4. きゅうしゅうに　いきます、フェリーが　いいと　お
   もいますよ
5. ヨーロッパを　りょこうします、5がつごろが　きれい
   で　いいですよ

Vocabulary

むかし	**mukashi**	old, long-time
かわいい	**kawaii**	cute
いぬ	**inu**	dog
でてくる	**dete kuru**	come out, appear
うんどうする	**undō suru**	exercise
うんどう	**undō**	exercise
せなか	**senaka**	back
ぜんいん	**zen'in**	all the staff, all members
そろう	**sorou**	be present, assemble, be/become complete
すむ	**sumu**	be finished
にほんじゅう	**Nihon-jū**	all over Japan
じゅう	**-jū**	all over, throughout
はんぶん	**hambun**	half
きふする	**kifu suru**	donate, contribute
きふ	**kifu**	donation, contribution
せかいじゅう	**sekai-jū**	all over the world
せかい	**sekai**	world, society, realm
るす	**rusu**	be out/away
しょうかいする	**shōkai suru**	introduce
フェリー	**ferī**	ferry

SHORT DIALOGUES

1. A: この　へんに　にもつを　あずける　ところは　ありません
   か。
   B: あそこに　コインロッカーが　あります。もし　いっぱいな
   ら、かいさつぐちの　そばにも　ありますよ。

   A: Isn't there a place to check baggage around here?
   B: There are pay lockers over there. If (they're) all full, there are some others near the ticket
   gate.

2. ホワイト：かいぎは　なかなか　おわりませんね。
   わたなべ：9じに　なったら　おわるでしょう。
   ホワイト：そうですか。そんなに　おそく　なるなら　おさき
   　　　　　に　しつれいします。

White:　　 The meeting still isn't over, is it?

Watanabe: It'll be over by nine, I suppose.

White:　　 Oh, will it? If it's going on so late, I'm going to leave now.

3. A: ちゅうごくごの　つうやくを　さがしているんですが。

   B: ちゅうごくごから　にほんごへの　つうやくですね。

   A: ええ、だれか　いい　ひとが　いたら　ぜひ　しょうかいして　ください。

A: I'm looking for an interpreter for Chinese.

B: From Chinese to Japanese?

A: Yes. If there's anyone good around, please introduce them to me.

Vocabulary		
この　へん	**kono hen**	around here, this vicinity
へん	**hen**	neighborhood, vicinity
コインロッカー	**koin rokkā**	pay locker
そば	**soba**	near, beside
そんなに	**sonna ni**	that much
つうやく	**tsūyaku**	interpreter, translator
さがす	**sagasu**	look for

QUIZ

I　Read this lesson's Opening Dialogue and answer the following questions.

1. ブラウンさんは　やまもとさんの　わすれた　かさを　だれから　あずかりましたか。

2. ブラウンさんは　どこで　やまもとさんに　その　かさを　わたしたいと　おもっていますか。

3. ブラウンさんは　スポーツクラブに　いった　とき、やまもとさんに　あう　ことが　できましたか。

4. やまもとさんは　この　スポーツクラブの　かいいんですか。

II　Put the appropriate particles in the parentheses.

1. ブラウンさんは　うけつけの　ひと（　　）にもつ（　　）あずけました。

2. かいいん（　　）やまもとさまは　きょう　ゆうがた　6じ（　　）いらっしゃいます。

3. やまもとさんが　かさ（　　）わすれて　かえりました。じゃ、わたし（　　）その　かさ（　　）あずかりましょう。

スポーツクラブ（　　）やまもとさん（　　）あったら、
わたします。

4. ちゅうしょく（　　）すんだら、きっぷ（　　）かい（　　）
いってください。

III Complete the questions so that they fit the answers.

1. もし　やまもとさんが　こなかったら、（　　）しましょう
か。
てがみで　しらせてください。

2. （　　）ひっこすんですか。
うちが　できたら　ひっこします。

3. （　　）に　しょうたいじょうを　わたしましたか。
ひしょに　わたしました。

4. （　　）パーティーに　いかないんですか。
パーティーは　たいくつなので　いきたくないんです。

IV Complete the sentences with the appropriate form of the words indicated.

1. ワープロを（　　）なら、いい　みせを　おしえましょう。
（かいます）

2. ぜんいんが（　　）たら、（　　）ください。（そろいます、
はじめます）

3. タクシーに（　　）たら、きぶんが（　　）なりました。
（のります、わるいです）

4. （　　）なら、えいがを（　　）に　いきませんか。（ひま
です、みます）

5. この　かばんは　つかっていません。
（　　）なら、（　　）ほうが　いいですよ。（つかいません、
すてます）

6. （　　）たら、すこし（　　）ください。（つかれます、や
すみます）

7. （　　）たら、ジュースを（　　）ください。（いそがしく
ないです、かってきます）

8. つくりかたが（　　）なら、（　　）のを　やめます。（めん
どうです、つくります）

9. あした（　　）たら、でかけません。（あめです）

10. きょうとに（　　）なら、この　ちずを（　　）ましょう。
　（いきます、あげます）
11. にもつが（　　）ので、（　　）ください。（おもいです、
　あずかります）

V　Answer the following questions.

1. さいふを　おとしたら、あなたは　どう　しますか。
2. 1かげつ　やすみが　あったら、なにを　しますか。
3. ともだちの　ガールフレンド／ボーイフレンド　から　ラブレ
　ターを　もらったら　どう　しますか。

NEW KANJI

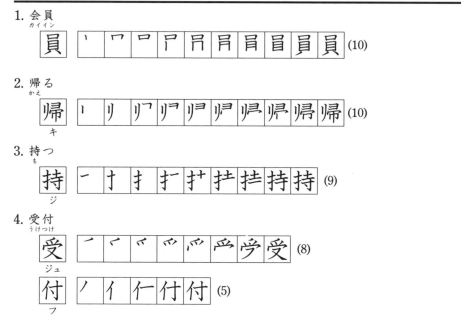

1. 会員
　カイイン
員　丶　冖　冂　尸　弖　冃　冐　冒　員　員　(10)

2. 帰る
　かえ
帰　丿　刂　刂'　刂''　刂'''　刂''''　帰　帰　帰　帰　(10)
　キ

3. 持つ
　も
持　一　十　扌　扌'　扩　拝　拝　持　持　(9)
　ジ

4. 受付
　うけつけ
受　丶　丷　爫　爫'　爫''　严　学　受　(8)
　ジュ
付　丿　イ　仁　付　付　(5)
　フ

Readings:

　山：　あそ山，山本　　　　　本：　日本語，山本
　　　　　サン　やまもと　　　　　　　　　ニ ホン ゴ　やまもと
　会：　会社，会う　　　　　　今：　今，今日中，今度
　　　　カイ シャ　あ　　　　　　　　　いま　キョウジュウ　コン ド

LESSON 16 THE NEW SHOWROOM DESIGN

Mr. Yamakawa asks Mr. Hayashi on the phone if he likes the new design for the showroom.

山川：もしもし、林部長ですか。こちらは　Mせっけいじむしょ
やまかわ　　　　はやしぶちょう
の　山川ですが、ごいらいの　ショールームの　せっけい
が　できあがりました。

林：ああ、さっき　ファックスで　ずめんを　いただきました。
はやし
なかなか　いいですね。

山川：何か　もんだいは　ありませんか。来週から　工事を
なに　　　　　　　　　　らいしゅう　こうじ
はじめれば、来月中に　できあがります。
らいげつちゅう

林：そうですねえ。

山川：もし　もんだいが　なければ、さっそく　はじめたいと
思いますが・・・。
おも

林：年末に　なると　ぎょうしゃも　いそがしく　なりますか
ねんまつ
らね。

山川：ええ。早ければ　早いほど　いいと　思うんですが・・・。
はや

林：すみませんが、はじめる　前に　ちょっと　そうだんした
まえ
い　ことが　あるんですが・・・。

山川：わかりました。そちらの　ごつごうが　よければ、これか
ら　うかがいます。

林：できれば　そう　してください。6時に　なると　おもての
じ
入口は　閉まります。はんたいがわに　まわると　うら口
いりぐち　し　　　　　　　　　　　　　　　　　　　　ぐち
が　ありますから、そこから　入ってください。
はい

山川：わかりました。

林：うら口は　10時まで　開いています。じゃ、よろしく
あ
おねがいします。

Yamakawa:　Hello, is this Mr. Hayashi? This is Yamakawa of the M Design Office. We have finished the showroom design you requested.

Hayashi:　Ah, yes. We received the blueprint by fax (just) a little while ago. It looks quite good
to me.

Yamakawa:	Are there any problems? If (we) start construction work next week, it'll be finished by the end of next month.
Hayashi:	I see.
Yamakawa:	If there are no problems we'd like to start without delay.
Hayashi:	As it gets near the end of the year, contractors get (quite) busy, don't they?
Yamakawa:	Yes. The earlier the better, I think.
Hayashi:	I'm afraid we'd prefer to meet (you) and have one more consultation before (you) start.
Yamakawa:	I understand. If you have time, I'll come (over) now.
Hayashi:	If you can, please do so. The front entrance is closed at six (lit. "when it gets to be six"). If you go around to the opposite side, there's a back entrance. Please come in that way.
Yamakawa:	Yes, of course.
Hayashi:	The back entrance is open until ten o'clock. I'll be expecting you then. (lit. "I request you to [act] properly.")

Vocabulary

せっけい	sekkei	design, plan
ごいらい	go-irai	someone else's request, commission
ショールーム	shōrūmu	showroom
できあがる	dekiagaru	be finished/ready/done
ずめん	zumen	blueprint, plan
いただきました	itadakimashita	(polite form of **moraimashita**)
なにか	nanika	some-/anything, some, any
こうじ	kōji	construction work
〜ば／〜ければ	-ba/-kereba	= if
さっそく	sassoku	without delay, directly
ねんまつ	nenmatsu	end of the year
ぎょうしゃ	gyōsha	contractor, supplier, trader, businessman
〜（けれ）ば〜ほど	-(kere)ba . . . hodo	if . . . -er/more/less, (then) . . .
うかがう	ukagau	visit, ask (polite)
〜と	to	when (particle)
おもて	omote	front, face, surface
しまる	shimaru	be closed
はんたいがわ	hantai-gawa	opposite side
はんたい	hantai	opposite, reverse
〜がわ	-gawa	side
うらぐち	uraguchi	back entrance
うら	ura	back, reverse (side)
よろしく	yoroshiku	properly, well, at one's discretion

GRAMMAR & LESSON OBJECTIVES

• **-ba/-kereba**
Raishū kara kōji o hajimereba raigetsu-chū ni dekiagarimasu.
Sochira no go-tsugō ga yokereba . . .

The **-ba/-kereba** form is called the conditional form and is made with verbs, the two types of adjectives, and nouns as shown below. Note also the negatives (in which practice is given in the Exercises in this lesson).

		aff.	neg.
verb	**omou** (Reg. I) **hajimeru** (Reg. II) **kuru** (Irr.) **suru** (Irr.)	omoeba hajimereba kureba sureba	omowanakereba hajimenakereba konakereba shinakereba
-i adj.	**hayai** **ii/yoi**	hayakereba yokereba	hayaku nakereba yoku nakereba
-na adj.	**benrina**	(benri de areba) benri nara(ba)/dattara	benri de/ja nakereba
noun	**ame**	(ame de areba) ame nara(ba)/dattara	ame de/ja nakereba

Naraba is found in written Japanese and is a formal way of speaking.

To see the conditional in relation to other forms, refer to the verb table in Appendix B.

- **-ba . . . hodo . . .**

Hayakereba hayai hodo ii.

This pattern uses the conditional form of an **-i** adjective with the dictionary form of the same adjective plus **hodo** and leads to a conclusion.

ex. **Ōkikereba ōkii hodo ii desu.** "The larger the better."

For **-na** adjectives the pattern is **Shizuka nara shizuka na hodo ii desu.** "The quieter the better."

Essentially the same pattern consists of the conditional form of a verb and the dictionary form of the same verb with **hodo** coming after it.

ex. **Mireba miru hodo hoshiku narimasu.** "The more (I) look at (it), the more (I) want it."

- Particle **to**

6-ji ni naru to omote no iriguchi wa shimarimasu.

Hantai-gawa ni mawaru to uraguchi ga arimasu.

A clause ending with **to** followed by a main clause with a present form is a way of saying if or when A happens, B occurs as a natural or habitual result. The sense is often "whenever." Two points to remember are that **to** comes after the dictionary or plain negative form of a verb, and this pattern is not appropriate for expressing one's own requests, suggestions, intentions or the granting of permission. Specifically, it is not used in sentences ending in **-te kudasai**, **-mashō**, **masen ka** and so on.

ex. 1. **Taiyō ga shizumu to, kuraku narimasu.** "When the sun sets, it gets dark."
2. **Kono botan o osu to, kikai ga ugokimasu.** "If you push this button, the machine will (start) running."

to, **-tara**, **nara** and **-ba** are in some cases interchangeable, as when they are translated by "if," but there are rules and restrictions in the usage of each word. Please refer to the grammar sections on each one.

NOTES

1. **Gyōsha**

This word refers to traders, suppliers and manufacturers who provide goods and services to larger enterprises and government organizations. It can be compared with **torihikisaki**, which implies a more equal relationship.

2. **Nenmatsu**

Nenmatsu—the final few days in December—has traditionally been regarded as the period for finishing the year's business or settling accounts. This feeling still pervades society, even though the fiscal year for the vast majority of companies now extends from April to March. People do their best to clear up any outstanding problems within the year so that they can relax during the New Year's holidays.

PRACTICE

KEY SENTENCES

1. ビールは　ありますか。
   いいえ、ありませんが、さかやに　でんわすれば　すぐ　もって
   きます。
2. はるに　なると　さくらの　はなが　さきます。
3. さかなは　あたらしければ　あたらしいほど　いいです。

1. Is there any beer?
   No. there isn't, but if I call the liquor store they'll bring some over right away.
2. When spring comes, the cherry blossoms come out.
3. As for fish, the fresher the better.

Vocabulary		
はる	**haru**	spring
さく	**saku**	blossom, flower

EXERCISES

I　Verbs: Study the examples, convert into the conditional form, and memorize.

ex. いく → いけば、いかなければ　　　たべる → たべれば、たべな
ければ

くる → くれば、こなければ　　　する → すれば、しなければ

1. あらう	4. たのむ	7. できる	10. しらせる
2. たつ	5. つかう	8. おりる	11. もってくる
3. うる	6. あるく	9. つとめる	12. でんわする

II   Practice the following patterns by changing the underlined parts as in the example given.

ex. うちから　えきまで　あるけば　**30**ぷん　かかります。

   1. めがねを　かけます、　よく　みえます
   2. ゆっくり　はなします、　わかります
   3. えきに　つく　じかんが　わかります、　むかえに
     いきます
   4. しつもんが　ありません、　これで　おわります
   5. はっきり　いいません、　わかりません
   6. かいいんに　なりません、　この　プールを　りよう
     する　ことが　できません

III   Adjectives: Study the example, convert into the conditional form, and memorize.

ex. あつい→あつければ、あつくなければ

   1. わるい　　　　4. おもい　　　　7. つごうが　いい
   2. おもしろい　　5. めずらしい　　8. あたまが　いたい
   3. かたい　　　　6. すくない　　　9. はなしたい

IV   Practice the following patterns by changing the underlined parts as in the examples given.

A. *ex.* やすければ　かいますが、たかければ　かいません。

   1. あたらしい、ふるい　　　3. いい、わるい
   2. おいしい、まずい　　　　4. おもしろい、つまらない

B. *ex.* つごうが　わるければ　でんわを　ください。

   1. おもしろい、わたしも　みたいと　おもいます
   2. いそがしい、ほかの　ひとに　たのみます
   3. むずかしい、しなくても　いいですよ
   4. いそがしくない、いっしょに　えいがに　いきませんか
   5. いきたくない、いかなくても　いいです

V   Make dialogues by changing the underlined parts as in the examples given.

A. *ex.* A: スポーツクラブに　はいりませんか。
    B: えきに　ちかければ　はいりたいと　おもいます。

   1. たかくないです
   2. プールが　あります

3. いい　コーチが　います
4. こんでいません
5. ゴルフの　れんしゅうが　できます
6. あさ　はやくから　あいています

B. *ex.* たなかふじん：　あなたも　フラワーショーに　いきますか。
スミスふじん：　<u>ひまが　あれば</u>　いきます。

1. じかんが　あります
2. えいごの　せつめいが　あります
3. ベビーシッターが　みつかります
4. その　ひに　ほかの　よていが　ありません
5. てんきが　わるくないです
6. おっとの　つごうが　いいです

VI Make dialogues by changing the underlined parts as in the examples given.

A. *ex.* **A:** <u>しごと</u>は　<u>はやければ</u>　<u>はやいほど</u>　いいですね。
B: ええ、わたしも　そう　おもいます。

1. やちん、やすい　　　　3. ぜいきん、すくない
2. きゅうりょう、おおい　　4. やすみ、ながい

B. *ex.* **A:** そんなに　<u>かいたい</u>んですか。
B: ええ、<u>みれば</u>　<u>みるほど</u>　<u>ほしく</u>　なります。

1. テニスが　すき、やる、おもしろい
2. けっこんしたい、あう、すき
3. むずかしい、かんがえる、わからない

VII Practice the following patterns by changing the underlined parts as in the example given.

ex. <u>まっすぐ　いくと</u>　<u>ひだりがわに　ポストが　あります</u>。

1. （お）さけを　のみます、たのしく　なります
2. かいさつぐちを　でます、めの　まえに　スーパーが
あります
3. さとうさんは　かいしゃに　つきます、まず　コーヒ
ーを　のみます
4. たばこを　たくさん　すいます、がんに　なりますよ
5. やすみません、びょうきに　なりますよ

VIII Make dialogues by changing the underlined parts as in the example given.

ex. Q: どうすると　<u>あく</u>んですか。

A: <u>ボタンを　おす</u>と　<u>あきます</u>。

1. ジュースが　でてきます、おかねを　いれます
2. でんきが　きえます、ドアを　しめます
3. まどが　あきます、レバーを　ひきます
4. ラジオの　おとが　おおきく　なります、これを　まわします

Vocabulary

しつもん	**shitsumon**	question
はっきり	**hakkiri**	clearly
りょうする	**riyō suru**	make use of, take advantage of
りょう	**riyō**	use
かたい	**katai**	hard
めずらしい	**mezurashii**	rarc, unusual
すくない	**sukunai**	a little, few
まずい	**mazui**	not delicious
はやくから	**hayaku kara**	(from) early
ふじん	**fujin**	Mrs., lady, woman
フラワーショー	**furawā shō**	flower show
ベビーシッター	**bebī shittā**	baby sitter
みつかる	**mitsukaru**	be found, find
おっと	**otto**	husband
やちん	**yachin**	(house) rent
きゅうりょう	**kyūryō**	salary
めの　まえ	**me no mae**	right in front of (*lit.* "in front of your eyes")
がん	**gan**	cancer
ボタン	**botan**	button
おす	**osu**	push
いれる	**ireru**	put in
きえる	**kieru**	go out, be extinguished, put out
レバー	**rebā**	lever
ひく	**hiku**	pull
おと	**oto**	sound
まわす	**mawasu**	turn

SHORT DIALOGUE

A: たいへん。もう　10じはんですか。ひこうきの　じかんに　まにあわないかもしれません。

B: くるまで　くうこうまで　おくりましょう。いそげば　まにあいますよ。

A: じゃ、ごめいわくでなければ　おねがいします。

A: Oh dear, it's 10:30 already. It looks like (I'll) be late for the plane.
B: I'll take (you) (lit. "send you off") to the airport by car. If (we) hurry, you'll be in time.
A: Thank you. (lit. "If it is not too much trouble for you to do so, please do so.")

Vocabulary

たいへん	**taihen**	Oh dear!
まにあう	**maniau**	be in/on time
おくる	**okuru**	take, see/send off, escort
ごめいわく	**go-meiwaku**	trouble, inconvenience

QUIZ

I　Read this lesson's Opening Dialogue and answer the following questions.

1. やまかわさんは　はやしさんに　ファックスで　なにを　お
くりましたか。
2. やまかわさんは　らいしゅうから　こうじを　はじめれば
いつ　できあがると　いいましたか。
3. はやしさんの　かいしゃに　なんじまでに　いけば　おもて
の　いりぐちから　はいる　ことが　できますか。
4. ABCの　うらぐちは　なんじに　なると　しまりますか。

II　Put the appropriate word or word parts in the parentheses.

1. なに（　　）のみものは　ありませんか。
2. いつまで（　　）はらわなければ　なりませんか。
はやけれ（　　）はやいほど　いいだろう（　　）おもいま
す。
3. この　みせは　ひるから　よる　12じ（　　）あいています。
4. あたらしい　じむしょ（　　）せっけいが　できあがりまし
たので、ファックス（　　）おくります。

III　Complete the questions so that they fit the answers.

1. さくらの　はなは（　　）さきますか。
4がつに　なると　さきます。
2. （　　）か　あいている　へやは　ないでしょうか。
かいぎしつが　あいていますよ。
3. やまださんが　かいた　えは（　　）でしたか。
なかなか　よかったですよ。

IV Convert the following verbs and adjectives into their **-ba/-kereba** forms.

1. あう　　　　4. ふる　　　　7. おくれる　　　10. ない
2. かく　　　　5. みえる　　　8. けっこんする　11. めずらしい
3. しまる　　　6. まにあう　　9. もってくる　　12. いい

V Complete the sentences with the appropriate form of the words indicated.

1. よく　（　　　）ば、げんきに（　　　）でしょう。（やすみます、なります）
2. とうきょうタワーに（　　　）ば、うみが（　　　）でしょう。（のぼります、みえます）
3. つぎの　かどを　みぎに（　　　）と　はなやが　あります。（まがります）
4. おさけを（　　　）と、（　　　）なります。（のみます、たのしいです）
5. ごつごうが（　　　）ば、ごご（　　　）たいと　おもいます。（いいです、うかがいます）
6. （　　　）ば、（　　　）なりません。（れんしゅうしません、じょうずです）
7. ボタンを（　　　）と　ドアが　しまります。（おします）
8. （　　　）ば、もっと（　　　）ましょう。（ほしいです、もってきます）
9. でんわで（　　　）ば、（　　　）と　おもいます。（たのみます、もってきます）
10. （　　　）ば、（　　　）ほど　わからなく　なります。（かんがえます、かんがえます）

VI Circle the correct words in the parentheses.

1. いつ　しょるいを　あずけたんですか。
   きのう（はっきり、たしかに、なかなか）うけつけに　あずけました。
2. なんじごろ　うかがいましょうか。
   ごぜんちゅうは　いそがしいので、（できれば、なかなか、さっき）ごご　2じごろ　きてくれませんか。
3. じかんが　ないので、（さっき、たしかに、さっそく）はじめてください。

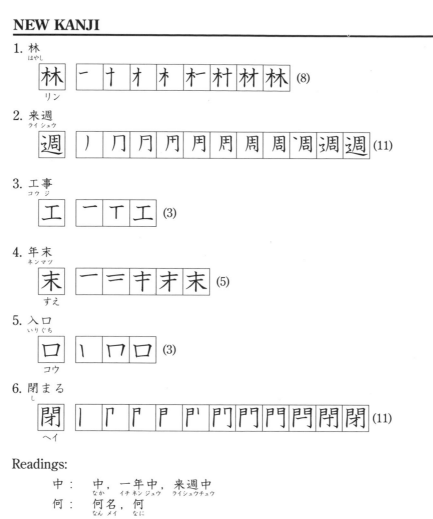

1. 林
   はやし
   林　一　十　才　木　朴　村　材　林 (8)
   リン

2. 来週
   ライ シュウ
   週　丿　刀　月　円　円　円　周　周　`周　凋　週 (11)

3. 工事
   コウ ジ
   工　一　丅　工 (3)

4. 年末
   ネンマツ
   末　一　二　キ　才　末 (5)
   すえ

5. 入口
   いりぐち
   口　丨　冂　口 (3)
   コウ

6. 閉まる
   し
   閉　丨　冂　冂　冃　門　門　門　門　閉　閉 (11)
   ヘイ

Readings:

中： 中，一年中，来週中
　　 なか　イチ ネン ジュウ　ライ シュウ チュウ
何： 何名，何
　　 なん メイ　なに

Mr. Brown has to keep a diary as a part of his Japanese study.

12月31日（水）はれ　のち　くもり

　今日は　大みそかだ。となりの　おおのさんの　うちでは、朝から　かぞく　全員で　そうじを　していた。みんなで　へいや車や、そして　いぬまで　あらっていた。

　午後は　日本語で　ねんがじょうを　書いたが、じが　へただから　よみにくいだろう。ゆうがた、たなかさん　一家と　そばを　食べに　行った。

　よるは　ふだんは　あまり　見ない　テレビを　見た。チャンネルを　つぎつぎに　かえると、さわがしい　ショーや　さむらいの　時代げきを　やっていた。3チャンネルでは　ベートーベンの　"第九"を　えんそうしていた。先日、中村さんが　「毎年、12月に　なると　日本かくちで　"第九"を　えんそうするんですよ」と　言っていたが、おもしろい　国だ。

1月1日（木）はれ

　日本で　新年を　むかえた。町は　人も　車も　少なくて、たいへん　しずかだ。こうじょうも　会社も　休みなので、いつもは　よごれている　東京の　そらが、今日は　きれいで　気持ちが　いい。近所の　店も　スーパーも　みんな　休みだった。

あの　ラッシュアワーの　サラリーマンや　学生は　どこに　行
ったのだろうか。
　　日本人の　どうりょうや　ともだちから　ねんがじょうが　と
どいた。ぎょうしゃからも　来た。いんさつの　ものが　多いが、
ふでで　書いた　ものも　ある。やはり　うつくしい。もらった
ねんがじょうは　ほとんど　全部　くじつきである。

Wednesday, December 31
Fair, later cloudy

　　Today is the (year's) final day. At the Ōno house next door, beginning in the morning, every member of the family did (some) cleaning up. Everybody washed (something)—the fence, the car, even the dog.

　　In the afternoon I wrote New Year's cards in Japanese, but they are probably difficult to read because of my poor handwriting. In the early evening we went to eat *soba* with the Tanakas.

　　(Later) in the evening, I watched television, which I do not ordinarily see very often. Switching channels one after another, I came across an uproarious show, a samurai period drama and such-like. On Channel 3 they were performing Beethoven's Ninth Symphony. The other day Nakamura told me, "Every year when December comes around Beethoven's Ninth Symphony is performed all over Japan." Interesting country!

Thursday, January 1
Fair

　　I salute the New Year in Japan! The city has few people or cars and is very quiet. Because factories and companies (are) on vacation, Tokyo's usually dirty air is clean. (What a) good feeling! The neighborhood stores and the supermarket are all closed, too. Where have those rush-hour, white-collar workers and students gone, I wonder?

　　New Year's cards came from Japanese colleagues and friends. They came from business associates, too. Most were printed ones, but some were written with a brush as well. Quite beautiful, as one would expect. Of the cards (I) received, almost all have lottery (numbers) on them.

Vocabulary

はれ	**hare**	clear
のち	**nochi**	later
くもり	**kumori**	cloudy
おおみそか	**ō-misoka**	last day of year
おおの	**Ōno**	Japanese surname
へい	**hei**	fence, wall
じ	**ji**	(hand)writing, character, letter
へた(な)	**heta(na)**	poor, unskillful
～にくい	**-nikui**	difficult, awkward
いっか	**ikka**	family, household
そば	**soba**	buckwheat noodles
よる	**yoru**	night
ふだん(は)	**fudan(wa)**	ordinarily
チャンネル	**channeru**	channel

つぎつぎに	**tsugi-tsugi ni**	one after another, in turn
さわがしい	**sawagashi**	uproarious, noisy
ショー	**shō**	show
さむらい	**samurai**	samurai
じだいげき	**jidai-geki**	period drama
げき	**geki**	drama
やる	**yaru**	show, play
ベートーベン	**Bētōben**	Beethoven
だいく	**Dai-ku**	Ninth (Symphony)
だい	**dai-**	(prefix for ordinal numbers)
えんそうする	**ensō suru**	perform
えんそう	**ensō**	performance, recital
せんじつ	**senjitsu**	the other day
まいとし	**maitoshi**	= **mainen**, every year
かくち	**kakuchi**	all over, various districts
しんねん	**shinnen**	new year
たいへん	**taihen**	very
こうじょう	**kōjō**	factory
よごれる	**yogoreru**	be/become dirty
そら	**sora**	sky
きもち	**kimochi**	feeling
きんじょ	**kinjo**	neighborhood
みんな	**minna**	all, everything
ラッシュアワー	**rasshu awā**	rush hour
サラリーマン	**sarariman**	white-collar (salaried) worker
(の)だろうか	**(no) darō ka**	I wonder
いんさつ	**insatsu**	printing
ふで	**fude**	brush
やはり	**yahari**	- **yappari**, (just) as we/you expected
うつくしい	**utsukushii**	beautiful
ほとんど	**hotondo**	almost
ぜんぶ	**zembu**	all, every
くじつき	**kuji-tsuki**	with lottery
くじ	**kuji**	lottery
〜つき	**-tsuki**	with, attached, included

GRAMMAR & LESSON OBJECTIVES

• Plain style

In this course, the plain forms of verbs have up to this point been used only in the middle of sentences. As the final verbs in sentences, the plain forms are tied into, and are the main indicators of, the level of politeness. The plain style is used, for example, in a diary, a thesis or in informal speech.

In informal speech there is a great variety of usage, related to the sex and age of the speakers and their relationships. Situation and topic may also be factors influencing the level of formality and politeness of forms and diction. Read the Short Dialogues in this and the following lessons carefully and note how the speech levels depend upon these factors.

The following table summarizes these expressions, most of which have already been introduced.

desu/-masu style	plain style
1. Sumō o mita koto ga arimasu.	Sumō o mita koto ga aru.
2. Kinō Ōsaka e ikimashita.	Kinō Ōsaka e itta.
3. Tanaka-san wa konai kamo shiremasen.	Tanaka-san wa konai kamo shirenai.
4. Ashita wa ame deshō.	Ashita wa ame darō.
5. Tōkyō wa omoshiroi machi desu.	Tōkyō wa omoshiroi machi da.
6. Kyō wa kimochi ga ii desu.	Kyō wa kimochi ga ii.

NOTES

1. **Ji ga heta da kara yominikui darō.**

   -nikui added to the **-masu** stem of a verb gives the meaning "difficult," "hard," "awkward," and so on. In this context the translation can be "illegible." The opposite is **-yasui**, as in **yomiyasui**, "legible, easy to read." Both **-yasui** and **-nikui** are themselves inflected in just the same way as **-i** adjectives, e.g., **yominikuku nai**, "not hard to read."

2. **Tanaka-san ikka to soba o tabe ni itta.**

   Soba in many varieties is everyday fare in Japan. The buckwheat noodles prepared especially for New Year's Eve go by the name of **toshikoshi soba**, signifying the passing (**koshi**) of the year (**toshi**), thus by implication the imminent arrival of the New Year.

3. **Channeru o kaeru to . . . jidai-geki o yatte ita.**

   In addition to the **to . . . -masu** pattern (p. 159), there is the **to. . . mashita** pattern meaning "A did X and then discovered Y" or "X happened and then Y occurred."

   ex. **Yamamoto-san ga kuru to, uketsuke no hito wa kasa o watashimashita.**
   "When Yamamoto came, the receptionist handed him (his) umbrella."

   In conversation, **yatte iru** is by far the most common way of saying something is on TV, is being produced on stage, and so on. If the time is the future, **yaru** is used.

4. **Ano rasshu awā no sararīman ya gakusei wa doko ni itta no darō ka.**

   As noted in Lesson 1, **ko-**, **so-** and **a-** words are not limited to the tangible or what is immediately at hand. The expanded usage of **a-** can denote "that which both you and I know about." In this sentence, **ano** underscores the unforgettableness of the rush hour subway experience.

5. **Moratta nengajō wa hotondo zembu kuji-tsuki de aru.**

   Christmas cards are sent in Japan but in nowhere near the quantities of the more traditional New Year's cards (over 3 billion in one recent year). These regular-size but specially printed postcards bearing lottery numbers go on sale at post offices in November. If mailed by the deadline (around December 20), they are delivered on New Year's Day. The lottery is held on January 15—**Seijin no Hi**, "Coming-of-Age Day"— and the lucky winners receive things like bicycles or portable radios or consolation prizes of commemorative postage stamps.

   The ending of this sentence, **de aru**, is the equivalent of **desu** and belongs to a bookish style of writing.

PRACTICE

KEY SENTENCES

1. きのうは　あつかったから、ともだちと　およぎに　いった。
2. はこを　あけると、なかは　からだった。

1. Yesterday was warm so I went swimming with my friend.
2. When I opened the box, it (the inside) was empty.

Vocabulary

から　　　　　　　　**kara**　　　　　empty

EXERCISES

I　Practice the following patterns by changing verbs and adjectives as in the examples given.

A. *ex.* わたしは　きょうとへ　<u>いきます</u>。
　　→わたしは　きょうとへ　いく。
　　わたしは　きょうとへ　いかない。
　　わたしは　きょうとへ　いった。
　　わたしは　きょうとへ　いかなかった。

1. スミスさんと　ダンスを　します
2. たなかさんは　10じに　きます
3. ジョンソンさんに　あいます
4. ともだちと　えいがを　みます
5. ここに　かぎが　あります

B. *ex.* たなかさんは　<u>いそがしいです</u>。
　　→たなかさんは　いそがしい。
　　たなかさんは　いそがしくない。
　　たなかさんは　いそがしかった。
　　たなかさんは　いそがしくなかった。

1. べんきょうは　たのしいです
2. くるまが　すくないです
3. あたまが　いいです
4. あの　レストランは　まずいです
5. つごうが　わるいです

C. ex. スミスさんは　げんきです。
　　　→スミスさんは　げんきだ。
　　　　スミスさんは　げんきでは　ない。
　　　　スミスさんは　げんきだった。
　　　　スミスさんは　げんきでは　なかった。

　　1. この　ホテルは　しずかです
　　2. スミスさんは　ビールが　すきです
　　3. スミスさんは　りょうりが　じょうずです
　　4. デパートは　やすみです
　　5. やまもとさんは　パイロットです

D. ex. きのう　がっこうを　やすんだ。
　　　→きのう　がっこうを　やすみました。

　　1. あした　ぜいむしょに　いかなければ　ならない
　　2. 6じに　うちに　かえる　ことが　できない
　　3. つきに　いった　ことが　ない
　　4. たいきんを　ひろった　ことが　ある
　　5. テニスを　したり　つりを　したり　した
　　6. たなかさんは　いくだろう
　　7. はやく　やすんだ　ほうが　いい
　　8. たなかさんは　スライドを　みていた
　　9. あしたは　ゆきかもしれない
　　10.まだ　ジョンソンさんに　あっていない

II　Make dialogues by changing the underlined parts as in the examples given.

A. ex. Q: あの　ひとの　はなしかたは　どうですか。
　　　A: はやくて　ききにくいです。

　　1. この　しんぶん、じが　ちいさい、よむ
　　2. この　テープ、おとが　わるい、きく
　　3. なっとう、くさい、たべる
　　4. この　くすり、にがい、のむ

B. ex. Q: その　くつは　いかがですか。
　　　A: はきやすくて　きに　いっています。

　　1. その　ペン、かく

172　LESSON 17

2. この　じしょ、ひく
3. その　スーツ、きる
4. あたらしい　ワープロ、つかう

III　Practice the following pattern by changing the underlined parts as in the example given.

ex. <u>へやに　はいると</u>　<u>でんわが　なっていました</u>。

1. まどを　あけました、すずしい　かぜが　はいってきました
2. そとに　でました、あめが　ふっていました
3. うちに　かえりました、ともだちが　まっていました
4. きんこを　あけました、なかは　からでした

Vocabulary

ダンス	**dansu**	dance, dancing
パイロット	**pairotto**	pilot
ぜいむしょ	**zeimusho**	tax office
〜しょ	**-sho**	office, bureau
たいきん	**taikin**	large sum of money
なっとう	**nattō**	fermented soybeans
くさい	**kusai**	smelly
にがい	**nigai**	bitter
はきやすい	**haki-yasui**	easy to put on
はく	**haku**	put on, wear (shoes, pants, etc.)
〜やすい	**-yasui**	easy to
ひく	**hiku**	consult, look up in
スーツ	**sūtsu**	suit
なる	**naru**	ring
かぜ	**kaze**	wind
はいってくる	**haitte kuru**	come in
そと	**soto**	outside, exterior, outer
きんこ	**kinko**	strong box, safe, vault

SHORT DIALOGUES

1. おとこA：もう　あの　えいが　みた？
　おとこB：ううん、まだ。きみは？
　おとこA：うん、もう　みた。
　おとこB：どうだった？
　おとこA：あんまり　おもしろくなかった。

Man A:　Have you already seen that movie?
Man B:　Uhn-un, not yet. How about you?
Man A:　Un, I saw (it).

Man B: How was it?
Man A: Not very interesting.

2. おんな ： もうすぐ　おしょうがつね。しごとは　いつまで？

おとこ ： 12がつ28にちまで。ねんまつは　いつも　いそがしく
て　いやなんだ。

おんな ： おしょうがつは　どっかに　いく？

おとこ ： ううん、どこにも。しょうがつは　のんびりしたいね。

Woman: New Year's will soon (be here), won't it? Which day do you work until? (*lit.* "[Your] work [is] until when?")
Man: Until December 28. The end of the year is always (so) busy. It's horrible!
Woman: Are you going someplace for New Year's?
Man: No, nowhere. (I) want to take it easy.

Vocabulary

ううん	**uun**	uhn-un, nope, no (informal)
きみ	**kimi**	you (informal men's speech)
うん	**un**	un, un-huh, yeah (informal)
あんまり	**ammari**	not very (colloquial for **amari**)
おしょうがつ	**o-shōgatsu**	New Year's
いや(な)	**iya(na)**	horrible, nasty, unwelcome
どっか	**dokka**	some-/anyplace (informal contraction of **doko ka**)
のんびりする	**nombiri suru**	take it easy

QUIZ

I Read this lesson's opening passage and answer the following questions.

1. ブラウンさんは　おおみそかの　ゆうがた　だれと　なにを
たべに　いきましたか。

2. 12がつには　にほんかくちで　ベートーベンの　"だいく"
を　えんそうすると　ブラウンさんに　はなしたのは　だれ
ですか。

3. おしょうがつに　ブラウンさんの　きんじょの　みせは
あいていましたか。

4. ブラウンさんは　だれから　ねんがじょうを　もらいました
か。

5. ブラウンさんは　ふでで　かいた　ねんがじょうを　うつく
しいと　おもっていますか。

II Complete the questions so that they fit the answers.

1. （　　　）に　でかける？
   9じに　でる。
2. きのうの　えいがは　（　　　）だった？
   あんまり　おもしろくなかった。
3. （　　　）に　すみたい？
   あんぜんな　ところが　いい。
4. かれは　（　　　）くる？
   あした　くるだろう。
5. （　　　）と　いっしょに　いく？
   ひとりで　いく。

III Complete the sentences with the appropriate form of the words indicated.

1. この　にくは　（　　　）、（　　　）にくい。（かたい、たべる）
2. かれの　せつめいは　（　　　）、（　　　）にくい。（ふくざつ、わかる）
3. この　きかいは　（　　　）、（　　　）やすい。（べんり、つかう）
4. ことしは　（　　　）、ねんがじょうを　ぜんぜん　（　　　）ことが　できなかった。（いそがしい、かく）
5. へやが　（　　　）、きもちが　いい。（きれい）

IV Answer the following questions.

1. あなたの　くにでは　おおみそかや　おしょうがつに　なにを　しますか。
2. おしょうがつの　やすみは　なんにちまでですか。
3. あなたの　すんでいる　まちでは　クリスマスと　おしょうがつと　どちらが　にぎやかですか。

V にほんごで　にっきを　かいて　ください。

NEW KANJI

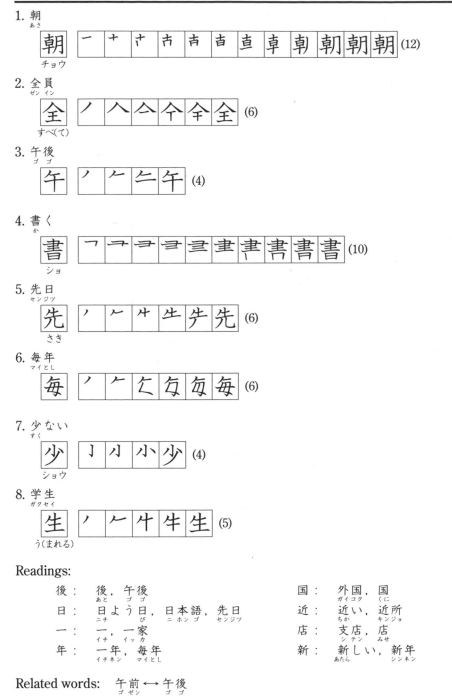

1. 朝
あさ
朝 一 十 产 古 吉 古 直 卓 卓 朝 朝 朝 (12)
チョウ

2. 全員
ゼン イン
全 ノ 入 入 仝 全 全 (6)
すべ(て)

3. 午後
ゴ ゴ
午 ノ 스 仁 午 (4)

4. 書く
か
書 フ ヨ ヨ ユ 聿 聿 書 書 書 (10)
ショ

5. 先日
センジツ
先 ノ 止 生 生 先 (6)
さき

6. 毎年
マイ とし
毎 ノ 仁 仁 句 句 毎 (6)

7. 少ない
すく
少 ノ 小 小 少 (4)
ショウ

8. 学生
ガクセイ
生 ノ 仁 牛 牛 生 (5)
う(まれる)

Readings:

後 : 後 , 午後
　　 あと　　ゴ ゴ
日 : 日 よう日 , 日本語 , 先日
　　 ニチ　　 び　　ニ ホン ゴ　センジツ
一 : 一 , 一家
　　 イチ　イッ カ
年 : 一年 , 毎年
　　 イチネン　マイ とし

国 : 外国 , 国
　　 ガイコク　くに
近 : 近い , 近所
　　 ちか　　 キンジョ
店 : 支店 , 店
　　 シ テン　みせ
新 : 新しい , 新年
　　 あたら　　 シンネン

Related words:　午前 ←→ 午後
　　　　　　　　 ゴ ゼン　　 ゴ ゴ

Kanji for recognition:　第九
　　　　　　　　　　　　 ダイ ク

LESSON 18 BIRTHDAY FLOWERS

Mr. Johnson wants to find out whether giving flowers to a woman friend is an acceptable practice in Japan.

ジョンソン： すずきさん、ちょっと。

すずき： 何でしょう。

ジョンソン： 日本の しゅうかんを 知らないので おしえてく
ださいませんか。友だちの たんじょう日に 花を
あげようと 思うんですが、おかしくないですか。

すずき： 女の人ですか。

ジョンソン： ええ、でも とくべつの 友だちでは ないんです
が・・・。

すずき： おかしくないですよ。だいじょうぶです。デートで
すか。いいですねえ。

ジョンソン： ううん、まあ。

At the florist.

ジョンソン： 友だちに 花を 送ろうと 思うんですが、お願い
できますか。

花屋： はい。おとどけですね。できます。何日の おとど
けでしょうか。

ジョンソン： あした とどけてください。

花屋： かしこまりました。

ジョンソン： この ばらは いくらですか。

花屋： 1本 250円です。

ジョンソン： じゃ、これを 20本 お願いします。たんじょう日
の プレゼントに する つもりですから、この
カードを つけて とどけてくれませんか。

> 田中けい子さま
> おたんじょう日 おめでとうございます。
>   マイケル

花屋：　　　　はい。おとどけ先は　どちらですか。
ジョンソン：よこはまです。
花屋：　　　　送料が　500円　かかりますが、よろしいですか。
ジョンソン：ええ。じゃ　お願いします。

Johnson:　Say, Mr. Suzuki.
Suzuki:　Yes, what is it?
Johnson:　Since I don't know Japanese customs, would you please tell me (something)? I'm think-
ing of giving flowers to a friend for (her) birthday. It wouldn't be strange, would it?
Suzuki:　Is it a woman friend?
Johnson:　Yes. But she's not a special girl friend.
Suzuki:　It's not strange. It's (quite) OK. (Are you going on) a date? That's nice. (I'm jealous.)
Johnson:　Umm well . . .

Johnson:　I'm thinking of sending flowers to a friend. Can you take care of it?
Florist:　Yes, of course. Delivered, you say? We can do that. What's the delivery day (you have in
mind)?
Johnson:　Please deliver (them) tomorrow.
Florist:　Certainly.
Johnson:　How much are these roses?
Florist:　¥250 each.
Johnson:　All right. I'd like twenty of them. (They're) meant to be a birthday gift, so would you
include this card and deliver (them)?

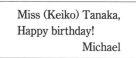

> Miss (Keiko) Tanaka,
> Happy birthday!
> 　　　　　Michael

Florist:　Yes, of course. Where should they be delivered to?
Johnson:　Yokohama.
Florist:　There'll be a ¥500 delivery charge. Is that all right?
Johnson:　OK.

Vocabulary

〜（よ）う	-(y)ō	(volitional form)
おかしい	okashii	strange, funny
とくべつの／な	tokubetsu no/na	special, extraordinary
だいじょうぶ（な）	daijōbu(na)	all right
ううん	uun	umm
おくる	okuru	send (a present)
おとどけ	o-todoke	delivery
つもり	tsumori	intention, purpose
つける	tsukeru	include (*lit.* "attach")
おめでとうございます	omedetō gozaimasu	congratulations
おとどけさき	o-todoke-saki	consignee, destination
よこはま	Yokohama	Yokohama (city)

| そうりょう | **sōryō** | delivery charge, postage |
| よろしい | **yoroshii** | all right |

GRAMMAR & LESSON OBJECTIVES

- **-(y)ō**, volitional form

  Tomodachi ni hana o ageyō to omou n desu ga, . . .

  Verbs ending in **-(y)ō** (plain form) and **-mashō** are in the volitional form and, in general, are translatable by "I'll," "we'll" or "let's." As in other cases, the usage of plain forms at the ends of sentences indicates familiar speech.

  ex. **Takushī de ikō ka.** "Shall we go by taxi?"

  Chikai kara arukō yo. "Since (it's) close, let's walk."

  As for the volitional form of Regular I verbs, note **arukō** in the example and keep in mind the correlation with the **a, i, u, e, o** vowel order.

		-*masu* form	dictionary form	volitional form
Reg. I		okurimasu kakimasu aimasu	okuru kaku au	okurō kakō aō
Reg. II		agemasu todokemasu mimasu	ageru todokeru miru	ageyō todokeyō miyō
Irreg.		kimasu shimasu	kuru suru	koyō shiyō

- **tsumori**

  Tanjōbi no purezento ni suru tsumori desu.

  Tsumori is actually a noun and is much used in this pattern to show intent or purpose.

  ex. 1. **Kyō Yoshida-san ga kimasu ga, awanai tsumori desu.** "Mr. Yoshida is coming today, but I don't plan to see him."

  2. **Ashita Tōkyō ni kaerimasu ka.** "Will you go back to Tokyo tomorrow?"

     Ee, sono tsumori desu. "Yes, I intend to."

- Polite expressions

  The polite expressions in this lesson can be compared with others previously introduced.

  Yoroshii desu ka is the same as **ii desu ka** but is more polite. The appropriate response is not **Yoroshii desu**, but **Kekkō desu, Ii desu**, or simply **Hai**.

  O-todoke desu ka. "Is it to be delivered?" In this case, too, prefacing the verb with the honorific **o-** is one way of expressing politeness or respect. (See p. 39.)

  ex. 1. **Itsu o-kaeri desu ka.** "When are you coming back?"

  2. **Hayashi-san wa taihen o-yorokobi deshita.** "Mrs. Hayashi was very pleased."

  Oshiete kudasaimasen ka. "Would you please tell me?" **-te kudasaimasen ka** has the same meaning as **-te kuremasen ka** but is more polite.

PRACTICE

1. まいにち にほんごを べんきょうしようと おもいます。
2. あした はれたら、テニスを する つもりです。

1. I intend to study Japanese every day.
2. If it clears up tomorrow, (I) plan to play tennis.

Vocabulary

はれる	**hareru**	clear up

EXERCISES

I Verbs: Study the examples, convert into the volitional form, and memorize.

ex. かく→かこう   たべる→たべよう   くる→こよう
いう→いおう   おきる→おきよう   する→しよう

1. かえる (return)   4. おぼえる   7. かりる
2. およぐ   5. あずける   8. かってくる
3. やすむ   6. みる   9. りょうりする

II Make dialogues by changing the underlined parts as in the example given.

ex. Q: きょう たなかさんに あいますか。
    A: ええ、あおうと おもいます。

1. たばこを やめる
2. しゃちょうに そうだんする
3. ともだちに こどもを あずける
4. ひこうきで いきます

III Practice the following patterns by changing the underlined parts as in the example given.

ex. この プロジェクトが おわったら なつやすみを とろう
と おもいます。

1. らいしゅう てんきが よければ ふじさんに のぼ
る
2. こどもが できたら しごとを かえる
3. ひまが できた とき この ほんを よむ
4. だいがくの にゅうがくしけんに しっぱいした
ばあいは もう 1ねん がんばる

IV Make dialogues by changing the underlined parts as in the examples given.

A. *ex.* Q: かいしゃを　やめて　なにを　するんですか。
 A: <u>ひとりで　しごとを　はじめる</u>　つもりです。

   1. だいがくに　はいって　もう　いちど　べんきょうします
   2. くにに　かえって　しょうらいの　ことを　かんがえます
   3. デザイナーに　なって　じぶんの　みせを　もちます
   4. もっと　きゅうりょうの　いい　しごとを　さがします

B. *ex.* Q: <u>けっこんしない</u>んですか。
 A: ええ、<u>けっこんしない</u>　つもりです。

   1. もう　たばこを　すいません
   2. だれにも　みせません
   3. カメラを　もっていきません
   4. こどもを　つれていきません

C. *ex.* Q: すみませんが、<u>しおを　とって</u>くださいませんか。
 A: はい。

   1. その　カメラを　みせる
   2. ここで　まっている
   3. クーラーを　けす
   4. いすを　はこぶのを　てつだう

| Vocabulary |

おぼえる	**oboeru**	remember, memorize
りょうりする	**ryōri suru**	cook
りょうり	**ryōri**	food
やすみを　とる	**yasumi o toru**	take a vacation
（こどもが）できる	**(kodomo ga) dekiru**	have a baby, become pregnant
（じかんが）できる	**(jikan ga) dekiru**	find spare time
しっぱいする	**shippai suru**	fail
しっぱい	**shippai**	failure, mistake
がんばる	**gambaru**	try hard
しょうらい	**shōrai**	future
デザイナー	**dezainā**	designer

つれていく	**tsurete iku**	take (a person)
つれる	**tsureru**	take, bring, be accompanied by
しお	**shio**	salt
とる	**toru**	pass
てつだう	**tetsudau**	help, assist

SHORT DIALOGUES

1. かちょう： かえりに どう？ いっぱい のもう。

   おがわ： きょうは かないが かぜを ひいている
   ので・・・。

   かちょう： ちょっとなら いいだろう。

   おがわ： いえ、やっぱり だめなんです。

   かちょう： そうか。じゃ、あきらめよう。

Section Chief:	On the way home shall we have a drink?
Ogawa:	My wife has a cold today.
Section Chief:	If it's just a short one, it'll be OK (I think).
Ogawa:	No, it's really out of the question.
Section Chief:	Is it now? Oh well then, I give up.

2. かとう： ことしの にほんごスピーチコンテストに でま
   すか。

   ブラウン： ええ、その つもりですが、じゅうぶん じゅん
   びが できなければ らいねんに するかもしれ
   ません。

Katō:	Are you going to take part in this year's Japanese speech contest?
Brown:	Yes, I intend to, but if I cannot do enough preparation, I will probably do it next year.

Vocabulary

そうか	**sō ka**	= **sō desu ka**
あきらめる	**akirameru**	give up, be resigned
スピーチコンテスト	**supīchi kontesto**	speech contest
スピーチ	**supīchi**	speech
コンテスト	**kontesto**	contest
でる	**deru**	participate, be a contestant
じゅうぶん	**jūbun**	enough
じゅんび	**jumbi**	preparation

I   Read this lesson's Opening Dialogue and answer the following questions.

1. ジョンソンさんは　おんなの　ともだちへの　プレゼントに　ついて　どうして　すずきさんに　そうだんしましたか。

2. ジョンソンさんは　だれに　プレゼントを　おくろうと　おもっていますか。

3. ジョンソンさんが　かった　ばらは　20ぽんで　いくらですか。

4. けいこさんは　どこに　すんでいますか。

II   Convert the following verbs into their volitional form.

1. はなす	4. やめる	7. わかれる	10. まつ
2. とどける	5. つくる	8. はらう	11. デートする
3. あう	6. あるく	9. しつもんする	12. もってくる

III   Complete the sentences with the appropriate form of the verbs indicated.

1. なにを　（　　　）いるんですか。
　たなの　うえの　はこを　（　　　）と　おもうんですが、てが（　　　）んです。（します、とります、とどきません）

2. どんな　ワープロを　（　　　）つもりですか。
　ちいさくて、つかいやすい　ワープロを　（　　　）と　おもうんですが、どれが　いいでしょうか。（かいます、かいます）

3. いまから　ゆうびんきょくへ　（　　　）と　おもうんですが、なにか　ようじは　ありませんか。
　すみませんが、この　てがみを　（　　　）くださいませんか。（いってきます、だします）

4. ほんとうに　かれと　（　　　）んですか。
　ええ、もう　（　　　）つもりです。（　　　）ば、また　けんかしますから。　（わかれました、あいません、あいます）

5. にほんごの　べんきょうを　（　　　）と　おもうんですが、どこか　いい　がっこうを　（　　　）くださいませんか。（はじめます、おしえます）

IV   Choose a sentence appropriate to the situation described.

A. Congratulate a friend for passing his examination.

1. ごうかくするでしょう。

2. ごうかく　おめでとうございます。

3. ごうかくしました。

B. You want to ask your section chief if it's all right to call him very late tomorrow evening.

1. あしたの　ばん　おそく　おでんわくださいませんか。
2. あしたの　ばん　おそく　かえってから　でんわする。
3. あしたの　ばん　おそく　でんわを　しても　よろしいで
   すか。

C. On the phone you ask the wife of an acquaintance of yours what time he will get home.

1. ごしゅじんは　なんじごろ　かえりましたか。
2. ごしゅじんは　なんじごろ　おかえりでしょうか。
3. しゅじんは　なんじごろ　かえる　つもりですか。

D. You answer a question by saying you really do intend to quit your job.

1. はい、ほんとうに　やめる　つもりです。
2. はい、たぶん　やめたと　おもいます。
3. はい、たぶん　やめるだろうと　おもいます。

V　Answer the following questions.

1. あなたは　あした　なにを　しようと　おもいますか。
2. にほんごの　べんきょうが　おわったら、にほんの　かい
   しゃで　はたらくつもりですか。
3. あなたは　せかいじゅうを　りょこうしたいと　おもいま
   すか。
4. あなたの　らいしゅうの　よていを　はなしてください。

NEW KANJI

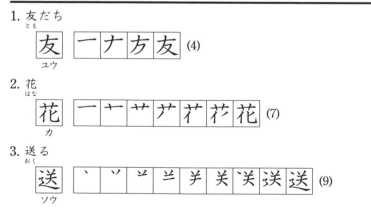

1. 友だち
   とも
   友　一ナ方友　(4)
   ユウ

2. 花
   はな
   花　一ナ艹ナ花花花　(7)
   カ

3. 送る
   おく
   送　丶丷丷丷关关送送　(9)
   ソウ

4. お願いする

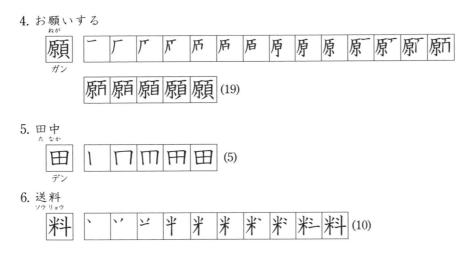

願 [ガン] 一 厂 厂 厃 厛 屑 盾 原 原 原 原 原 原 願

願 願 願 願 願 (19)

5. 田中 [たなか]

田 [デン] 丨 冂 冊 田 田 (5)

6. 送料 [ソウリョウ]

料 丶 丷 丷 半 米 米 米 米 料 料 (10)

Readings:

女 :　女性，女
　　　ジョセイ　おんな

送 :　送る，送料
　　　おく　　ソウリョウ

本 :　日本語，20本
　　　ニ　ホン　ゴ　　　ボン

LESSON **19**   THE PUBLIC LIBRARY

Mr. Chang and his neighbor, Daisuke, go for a walk together.

チャン ：　あれは　何ですか。

だいすけ：図書館です。

チャン ：　だれでも　りようできますか。

だいすけ：ええ、もちろんです。だれでも　入れますよ。あそこ
　　　　　は　自分で　本を　手に　とって　見られますから、
　　　　　とても　りようしやすいですよ。

チャン ：　それは　いいですね。ぼくは　カードを　見て　えら
　　　　　ぶのは　にがて　なんです。

だいすけ：でも　チャンさんは　かんじが　読めるでしょう。

チャン ：　ええ、いみは　わかります。でも、ぼくは　自分で
　　　　　本を　見ながら　えらべる　図書館が　好きなんです。

だいすけ：ちょっと　ふべんな　所に　あるけど、広いし　しず
　　　　　かだし、いいですよ。

チャン ：　本を　かりたり　コピーしたり　する　ことも　でき
　　　　　ますか。

だいすけ：ええ。てつづきを　すれば　かりられます。ぼくも
　　　　　今　2さつ　かりています。

チャン ：　新聞や　ざっしも　かりられますか。

だいすけ：いいえ、本しか　かりられません。でも、新聞や
　　　　　ざっしは　コピーを　たのめます。2、3分で　行けま
　　　　　すから、これから　いっしょに　行きませんか。

Chang: What's that?

Daisuke: It's a library.

Chang: Can anyone use it?

Daisuke: Yes, of course. Anyone can go in. You can get books and look at them, so it's very easy to use.

Chang: That's nice. Choosing books by looking through (the card catalogue) is difficult for me.

Daisuke: But I suppose you can read *kanji*, can't you?

Chang: Yes. I understand the meanings. But I like libraries where I myself can look at the books and choose.

Daisuke: It's in a slightly inconvenient location, but it's roomy and quiet, so it's a pleasant (place).

186

Chang: Can you borrow books and make photocopies?

Daisuke: Yes. If you go through the formalities, you can borrow books. At present I have borrowed two books.

Chang: Can you borrow newspapers and magazines, too?

Daisuke: No, you can only borrow books. But you can ask for photocopies of newspapers and magazines. We can get there in a couple of minutes, so shall we go (there) now?

Vocabulary

だいすけ	**Daisuke**	male given name
だれでも	**dare demo**	anyone, everyone, someone
もちろん	**mochiron**	of course
はいれる	**haireru**	can go in
てに とる	**te ni toru**	get, take in one's hands
みられる	**mirareru**	can see
にがて	**nigate**	difficult, poor at
よめる	**yomeru**	can read
いみ	**imi**	meaning
えらべる	**eraberu**	can choose
～けど	**kedo**	but, however
てつづき	**tetsuzuki**	formality, procedure
かりられる	**karirareru**	can borrow
～さつ	**-satsu**	(counter for books)
～しか～ない	**shika . . . nai**	only
たのめる	**tanomeru**	can ask
いける	**ikeru**	can get to, reach, can go

GRAMMAR & LESSON OBJECTIVES

- Potential form of verbs

  Dare demo riyō dekimasu ka.

  Dare demo hairemasu.

  Ano toshokan de hon ga kariraremasu.

  2, 3-pun de ikemasu.

  Potentiality can be expressed by the verb **dekiru** and also by the pattern **koto ga dekiru.** (See Book I for the first and p. 38 for the latter.) In addition, many verbs have a potential form made by conjugation. It will be noted that in terms of pronunciation, the final **u** of Regular I verb is replaced by **eru**, for example, **yomu** → **yomeru**, "can read," "be readable." And **erabu** → **eraberu**, "can choose," "can be chosen." (Although it is technically correct to call **yomeru** and **eraberu** dictionary forms, in the great majority of cases this form does not appear in bilingual dictionaries since the verbs are made by regular transformations of other verbs.)

Regular I

	-nai	-masu	conditional	-te	-ta
yomeru eraberu	yomenai erabenai	yomemasu erabemasu	yomereba erabereba	yomete erabete	yometa erabeta

Potential verbs conjugate the same as Regular II verbs but have no volitional form. Other examples: **iku** → **ikeru, hanasu** → **hanaseru, kaeru** → **kaereru, okuru** → **okureru, kaku** → **kakeru, hairu** → **haireru**

The following sentences compare the meanings of the verb and its potential form:

ex. 1. **Chan-san wa toshokan ni hairimasu.** "Chang enters the library."

　　2. **Chan-san wa toshokan ni hairemasu.** "Chang can enter the library."

For Regular II verbs add **-rareru** to the stem of the **-nai** form as, for example, **minai** → **mirareru**, "can see," "can be seen," and **karinai** → **karirareru**, "can borrow," "can be borrowed." The Irregular **kuru** becomes **korareru**, "can come," and **suru** is replaced by **dekiru**.

An easier, more practical way to make this form is to insert **-rare** (or sometimes only **-re** in colloquial usage) between the stem and the final **-ru, -masu, -ta**, etc.

ex. **taberareru, taberarenai, taberaremasu, taberareta**

Regular II and Irregular

	-nai	-masu	conditional	-te	-ta
mirareru karirareru	mirarenai karirarenai	miraremasu kariraremasu	mirarereba karirarereba	mirarete karirarete	mirareta karirareta
korareru dekiru	korarenai dekinai	koraremasu dekimasu	korarereba dekireba	korarete dekite	korareta dekita

Other examples: **taberu** → **taberareru, todokeru** → **todokerareru, iru** → **irareru**

suru → **dekiru:** *ex.* **Kodomo mo riyō shimasu.** "Children use (it) too."

Kodomo mo riyō dekimasu. "Children can use (it) too."

The topic or subject of a potential verb can be either animate or inanimate. For example, **Kono naifu wa yoku kiremasu.** "This knife cuts well."

ex. 1. **Sumisu-san wa kanji ga yomemasu.** "Smith can read Sino-Japanese characters."

　　2. **Kono ji wa totemo chiisakute yomemasen** means "the letters are unreadable."

Potential verbs have customarily taken the particle **ga**, but recently **o** has also come into use.

ex. 1. **Chan-san wa kanji ga/o yomemasu.** "Chang can read Sino-Japanese characters."

　　2. **Hon ga/o kariraremasu.** "You can borrow books."

　　3. **Kopī ga/o tanomemasu.** "(You) can ask for copies."

When it comes to a choice between the potential form and **koto ga dekiru**, it can be said that the former, being slightly shorter, is often preferred. **Chan-san wa toshokan ni hairu koto ga dekimasu**, although grammatically correct, sounds a bit stilted. Still the forms are interchangeable, and it is not necessary to be overly cautious concerning the differences between them.

ex. 1. **Sumisu-san wa shimbun ga yomemasu.** "Smith can read a (Japanese) newspaper."

　　2. **Toshokan ni ikeba, jūnen mae no shimbun o yomu koto ga dekimasu.** "If (you) go to the library, (you) can read newspapers from ten years ago."

NOTES

1. **Demo Chan-san wa kanji ga yomeru deshō.**
   When used like this, **desho/deshō** normally have a rising tone and imply, "I suppose (something). Aren't I right?"

2. **Chotto fubenna tokoro ni aru kedo.**
   Kedo is a colloquial shortening of **keredo** and **keredomo**, meaning "although," "but." In some contexts all these are comparable to the particle **ga** and convey no particular meaning. (See Book I, p. 88.)
   ex. **Moshi moshi, Jonson desu ga/kedo/keredo/keredomo, Keiko-san wa irasshaimasu ka.**

3. **Hiroi shi shizuka da shi ii desu yo.**
   Before the connective **shi**, plain forms can occur as well as **desu** and the **-masu** form. (See p. 55.)

4. **Hon shika kariraremasen.**
   Shika with a negative means "only," "merely," emphasizing that besides X there's nothing else. This contrasts with the usage of **mo** to emphasize how many or much. (See p. 198, Note 4.)
   ex. 1. **Saifu no naka ni 2000-en shika arimasen.** "I only have ¥2000 in my purse."
   2. **Kyōto ni shika ikimasen deshita.** "I visited Kyoto only."

5. **2, 3-pun de ikemasu yo.**
   One way to indicate the time or money required is with the pattern **de** plus potential form. In meaning, this sentence forms a pair with **2, 3-pun shika kakarimasen**, rather than **2, 3-pun kakarimasu.**
   ex. **Ano mise ni ikeba 4000-en de kaemasu yo.** "At that store (it) can be bought for ¥4000."

PRACTICE

KEY SENTENCES

1. ブラウンさんは　にほんごが　はなせます。
2. てつづきを　すれば、だれでも　ほんが　かりられます。
3. わたなべさんは　やさいしか　たべません。

1. Mr. Brown can speak Japanese.
2. If they go through the formalities, anybody can borrow books.
3. Watanabe eats only vegetables.

EXERCISES

I Verbs: Study the examples, convert into the potential form, and memorize.

ex. かく→かける　　いる→いられる　　　　　くる→こられる
　　　かけない　　　　いられない　　　　　　こられない
　　かう→かえる　　おぼえる→おぼえられる　する→できる
　　　かえない　　　　おぼえられない　　　　できない

1. きく 　　　 4. はいる 　　　 7. つとめる
2. とぶ 　　　 5. おしえる 　　　 8. もってくる
3. あらう 　　　 6. おきる 　　　 9. れんしゅうする

II　Make dialogues by changing the underlined parts as in the examples given.

A. *ex.* **Q:** がいこくごで　うたが／を　うたえますか。
　　　　 A: はい、うたえます。

　　 1. この　かんじを　よむ
　　 2. あした　あさ　7じに　でかける
　　 3. がいこくじんの　なまえを　すぐ　おぼえる
　　 4. にほんごで　せつめいする

B. *ex.* **Q:** えきまえに　くるまが／を　とめられますか。
　　　　 A: いいえ、とめられません。

　　 1. すぐ　しりょうを　あつめる
　　 2. あの　ひとの　はなしを　しんじる
　　 3. この　でんわで　こくさいでんわを　かける
　　 4. 100メートルを　10びょうで　はしる

C. *ex.* **Q:** ひらがなも　かんじも　かけますか。
　　　　 A: ひらがなは　かけますが、かんじは　かけません。

　　 1. じてんしゃ、オートバイ、のる
　　 2. さかな、にく、たべる
　　 3. たなかさん、やまもとさん、くる
　　 4. テニス、ゴルフ、する

D. *ex.* **Q:** なんじごろ　かえれますか。
　　　　 A: 8じまでに　かえれると　おもいます。

　　 1. だれが　なおす、たなかさんが　なおす
　　 2. だれに　あずける、だれにも　あずけない
　　 3. いつ　たなかさんに　あう、らいしゅうの　もくよう
　　　　 びに　あう
　　 4. どこで　かりる、としょかんで　かりる
　　 5. なんメートル　およぐ、10メートルも　およがない

E. ex. Q: にほんで　イギリスの　しんぶんが　かえますか。

A: ホテルに　いけば　かえます。

1. にほんごの　しんぶんを　よむ、じしょを　つかう
2. コンピューターを　つかう、せつめいを　よむ
3. あした　パーティーに　いく、しごとが　ない
4. この　かいわを　おぼえる、もう　すこし　みじかい

F. ex. Q: てつづきは　いつが　いいですか。

A: こんしゅうちゅうなら　いつでも　いいです。

1. りょうり、なに、ぶたにくで　なければ
2. とまる　ところ、どこ、べんりな　ところだったら
3. あつまる　じかん、なんじ、へいじつの　ゆうがたなら
4. うけつけを　てつだう　ひと、だれ、えいごが　できれば

G. ex. Q: おこさんは　なんにん　いますか。

A: ひとりしか　いません。

1. いま　おかねを　たくさん　もっている、500えん
2. よく　れんしゅうできた、1じかん
3. なんでも　たべる、やさい
4. あの　としょかんは　だれでも　りようできる、15さいいじょうの　ひと

Vocabulary		
がいこくご	**gaikoku-go**	foreign language
しんじる	**shinjiru**	believe
こくさいでんわ	**kokusai-denwa**	international telephone call
こくさい	**kokusai**	international
メートル	**mētoru**	meter
～びょう	**-byō**	second (counter)
じてんしゃ	**jitensha**	bicycle
オートバイ	**ōtobai**	motorcycle
ぶたにく	**buta-niku**	pork
へいじつ	**heijitsu**	weekday

A: かいぎの　うけつけが　ひとり　たりないんですが、あさって
　　てつだいに　こられる　ひとは　いないでしょうか。
B: わたしで　よければ　おてつだいします。
A: たすかります。ぜひ　おねがいします。

A: I have to find one more receptionist for the meeting. Can anyone come to help the day after tomorrow?
B: (If I'm good enough) I can come.
A: Thank you (*lit.* "you save me"). Please do.

Vocabulary

てつだい　　　　　　　　　**tetsudai**　　　　　　　　help, assistance
たすかる　　　　　　　　　**tasukaru**　　　　　　　　be relieved, be saved

QUIZ

I Read this lesson's Opening Dialogue and answer the following questions.

1. チャンさんは　どんな　としょかんが　すきですか。
2. この　としょかんは　ひろくて　しずかですか。
3. ほんを　かりたい　ひとは　どう　すれば　かりられますか。
4. としょかんでは　しんぶんや　ざっしも　かりられますか。

II Put the appropriate words in the parentheses.

1. かいいんしか　その　スポーツクラブを　りようできませんか。
　　いいえ、だれ（　　）りようできます。
2. この　へやは　ひろい（　　）きれいだ（　　）、きもちが
　　いい。
3. この　はなは　ジョンソンさんから　けいこさん（　　）の
　　プレゼントです。
4. ここ（　　）ぎんざ（　　）どのぐらい　かかりますか。
　　15ふん（　　）いけますよ。
5. ゆうべは　1じかん（　　）べんきょうしませんでした。
6. さむいけど　くうきが　わるい（　　）、まど（　　）　あ
　　けましょう。

III Without changing the level of politeness, convert the following verbs into the potential form.

1. まちます　　　　　5. いいません　　　9. わすれない
2. かきません　　　　6. えらびます　　　10. きる (wear)
3. はなします　　　　7. うたう　　　　　11. もってくる
4. やくそくしません　8. あわない　　　　12. やすまない

IV Complete the questions so that they fit the answers.

1. （　　　）およげますか。
   100メートルぐらい　およげます。
2. つぎの　かいぎは（　　　）が　いいですか。
   いつでも　けっこうです。
3. （　　　）に　いけば　かえますか。
   デパートで　うっていますよ。
4. （　　　）きょうは　はやく　かえるんですか。
   つまの　たんじょうびなので、はやく　かえります。

V Complete the sentences with the potential form of the verbs indicated.

1. ここは　ちゅうしゃきんしなので、くるまは（　　　）。（とめ
   ません）
2. スキーに　いって　けがを　したので（　　　）。（あるきませ
   ん）
3. 1ねんに　なんにち　かいしゃを（　　　）か。（やすみます）
4. らいねん（　　　）か。（そつぎょうします）
5. いますぐ（　　　）か。（でかけます）
6. ホワイトさんは　みそしるが（　　　）か。（つくります）
7. うけつけに　ある　でんわは（　　　）か。（つかいます）
8. どこに　いけば　おいしい　すしが（　　　）か。（たべます）
9. しけんに　ごうかくしなければ、この　だいがくに（　　　）。
   （はいります）
10. テレビで　にほんの　ふるい　えいがが（　　　）。（みます）

VI Answer the following questions.

1. あなたは　フランスごが　はなせますか。
2. あなたは　かんじが　いくつぐらい　よめますか。
3. あなたは　ゆうべ　よく　ねられましたか。

4. あなたは　にほんごの　じしょが　ひけますか。
5. あなたは　にほんごで　てがみが　かけますか。

NEW KANJI

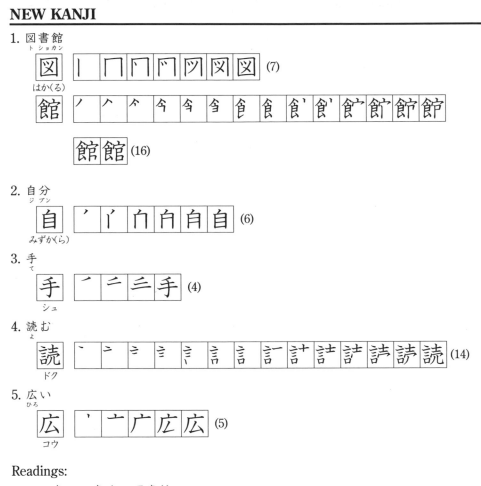

1. 図書館
トショカン

図 ｜ 冂 冂 冈 図 図 図 (7)

はか(る)

館 ノ 𠆢 𠆢 今 今 食 食 食 食` 食` 飣 飣 飣 飣

館 館 (16)

2. 自分
ジブン

自 ＇ 丨 自 自 自 自 (6)

みずか(ら)

3. 手
て

手 ＇ 二 三 手 (4)

シュ

4. 読む
よ

読 ＇ 二 三 言 言 言 計 計 計 読 読 読 (14)

ドク

5. 広い
ひろ

広 ＇ 亠 广 広 広 (5)

コウ

Readings:

書： 書く，図書館
　　　か　　　トショカン
所： 住所，所
　　　ジュウショ　ところ
聞： 聞く，新聞
　　　き　　シンブン

194　LESSON 19

LESSON 20 CHERRY BLOSSOMS

　桜前線と　いう　ことばを　聞いた　ことが　ありますか。
　日本の　春を　だいひょうする　花は　何と　いっても　桜で
しょう。人々は　春が　近づくと、桜の　さく　日を　よそくし
たり、友だちと　お花見に　行く　日を　やくそくしたり　しま
す。
　ところで、日本は　南から　北へ　長く　のびている　しま国
です。きゅうしゅう、しこく、ほんしゅう、ほっかいどうでは
ずいぶん　きおんの　さが　ありますから、桜の　さく　日も
少しずつ　ことなっています。きゅうしゅうの　南部では、3月の
末ごろ　さきますが、ほっかいどうでは　5月の　はじめごろ　さ
きます。このように　やく　40日も　かかって、日本れっとうを
南から　北へ　花が　さいていく　ようすを　線で　あらわした
ものが　桜前線です。
　桜前線の　ほかに　うめ前線や　つつじ前線などの　花前線も
あります。うめは　桜より　ずっと　早く　きゅうしゅうを
出発しますが、ほっかいどうに　着くのは　だいたい　桜と　同
じころです。ですから、5月の　上じゅんから　中じゅんに　かけて

ほっかいどうへ　りょこうすれば、一度に　春の　花が　見られ
るのです。これとは　はんたいに、秋に　なると、こうよう前線
は　山の　木々を　あかや　きいろに　そめながら、北から　南
へ　すすんでいきます。

　人々は　春には　お花見、秋には　もみじがりなどを　して、
きせつを　たのしみます。

桜前線
（そめいよしのの　開花日）

紅葉前線
（いろはかえでの　紅葉日）

Have you heard the term *sakura zensen*? The flower typifying spring in Japan is, undoubtedly, *sakura*, the cherry blossom. As spring approaches, people predict the day the cherry (trees) will blossom and agree with friends on a day to go blossom viewing.

Japan is an island country extending in a long (line) from south to north. Kyushu, Shikoku, Honshu, Hokkaido—there's quite a difference in temperatures, so the day the cherries blossom differs somewhat, too. In the southern part of Kyushu the cherries bloom around the end of March, but in Hokkaido they bloom around the beginning of May. Thus, the cherry blossom "front," a line starting in the south of the Japanese archipelago and (moving) north, shows the state of the cherry trees' blossoming. This takes as long as forty days.

In addition to the cherry blossom front there are other flower fronts, such as the apricot blossom front and the azalea front. Apricots start in Kyushu a whole lot earlier than the cherry trees, but they reach Hokkaido at almost the same time (as the cherries). Therefore, if (you) travel to Hokkaido in early or mid May, (you) can see (various) spring flowers at the same time. On the other hand, when it gets to be autumn the autumn leaves front makes its way from north to south, dyeing the trees in the mountains crimson or yellow.

With flower viewing in the spring, maple (leaf) excursions in the autumn and so on, people enjoy each season (in turn).

Vocabulary

さくらぜんせん	**sakura zensen**	cherry blossom front
ぜんせん	**zensen**	front
ことば	**kotoba**	word
だいひょうする	**daihyō suru**	typify, represent
だいひょう	**daihyō**	representation
なんと いっても	**nan to itte mo**	undoubtedly
ひとびと	**hito-bito**	people
ちかづく	**chikazuku**	approach
よそくする	**yosoku suru**	predict
よそく	**yosoku**	prediction, estimate
おはなみ	**o-hanami**	(cherry) blossom viewing
ところで	**tokorode**	well, incidentally
のびる	**nobiru**	extend, stretch, postpone
しまぐに	**shima-guni**	island country
しこく	**Shikoku**	Shikoku (place name)
ほんしゅう	**Honshū**	Honshu (place name)
ずいぶん	**zuibun**	quite
きおん	**kion**	(air) temperature
さ	**sa**	difference
ことなる	**kotonaru**	differ, be different
なんぶ	**nambu**	southern part
すえ	**sue**	end
はじめ	**hajime**	beginning, first
このように	**kono yō ni**	thus, in this way
～よう	**yō**	way, manner
やく	**yaku**	about
れっとう	**rettō**	archipelago
さいていく	**saite iku**	be (in the process of) blooming
ようす	**yōsu**	state, circumstance, appearance
せん	**sen**	line
あらわす	**arawasu**	show, express
～の ほかに	**no hoka ni**	in addition to
うめ	**ume**	apricot, Japanese plum
つつじ	**tsutsuji**	azalea
～などの	**nado no**	such as
～など	**nado**	and so forth
ずっと	**zutto**	a whole lot, all the time/way
だいたい	**daitai**	almost
ですから	**desu kara**	therefore (same as **da kara**)
じょうじゅん	**jōjun**	first third of the month
ちゅうじゅん	**chūjun**	second third of the month
～から ～に かけて	**kara ... ni kakete**	from ... to ...

こうよう	**kōyō**	autumn (*lit.* "red") leaves
きぎ	**kigi**	trees
あか	**aka**	red
きいろ	**kiiro**	yellow
そめる	**someru**	dye
すすんでいく	**susunde iku**	be advancing
もみじがり	**momiji-gari**	maple leaf excursion
もみじ	**momiji**	maple
かり/がり	**kari/-gari**	excursion, hunting
きせつ	**kisetsu**	season
たのしむ	**tanoshimu**	enjoy

Supplemental vocabulary

そめいよしの	**somei yoshino**	a species of cherry
かいかび	**kaika-bi**	day of blooming
いろはかえで	**iroha kaede**	a species of maple
こうようび	**kōyō-bi**	day the leaves turn

NOTES

1. **Sakura zensen, kōyō zensen**
   These **zensen** are analogous to warm and cold weather fronts, so perhaps it is not surprising that information on their progress comes from the **Kishō-chō**, the Meteorological Agency. Among its weather-related functions are predicting the harvest time of fruits, but predictions and reports on the **sakura** and **kōyō** are the most eagerly awaited. The harbinger for the many varieties of cherry blossoms is the species known as **somei yoshino**, and for maples it is **iroha kaede**.

2. **Sakura**
   Somei yoshino only blooms for a very short period, from five to ten days. If it rains or is windy, which is typical spring weather in Japan, the blossoms may all fall overnight.

3. **Nan to itte mo**
   More literally this means "No matter what anyone says . . ."

4. **Yaku 40-nichi mo kakatte . . .**
   The particle **mo** here emphasizes the number of days the cherry blossom front takes as it moves from the south to the north of Japan. This use of **mo** reflects the speaker's feelings of "so many" or "so much."

5. **Hana ga saite iku.** (*lit.*) "The flowers bloom progressively."
   Adding **iku**, which means "to go," to the **-te** form of verbs indicates the continuous progress of the action.
   ex. **Tsubame wa 10-gatsu goro minami e tonde ikimasu.** "Swallows fly (*lit.* "go flying") south in October."

6. **Ichido ni haru no hana ga mirareru no desu.**
   no desu is equivalent to **n desu** but less colloquial. (See p. 108.)

7. 木々 (**kigi**)
   The kanji 々 indicates the repetition of the syllable(s) coming immediately before it,

sometimes with a phonetic change. Nouns in Japanese are generally written and pronounced the same whether singular or plural (as noted in Characteristics of Japanese Grammar in Book I), but this is one way of specifying plurality. Other examples: 花々 **hanabana**, "flowers"; 国々 **kuniguni**, "countries"; 島々 **shimajima**, "islands"; 山々 **yamayama**, "mountains"; 我々 **wareware**, "we." (See Book III, Lesson 1.)

Words made plural with suffixes are comparatively few and must be learned as they are encountered. **Anata-gata**, for example, is one way of pluralizing "you." From familiar to formal, there are a number of words for "we," such as **boku-ra**, **wata(ku)shi-tachi** (the most common) and **watashi-domo** (humble/formal).

8. **Haru ni wa o-hanami, aki ni wa momiji-gari**

When things are listed or enumerated, it is sometimes permissible to omit predicates and, in fact, this can create a dramatic effect.

QUIZ

I Read this lesson's opening passage and answer the following questions.

1. にほんの　はるを　だいひょうする　はなは　さくらです
   か、つつじですか。
2. にほんじんは　はるに　なると　よく　なにを　しますか。
3. きゅうしゅうの　なんぶでは　いつごろ　さくらが　さきま
   すか。
4. きゅうしゅうでは　さくらと　うめと　どちらが　さきに
   さきますか。
5. ほっかいどうでは　いつごろ　うめが　さきますか。
6. さくらぜんせんと　いうのは　なんですか。
7. こうようぜんせんも　みなみから　きたへ　すすみますか。

II あなたの　くにの　きせつに　ついて　かいてください。

NEW KANJI

1. 前線
   ゼンセン

2. 春
   はる

   シュン

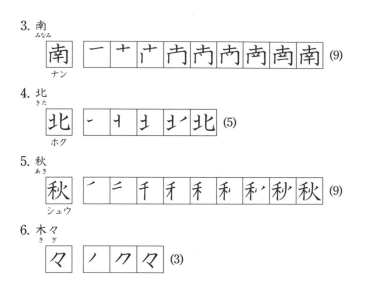

3. 南
みなみ
南 一 十 十 内 内 内 南 南 南 (9)
ナン

4. 北
きた
北 ゝ イ キ ゴ 北 (5)
ホク

5. 秋
あき
秋 ノ 二 千 禾 禾 禾 秋 秋 秋 (9)
シュウ

6. 木々
き ぎ
々 ノ ク 々 (3)

Readings:

前 ： 前，桜前線
　　　まえ　さくらゼンセン

長 ： 社長，長い
　　　シャチョウ　なが

少 ： 少ない，少し
　　　すく　　　すこ

南 ： 南，南部
　　　みなみ　ナンブ

末 ： 年末，末ごろ
　　　ネンマツ　すえ

上 ： 上，上じゅん
　　　うえ　ジョウ

木 ： 木よう日，木々
　　　モク　び　きぎ

Related words:　春 — 夏 — 秋 — 冬
　　　　　　　　　はる　なつ　あき　ふゆ
　　　　　　　　　シュン　カ　シュウ　トウ

　　　　　　　　　東 — 西 — 南 — 北
　　　　　　　　　ひがし　にし　みなみ　きた
　　　　　　　　　トウ　セイ・サイ　ナン　ホク

Kanji for recognition:　桜
　　　　　　　　　　　　さくら

APPENDICES

A: Plain Forms and Connective Patterns

The plain adjective and verb forms given in the charts below are used in a number of patterns. Exceptions, which occur only in the case of a **-na** adjective or a noun followed by **da**, are shown in boxes.

Verbs

	Present		Past	
	aff.	neg.	aff.	neg.
Reg. I	**tsukau**	**tsukawanai**	**tsukatta**	**tsukawanakatta**
Reg. II	**iru**	**inai**	**ita**	**inakatta**
Irr.	**kuru**	**konai**	**kita**	**konakatta**
	suru	**shinai**	**shita**	**shinakatta**

Adjectives, Noun + **desu**

	Present		Past	
	aff.	neg.	aff.	neg.
-i adj.	**akai**	**akaku nai**	**akakatta**	**akaku nakatta**
-na adj.	**shizuka da**	**shizuka dewa/ja nai**	**shizuka datta**	**shizuka dewa/ja nakatta**
N + **desu**	**N da**	**N dewa/ja nai**	**N datta**	**N dewa/ja nakatta**

Four connective patterns using the following words and phrases are encountered in Book II.

1. Basic Pattern

Before **to omou, to iu, to kiku**, etc., verbs and adjectives end in the plain form without exception.

2. Noun-modifying Pattern

Nouns (Lesson 7), **toki, baai** (Lesson 12), **tsumori** (Lesson 18).
When these words are modified, the following exceptions occur:
After **-na** adj.: **shizukana kōen/toki**, etc.
After noun: **kodomo no hon/toki**, etc.

3. **Deshō** Pattern

Deshō (Lesson 8), **darō** (Lesson 13), **kamo shiremasen** (Lesson 13)
-na adjectives and nouns plus **da** are exceptions. The stem of **-na** adjectives and nouns comes directly before these words.
-na adj.: **shizuka deshō** (after the stem)
noun: **kodomo deshō**

4. **Na node** Pattern

No/n desu (Lesson 11), **node** (Lesson 13).

-na adjectives and nouns plus **da** are exceptions.

-na adj.: **shizukana node**

noun: **kodomo na node**

Index: **baai** (2), **darō** (3), **deshō** (3), **kamo shiremasen** (3), **node** (4), **no/n desu** (4), noun (2), **to iu/kiku/omou/tsutaeru** (1), **toki** (2), **tsumori** (2).

Notes: The number in the parentheses refer to the pattern number.

    For other words and phrases, such as **-nagara, -nakute mo ii, koto ga aru,** which follow other forms, refer to their connective pattern in the grammar sections of the respective lessons.

B: Grammatical Patterns and Common Constructions

Lesson 1	1	～と～と　どちらが～か	とうきょうとおおさかとどちらがおおきいですか。
	2	～より～の　ほうが～	おおさかよりとうきょうのほうがおおきいです。
	3	～は～より～	とうきょうはおおさかよりおおきいです。
	4	～の　なかで～がいちばん～	スポーツのなかでテニスがいちばんすきです。
	5	～も～も～	あさもゆうがたもこんでいます。
Lesson 2	6	～くて／で、～です	ここはひろくてしずかなこうえんです。
	7	～く／に　～ます	かんじをきれいにかいてください。
	8	～に　いきます	レストランにひるごはんをたべにいきます。
	9	～もの	わすれものをしました。
Lesson 3	10	～る　ことが　できます	いちねんじゅうおよぐことができます。
	11	～る　まえに～	かいしゃにいくまえに、しんぶんをよみます。
	12	～でも	どれでもいいです。
	13	お／ご～ください	ごそうだんください。
	14	～に～かい	1しゅうかんに2かいにほんごのクラスがあります。
Lesson 4	15	～た　ことが　あります	ホンコンにいったことがあります。
	16	～たり～たり　します	ほんをよんだり、おんがくをきいたりします。
	17	～を～ます	ほっかいどうをまわります。
	18	～たことは　ありますが、～たことは　ありません	しゃしんをみたことはありますが、いったことはありません。

Lesson 5	19	〜く／に　なります	セーターがやすくなりました。
	20	〜に　します	プレゼントはセーターにします。
	21	〜てから、〜ます	てをあらってから、サンドイッチをたべます。
	22	まだ〜ていません	まだきめていません。
	23	〜ですし、〜ですし、〜	おいしいですし、きれいですし、あのレストランはいいですよ。
	24	くれます	セールスのひとがくれました。
	25	〜が　ほしいです	ワープロがほしいです。
	26	〜かた	つかいかたがわかりません。
Lesson 6	27	〜た／ない　ほうが　いいです	けいさつにでんわしたほうがいいです。むりをしないほうがいいです。
	28	〜てきます	たばこをかってきます。
	29	なかなか〜ません	なかなかじょうずになりません。
	30	〜た　ばかりです	にほんにきたばかりです。
Lesson 7	31	〜noun (Noun Modifiers)	スミスさんはABCではたらいているべんごしです。
	32	〜る　ことも　あります	ひこうきははやくつくこともあります。
	33	〜てくれませんか	むかえにいってくれませんか。
	34	〜か	だれかきました。
	35	〜も　ありません	てがみをかくじかんもありません。
Lesson 8	36	〜と　おもいます／いっていました	でんしゃもバスもうごかないとおもいます。きむらさんはさっぽろをしっているといっていました。
	37	〜でしょう	あしたはあめでしょう。
	38	もう〜ません	きっぷはもうありません。
Lesson 9	39	〜なければ　なりません	きょうじゅうにもうしこみをしなければなりません。
	40	〜なくても　いいです	あしたいかなくてもいいです。
	41	〜ては　いけませんか	ゆうびんでおくってはいけませんか。
	42	〜ては　いけません	びょういんでたばこをすってはいけません。
	43	〜でも　いいです	ゆうびんでもいいです。
	44	〜で　いいですか	しょるいはこれでいいですか。
Lesson 10	45	〜ながら、〜ます	ラジオをききながら、しんぶんをよんでいます。
	46	〜た　あと、〜ます	くまもとをけんぶつしたあと、ながさきへいきます。

Lesson 11	47	〜んです	あしたかいぎがありますから、しりょうをコピーしているんです。
	48	〜こと	スミスさんがおおさかへいったことをしっていますか。
	49	〜からです	じこでけがをしたからです。
Lesson 12	50	〜とき、〜	スミスさんはほんをよむとき、めがねをかけます。
	51	〜ばあい、〜	おそくなるばあいはれんらくします。
	52	〜と いいます	わたしはスミスといいます。
Lesson 13	53	〜かもしれません	あさっておおさかへいくかもしれません。
	54	〜だろうと おもいます	すずきさんはリンダさんをしらないだろうとおもいます。
	55	〜ので、〜	ひこうきがとばないので、りょこうにいくことができません。
	56	〜から／まで／へ／で／との	わたなべさんからのてがみです。
Lesson 14	57	〜て／で、〜	そのはなしをきいて、あんしんしました。
	58	〜て、〜	きむらさんはあるいてかいしゃにいきます。
	59	〜の	スミスさんをくうこうまでむかえにいったのはすずきさんです。
	60	〜が みえます／きこえます	ホテルのまどからふじさんがみえます。
	61	〜る まで、〜	かいぎがおわるまでまちます。
Lesson 15	62	〜たら、〜ました	きょうとまでくるまでいったら、10じかんかかりました。
	63	〜たら、〜ます	よていがかわったら、しらせます。
	64	〜なら、〜	ひこうきでいくなら、はやくきっぷをかったほうがいいですよ。
Lesson 16	65	〜ば／ければ、〜	さかやにでんわすれば、すぐビールをもってきます。
	66	〜と、〜ます	はるになると、さくらのはながさきます。
	67	〜ば／ければ〜ほど〜	さかなはあたらしければあたらしいほどいいです。
Lesson 17	68	Plain Style	きのうはあつかったから、ともだちとおよぎにいった。
	69	〜と、〜ました	へやにはいると、でんわがなっていました。
	70	〜やすい／にくい	このくつははきやすいです。

Lesson 18	71	〜う／よう	ちかいからえきまであるこう。
	72	〜う／ようと　おもいます	まいにちべんきょうしようとおもいます。
	73	〜つもりです	あしたはれたら、テニスをするつもりです。
Lesson 19	74	Potential	ブラウンさんはにほんごがはなせます。
	75	〜しか〜ません	わたなべさんはやさいしかたべません。
	76	〜でしょう	チャンさんはかんじがよめるでしょう。
	77	〜し、〜し、〜	ひろいし、しずかだし、いいですよ。
Lesson 20	78	〜ていきます	みなみからきたへはながさいていきます。
	79	〜も	8じかんもかいぎをしています。

C: Verb Conjugations

Except for the two irregular verbs **kuru** and **suru**, all verbs belong to either the Regular I or Regular II category and conjugate as in the following tables. The **-te/-ta** form comes from the **-masu** form, but euphonic changes occur in the case of most Regular I verbs. Note the last sound of the **-masu** stem is underlined.

Regular I

	-nai	-masu	dictionary	conditional	volitional	-te	-ta	type
walk	arukanai	aru<u>ki</u>masu	aruku	arukereba	arukō	aruite	aruita	-ite/-ita
swim	oyoganai	oyo<u>gi</u>masu	oyogu	oyogeba	oyogō	oyoide	oyoida	-ide/-ida
buy	kawanai	ka<u>i</u>masu	kau	kaeba	kaō	katte	katta	-tte/-tta
wait	matanai	ma<u>chi</u>masu	matsu	mateba	matō	matte	matta	-tte/-tta
get on	noranai	no<u>ri</u>masu	noru	noreba	norō	notte	notta	-tte/-tta
live	sumanai	su<u>mi</u>masu	sumu	sumeba	sumō	sunde	sunda	-nde/-nda
die	shinanai	shi<u>ni</u>masu	shinu	shineba	shinō	shinde	shinda	-nde/-nda
call	yobanai	yo<u>bi</u>masu	yobu	yobeba	yobō	yonde	yonda	-nde/-nda
push	osanai	o<u>shi</u>masu	osu	oseba	osō	oshite	oshita	no euphonic change

Note: Remember one exception. The **-te** form of **iku** is **itte**.

Regular II

	-nai	-masu	dictionary	conditional	volitional	-te	-ta	
eat	tabenai	tabemasu	taberu	tabereba	tabeyō	tabete	tabeta	
get off	orinai	orimasu	oriru	orireba	oriyō	orite	orita	

Irregular

	-nai	-masu	dictionary	conditional	volitional	-te	-ta	
come	konai	kimasu	kuru	kureba	koyō	kite	kita	
do	shinai	shimasu	suru	sureba	shiyō	shite	shita	

JAPANESE-ENGLISH GLOSSARY

abiru, bathe, 41
abunai, dangerous, 111
ageru, raise, 78
aisatsu, greeting, address, 46
aka(i), red, crimson, scarlet, 198
akarui, cheerful, bright, 30, 59
akirameru, give up, be resigned, 182
aku, be vacant, be empty, (be) open, 117
ame, rain, 87
ammari, not very, 174
anaunsu, announcement, 138
annai, guidance; *annai suru*, show around, 36
anō, er, 36
anshin, peace of mind; *anshin suru*, be relieved/
  relaxed, 46
anzen(na), safe, 111
apāto, apartment, 60
ara, Oh! (women's speech), 94
arau, wash, 41
arawasu, show, express, 197
ashi, leg, foot, 70
asobu, play, 41
atama ga ii, bright, clever, 30
atatakai, warm, 59
ato, rest, 65
ato de, later, afterward, 94
atsumeru, gather, collect, assemble, 144
azukaru, take care of, keep, 128
azukeru, deposit, entrust, 149

-ba/-kereba, if, 158
baai, (in) case, occasion, circumstance, 118
bābekyū, barbecue, 112
-(kere)ba . . . hodo, if . . . -er/more/less, (then) . . . ,
  158
(-ta) bakari, (have) just, 65
-bamme (counter for ordinal numbers), 26
-bansen (counter for tracks), 90
bara, rose, 122
Barentain dē, Valentine's Day, 128
bebī shittā, baby sitter, 163
benkyō suru, study, 18
bentō, box lunch, 41
betsu(na/no), some other (thing), 65; *(na/no)*
  extra, distinctive, 117
bideo, video, 50
bimbō(na), poor, 59

biza, visa, 98
bōeki, trading, 103
boku, I (informal men's speech), 54
bōru pen, ball-point pen, 122
botan, button, 163
bu, department, division; *buchō*, department
  head, division chief, 29
-bun, portion, share, 94
buta-niku, pork, 191
-byō, second (counter), 191
byōki, sickness, 59

channeru, channel, 168
chikazuku, approach, 197
chikyū, earth, globe, 21
chokorēto, chocolate, 128
-chū/-jū, all over, throughout, 36, 153
-chū/-jū ni, within, 26
chūjun, second third of month, 197
Chūka ryōri, Chinese cooking, 69
chūshi, discontinuance, interruption, 123
chūshoku, lunch, 74

dai- (prefix for ordinal numbers), 169
daibu, considerably, greatly, 69
daigaku, university, 31
daihyō, representation; *daihyō suru*, typify,
  represent, 197
daijin, minister (of state), 89
daijobu(na), all right, 178
Dai-ku, Ninth (Symphony), 169
daitai, almost, 197
daitōryō, president, 50
dame(na), not good, 99
dansei, male, man, 128
dansu, dance, dancing, 173
dare demo, anyone, everyone, someone, 187
dare ka, someone, anyone, 74
darō (plain form of *deshō*), 128
(no) darō ka, I wonder, 169
dasu, mail, 60
de gozaimasu (polite for *desu*), 112
dekakeru, go out, 41
dekiagaru, be finished/ready/done, 158
(kodomo ga) dekiru, have a baby, became preg-
  nant, 181; *(jikan ga) dekiru*, find spare time,
  181

demo, any, 36

demo, let's say, for example, 138

demo, though, 18

demo ii, all right, 94

denwa o kakeru, telephone, 26

denwa ga tōi, I can't hear (you), 144

deru, graduate, leave, 59; attend, 89; participate, 182

desu kara, therefore (same as *da kara*), 197

dete kuru, come out, appear, 153

dēto, date, 133

dezainā, designer, 181

dochira, which, 20; *dochira-sama*, who, 36; *dochira demo*, either, 95; *dochira mo*, both, 22

dōgu, implement, machine, appliance, tool, 78

dohyō, *sumō* ring, 138

dō iu, what kind of, 139

dōka suru, something is wrong, 70

dokka, informal contraction of *dokoka*, some-/any place, 174

Dō narimashita ka, (*lit.*) "How have things become?", 59

dore demo, anything, 36

dōryō, coworker, 128

dotchi = dochira, which, 21

e, Oh dear (excalamation of surprise), 128

Edo jidai, Edo period, 103

eikaiwa, spoken English, 111

ekiin, station employee, 26

empitsu, pencil, 99

enryo, reserve, restraint, diffidence; *enryo naku*, without hesitation/reserve, 133

ensō, performance, recital; *ensō suru*, perform, 169

erabu, choose, 79

erai, important, illustrious, eminent, 139

ēto, let me see, 144

fakkusu, facsimile, 21

ferī, ferry, 153

fuben(na), inconvenient, 30

fudan (wa), ordinarily, 168

fude, brush, 169

fueru, proliferate, increase, 103

fūfu, husband and wife, 79

fūfu-genka, marital disagreement, 79

fujin, Mrs., lady, woman, 163

fukuro, bag, 26

fukuzatsu(na), complicated, 30

furawā shō, flower show, 163

furikomu, transfer, 94

furu, fall, 76

fuyu, winter, 57

fuyu-mono, winter goods/wear, 57

gaikoku-go, foreign language, 191

gakkari suru, be disappointed, 144

gaman suru, endure, be patient, 99

gambaru, try hard, 181

gamen, screen, 54

gan, cancer, 163

gāru furendo, girl friend, 129

-gawa, side, 158

geki, drama, 169

genkin, cash, 32; *genkin kakitome*, registered mail (for cash), 94

getsuyō, Monday, 69

go-busata, remiss (in not writing, not visiting, etc.); *go-busata shite imasu*, I have been remiss in not writing to you, 103

giri-choko, *giri* chocolate; *giri* (sense of) obligation, 128

go-chisōsama deshita (phrase used after eating), 122

go-irai, (someone else's) request, commission, 158

gōkaku, success, eligibility; *gōkaku suru*, pass, succeed, 94

go-meiwaku, trouble, inconvenience, 164

gomen-nasai, I'm sorry, Excuse me, 94

gomi, rubbish, 98

(go-)tōchaku, arrival, 118

gozaimasu (polite for *arimasu*), 117

guai, condition, 111

gyōji, *sumō* referee, 139

gyōsha, contractor, supplier, trader, businessman, 158

hade(na), flashy, gorgeous, 138

hairu, contain, include, 32; join, become a member, 133

haitte kuru, come in, 173

hajimaru, start, 65

hajime, beginning, first, 197

hajimeru, begin, start, 37

hajimete, for the first time, 18

hakkiri, clearly, 163

hakobu, carry, transport, 79

-haku/-paku, night (counter), 117

haku, put on, wear (shoes, pants, etc.), 173

hambun, half, 153

hanami, (cherry) blossom viewing, 197

hanasu, talk, speak, tell, 41

hanataba, bouquet, 60

hanko, seal, 98

hansamu(na), handsome, 59

hantai, opposite, reverse; *hantai-gawa*, opposite side, 158

happyō, announcement; *happyō suru*, announce, publicize, 69

harau, pay, 69

hare, fair, clear, 168
hareru, clear up, 180
haru, spring, 160
hashiru, run, 144
hataraku, work, 21
-hatsu, departure, 90
hatsugen, view, observation, utterance; *hatsugen-ken*, right to say one's views, 139
hayai, fast, 18; early, 30
hayame ni, early, 74
hei, fence, wall, 168
heijitsu, weekday, 191
hen, neighborhood, vicinity, 154
henji, reply, answer, 143
heta(na), poor, unskillful, 168
hikkosu, move (house), 60
hiku, pull, 163; consult, look up in, 173; play (a musical instrument), 144
hiroi, spacious, wide, 21
hirou, find, pick up, 32
hītā, heater, 59
hito-bito, people, 197
hitsuyō(na), necessary, 89
hō, oh, 54
hō ga ii, it's better to . . ./(you) had better, 65
honsha, head office, main company, 104
hontō (no), real, 139
hora, Look!, There!, 138
hoshii, want, desire, 54
hotaru, firefly, 103
hotondo, almost, 169

ichiban, most, number one, 18
ichi-nen-jū, all year round, 36
ichi-nichi, (in) a day, 21
ie, house, home, 84
ijō, more than, 84
ikebana, flower arranging, 42
(-te wa) ikenai, must not 94
iki, going, 18
-iki, bound for, 90
ikka, family, household, 168
ikutsu, how old (for a person), 61
ima no uchi ni, right away, before it's too late, 65
imi, meaning, 187
insatsu, printing, 169
insutorakutā, instructor, 37
inu, dog, 153
ippai (no/na), full, 133
irai, request, commission, 158
irassharu (polite form of *kuru, iku, iru*), 149
ireru, put in, 163
iro, color, 65
iroha kaede, a species of maple, 198
iru, need, 98

isogu, hurry, 41
isshōkemmei, as hard as one can, 59
itadakimasu (phrase used before eating), 122
itadaku, accept, receive (politer than *morau*), 133
itsu demo, any-/sometime, 123
itsumo, always, 138
itte mairimasu, good-bye, 94
itte rasshai, good-bye, 94
iya(na), horrible, nasty, unwelcome, 174

jajji, judge, 139
ji, (hand) writing, character, letter, 168
jibun, oneself; *jibun de*, by oneself, 79
jidai, period, 103
jidai-geki, period drama, 169
jiko, accident, 132
jimu-shitsu, clerks' office, 26
jimusho, office, 74
jishin, earthquake, 122
jitensha, bicycle, 191
jitsu wa, as a matter of fact, in fact, actually, 128
-jō , letter, 111
jōdan, joke; *jodan o iu*, crack a joke, 144
jōjun, first third of the month, 197
josei, woman, female, 128
jōshi, superior, 128
-jū, throughout, 36, 153
jūbun, enough, 182
jūdō, judo, 50
jugyō, instruction, lesson; *jugyō-ryō*, tuition, 94
jumbi, preparation, 182
jūtai, congestion, traffic jam, 84

ka, section, 54
ka, or (particle), 65
ka, Tuesday, 42
-ka, lesson (counter), 78
kachō, section chief, 80
kādo, credit card, 99; greeting card, 128
kaeri, coming back, returning, 18
kaeru, change, 54
kago, cage, basket, 103
kai, time(s) (counter), 42
kaiin, club/society member, 149
kaika-bi, day of blooming, 198
kaiwa, conversation, 111
kakari-/gakari, person in charge, 117
kakeru, call, 26; wear, put on (glasses), 79
kakitome, registered mail, 94
kakuchi, all over, various districts, 169
kami, hair, 30
kami, paper, 26
kamo shiremasen, may be, 128
kanarazu, be sure to, certainly, 118

kangaeru, think, consider, 41
kangofu(-san), nurse, 89
kantan(na), simple, easy, 54
kao, face, 65
kaoiro, complexion, 65
(-te) kara, after, 54
kara, empty, 171
karada, body, health, 111; *karada ni ii*, good for the health, 112
kara . . . ni kakete, from . . . to, 197
karaoke, karaoke, 132
kare, he, 78
kari-/gari, excursion, hunting, 198
kariru, borrow, rent, 133
karui, light, 60
kashikomarimashita, certainly, 118
kashi-ya, confectioner, confectionary, 129
kasu, lend, 80
-kata, way, how to, 54
katai, hard, 163
katazukeru, put away, tidy up, 80
kawa, leather, 32
kawa, river, creek, stream, 103
kawaii, cute, 153
kawaru, change, 98
kayō, Tuesday, 69
kaze, a cold; *kaze o hiku*, catch a cold, 59
kaze, wind, 173
kedo/keredo, but, however, 187
kega, injury, wound; *kega o suru*, (be) hurt, 70
keisatsu, police, 67
keiyaku, contract, 122
kekka, result, 89
kekkō(na), fine, 95
kembutsu, sightseeing, visit; *kembutsu suru*, sightsee, 103
ken, ticket, 84
-ken, power, authority, right, 139
kenka, quarrel, fight, 79
kenkō, health, 68
kenkyū, research, study, 89
kenshū, training program; *kenshū suru*, study, train, 108
-(kere)ba . . . hodo, if . . . -er/more/less, then . . . , 158
kesa, this morning, 18
keshigomu, eraser, 122
kettei, decision, conclusion; *kettei-ken*, decisive say, authority, 139
ki, feeling; *ki ni irimashita*, was/is satisfactory, 37
kieru, go out, be extinguished, put out, 163
kifu, donation, contribution; *kifu suru*, donate, contribute, 153
kigi, trees, 198
kiiro, yellow, 198

kikai, machine, equipment, 133
kikai, opportunity, occasion, 112
kikan, system, 18
kikoeru, can hear, be audible, 138
kimeru, decide, 54
kimi, you (informal men's speech), 174
kimochi, feeling, 169
kimono, kimono, 138
kinjo, neighborhood, 169
kinko, strong box, safe, vault, 173
kinu, silk, 60
kion, (air) temperature, 197
kirai(na), dislike, unlike, 132
kiru, cut, 78
kiru, wear, put on, 50
kisei, homecoming; *kisei suru*, return to one's home/birthplace, 84
kisetsu, season, 198
kita, north, 21
kitanai, dirty, 59
-kō, port, 103
kōchi, coach, 36
koe, voice, 79
koin rokkā, pay locker, 154
kōji, construction work, 158
kōjō, factory, 169
kokusai, international, 191
kokusai-denwa, international telephone call, 191
kokusai-teki(na), international, 104
komaru, be inconvenienced/ troubled/ embarrassed, 123
kompyūtā, computer, 108
kondo, next (time), 42
konna, like this, this sort of, 54
kono hen, around here, this vicinity, 154
kono yō ni, thus, in this way, 197
kontesuto, contest, 182
kon'yaku, engagement; *kon'yaku suru*, become engaged, 111
korekara, from now (on), 69
koro, time, 46
kōto, coat, 57
koto, matter, fact, 108
. . . koto ga aru, have the experience of, 46
. . . koto ga dekiru, can, 36
kotoba, word, 197
kotonaru, differ, be different, 197
kotowaru, decline, reject, 133
kōtsū, transportation, 18
kōyō, autumn (*lit.* "red") leaves; *kōyō-bi*, day the leaves turn, 198
kuji, lottery, 169
kumori, cloudy, 168
-kun, Mr., Master (informal men's speech), 65
kuni, home town, birthplace, country, 84
kūrā, air conditioner, 98

kurabu, club, 36
kurasu, class, 42
kureru, give, 54
kuro, black(ness), 26
kusai, smelly, 173
kuwashii, detailed, precise; *kuwashiku*, in detail, 26
kyōju, professor, 31
kyō-jū ni, within today, 26
kyōmi, interest; *(ni) kyōmi ga aru*, be interested in, 104
kyū ni, suddenly, 111
kyūryō, salary, 163

madoguchi, window, clerk, 90
mae, before, 26
mafurā, scarf, muffler, 26
maitoshi, every year, 169
majime(na), serious, diligent, 30
mamoru, keep (a promise), obey, 79
man-, full (prefix); *man'in*, full (of people), 138
maniau, be in/on time, 164
mannaka, middle, 21
mashin, machine, 36
matomaru, be brought together, be in order, 89
mawaru, tour, go round, 46
mawasu, turn, 163
mazu, before anything (else), 54
mazui, awkward, unsavory, 54
mazui, not delicious, 163
-mei (-sama) (counter for people), 117
meiwaku, trouble, inconvenience, 164
mendō(na), troublesome, annoying, a nuisance, 144
me no mae, right in front of, 163
mētoru, meter, 191
mezurashii, rare, unusual, 163
michi, road, street, way, 18
midori, green, 90
Midori no Madoguchi, Green Ticket Office, 90
mieru, can see, be visible, 138
migaku, brush, polish, 41
mijikai, short, 79
minami, south, 104
minna, all, everything, 169
miso, soybean paste, 59
misoshiru, miso soup, 59
mitsukaru, be found, 163
miyage, souvenir, 122
mo, even (emphasis), 79
mochiron, of course, 187
moku, Thursday, 42
momiji, maple; *momiji-gari*, maple leaf excursion, 198
mo . . . mo, both . . . and, 18

mō . . . nai, any/no more, any/no longer, 84
mondai, problem, 30
mono, thing, goods, wear, 36, 57
moshi, if, 149
mōshikomi, application; *mōshikomi-sho*, application form, 37; *mōshikomu*, apply, propose, 79
mōshiwake arimasen, I'm sorry, (*lit.* "There's no excuse"); *mōshiwake*, excuse, apology, 65
motsu, have, hold, 41
motte iku, take (things), 122
motto, -er, more, less, 65
moyō, pattern, design, 26
mukae ni iku, go to meet, 74
mukaeru, meet, greet, 74
mukashi (no), old, 153
mune, chest, 26
muri o suru, overdo, 65
myūjikaru, musical, 89

nado, and so forth; *nado no*, such as, 197
nagai, long, 30
nagame, view, 103
-nagara, while . . . -ing, at the same time, 103
naka-goro, around the middle, 84
nakami, contents, 26
nakanaka, quite, very, 46; *nakanaka . . . nai*, not any/at all, 65
-nakereba naranai, must, 94
nakunaru, pass away, be lost/missing, disappear, 111
nambu, southern part, 197
nan to itte mo, undoubtedly, 197
nanika, some-/any(thing), some, any, 158
naoru, get well, be fixed, 68
naosu, correct, improve, repair, 41
-nara, if, 149
narau, learn, 36
nureru, get used to, 123
naru, become, 54
naru, ring, 173
naruhodo, I see, 84
nattō, fermented soybeans, 173
nattoku, understanding, consent, 139
naze, why, 108
nemmatsu, end of the year, 158
nemui, sleepy, 122
neru, sleep, go to bed, 41
nigai, bitter, 173
nigate, difficult, poor at, 187
-nikui, difficult, awkward, 168
ni kyōmi ga aru, be interested in, 104
nimotsu, baggage, cargo, 60
ni suru, decide, make/do (it), 54
nobiru, extend, stretch, postpone, 197
noboru, climb, 50

nochi, later, 168
(no) darō ka, I wonder, 169
node, since, because, 128
no hō ga, -er/more/less, 18
no hoka ni, in addition to, 197
no mawari ni, around, 139
nombiri suru, take it easy, 174
no naka de, of all, among, 18
nōyaku, agricultural chemical, 103
nugu, take off, 41
nyūgaku, matriculation; *nyūgaku-kin*, matriculation fee, 94

o-bentō, box lunch, 41
ōbī, OB (old boy), alumnus/i, 139
oboeru, remember, memorize, 181
O-Bon, O-Bon (midsummer festival), 84
ochiru, drop, fall, 32; fail, 143
o-daiji ni, Take care of yourself, 65
odoroku, be surprised, 143
o-hanami, (cherry) blossom viewing, 197
ōi, many, much, 84
o-ikutsu, how old (for a person), 61
okaeri nasai, welcome home, 99
o-kage-sama de, Thank you, 69
okā-sama, (someone else's) mother (polite), 111
okashii, strange, funny, 178
okiru, get up, wake up, 30; happen, occur, 133
o-ko-san, (someone else's) child(ren), 61
oku, put, set up, 50
okureru, be late, 98
okurimono, gift, 128
okuru, send (a present), 178
okuru, take, see/send off, escort, 164
oku-sama, (someone else's) wife (polite), 104
o-kyaku-san, client, guest, visitor, 89
omedetō gozaimasu, congratulations, 178
ō-misoka, last day of year, 168
o-miyage, souvenir, 122
omoi, heavy, 79
omote, front, face, surface, 158
omou, think, 84
onaji, same, 128
onsui, warm water; *onsui pūru*, heated (swimming) pool, 36
orosu, withdraw, 98
o-saki ni shitsurei shimasu, good-bye, 65
o-sewa ni naru, be under the care of, be indebted to, 128
o-shaberi suru, chat, 79
o-shōgatsu, New Year's, 174
osoreirimasu, excuse me, be sorry (polite), 118
o-sōshiki, funeral, 122
osu, push, 163
o-sukina mono, thing(s) you like, 36
oto, sound, 163

ōtobai, motorcycle, 191
o-todoke, delivery, 178
o-todoke-saki, consignee, destination, 178
otona, adult, 90
otosu, lose, drop, 32
ototoshi, year before last, 108
otto, husband, 163
oyogu, swim, 36
ōzei, hordes/lots of people, 84

pairotto, pilot, 173
pasokon, personal computer, 133
pasupōto, passport, 98
pianisuto, pianist, 59
piano, piano, 111
pīku, peak, 18
purezento, present, 128
purojekuto, project, 65
pūru, pool, 36

rabu retā, love letter, 128
rasshu, rush, 84; *rasshu awā*, rush hour, 169
rebā, lever, 163
renraku, contact, communication, connection; *renraku suru*, contact, 108
renshū, practice; *renshū suru*, practice, 50
ressun, lesson, 78
rettō, archipelago, 197
rikishi, *sumō* wrestler, 139
risāchi, research, 89
riyō, use; *riyō suru*, make use of, take advantage of, 163
rombun, paper, thesis, 122
rusu, be out/away, 153
-ryō, fee, charge, 94
ryokan, inn, 103
ryōkin, charge, fee, 118
ryōri, food; *ryōri suru*, cook, 181
ryōtei, Japanese restaurant, teahouse, 103

sa, difference, 197
sā, come now, 138
sābisu-ryō, service charge, 117
sagasu, look for, 154
saiensu, science, 108
saifu, wallet, purse, 32
sain, signature, 99
saite iku, be (in the process of) blooming, 197
saki, before, ahead, beyond, future, 65
sakki, a short time ago, 65
saku, blossom, flower, 160
sakura, cherry blossom, 31
sakura zensen, cherry blossom front, 197
samā kōsu, summer course, 94
samurai, samurai, 169
-san, Mount (with names), 50

sararīman, white-collar (salaried) worker, 169
sassoku, without delay, directly, 158
-satsu (counter for books), 187
sawagashii, uproarious, noisy, 169
sayōnara, good-bye, 122
se, back; *se ga takai*, tall, high, 30
seikatsu, living, life, 123
sekai, world, society, realm; *sekai-jū*, all over the world, 153
seki, coughing, cough, 69; *seki o suru*, cough, 79
sekkei, design, plan, 158
sekken, soap, 144
semai, small, narrow, 60
semmon, specialty, 108
sen, line, 197
senaka, back, 153
senjitsu, the other day, 169
sensō, war, 122
sērusu, sales; *sērusu no hito*, salesperson, 54
setsumei, explanation; *setsumei suru*, explain, 26
sewa, help, kindness, good offices; *sewa ni naru*, under the care of, indebted to, 128
-sha, person, 133
shachō, president of a company, 21
sharyō, car, vehicle, 26
shatsu, shirt, 60
shawā, shower; *shawa o abiru*, take a shower, 41
shi, and, moreover, 54
shibai, play, 89
shiharai, payment, 94
shika . . . nai, only, 187
shiken, examination, test, 61
shima, stripe, 26
shima-guni, island country, 197
shimaru, be closed, 158
shinai, within a city, 46
shinjiru, believe, 191
shinnen, new year, 169
shinu, die, 41
shio, salt, 182
shippai, failure, mistake; *shippai suru*, fail, 181
shiranai hito, stranger, 78
shiraseru, inform, 68
shiro, white (ness), 26
shiru, soup, 59
shiryō, papers, documents, 80
shisutemu, system; *shisutemu-bu*, systems department, 54
shitei, appointment, designation, specification; *shitei-ken*, reserved ticket, 84
shiten, branch (office/store), 46
shitsumon, question, 163
shiyō, using, use, application, 103
shizen, nature, 103

shō, show, 169
-sho, book, document, note, 37
-sho, office, bureau, 173
shōgakkō, elementary school, 111
shōgatsu, New Year's, 174
shōkai suru, introduce, 153
-shoku, meal (counter), 117
shokuba, workplace, 128
shonichi, first/opening day, 138
shōrai, future, 181
shorui, document, 60
shōrūmu, showroom, 158
shōsha, trading company, 108
shōtai, invitation; *shōtai-jō*, invitation card/letter, 111
shujin, proprietor, 103
shūkai, gathering, assembly, 89
shūkan, custom, habit, 128
shūkan-shi, weekly magazine, 69
shukudai, homework, 144
shuppatsu, departure; *shuppatsu suru*, leave, 74
shushō, prime minister, 89
shusseki, attendance; *shusseki suru*, attend, 79
shutchō, business/official trip, 46; *shutchō suru*, take a business trip, 108
soba, buckwheat noodles, 168
soba, near, beside, 154
sōdan, consultation, 37; *sōdan suru*, consult, 54
sōji, cleaning; *sōji o suru*, clean, 59
sō ka (informal) = *sō desu ka*, 182
somei yoshino, a species of cherry, 198
someru, dye, 198
sonna ni, that much/many, 154
sora, sky, 169
sorede, and then, 118
sore dewa, well then, 65
sore-ja, in that case, 65
sore ni, moreover, 108
sorou, be present, assemble, be/become complete, 153
sōryō, delivery charge, postage, 179
sōshiki, funeral, 122
sōsō, oh yes, 149
soto, outside, exterior, outer, 173
sotsugyō, graduation; *sotsugyō suru*, graduate, 89
sue, end, 197
sugoi, terrible, wonderful; *sugoku*, very, terrible, 18
sugu, immediately, 61
suiei, swimming, 89
sukāfu, scarf, 60
sukoshi-zutsu, little by little, 123
suku, be/become empty/uncrowded, 18
sukunai, a little, few, 163

sumaseru, finish, 74
sumō, Japanese wrestling, 138
sumu, be finished, 153
Supein-go, Spanish, 133
supīchi, speech; *supīchi kontesuto*, speech contest, 182
supōtsu, sports, 20
supōtsu kurabu, health club, 36
susunde iku, be advancing, 198
suteru, throw away, 98
suto, strike, 87
sutōbu, (heating) stove, 68
sutoraiki, strike, 111
sūtsu, suit, 173
suwaru, sit, take a seat, 50
suzushii, cool, 122

tabun, probably, perhaps, 87
tadaima, I'm back!, I'm home!, 99
taifū, typhoon, 93
taihen, Oh dear!, 164; very, 169
taihen(na), hard, difficult, 60
taikai, (big) meeting, conference, tournament, 123
taikin, large sum of money, 173
taikutsu(na), boring, 89
taishita, serious, important, 69
taitei, usually, most of the time, 59
takai, tall, high, 30
tama ni, once in a while, 79
tanomu, request, 65
tanoshimu, enjoy, 198
tantō-sha, person in charge, 133
-tara, when, if, 149
tariru, be enough, 122
-tari . . . -tari suru, do X, Y, etc., 46
tashikameru, make sure, 123
tashika ni, certainly, 149
tasukaru, be relieved, be saved, 192
tatsu, stand up, 79
tatta, only; *tatta hitotsu*, one only, 103
tawā, tower, 144
tazuneru, visit, 59
te, hand, arm, 41; *te o kasu*, lend a hand, 80; *te ni toru*, get, take in one's hands, 187
teire, care, trimming, mending, 89
-teki, like, resembling, 104
tekitō(na), suitable, appropriate, 89
tempura, tempura, 21
tenisu kōto, tennis court, 36
tetsudai, help, assistance, 192; *tetsudau*, help, 182
tetsuzuki, formality, procedure, 187
to, when, 158
tōchaku, arrival, 118
tobu, fly, 50
todoku, arrive, reach, 26

tōfu, tofu, 50
toire, toilet, 79
toki, when, while, 118
tokkyū, special/limited express, 90
tokorode, by the way, 54; well, incidentally, 197
tōku, long distance, 144
tokubetsu (no/na), special, extraordinary, 178
tomaru, stop, 69; stay, stop at, 74
tonari, next, neighboring, 89
torihikisaki, business contact, 46
torikumi, bout, 138
toru, pick up, get, take, pass, 26, 182
tōru, go through/past, 79
to shite, as, in the capacity of, 118
tsugi-tsugi ni, one after another, in order, 169
tsukai-kata, way of using, 54
tsukareru, get tired, 122
tsukeru, include, 178
-tsuki, included, attached, with, 117, 169
tsuki, moon, 21
tsūkōnin, passerby, 90
tsukuru, cook, prepare, make, 41
tsuma, (one's own) wife, 79
tsumaranai, trifling, worthless, 133
tsumetai, cold, cool, chilled, 111
tsumori, intention, purpose, 178
tsureru, take, bring, be accompanied by; *tsurete iku*, take (a person), 181
tsuri, fishing; *tsuri o suru*, fish, 50
tsutaeru, give, convey, impart, 104
tsutsuji, azalea, 197
tsūyaku, interpreter, translator, 154
tsuyoi, strong, 59
tte (informal for *to iu no wa*); *tte nan desu ka*, What do you/does it mean?, 128

uchikin, deposit, partial payment, 118
uchi no, our, 54
uchū, universe; *uchū hikōshi*, astronaut, 59
ugokimawaru, move around, 139
ugoku, run, move, operate, 87
uisukī, whiskey, 60
ukagau, visit, ask (polite), 158
ukeru, take (an examination), receive, undergo, have, 94
uma, horse, 26
umareru, be born, 111
ume, apricot, Japanese plum, 197
undō, exercise; *undō suru*, exercise, 153
unten, driving; *unten suru*, drive, 41
ura, back, reverse (side); *uraguchi*, back entrance, 158
ureshii, delighted, happy, 128
urikire, sold out, 84
ūru, wool, 26
ushiro, back, 26

uta, song; *utau*, sing, 41
utsukushii, beautiful, 169

wakai, young, 30
wakareru, part, split up, 122
wāpuro, word processor, 54
warau, laugh, smile, 79
wasureru, forget, 26
wasuremono, forgotten or lost article, 26
watasu, hand (over), 99
wazawaza, especially; *wazawaza suru*, go to the trouble of, 94

yachin, (house) rent, 163
yahari (= *yappari*), (just) as you/we expected, 129, 169
yakimono, pottery, 60
yakitori, grilled chicken, 138
yaku, about, 197
yaku, bake, grill, roast, 79
yakusoku, promise, appointment, 79
yamanobori, mountain climbing, 111
yameru, give up, stop, 84, 103; quit, 168
yamu, stop, 123
yappari, (just) as you/we expected, 129
yaru, do, give, play, 112; show, play, 169
yaseru, lose weight, become thin, 133
-yasui, easy to, 173
yasumi o toru, take a vacation, 181
yasumu, rest, 31
yattsu, eight years old, 61
yō, way, manner, 197
yobikō, preparatory school, 94
yobu, call, invite, 41
yogoreru, be/become dirty, 169
yoku, much, a great deal, 21
yōji, work, business, 65
yonaka, middle of the night, midnight, 143
yori, than, 12
yorokobu, be happy, be pleased, 129
yoroshii, all right, 179; *yoroshiku*, properly, well, at one's discretion, 158
yoru, stop by, drop in, 70
yoru, night, 168
yosoku, prediction, estimate; *yosoku suru*, predict, 197
yōsu, state, circumstance, appearance, 197
yotei, plan, schedule, 122
yoyaku-gakari, reservation clerk, 117
yūbe, last night/evening, 30
yūbin, mail, 94
yude tamago, boiled egg, 78
yūfō, UFO, 50
yuki, snow; *yuki ga furu*, it snows, 76

zangyō, overtime, 60

zannen(na), disappointing, 50
zaseki, seat, 90
zehi, please, 112
zeikin, tax, 117
zeimusho, tax office, 173
zembu, all, every, 169
zen'in, all the staff, all members, 153
zensen, front, 197
zubon, trousers, 122
zuibun, quite, 197
zumen, blueprint, plan, 158
zutto, a whole lot, all the time/way, 197

ENGLISH-JAPANESE GLOSSARY

accident, *jiko*, 132
a little, *sukunai*, 163
almost, *hotondo*, 169
about, *yaku*, 197
accept, *itadaku*, 133
adult, *otona*, 90
air conditioner, *kūrā*, 98
all over the world, *sekai-jū*, 153
all right, *daijōbu(na)*, 178
all, *minna*, 169
all, *zembu*, 169
all, *zen'in*, 153
always, *itsumo*, 138
and then, *sorede*, 118
announcement, *anaunsu, happyō suru*, 138
announcement, *happyō*, 69
anyone, *dare demo*, 187
apartment, *apāto*, 60
application form, *mōshikomi-sho*, 37
apply, *mōshikomu*, 79
approach, *chikazuku*, 197
appropriate, *tekitō(na)*, 89
archipelago, *rettō*, 197
around here, *kono hen*, 154
arrival, *tōchaku*, 118
as a matter of fact, *jitsu wa*, 128
attend, *shusseki suru*, 79
attendance, *shusseki*, 79
awkward, *mazui*, 54
azalea, *tsutsuji*, 197

back, *senaka*, 153
back, *ura*, 158
back, *ushiro*, 26
bag, *fukuro*, 26
baggage, *nimotsu*, 60
bake, *yaku*, 79
ball-point pen, *bōru pen*, 122
barbecue, *bābekyū*, 112
bathe, *abiru*, 41
beautiful, *utsukushii*, 169
become, *naru*, 54
before anything else, *mazu*, 54
before, *mae*, 26
begin, *hajimeru*, 37
beginning, *hajime*, 197
believe, *shinjiru*, 191

beside, *soba*, 154
bicycle, *jitensha*, 191
bitter, *nigai*, 173
black, *kuro(i)*, 26
blossom, *saku*, 160
blueprint, *zumen*, 158
body, *karada*, 111
boiled egg, *yude tamago*, 78
boring, *taikutsu(na)*, 89
(be) born, *umareru*, 111
borrow, *kariru*, 133
bouquet, *hanataba*, 60
box lunch, *bentō*, 41
branch (office/store), *shiten*, 46
bright, *akarui*, 59
bright, *atama ga ii*, 30
brush, *fude*, 169
buckwheat noodles, *soba*, 168
business trip, *shutchō*, 46
button, *botan*, 163
by the way, *tokorode*, 54

cage, *kago*, 103
call, *yobu*, 41
cancer, *gan*, 163
car, *sharyō*, 26
carry, *hakobu*, 79
case, *baai*, 118
cash, *genkin*, 32
catch a cold, *kaze o hiku*, 59
certainly, *kanarazu*, 118
certainly, *tashika ni*, 149
change, *kaeru*, 54
change, *kawaru*, 98
channel, *channeru*, 168
charge, *ryōkin*, 118
chat, *o-shaberi suru*, 79
cheerful, *akarui*, 30
cherry blossom, *sakura*, 31
chest, *mune*, 26
chocolate, *chokorēto*, 128
choose, *erabu*, 79
class, *kurasu*, 42
clean, *sōji o suru*, 59
clear up, *hareru*, 180
clearly, *hakkiri*, 163
client, *o-kyaku-san*, 89

climb, *noboru*, 50
(be) closed, *shimaru*, 158
cloudy, *kumori*, 168
club member, *kaiin*, 149
coach, *kōchi*, 36
coat, *kōto*, 57
cold, *tsumetai*, 111
color, *iro*, 65
complexion, *kaoiro*, 65
complicated, *fukuzatsu(na)*, 39
computer, *kompyūtā*, 108
condition, *guai*, 111
congratulations, *omedetō gozaimasu*, 178
construction work, *kōji*, 158
consult, *sōdan suru*, 54
contact, *renraku*, 108
contents, *nakami*, 26
contest, *kontesuto*, 182
contract, *keiyaku*, 122
conversation, *kaiwa*, 111
convey, *tsutaeru*, 104
cook, *ryōri suru*, 181
cool, *suzushii*, 122
correct, *naosu*, 41
cough, *seki o suru*, 79
cough, *seki*, 69
coworker, *dōryō*, 128
custom, *shūkan*, 128
cut, *kiru*, 78
cute, *kawaii*, 153

dance, *dansu*, 173
dangerous, *abunai*, 111
decide, *kimeru*, 54
decision, *kettei*, 139
decline, *kotowaru*, 113
delighted, *ureshii*, 128
delivery charge, *sōryō*, 179
delivery, *o-todoke*, 178
department, *bu*, 29
departure, *-hatsu*, 90
departure, *shuppatsu*, 74
deposit, *azukeru*, 149
deposit, *uchikin*, 118
design, *sekkei*, 158
designer, *dezainā*, 181
detailed, *kuwashii*, 26
die, *shinu*, 41
differ, *kotonaru*, 197
difficult, *taihen(na)*, 60
dirty, *kitanai*, 59
(become) dirty, *yogoreru*, 169
(be) disappointed, *gakkari suru*, 144
disappointing, *zannen(na)*, 50
discontinuance, *chūshi*, 123
dislike, *kirai(na)*, 132

do, *yaru*, 112
document, *shorui*, 60
dog, *inu*, 153
donation, *kifu*, 153
drama, *geki*, 169
drive, *unten suru*, 41
drop, *ochiru*, 32
drop, *otosu*, 32
dye, *someru*, 198

earthquake, *jishin*, 122
elementary school, *shōgakkō*, 111
empty, *kara*, 171
end of the year, *nemmatsu*, 158
end, *sue*, 197
endure, *gaman suru*, 99
engagement, *kon'yaku*, 111
enjoy, *tanoshimu*, 198
enough, *jūbun*, 182
(be) enough, *tariru*, 122
eraser, *keshigomu*, 122
every year, *maitoshi*, 169
examination, *shiken*, 61
exercise, *undō*, 153
explanation, *setsumei*, 26
express train, *tokkyū*, 90
express, *arawasu*, 197
extend, *nobiru*, 197

face, *kao*, 65
facsimile, *fakkusu*, 21
factory, *kōjō*, 169
fail, *ochiru*, 143
failure, *shippai*, 181
fair, *hare*, 168
fall, *furu*, 76
fast, *hayai*, 18
feeling, *ki*, 37
feeling, *kimochi*, 169
female, *josei*, 128
ferry, *ferī*, 153
few, *sukunai*, 163
fine, *kekkō(na)*, 95
finish, *sumaseru*, 74
fish, *tsuri o suru*, 50
flashy, *hade(na)*, 138
flower, *saku*, 160
fly, *tobu*, 50
foot, *ashi*, 70
for the first time, *hajimete*, 18
foreign language, *gaikoku-go*, 191
forget, *wasureru*, 26
front, *omote*, 158
full, *ippai (no/na)*, 133
funeral, *(o-)sōshiki*, 122
funny, *okashii*, 178

future, *shōrai*, 181

gather, *atsumeru*, 144
gathering, *shūkai*, 89
generally, *daitai*, 197
get up, *okiru*, 30
get well, *naoru*, 68
gift, *okurimono*, 128
give a gift to someone, *okuru*, 164
give up, *akirameru*, 182
give up, *yameru*, 84
give, *kureru*, 54
globe, *chikyū*, 21
go out, *dekakeru*, 41
go out, *kieru*, 163
go round, *mawaru*, 46
go through/past, *tōru*, 79
good-bye, *sayōnara*, 122
graduate, *deru*, 59
graduate, *sotsugyō suru*, 89
greatly, *daibu*, 69
green, *midori*, 90
greeting, *aisatsu*, 46
grill, *yaku*, 79
grilled chicken, *yakitori*, 138
guest, *o-kyaku-san*, 89
guidance, *annai*, 30

hair, *kami*, 30
half, *hambun*, 153
hand over, *watasu*, 99
hand, *te*, 41
handsome, *hansamu(na)*, 59
handwriting, *ji*, 168
happen, *okiru*, 133
(be) happy, *yorokobu*,129
hard, *katai*, 163
have, *motsu*, 41
health, *kenkō*, 79
heater, *hītā*, 59
heavy, *omoi*, 79
help, *tetsudau*, 182
high, *takai*, 30
home town, *kuni*, 84
home, *ie*, 84
homework, *shukudai*, 144
horse, *uma*, 26
house, *ie*, 84
how old (for a person), *ikutsu*, 61
hurry, *isogu*, 41
husband, *otto*, 163

I (informal men's speech), *boku*, 54
if, *moshi*, 149
immediately, *sugu*, 61
important, *erai*, 139

important, *taishita*, 69
inconvenient, *fuben(na)*, 30
increase, *fueru*, 103
inform, *shiraseru*, 68
injury, *kega*, 70
inn, *ryokan*, 103
instruction, *jugyō*, 94
intention, *tsumori*, 178
interest, *kyōmi*, 104
international, *kokusai*, 191
international, *kokusai-teki(na)*, 104
interpreter, *tsūyaku*, 154
introduce, *shōkai suru*, 153
invitation, *shōtai*, 111

Japanese plum, *ume*, 197
join, *hairu*, 133
joke, *jōdan*, 144

karaoke, *karaoke*, 132
keep (promise), *mamoru*, 79

last night, *yūbe*, 30
(be) late, *okureru*, 98
later, *ato de*, 94
laugh, *warau*, 79
learn, *narau*, 36
leave, *shuppatsu suru*, 74
leg, *ashi*, 70
lend, *kasu*, 80
lesson, *ressun*, 78
life, *seikatsu*, 123
light, *karui*, 60
like, *ki ni iru*, 37
line, *sen*, 197
little by little, *sukoshi-zutsu*, 123
long, *nagai*, 30
look after, *azukaru*, 128
look for, *sagasu*, 154
look up in, *hiku*, 173
lose weight, *yaseru*, 133
(be) lost, *nakunaru*, 111
lots of people, *ōzei*, 84
lottery, *kuji*, 169
lunch, *chūshoku*, 74

machine, *kikai*, 133
machine, *mashīn*, 36
mail, *(tegami o) dasu*, 60
mail, *yūbin*, 94
make sure, *tashikameru*, 123
make, *tsukuru*, 41
male, *dansei*, 128
many, *ōi*, 84
maple, *momiji*, 198
matriculation fee, *nyūgaku-kin*, 94

meaning, *imi*, 187
memorize, *oboeru*, 181
meter, *mētoru*, 191
middle, *mannaka*, 21
midnight, *yonaka*, 143
minister, *daijin*, 89
moon, *tsuki*, 21
more, *motto*, 65
moreover, *sore ni*, 108
most, *ichiban*, 18
motorcycle, *ōtobai*, 191
mountain climbing, *yamanobori*, 111
move (house), *hikkosu*, 60
move around, *ugokimawaru*, 139
move, *ugoku*, 87
much, *yoku*, 21
much, *ōi*, 84
musical, *myūjikaru*, 89

narrow, *semai*, 60
nasty, *iya(na)*, 174
nature, *shizen*, 103
near, *soba*, 154
necessary, *hitsuyō(na)*, 89
need, *iru*, 98
neighborhood, *kinjo*, 169
New Year's, *o-shōgatsu*, 174
new year, *shinnen*, 169
next, *tonari*, 89
night, *yoru*, 168
noisy, *sawagashii*, 169
north, *kita*, 21
not any/at all, *nakanaka . . . nai*, 65
not good, *dame(na)*, 99
not very, *ammari*, 174
nurse, *kangofu*, 89

occur, *okiru*, 133
of course, *mochiron*, 187
office, *jimusho*, 74
old, *mukashi (no)*, 153
oneself, *jibun*, 79
only, *tatta*, 103
(be) open, *aku*, 117
opportunity, *kikai*, 112
opposite, *hantai*, 158
or, *ka*, 65
ordinarily, *fudan (wa)*, 168
(be) out/away, *rusu*, 153
outside, *soto*, 173
overdo, *muri o suru*, 65
overtime, *zangyō*, 60

paper, *kami*, 26
part, *wakareru*, 122
pass away, *nakunaru*, 111

passerby, *tsūkōnin*, 90
passport, *pasupōto*, 98
pattern, *moyō*, 26
pay, *harau*, 69
payment, *shiharai*, 94
pencil, *empitsu*, 99
people, *hito-bito*, 197
performance, *ensō*, 169
perhaps, *tabun*, 87
period, *jidai*, 103
person in charge, *kakari*, 117
personal computer, *pasokon*, 133
piano, *piano*, 111
pick up, *toru*, 26,
pilot, *pairotto*, 173
play (a musical instrument), *hiku*, 144
play, *asobu*, 41
play, *shibai*, 89
police, *keisatsu*, 67
polish, *migaku*, 41
pool, *pūru*, 36
poor, *bimbō(na)*, 59
pork, *butaniku*, 191
portion, *bun*, 94
pottery, *yakimono*, 60
practice, *renshū*, 50
prediction, *yosoku*, 197
preparation, *jumbi*, 182
present, *purezento*, 128
president of a company, *shachō*, 21
president, *daitōryō*, 50
prime minister, *shushō*, 89
printing, *insatsu*, 169
problem, *mondai*, 30
procedure, *tetsuzuki*, 187
professor, *kyōju*, 31
project, *purojekuto*, 65
promise, *yakusoku*, 79
proprietor, *shujin*, 103
pull, *hiku*, 163
purse, *saifu*, 32
push, *osu*, 163
put away, *katazukeru*, 80
put in, *ireru*, 163
put on (glasses), *kakeru*, 79
put, *oku*, 50

quarrel, *kenka*, 59
question, *shitsumon*, 163
quit, *yameru*, 168
quite, *nakanaka*, 40
quite, *zuibun*, 197

rain, *ame*, 87
raise, *ageru*, 78
rare, *mezurashii*, 163

reach, *todoku*, 26
real, *hontō (no)*, 139
red, *aka(i)*, 198
registered mail, *kakitome*, 94
(be) relieved/relaxed, *anshin suru*, 46
rent (house), *yachin*, 163
reply, *henji*, 143
represent, *daihyō suru*, 197
request, *irai*, 158
request, *tanomu*, 65
research, *kenkyū*, 89
research, *risāchi*, 89
reserve, *enryo*, 133
reserved ticket, *shitei-ken*, 84
rest, *yasumu*, 23
result, *kekka*, 89
ring, *naru*, 173
river, *kawa*, 103
road, *michi*, 18
roast, *yaku*, 79
rose, *bara*, 122
rubbish, *gomi*, 98
run, *hashiru*, 144

safe, *anzen(na)*, 111
salary, *kyūryō*, 163
sales, *sērusu*, 54
salt, *shio*, 182
same, *onaji*, 128
samurai, *samurai*, 169
scarf, *mafurā*, 26
scarf, *sukāfu*, 60
schedule, *yotei*, 122
science, *saiensu*, 108
screen, *gamen*, 54
seal, *hanko*, 98
season, *kisetsu*, 198
seat, *zaseki*, 90
second, *-byō*, 191
section chief, *kachō*, 80
section, *ka*, 54
send (a present), *okuru*, 178
serious, *majime(na)*, 30
shirt, *shatsu*, 60
short, *mijikai*, 79
shower, *shawā*, 41
showroom, *shōrūmu*, 158
sickness, *byōki*, 59
side, *-gawa*, 158
sightseeing, *kembutsu*, 103
signature, *sain*, 99
silk, *kinu*, 60
simple, *kantan(na)*, 54
sing, *utau*, 41
sit, *suwaru*, 50
sky, *sora*, 169

sleep, *neru*, 41
sleepy, *nemui*, 122
small, *semai*, 60
smelly, *kusai*, 173
smile, *warau*, 79
snow, *yuki*, 76
so forth, *nado*, 197
soap, *sekken*, 144
sold out, *urikire*, 84
some other (thing), *betsu(na)*, 65
someone, *dare ka*, 74
song, *uta*, 41
sound, *oto*, 163
south, *minami*, 104
souvenir, *o-miyage*, 122
spacious, *hiroi*, 21
speak, *hanasu*, 41
special, *tokubetsu (no/na)*, 178
specialty, *semmon*, 108
sports, *supōtsu*, 20
spring, *haru*, 160
stand up, *tatsu*, 79
start, *hajimaru*, 65
start, *hajimeru*, 37
state, *yōsu*, 197
station employee, *ekiin*, 26
station staff, *ekiin*, 26
stop by, *yoru*, 70
stop, *tomaru*, 69,
stop, *yamu*, 123
stove, *sutōbu*, 68
strange, *okashii*, 178
stranger, *shiranai hito*, 78
street, *michi*, 18
strike, *suto, sutoraiki*, 87
stripe, *shima*, 26
strong, *tsuyoi*, 59
study, *benkyō suru*, 18
suddenly, *kyū ni*, 111
suit, *sūtsu*, 173
suitable, *tekitō(na)*, 89
(be) surprised, *odoroku*, 143
superior, *jōshi*, 128
swim, *oyogu*, 36
swimming, *suiei*, 89
system, *shisutemu*, 54

take (a person), *tsureru*, 181
take (an examination), *ukeru*, 94
take off, *nugu*, 41
talk, *hanasu*, 41
tall, *se ga takai*, 30
tax, *zeikin*, 117
telephone, *denwa o kakeru*, 26
temperature (air), *kion*, 197
tempura, *tempura*, 21

terrible, *sugoi*, 18
therefore, *desu kara*, 197
thesis, *rombun*, 122
thing, *mono*, 36,
think, *kangaeru*, 41
think, *omou*, 84
this morning, *kesa*, 18
though, *demo*, 18
throw away, *suteru*, 98
ticket, *ken*, 84
(be in/on) time, *maniau*, 164
(get) tired, *tsukareru*, 122
tofu, *tōfu*, 50
toilet, *toire*, 79
tool, *dōgu*, 78
tower, *tawā*, 144
trading company, *shōsha*, 108
trading, *bōeki*, 103
traffic jam, *jūtai*, 84
training, *kenshū*, 108
transfer, *furikomu*, 94
transportation, *kōtsū*, 18
trifling, *tsumaranai*, 133
trouble, *meiwaku*, 164
(be) troubled, *komaru*, 123
troublesome, *mendō(na)*, 144
trousers, *zubon*, 122
try hard, *gambaru*, 181
turn, *mawasu*, 163
typhoon, *taifū*, 93
typify, *daihyō suru*, 197

uchū, universe, 59
(be) uncrowded, *suku*, 18
undelicious, *mazui*, 163
university, *daigaku*, 31
unskillful, *heta(na)*, 168
unusual, *mezurashii*, 163
uproarious, *sawagashii*, 169
use, *riyō suru*, 163
use, *shiyō*, 103
usually, *taitei*, 59

(be) vacant, *aku*, 117
video, *bideo*, 50
view, *nagame*, 103
visa, *biza*, 98
visit, *tazuneru*, 59
visit, *ukagau*, 158
voice, *koe*, 79

want, *hoshii*, 54
war, *sensō*, 122
warm, *atatakai*, 59
wash, *arau*, 41
wear (shoes, pants, etc.), *haku*, 173

wear, *kiru*, 50
weekday, *heijitsu*, 191
weekly magazine, *shūkan-shi*, 69
which, *dochira*, 20
which, *dotchi*, 21
whiskey, *uisukī*, 60
white, *shiro*, 26
why, *naze*, 108
wife, *tsuma*, 79
wind, *kaze*, 173
winter, *fuyu*, 57
withdraw, *orosu*, 98
within (today), *kyō-jū ni*, 26
wool, *ūru*, 26
word processor, *wāpuro*, 54
word, *kotoba*, 197
work, *hataraku*, 21
workplace, *shokuba*, 128
world, *sekai*, 153

year before last, *ototoshi*, 108
yellow, *kiiro*, 198
you (informal men's speech), *kimi*, 174
young, *wakai*, 30

INDEX

accumulation, noun *mo* noun *mo* (noun *mo*), 18; noun *shi* noun *shi* (noun *shi*), 55

adjective, into adverb, *-ku/ni* form, 27

adjective, *-te* form, 27

adverbial form, *-i* adjective, 27; with verbs, 54

all right, satisfactory, *de ii*, 96, 140; noun *demo ii*, 95

alternative action, noun *ka* noun, 66; *-tari . . . -tari suru*, 47

anything (-place, -time, -body), *dore demo*, 38

apology, *mōshiwake arimasen*, 64

baai, 118

become, *-ku/ni naru*, 54

cause and effect, *-tara . . .-mashita*, 149; *to . . . -masu/mashita*, 159, 170

comparison, *no hō ga . . . yori, wa . . . yori*, 17; *no naka de . . . ichiban*, 17

completion, *-tara*, 148

complex sentence, 118

compound verb, *ugokimawaru*, 137; *-te iku, -te kuru*, 64, 198

conditional form, 158; *-ba/reba*, 158; *-nara*, 148; *-tara*, 149; *to*, 159

connective, *de (desu)*, 26; *-nagara*, 104; *. . . shi . . . shi*, 55; *-te/-de* form of adjectives, 27; *-te* form of verb, 27

contraction/abbreviation, *dokka*, 174; *kedo/ keredo (keredomo)*, 186; *tte (to iu no wa)*, 129

counters: *-bamme*, 26; *-bansen*, 90; *-byō*, 191; *-fun/pun*, 189; *-haku/paku*, 117; *-ka*, 78; *-kai*, 42; *-mei(-sama)*, 117; *-satsu*, 187; *-shoku*, 117

de ii, 96, 140

demo, 38, 95, 140

dewa/ja nai, 66

dō iu/donna, 140

dōzo, 105

Edo jidai, 104

emphasis, *-kereba. . . . hodo* (adj. conditional + adj. + *hodo*), 159; *mo*, 198; *nā*, 56; *(ni)wa/ (de)wa*, 38, 47

expected, supposed to be, *yahari/yappari*, 129

experience/occurrence, *-ta koto ga aru*, 46

familiar conversation, 173, 182

familiar speech, *boku*, 56; *-kun*, 66

giri-choko, 129

greeting, *dōzo yoroshiku o-tsutae kudasai*, 105; *itte rasshai, itte mairimasu, tadaima, o- kaeri nasai*, 95; *o-dekake desu ka*, 95; *o-daiji ni*, 65; *o-saki ni shitsurei shimasu*, 66; *yoroshiku o-negai shimasu*, 157

guessing, probability, supposition, *darō to omou*, 129; *deshō*, 85; *kamo shirenai*, 129; *to omou*, 84

hesitation, *anō*, 38

if it's all right (for you), *go-meiwaku de nakereba*, 164

in case, *baai*, 118

informal speech, *see* familiar conversation/ speech

intent, purpose, *ni ikimasu/kimasu/kaerimasu*, 28; *ni suru*, 55; *ō/yō*, volitional verb ending, 179; *tsumori*, 179; adj.-*ku/ni suru/naru*, 54

interrogative, *dare, nani, itsu, doko ka*, 38; *itte irrashai/mairimasu*, 95

isn't it? I suppose, *desho/deshō*, 189

just happened, *-ta bakari*, 66

kikoeru, 140

ko-, so-, a-, do- (contextual meaning), 19, 170; *ano*, 170

koto (matter), 109

koto ga aru, 46

koto ga dekiru, 38

koto mo aru, 75

manner (in this way/condition), *-te*, 139

-masu stem, as noun, 19; *-masu* stem + *kata* ("how to"), 56; *-masu* stem + *mono*, 28; *-masu* stem + *nagara*, 104; *-masu* stem + *-nikui/ -yasui*, 170; *see also* compound verbs follow- ing *-masu* stem

men's speech, 173

mieru, 140

mō, mō nai, mada, 86

mo, 77

-mono, 28
modifying clause, 74
modifying nouns, *e no* noun , 129

-na adjective, *-teki*, 104
naru: *-ku/ni ni naru*, 54
n desu, 108; *no desu*, 198; *-tai (hoshii) n desu*, 56, 119
negation, *(dewa/a) nai, nakanaka . . . -masen*, 66
negative question: *nai n desu ka*, 141; *-te wa ikemasen ka*, 95
negative sentence pattern: *nakanaka . . . nai*, 66; *shika . . . nai*, 189
New Year's card, 167
ni iku/kuru/kaeru, 28, 48
-nikui, 170
no (noun equivalent): *atarashii no* ("one"), 55; to make noun clause, for person or scene, etc., 139
noun modification, noun clause, 74; with *no*, 74

o-/go-, honorific prefix: + noun (*go-shōkai/go-sōdan*, etc.)/*o* + verb + *kudasai*, 39
obligations, orders and prohibitions (must, must not): *dame*, 99; *-nakareba narimasen, -te wa ikimasen*, 95; *see also* imperative (do, don't)
O-Bon, 86

particle, *o*, 47; *wa*, 47; *ni/de/kara wa*, 48; *ni*, 48, 54; *to/ni*, 159
permission, *de ii*, 96, 140; *-nakute mo ii*, 96; *-temo/noun demo ii*, 95; *-te wa ikemasen ka*, 95
phonetic change, 119
plain forms, table, 85; dictionary form, 37; modifying noun, 74; *see also* plain style
plain style, 170; *see also* familiar speech
polite expressions, *(ga) gozaimasu*, 117, 179; *de gozaimasu*, 112; *kekkō*, 96; *nan-mei-sama*, 119; *o-* + *-masu* stem, 179; *-sama*, 38, 149; *yoroshii desu/deshō ka*, 28, 179
potential form (can), *koto ga dekiru*, 38; *-rareru* (potential form of verbs), 188
prefixes, *dai-*, 170; *man-*, 138
probability, *deshō*, 85
progressive action, *-te iku, -te kuru*, 198
purpose, *see* intent

quotation, *to omou/kiku/iu*, 84, 119; *tte*, 129

reason (cause), adj./verb *-te*, 139; *node, na node*, 129
request: *o-/go- . . . kudasai*, 39, 179; *-te kudasaimasen ka*, 179; *-te kuremasen ka*, 75

repeated action, *-tari . . . -tari suru*, 47
respect language, *o-/go-* + noun, 39

Seijin no Hi, 170
simultaneous action, *-nagara*, 103, 136
some(any)body/-time/-where/-thing, *dare ka*, 75
(it) sometimes happens that, . . . *koto mo aru*, 75
state, condition, *-te iru*, 28
suffixes, *-bun*, 94; *-chū-/jū*, 21, 28; *-kun*, 66; *-ra*, 199; *-ryō* , 94; *-sama*, 148; *-sha*, 133; *-sho*, 37; *-tachi, -gata, -ra, -domo*, 199; *-teki(na)*, 104; *-zutsu*, 123
suggestion, *hō ga ii*, 65
sumō, 140
supposition, *deshō*, 85

tadaima, okaeri nasai, 95
-ta form: *-ta ato*, 104; *-ta bakari*, 66; *-ta hō ga ii*, 65; *-ta koto ga aru*, 46; *-tara*, 149; *-tari . . . -tari suru*, 47
-te form, *-te iku/kuru*, 66; *-te kara*, 55; *-te kudasai/kuremasen ka*, 75; *-te kuru*, 66; *-te imasen*, 55; *-te mo*, 95
-teki, 104
to iu no wa, defining, 129; *to iu/mou/kiku*, 84
time expressions: *made*, 140; *-nagara*, 104; *-te imasen*, 55; *-te kara*, 55; *-ta ato*, 104; *-ta bakari*, 66; *-tara*, 150; *-to*, 159, 170; *toki*, 118, 149
to omou, 129
toshikoshi soba, 170
to shite, 119

uchi (no), 54
uncertainty, *kamo shiremasen/darō to omou*, 128; *nara*, 150

verbs: compound, *ugokimawaru*, 139; conjugations, 37; conditional, 159; dictionary form, 37; form, *-nakereba narimasen, -te wa ikemasen*, 95; *-te mo ii desu*, 95; into noun, 19; potential, 187; *-te* form, *-ta* form, 46; tenses, 118; volitional, 179

wa for contrast: *(ni) wa/(de) wa*, 38; *. . . wa . . . wa*, 47
want, noun *ga hoshii*, 56
way of doing, *-kata*, 56
written style: diary, 167; letter, 102; essay, report, 195

-yasui, 170

supplement to the text

QUIZ ANSWERS ◼||||||||||

Lesson 1

I 1. Asa no hō ga (yūgata yori) konde imasu. 2. Michi ga konde imasu kara (densha no hō ga kuruma yori hayai desu). 3. Maiasa 7-ji ni uchi o dete, chikatetsu de kaisha ni ikimasu. 4. Asa no 8-ji han goro ga ichiban konde imasu. 5. Hai, chikatetsu no naka de Nihongo o benkyō shite imasu.

II 1. yori 2. ni, o, de, ni 3. mo 4. ga, de 5. no, de

III 1. dochira/dotchi 2. itsu 3. Dare 4. nani 5. dochira/dotchi

IV 1. suite 2. ko 3. hataraite 4. konde, orite, aruki 5. tsukatte, tsukai, tsukawa

Lesson 2

I 1. Kurokute ōkii kami no fukuro o wasuremashita. 2. Ushiro kara 2-bamme no sharyō ni wasuremashita. 3. Hai, (uma no moyō ga) arimasu. 4. Tōkyō Eki ni denwa o kakete, kikimashita. 5. Tōkyō eki (no jimushitsu) ni tori ni ikimasu.

II 1. no, to, o 2. kara, no 3. to, no, ni, ga 4. ni, kara, ni, ni

III 1. Donna 2. Doko 3. nani 4. Doko

IV 1. jōzu ni 2. Kuwashiku 3. hayaku 4. itakute 5. shizuka ni 6. furukute, yūmeina 7. ōkiku

V 1. Kono densha ni notte, Tōkyō Eki de orite kudasai. 2. Ano resutoran wa hirokute akarui desu. 3. Kono mise wa atarashikute kirei de suiteimasu. 4. Sore wa aoi sētā de, hana no moyō ga arimasu. 5. Watanabe-san wa atama ga yokute shinsetsu desu. 6. Chan-san wa majime de yoku hatarakimasu. 7. Jimu-shitsu ni denwa o kakete kikimasu.

Lesson 3

I 1. Mōshikomi o shi ni ikimashita. / Supōtsu kurabu o mi ni ikimashita. 2. Supōtsu kurabu no hito ga annai shimashita. 3. Hai, (ichinenjū oyogu koto ga) dekimasu. 4. Iie, mōshikomi o suru mae ni, naka o mimashita.

II 1. de, ni, o 2. demo, o, ga, ga, ni, ni 3. ni, to, o 4. ni, ni/e

III 1. iku 2. au 3. annai suru 4. oshieru 5. wasureru 6. miru 7. aru 8. kesu 9. tomeru 10. magaru 11. kuru 12. taberu 13. benkyō suru 14. denwa o kakeru 15. mottekuru

IV 1. miru 2. tabe, itte 3. Kuru, kakete 4. ai, iku 5. Dekakeru 6. tomeru, tomenai

Lesson 4

I 1. Katō-san to ikimasu. 2. Iie, itta koto ga arimasen. 3. Iie, Kimura-san wa (issho ni) ikimasen. 4. (Sapporo shinai no) torihiki-saki o mawattari, ginkō ni aisatsu ni ittari shimasu.

II 1. ni/e, ni 2. de, o 3. wa, ga, wa 4. de, o

III 1. nobotta 2. atta 3. tabeta 4. kiita 5. ita 6. otoshita 7. yonda 8. wasureta 9. mita 10. asonda 11. mawatta 12. setsumei shita 13. oyoida 14. naratta 15. dekaketa

IV 1. nobotta 2. atta 3. kiku 4. yon, kai 5. mi, at-

Lesson 5

I   1. Sērusu no hito ni moraimashita.   2. Yasuku narimashita.   3. Shisutemu-bu no hito desu. 4. Hai, kantan desu.

II   1. ni, no, o 2. ni 3. ga, ga, shi 4. no, no, ga 5. o, o 6. no, ni 7. shi, shi 8. ga, ni 9. ga

III 1. Dono 2. Itsu 3. Dare

IV 1. tsukuri, oshiete 2. todoite 3. kaette 4. kangaete, kimete 5. hanasu 6. utau

Lesson 6

I   1. Isha ni moraimashita.   2. 38-do netsu ga arimashita.   3. Iie, nakanaka yoku nari-masen deshita. 4. Hai, hayaku uchi ni kaerimasu.

II   1. ni, ga 2. ka, ni 3. ni, no 4. ga, ga, ni 5. ni

III 1. isoida 2. tabenai 3. naotte, yasunde 4. shiraseta 5. itte, tanonde 6. konde, ikanai

IV 1. taitei 2. nakanaka 3. mazu, sorekara 4. sakki

V   A. 2 B. 2

Lesson 7

I   1. Suzuki-san ga mukae ni ikimasu.   2. Rondon no jimusho ni ita hito desu.   3. Iie, shiri-masen. 4. Iie, (shashin de mita koto wa arimasu ga, atta koto wa) arimasen.

II   1. ga/no 2. ni 3. ni, de/o 4. o 5. de, ni 6. de, to, mo

III 1. dekiru 2. au 3. minakatta 4. wakaranai 5. konakatta 6. katta 7. tomatte iru 8. yaku 9. harau, haratte 10. eranda

IV 1. Sumisu-san no okusan desu. 2. Tanaka-san desu. 3. Tanaka-san desu. 4. Sumisu-san desu. 5. Tanaka-san to Sumisu-san desu.

Lesson 8

I   1. Kyōto e asobi ni ikitai to omotte imasu.   2. O-bon no koro wa kuni e kaeru hito ga ōzei imasu kara. 3. Kuruma de kaerimashita. 4. Katō-san ga iimashita. 5. Ikanai to omoimasu/Wakarimasen.

II   1. o, to 2. o, ni, to 3. shi, shi, to 4. ni, no, ni, to

III 1. dochira/dotchi 2. itsu 3. nan 4. dō 5. dōshite

IV 1. ikanakatta 2. konai 3. genki datta 4. nai 5. omoshiroku nakatta 6. okusan dewa nai 7. furanai 8. owatte inai

Lesson 9

I   1. Iie, gōkaku shimasen deshita.   2. Yobikō ni ikanakereba narimasen.   3. Iie, (waza-waza) yobikō made ikanakute mo ii desu. 4. Hai, genkin kakitome demo ii desu. 5. Genkin kakitome de okuru to omoimasu./Wakarimasen.

II   1. de 2. no, ni 3. de, de 4. kara 5. ni

III 1. Itsu 2. Ikura 3. Dōshite 4. dochira/dotchi 5. Nankagetsu

IV 1. oki 2. wasurete 3. yoma 4. kaka 5. harawa 6. katazukete, katazuke 7. tomete

Lesson 10

1. Tanaka-san ni tegami o dashimashita. 2. Iie, kazoku to ryokō o shite imasu. 3. Aso-san desu. 4. Iie, mae ni Tōkyō no ryōtei de mita koto ga arimasu. 5. Nōyaku no shiyō o yamete kara, kawa ga kirei ni natte, hotaru ga fueta to itte imashita. 6. Kumamoto to Nagasaki o kembutsushite kara, Tōkyō ni kaerimasu. 7. Nihon de tatta hitotsu no bōeki-kō de, Nihon no naka de ichiban kokusai-teki na machi deshita. 8. Buraun-san no okusan desu. 9. Raishū moku-yōbi ni Amerika honsha kara shachō ga kimasu kara. 10. Iie, ikanai to omoimasu.

Lesson 11

I   1. Ototoshi sotsugyō shimashita. 2. Mae ni tsutomete ita shōsha dewa semmon no shigoto ga dekimasendeshita kara. 3. Kompūtā saiensu desu. 4. Hai, sukina shigoto ga dekiru to omotte imasu. 5. Hai, shitte imashita.

II   1. ni 2. ni,o 3. ni,o 4. de 5. o, ga, to, kara

III 1. Naze/Dōshite 2. Dō/Dōka 3. dōyatte 4. Nani

IV 1. kaetta 2. shirasenakatta, yasumi datta 3. itte ita 4. tabenai, tabetakunai 5. dekakeru, nai 6. byōki na 7. itta, hanashite 8. oboeru

V   A. 3 B. 1 C. 2

Lesson 12

I   1. (Kyōto no) Miyako Ryokan ni denwa o shimashita. 2. Hai, heya ga aite iru to iimashita. 3. 10-pun gurai kakarimasu. 4. Zeikin to sābisuryō o harawanakereba narimasen. 5. Hai, tomaru mae ni uchikin o harawanakereba narimasen.

II   1. de 2. to 3. ni, made, ni 4. yori 5. de 6. to 7. no

III 1. itsu/nan-ji ni 2. nan 3. Dōshite/Naze

IV 1. itta 2. inai 3. okita, futte 4. dekinai, shite 5. umareta 6. kuru, shirasete 7. tabete ita, itaku 8. nai 9. Wakai, ryokō shita 10. Himana, yon, ason

V   A. 1. B. 3 C. 2

Lesson 13

I   1. Watanabe-san kara no purezento desu. 2. Hai, (Chan-san mo) moraimashita. 3. Barentain dē desu. 4. Iie, okusan ya gāru furendo ga taberu darō to iimashita.

II   1. e 2. de 3. kara 4. ni, kara 5. te

III 1. dōshite/naze 2. nani 3. donna 4. nan

IV 1. genkina 2. Sumisu-san no mono dewa nai 3. byōki 4. matsuri datta, nigiyaka datta 5. motte ikanakatta 6. tōranai 7. oita 8. nareru 9. ugokanakatta 10. yorokobu

V   A. 3 B. 1 C. 3

Lesson 14

I   1. (Sumō o minagara) yakitori o tabete imasu. 2. Sumisu-san desu. 3. Gyōji desu. 4. Kuroi kimono o kite, dohyō no mawari ni suwatte imasu.

II   1. ga, ga 2. ga, no 3. no, ga 4. o, no 5. no

III 1. dō iu 2. Itsu 3. Nani 4. dō iu

IV 1. kiite 2. kiki 3. tsuri o shite iru, tōku 4. dasu 5. naku 6. dekiru 7. fukuzatsu 8. shi, untensuru

V   1. demo 2. kanarazu 3. yappari 4. jitsuwa

Lesson 15

I   1. Watanabe-san kara azukarimashita. 2. Supōtsu kurabu de watashitai to omotte imasu. 3. Iie, Yamamoto-san ni au koto ga dekimasen deshita. 4. Hai, kono supōtsu kurabu no kaiin desu/Hai, sō desu.

II   1. ni, o 2. no, ni 3. o, ga, o, de, ni 4. ga, o, ni

III 1. dō 2. Itsu 3. Dare 4 Dōshite/Naze

IV 1. kau 2. sorot-, hajimete 3. not-, waruku 4. Hima, mi 5. Tsukawanai, suteta 6. Tsukare, yasunde 7. Isogashikunakat-, kattekite 8. mendō, tsukuru 9. ame dat- 10. iku, age 11. omoi, azukatte

Lesson 16

I   1. Shōrūmu no sekkei no zumen o okurimashita.   2. Raigetsu-chū ni dekiagaru to iimashita.   3. 6-ii made ni ikeba omote no iriguchi kara hairu koto ga dekimasu.   4. 10-ji ni naru to shimarimasu.

II   1. ka 2. ni, -ba, to 3. made 4. no, de

III 1. itsu 2. Doko 3. dō

IV 1. aeba 2. kakeba 3. shimareba 4. fureba 5. miereba 6. maniaeba 7. okurereba 8. kekkon sureba 9. mottekureba 10. nakereba 11. mezurashikereba 12. yokereba

V   1. yasume, naru 2. nobore, mieru 3. magaru 4. nomu, tanoshiku 5. yokere, ukagai 6. Renshū shinakere, jōzu ni 7. osu 8. Hoshikere, motteki 9. tanome mottekuru 10. Kangaere, kangaeru

VI 1. tashikani 2. dekireba 3. sassoku

Lesson 17

I   1. Tanaka-san ikka to soba o tabe ni ikimashita.   2. Nakamura-san desu.   3. Iie, aite imasen deshita.   4. Nihon-jin no dōryō ya tomodachi ya gyōsha kara moraimashita.   5. Hai, utsukushii to omotte imasu/Hai, sō omotte imasu.

II   1. Nanji 2. dō 3. Doko 4. itsu 5. Dare

III 1. katakute, tabe 2. fukuzatsu de, wakari 3. benri de, tsukai 4. isogashikute, kaku 5. kirei de

Lesson 18

I   1. Nihon no shūkan o shiranai node, sōdan shimashita.   2. Tanaka Keiko-san ni okurō to omotte imasu.   3. 5000 en desu.   4. Yokohama ni sunde imasu.

II   1. hanasō 2. todokeyō 3. aō 4. yameyō 5. tsukurō 6. arukō 7. wakareyō 8. haraō 9. shitsumon shiyō 10. matō 11. dēto shiyō 12. mottekoyō

III 1. shite, torō, todokanai 2 kau, kaō 3. ittekoyō, dashite 4. wakareta, awanai, ae 5. hajimeyō, oshiete

IV A. 2 B. 3 C. 2 D. 1

Lesson 19

I   1. Jibun de hon o minagara eraberu toshokan ga suki desu.   2. Hai, hirokute shizuka desu.   3. Tetsuzuki o sureba, kariraremasu.   4. Iie, kariraremasen ga, kopī o tanomemasu.

II   1. demo 2. shi, shi 3. e 4. kara, made, de 5. shika 6. kara, o

III 1. matemasu 2. kakemasen 3. hanasemasu 4. yakusoku dekimasu 5. iemasen 6. erabemasu 7. utaeru 8. aenai 9. wasurerarenai 10. kirareru 11. mottekorareru 12. yasumenai

IV 1. Dono gurai 2. itsu 3. Doko 4. Dōshite/Naze

V   1. tomeraremasen 2. arukemasen 3. yasumemasu 4. sotsugyō dekimasu 5. dekakeraremasu 6. tsukuremasu 7. tsukaemasu 8. taberaremasu 9. hairemasen 10. miraremasu

Lesson 20

1. Sakura desu. 2. Hanami o shimasu. 3. 3-gatsu no sue goro sakimasu. 4. Ume no hō ga saki ni sakimasu. 5. 5-gatsu no hajime goro sakimasu. 6. Nihon rettō o minami kara kita e sakura no hana ga saite iku yōsu o sen de arawashita mono desu. 7. Iie, kōyō zensen wa kita kara minami e susumimasu.

ROMANIZED TEXT

1. RUSH HOUR

Opening Dialogue

Chan: Kesa hajimete densha de kaisha ni kimashita. Totemo konde imashita. Sugokatta desu yo.

Sumisu: Demo densha no hō ga kuruma yori hayai desu yo. Michi ga konde imasu kara.

Chan: Sumisu-san wa mainichi nan de kaisha ni kimasu ka.

Sumisu: Watashi wa iki mo kaeri mo chikatetsu desu. Tōkyō no kōtsū kikan no naka de chikatetsu ga ichiban benri desu yo.

Chan: Chikatetsu wa asa mo yūgata mo konde imasu ka.

Sumisu: Ee. Demo asa no hō ga yūgata yori konde imasu. Asa no 8-ji han goro ga pīku desu kara, watashi wa maiasa 7-ji ni uchi o demasu.

Chan: Sono jikan wa suite imasu ka.

Sumisu: Ee, 7-ji goro wa 8-ji goro yori suite imasu. Watashi wa maiasa chikatetsu no naka de Nihongo o benkyō shite imasu.

Chan: Sō desu ka.

Key Sentences ————————————

1. Tōkyō to Ōsaka to dochira ga ōkii desu ka.
   Tōkyō no hō ga [Ōsaka yori] ōkii desu.
2. [Watashi wa] supōtsu no naka de tenisu ga ichiban suki desu.
3. Tōkyō wa Ōsaka yori ōkii desu.

EXERCISES ————————————

I. Make dialogues by changing the underlined parts as in the examples given.

   A. *ex.* Q: <u>Tori-niku</u> to <u>gyū-niku</u> to dochira/dotchi ga <u>yasui desu</u> ka.
   　　　 A: <u>Tori-niku</u> no hō ga <u>yasui desu</u>.
   　　　　1. fakkusu, tegami, benri desu　2. asa, yūgata, konde imasu　3. Katō-san, Suzuki-san, takusan o-sake o nomimasu.

   B. *ex.* Q: <u>Nomimono</u> wa <u>kōhī</u> to <u>kōcha</u> to dochira/dotchi ga <u>ii desu</u> ka.
   　　　 A: <u>Kōhī</u> no hō ga <u>ii desu</u>.
   　　　　1. ryōri, tempura, shabu-shabu　2. jikan, gozen, gogo　3. dezāto, aisukurīmu, kuda-mono　4. pātī, kin-yōbi, do-yōbi

   C. *ex.* Q: <u>Supōtsu</u> no naka de <u>nani</u> ga ichiban <u>suki desu</u> ka.
   　　　 A: <u>Tenisu</u> ga ichiban <u>suki desu</u>.
   　　　　1. shisha, doko, ōkii desu, Nyū Yōku　2. kono mittsu no e, dore, suki, mannaka no e　3. ichi-nichi, itsu, konde imasu, asa 8-ji goro　4. kaisha, dare, yoku hatarakimasu, shachō

II. Practice the following pattern by changing the underlined parts as in the example given.
   ex. <u>Chikyū</u> wa <u>tsuki</u> yori <u>ōkii desu</u>.

1. hikōki, Shinkansen, hayai desu   2. Amerika, Nihon, hiroi desu   3. Sapporo, Tōkyō, kita ni arimasu   4. Chan-san, Jonson-san, yoku benkyō shimasu

Short Dialogue ————————————————————————————————

A: Kōhī to kōcha to dochira ga suki desu ka.
B: Dochira mo suki desu.

Quiz ————————————————————————————————————

I. Read this lesson's Opening Dialogue and answer the following questions.
1. Chikatetsu wa asa to yūgata to dochira ga konde imasu ka.   2. Dōshite densha no hō ga kuruma yori hayai desu ka.   3. Sumisu-san wa maiasa nan-ji ni uchi o dete, nan de kaisha ni ikimasu ka.   4. Chikatetsu wa asa no nan-ji goro ga ichiban konde imasu ka.   5. Sumisu-san wa chikatetsu no naka de Nihongo o benkyō shite imasu ka.

II. Put the appropriate particles or inflections in the parentheses.
1. Shinkansen wa kuruma (   ) hayai desu.   2. Kesa 7-ji (   ) uchi (   ) dete, chikatetsu (   ) kaisha (   ) kimashita.   3. Densha wa asa mo yūgata (   ) konde imasu.   4. Kochira no hō (   ) shizuka desu kara, koko (   ) hanashi o shimashō.   5. Kaisha (   ) naka (   ) dare ga ichiban yoku hatarakimasu ka.

III. Complete the questions so that they fit the answers.
1. Chikatetsu to basu to (   ) ga benri desu ka./Chikatetsu no hō ga benri desu.   2. Chikatetsu wa (   ) ga ichiban konde imasu ka./Asa ga ichiban konde imasu.   3. (   ) ga ichiban tenisu ga jōzu desu ka./Rinda-san ga ichiban jōzu desu.   4. Kudamono no naka de (   ) ga ichiban suki desu ka./Mikan ga ichiban suki desu.   5. Nomimono wa kōhī to kōcha to (   ) ga ii desu ka./Kōhī o onegaishimasu.

IV. Complete the sentences with the appropriate form of the verbs indicated.
1. Sono resutoran wa (   ) imasu ka. (sukimasu)   2. Kuruma de (   ) naide kudasai.(kimasu)   3. Chichi wa ima Nyūyōku de (   ) imasu. (hatarakimasu)   4. Michi ga (   ) imasukara, takushī o (   ), (   ) mashō. (komimasu, orimasu, arukimasu)   5. Kono kuruma o (   ) mo ii desu ka. (tsukaimasu)/Watashi ga (   ) masu kara, (   ) naide kudasai. (tsukaimasu, tsukaimasu)

V. Answer the following questions.
1. Anata wa supōtsu no naka de nani ga ichiban suki desu ka.   2. Go-kazoku no naka de donata ga ichiban yoku hatarakimasu ka.   3. Sushi to sukiyaki to dochira ga suki desu ka.   4. Anata no machi no kōtsū kikan no naka de nani ga ichiban benri desu ka.

2. LOST AND FOUND

Opening Dialogue

Chan: Sumimasen.
Ekiin: Hai, nan deshō ka.
Chan: Wasuremono o shimashita.
Ekiin: Dono densha desu ka.
Chan: 20-pun gurai mae no densha de, ushiro kara 2-bamme no sharyō desu.
Ekiin: Nani o wasuremashita ka.
Chan: Kurokute ōkii kami no fukuro desu.
Ekiin: Nakami wa nan desu ka. Kuwashiku setsumei shite kudasai.
Chan: Mafurā to sētā desu. Mafurā wa ūru de, kuro to shiro no shima no moyō desu. Sētā wa akakute, mune ni uma no moyō ga arimasu.

Ekiin: Ima Tōkyō eki ni denwa o kakete kikimasu kara, chotto matte kudasai.
Chan: Sumimasen.

Ekiin: Arimashita. Tōkyō eki no jimu-shitsu ni todoite imasu kara, kyō-jū ni tori ni itte kudasai.

Key Sentences

1. Hayashi-san wa Nihon-jin de ABC no buchō desu.
2. Koko wa hirokute shizukana kōen desu.
3. Kanji o kirei ni kaite kudasai.
4. Resutoran ni hiru-gohan o tabe ni ikimashita.

EXERCISES

Make dialogues by changing the underlined parts as in the examples given.

A. *ex.* Q: Donna tokoro desu ka.
   A-1: Hirokute shizukana tokoro desu.
   A-2: Shizukade kireina tokoro desu.
      1. tokoro, tōi, fubenna tokoro   2. tokoro, nigiyaka, omoshiroi tokoro   3. mondai, yasashii, omoshiroi mondai   4. mondai, fukuzatsu, muzukashii mondai

B. *ex.* Q: Yamada-san wa donna hito desu ka.
   A-1: Wakakute genkina hito desu.
   A-2: Majimede akarui hito desu.
      1. akarui, se ga takai   2. atama ga ii, shinsetsu   3. tenisu ga jōzu, genki   4. shizuka, kami ga nagai

C. *ex.* Q: Suzuki-san wa michi o setsumei shimashita ka.
   A-1: Ee, kuwashiku setsumei shimashita.
   A-2: Ee, shinsetsu ni setsumei shimashita.
      1. mō okimashita, asa hayai   2. tsukimashita, yūbe osoi   3. shigoto o shiteimasu, shizuka   4. chizu o kakimashita, jōzu

D. *ex.* A: Doko ni ikimasu ka.
   B: Ginza ni ikimasu.
   A: Nani o shi ni ikimasu ka.
   B: Eiga o mi ni ikimasu.
      1. Kyōto, furui o-tera o mimasu   2. depāto, kutsu o kaimasu   3. Katō-san no heya, tegami o todokemasu   4. kōen, shashin o torimasu

E. *ex.* Q: Raishū nani o shimasuka.
   A: Depāto ni kagu o kai ni ikimasu.
      1. Kyōto, sakura o mimasu, ikimasu   2. daigaku, Itō kyōju ni aimasu, ikimasu   3. ryōshin no uchi, yasumimasu, kaerimasu   4. mata koko, hanashi o shimasu, kimasu

Short Dialogues

1. Howaito: O-kane o hiroimashita.
   Keikan: Doko ni ochite imashita ka.
   Howaito: Sūpā no mae no michi ni ochite imashita.
   Keikan: Nan-ji goro hiroimashita ka.
   Howaito: 15-fun gurai mae desu.

2. Suzuki: Saifu o otoshimashita.
   Keikan: Donna saifu desu ka.
   Suzuki: Ōkii kawa no saifu desu.
   Keikan: Naka ni nani ga haitte imasu ka.
   Suzuki: Genkin ga 30,000-en gurai to meishi desu.

I. Read this lesson's Opening Dialogue and answer the following questions.

1. Chan-san wa donna fukuro o wasuremashita ka. 2. Ushiro kara nan-bamme no sharyō ni wasuremashita ka. 3. Akai sētā wa mune ni uma no moyō ga arimasu ka. 4. Ekiin wa Chan-san no setsumei o kiite, nani o shimashita ka. 5. Chan-san wa wasuremono o doko ni tori ni ikimasu ka.

II. Put the appropriate particles in the parentheses.

1. Chan-san wa ūru (　) mafurā (　) akai sētā (　) wasuremashita. 2. Mae (　) 3-bamme (　) sharyō desu. 3. Kuro (　) shiro (　) shima no sētā de, mune (　) chīsai kasa no moyō (　) arimasu. 4. Jimu-shitsu (　) todoite imasu (　), kyō-jū (　) tori (　) kite kudasai.

III. Complete the questions so that they fit the answers.

1. Saifu o otoshimashita./(　) saifu desu ka./Kuroi kawa no saifu desu. 2. (　) de otoshimashita ka./ Kōen de otoshimashita. 3. Naka ni (　) ga haitte imasu ka./Okane to meishi ga haitte imasu. 4. (　) ni mafurā o kai ni ikimasu ka./Depāto ni kai ni ikimasu.

IV. Complete the sentences with the appropriate form of the words in parentheses.

1. Buraun-san wa (　) kanji o kakimasu. (jōzu) 2. (　) setsumei shite kudasai. (kuwashii) 3. Kyō wa (　) kaisha ni ikimasu. (hayai) 4. Atama ga (　), netsu ga arimasu. (itai) 5. Kodomo wa (　) hon o yonde imasu. (shizuka) 6. Rekishi ga (　), (　) machi desu. (furui, yūmei) 7. Kanji o (　) kaite kudasai. (ōkii)

V. Connect the following sentences using the appropriate verb or adjective form.

1. Kono densha ni norimasu. Tōkyō eki de orite kudasai. 2. Ano resutoran wa hiroi desu. Akarui desu. 3. Kono mise wa atarashii desu. Kirei desu. Suite imasu. 4. Sore wa aoi sētā desu. Hana no moyō ga arimasu. 5. Watanabe-san wa atama ga ii desu. Shinsetsu desu. 6. Chan-san wa majime desu. Yoku hatarakimasu. 7. Jimu-shitsu ni denwa o kakemasu. Kikimasu.

VI. Answer the following questions.

1. Anata no otō-san wa donna hito desu ka. 2. Anata no machi wa donna tokoro desu ka. 3. Kōen ni nani o shi ni ikimasu ka. 4. Anata wa ashita doko ni ikimasu ka. Nani o shi ni ikimasu ka.

3. THE HEALTH CLUB

Opening Dialogue

Buraun: Anō, chotto onegaishimasu. Kochira no supōtsu kurabu ni mōshikomi o suru mae ni, naka o miru koto ga dekimasu ka.

Kurabu
no hito: Hai. Shitsurei desu ga, dochira-sama deshō ka.

Buraun: Buraun desu.

Kurabu: Buraun-sama desu ka. Dewa go-annai shimashō.

Buraun: Totemo hirokute kireina tokoro desu ne.

Kurabu: Kochira no tenisu-kōto niwa kōchi ga imasu kara, kōchi ni narau koto mo dekimasu. Kochira wa onsui pūru de, ichinen-jū oyogu koto ga dekimasu.

Buraun: Kochira dewa minna iroirona mashīn o tsukatte imasu ne.

Kurabu: Ee. Dore demo o-sukina mono o tsukau koto ga dekimasu ga, hajimeru mae ni insutorakutā ni go-sōdan kudasai.

Buraun: Ee, sō shimasu.

Kurabu: Ikaga deshita ka.

Buraun: Totemo ki ni irimashita. Mōshikomi-sho ga arimasu ka.

Kurabu: Hai. Kochira ni o-namae to go-jūsho o o-kaki kudasai.

Key Sentences

1. Kono pūru dewa ichinen-jū oyogu koto ga dekimasu.
2. Maiasa kaisha ni iku mae ni, shimbun o yomimasu.

EXERCISES

I. Verbs: Study the examples, convert into the dictionary form, and memorize.
   A. Regular I: *ex.* ikimasu → iku; nomimasu → nomu; shinimasu → shinu; asobimasu → asobu; hanashimasu → hanasu; machimasu → matsu; iimasu → iu; arimasu → aru

   1. aimasu 2. otoshimasu 3. urimasu 4. kikimasu 5. suimasu 6. hairimasu
   7. isogimasu 8. yobimasu 9. moraimasu 10. todokimasu 11. naoshimasu
   12. mochimasu 13. wakarimasu 14. nugimasu 15. kaimasu 16. torimasu
   17. sukimasu 18. komimasu 19. okurimasu 20. hatarakimasu

   B. Regular II: *ex.* tabemasu → taberu; mimasu → miru

   1. misemasu 2. okimasu (get up) 3. orimasu 4. agemasu 5. kangaemasu
   6. ochimasu 7. imasu 8. tomemasu 9. shimemasu

   C. Irregular: *ex.* kimasu → kuru; shimasu → suru

   1. kekkon shimasu 2. mottekimasu 3. annai shimasu 4. setsumei shimasu

II. Make dialogues by changing the underlined parts as in the examples given.
   A. *ex.* Q: <u>Kono pūru de ima oyogu</u> koto ga dekimasu ka.
      Aa: Hai, dekimasu.
      An: Iie, dekimasen.

      1. kono heya o tsukaimasu 2. kyō-jū ni todokemasu 3. Tōkyō eki ni tori ni ikimasu
      4. O-taku no chikaku ni kuruma o tomemasu

   B. *ex.* Q: [Anata wa] <u>Nihon-go o hanasu</u> koto ga dekimasu ka.
      A: Ee, dekimasu ga, amari jōzu dewa arimasen.

      1. Nihon no uta o utaimasu 2. kanji o kakimasu 3. kuruma o unten shimasu
      4. Nihon ryōri o tsukurimasu

   C. *ex.* Q: Itsu <u>ha o migakimasu</u> ka.
      A: <u>Neru mae ni</u> <u>ha o migakimasu</u>.

      1. sake o nomimasu, nemasu 2. te o araimasu, shokuji o shimasu 3. shawā o abimasu, dekakemasu 4. kaerimasu, michi ga komimasu

   D. *ex.* Q: <u>Mōshikomi o suru</u> mae ni <u>naka o miru</u> koto ga dekimasu ka.
      A: Ee, dekimasu yo.

      1. hajimemasu, insutorakutā ni sōdan shimasu 2. Ōsaka ni ikimasu, Hayashi-san ni aimasu. 3. Shinkansen ni norimasu, o-bentō o kaimasu

Short Dialogue

Howaito: Ikebana no kurasu o mi ni itte mo ii deshō ka.
Nakamura: Ee. Kondo issho ni ikimashō.
Howaito: Itsu kurasu ga arimasu ka.
Nakamura: 1-shūkan ni 2-kai, ka, moku ni arimasu.

Quiz

I. Read this lesson's Opening Dialogue and answer the following questions.
   1. Buraun-san wa supōtsu kurabu ni nani o shi ni ikimashita ka. 2. Dare ga Buraun-san o annai shimashita ka. 3. Kono supōtsu kurabu dewa ichinen-jū pūru de oyogu koto ga dekimasu ka. 4. Buraun-san wa supōtsu kurabu no naka o miru mae ni, mōshikomi o shimashita ka.

II. Put the appropriate particles in the parentheses.
1. Watashi wa America (　) Nihon-jin no sensei (　) Nihon-go (　) naraimashita.　2. Dore (　) o-sukina mono (　) tsukau koto (　)dekimasu (　), hajimeru mae (　) insutorakutā (　) go-sōdan kudasai.　3. Kono kami (　) o-namae (　) go-jūsho (　) o-kaki kudasai. 4. 1-kagetsu (　) 1-kai Ōsaka (　) ikimasu.

III. Convert the following verbs into the dictionary form.
1. ikimasu　2. aimasu　3. annai shimasu　4. oshiemasu　5. wasuremasu　6. mimasu　7. arimasu　8. keshimasu　9. tomemasu　10. magarimasu　11. kimasu　12. tabemasu　13. benkyō shimasu　14. denwa o kakemasu　15. mottekimasu

IV. Complete the sentences with the appropriate form of the verbs indicated.
1. Koko de suraido o (　) koto ga dekimasu ka. (mimasu)　2. Hiru-gohan o (　) ni (　) mo ii deshō ka. (tabemasu, ikimasu)　3. (　) mae ni denwa o (　) kudasai. (kimasu, kakemasu) 4. Ashita Tanaka-san ni (　) ni (　) koto ga dekimasu ka. (aimasu, ikimasu)　5. (　) mae ni shawā o abimasu. (dekakemasu)　6. Koko ni kuruma o (　) koto ga dekimasu ka. (tomemasu)/Iie, koko wa chūsha kinshi desu kara, kuruma o (　) de kudasai. (tomemasu)

V. Answer the following questions.
1. Anata wa oyogu koto ga dekimasu ka.　2. Anata wa kanji o yomu koto ga dekimasu ka. 3. Anata wa mainichi neru mae ni ha o migakimasu ka.　4. Anata wa asa-gohan o taberu mae ni nani o shimasu ka.　5. 1-shūkan ni nan-kai Nihon-go no jugyō ga arimasu ka.

4. A BUSINESS TRIP

Opening Dialogue

Kimura: Buraun-san, shutchō desu ka.
Buraun: Ee, ashita kara Sapporo shiten ni shutchō desu. Kimura-san wa Hokkaidō ni itta koto ga arimasu ka.
Kimura: Ee, gakusei no koro ichi-do Hokkaidō e ryokō ni itta koto ga arimasu. Kuruma de Hokkaidō o mawarimashita.
Buraun: Sapporo wa donna tokoro desu ka.
Kimura: Sapporo no machi wa nigiyaka de, nakanaka omoshiroi desu yo. Buraun-san wa hajimete desu ka.
Buraun: Ee, shashin o mita koto wa arimasu ga, itta koto wa arimasen.
Kimura: Hitori de shutchō desu ka.
Buraun: Katō-san mo issho desu. Futari de Sapporo shinai no torihikisaki o mawattari, ginkō ni aisatsu ni ittari shimasu.
Kimura: Katō-san wa sunde ita koto ga arimasu kara, Sapporo o yoku shitte imasu yo.
Buraun: Sō desu ka. Anshin shimashita.

Key Sentences

1. Watanabe-san wa Honkon ni itta koto ga arimasu.
2. Nichi-yōbi wa hon o yondari, ongaku o kiitari shimasu.

EXERCISES

I. Verbs: Study the examples, convert into -te and -ta forms, and memorize.
A. Regular I
ex. kakimasu → kaku → kaite → kaita; yomimasu → yomu → yonde → yonda; aimasu → au → atte → atta; owarimasu → owaru → owatte → owatta
1. naraimasu　2. oyogimasu　3. shinimasu　4. asobimasu　5. tachimasu　6. noborimasu

7. okimasu (put) 8. migakimasu 9. mochimasu 10. tobimasu 11. nugimasu 12. otoshi-masu 13. hatarakimasu 14. kaimasu 15. ikimasu 16. hanashimasu 17. suwari-masu 18. naoshimasu 19. arukimasu 20. yasumimasu

B. Regular II and Irregular

ex. Reg. II: tsukemasu → tsukeru → tsukete → tsuketa; okimasu (get up) → okiru → okite → okita
Irreg: kimasu → kuru → kite → kita; shimasu → suru → shite → shita

1. kimasu (wear) 2. kangaemasu 3. ochimasu 4. nemasu 5. anshin shimasu 6. wasure-masu 7. misemasu 8. dekakemasu 9. mottekimasu 10. sunde imasu 11. renshū shi-masu 12. utte imasu 13. demasu 14. hajimemasu 15. orimasu

II. Make dialogues by changing the underlined parts as in the examples given.

A. *ex.* Q: Sumisu-san wa mae ni <u>Kyūshū ni itta</u> koto ga arimasu ka.
    A: Hai, ichi-do <u>itta</u> koto ga arimasu.
      1. Hayashi-san no okusan ni aimashita. 2. Fuji-san ni noborimashita 3. Shinkansen ni norimashita 4. Yōroppa o mawarimashita

B. *ex.* Q: Sumisu-san wa <u>yūfō o mita</u> koto ga arimasu ka.
    A: Iie, zannen desu ga, <u>mita</u> koto ga arimasen.
      1. Afurika e ikimashita 2. jūdō o naraimashita 3. daitōryō ni aimashita

C. *ex.* Q: <u>Sapporo no machi</u> o shitte imasu ka.
    A: <u>Shashin o mita</u> koto wa arimasu ga, <u>itta</u> koto wa arimasen.
      1. Jonson-san, namae o kikimashita, aimashita 2. tōfu, sūpā de mimashita, tabe-mashita 3. Shēkusupia no Hamuretto, eiga o mimashita, hon o yomimashita

D. *ex.* Q: Shūmatsu ni nani o shimashita ka.
    A: <u>Kaimono ni ittari</u>, <u>tomodachi ni attari</u> shimashita.
      1. tenisu o suru, sampo o suru 2. bideo o miru, kodomo to asobu 3. tegami o kaku, zasshi o yomu 4. tomodachi to hanasu, rekōdo o kiku 5. umi de oyogu, tsuri o suru

Short Dialogues

1. A: Kyōto ni itta koto ga arimasu ka.
   B: Hai, arimasu.
   A: Itsu ikimashita ka.
   B: Kyonen no 8-gatsu ni ikimashita.
2. Tanaka: Yoku Ōsaka ni shutchō shimasu ne.
   Katō: Ee. 1-kagetsu ni 5-kai gurai Tōkyō to Ōsaka o ittari kitari shite imasu.

Quiz

I. Read this lesson's Opening Dialogue and answer the following questions.
   1. Buraun-san wa dare to Hokkaidō ni ikimasu ka. 2. Buraun-san wa Hokkaidō ni itta koto ga arimasu ka. 3. Kimura-san mo issho ni Sapporo shiten ni ikimasu ka. 4. Buraun-san wa Sapporo e itte nani o shimasu ka.

II. Put the appropriate particles in the parentheses.
   1. Yōroppa ( ) ryokō ( ) itta koto ga arimasu. 2. Kuruma ( ) Hokkaidō ( ) mawari-mashita. 3. Sushi o tabeta koto ( ) arimasu ( ), tsukutta koto ( ) arimasen. 4. Sumisu-san wa hitori ( ) kōen ( ) aruite imasu.

III. Convert the following verbs into the -ta form.
   1. noborimasu 2. aimasu 3. tabemasu 4. kikimasu 5. imasu 6. otoshimasu 7. yomi-masu 8. wasuremasu 9. mimasu 10. asobimasu 11. mawarimasu 12. setsumei shimasu 13. oyogimasu 14. naraimasu 15. dekakemasu

IV. Complete the sentences with the appropriate form of the verbs indicated.
   1. Fuji-san ni ( ) koto ga arimasu ka. (noborimasu) 2. Pātī de ichi-do Sumisu-san no oku-

san ni ( ) koto ga arimasu. (aimasu)   3. Kono rajio de gaikoku no nyūsu o ( ) koto ga dekimasu ka. (kikimasu)   4. Kinō no ban hon o ( ) dari, tegami o ( ) tari shimashita. (yomimasu, kakimasu)   5. Shūmatsu ni eiga o ( ) tari, tomodachi ni ( ) tari shimasu. (mimasu, aimasu)

V. Answer the following questions.
1. Anata wa kabuki o mita koto ga arimasu ka.   2. Anata wa Chūgoku ni itta koto ga arimasu ka.   3. Anata wa Shinkansen ni notta koto ga arimasu ka.   4. Anata wa Nichi-yōbi ni nani o shimasu ka. (Use . . . tari . . . tari shimasu.)   5. Anata wa kyonen no natsu-yasumi ni nani o shimashita ka. (Use . . . tari . . . tari shimashita.)

5. A NEW WORD PROCESSOR

Opening Dialogue

Hayashi: Wāpuro no katarogu ga takusan arimasu ne.
Chan: Ee, kinō sērusu no hito ga kuremashita. Uchi no ka no wāpuro ga furuku narimashita kara atarashii no ni kaetai desu.
Hayashi: Hō, dore ni shimasu ka.
Chan: A-sha no 45S ga yasuku narimashita ga, mada kimete imasen.
Hayashi: Tokorode, shisutemu-bu no Ogawa-san ni hanashimashita ka?
Chan: Iie, mada hanashite imasen.
Hayashi: Chotto mazui desu ne. Mazu Ogawa-san to sōdan shite kara kimete kudasai.
Chan: Wakarimashita.

Suzuki: A, atarashii wāpuro ga kimashita ne.
Chang: Ee. Kore wa tsukai-kata ga kantan desu shi, gamen mo ōkii desu shi, ii desu yo.
Suzuki: Boku mo konna wāpuro ga hoshii nā.

Key Sentences

1. Fuyu mono no kōto ya sētā ga yasuku narimashita.
2. Tanjōbi no purezento wa sētā ni shimasu.
3. Te o aratte kara sandoitchi o tabemashō.
4. Mō kimemashita ka./Iie, mada kimete imasen.
5. Oishii desu shi, kirei desu shi, ano resutoran wa ii desu yo.

EXERCISES

I. Make dialogues by changing the underlined parts as in the examples given.
A. *ex.* Q: Dō narimashita ka.
    A: <u>Yoku</u> narimashita./<u>Genki</u> ni narimashita.
       1. ōkii   2. nigiyaka   3. tsumaranai   4. kurai   5. akarui   6. shizuka   7. fukuzatsu
       8. benri   9. jōzu   10. kantan   11. tsuyoi   12. kirei

B. *ex.* 1. Q: <u>Kurai desu</u>. <u>Denki o tsukemashita</u>. Dō narimashita ka.
       A: <u>Akaruku</u> narimashita.
   ex. 2. Q: <u>Heya ga kitanai desu</u>. <u>Sōji o shimashita</u>. Dō narimashita ka.
       A: <u>Kirei</u> ni narimashita.
          1. samui desu, hītā o tsukemashita, atatakai   2. kaze o hikimashita, kusuri o nomi-mashita, ii   3. Pātī ga owarimashita, shizuka   4. Nihon-go o isshōkenmei benkyō shimashita, jōzu

II. Practice the following pattern by changing the underlined parts as in the example given.

　　ex. Watashi wa <u>pianisuto ni naritai</u> desu.
　　　1. yūmei, naritai　2. atama ga ii, naritai　3. uchū hikōshi, naritakatta　4. byōki, naritaku nai
　　　5. bimbō, naritaku nakatta

III. Make dialogues by changing the underlined parts as in the examples given.

　A. *ex.* Q:　<u>Nani o tabemashō ka</u>.
　　　　　A:　<u>Tempura</u> ni shimashō.
　　　　　　1. doko de, o-cha o nomimasu, ano kissaten　2. nan de, ikimasu, takushī　3. nani o,
　　　　　　tsukurimasu, tōfu no misoshiru　4. doko de, suraido o mimasu, 2-kai no kaigi-shitsu
　　　　　　5. dare ni, agemasu, hansamuna hito

　B. *ex.* Q:　Itsu kara <u>Nihon-go no benkyō</u> o hajimemashita ka.
　　　　　A:　<u>Nihon ni kite</u> kara hajimemashita.
　　　　　　1. gorufu, kekkon suru　2. tenisu, supōtsu kurabu ni hairu　3. kono shigoto, daigaku
　　　　　　o deru　4. unten, 30-sai ni naru

　C. *ex.* Q:　Itsumo <u>sōdan shite</u> kara <u>kimemasu</u> ka.
　　　　　A:　Hai, taitei <u>sōdan shite</u> kara <u>kimemasu</u>.
　　　　　　1. katarogu o miru, kau　2. kōhī o nomu, shigoto o hajimeru　3. yoyaku o suru,
　　　　　　resutoran ni iku　4. denwa o kakeru, tomodachi o tazuneru

　D. *ex.* Q:　Mō <u>kono hon o yomimashita</u> ka.
　　　　　A:　Iie, mada <u>yonde</u> imasen.
　　　　　　1. kippu o kau　2. denwa o kakeru　3. nimotsu ga todoku　4. tegami o dasu

　E. *ex.* Q:　<u>Atarashii uchi</u> wa dō desu ka.
　　　　　A:　<u>Hiroi</u> desu shi, <u>kirei</u> desu shi, <u>subarashii desu</u>.
　　　　　　1. atarashii kamera, karui, benri, ki ni itte imasu　2. ima no shigoto, isogashii,
　　　　　　zangyō ga arimasu, taihen desu　3. ima no apāto, semai, urusai, hikkoshitai desu

　F. *ex.* Sumisu:　　Tanaka-san wa Katō-san ni nani o agemashita ka.
　　　　　Watanabe:　<u>Nekutai</u> o agemashita.
　　　　　Sumisu:　　Anata niwa.
　　　　　Watanabe:　Watashi niwa <u>kabin</u> o kuremashita.
　　　　　　1. Kyōto no okashi, Kyōto no yakimono　2. shima no shatsu, kinu no sukāfu
　　　　　　3. eiga no kippu, kabuki no kippu　4. uisukī, hanataba

Short Dialogues ────────────────────────────────────

1. A:　Nan ni shimasu ka.
　 B:　Boku wa kōhī ni shimasu.
　 C:　Sō desu nē. Watashi wa jūsu ga ii desu.
　 D:　Watashi wa aisukurīmu desu.

2. A:　Kono shorui wa dō shimashō ka.
　 B:　Kopī shite kara sugu okutte kudasai.

3. A:　Konban eiga ni ikimasen ka.
　 B:　Ashita shiken ga arimasu shi, zannen desuga . . .

4. A:　O-kosan wa o-ikutsu desu ka.
　 B:　Raigetsu yattsu ni narimasu.

I. Read this lesson's Opening Dialogue and answer the following questions.
1. Chan-san wa dare ni wāpuro no katarogu o moraimashita ka.
2. A-sha no wāpuro no 45S wa takaku narimashita ka, yasuku narimashita ka.
3. Ogawa-san wa nani bu no hito desuka.
4. Atarashii wāpuro wa tsukai-kata ga kantan desu ka.

II. Put the appropriate particles in the parentheses.
1. Tomodachi ga watashi (　) shima (　) shatsu (　) kuremashita.　2. Dezāto wa aisukurīmu (　) shimashō.　3. Kyō atarashī wāpuro (　) kimashita. Tsukai-kata (　) kantan desu (　), totemo benri desu.　4. Torihikisaki (　) jūsho wa watashi yori hisho (　) hō (　) yoku shitte imasu.　5. Hirugohan (　) tabete kara, kōen (　) sampo shimashō.　6. Watashi wa kodomo (　) koro pianisuto (　) naritakatta desu.　7. Michi ga konde imasu (　), hito ga ōi desu (　), ikitaku nai desu.　8. Terebi (　) furuku narimashita kara, atarashii no (　) kaemasu.　9. Atarashii kamera (　) hoshii nā.

III. Complete the questions so that they fit the answers.
1. (　) wāpuro o kaimasu ka./45S ni shimasu.　2. (　) denwa o kakemasu ka./Uchi ni kaette kara kakemasu.　3. (　) ni sōdan shimashita ka./Shisutemu-bu no Ogawa-san ni sōdan shimashita.

IV. Complete the sentences with the appropriate form of the verbs indicated.
1. Miso shiru no (　) kata o (　) kudasai. (tsukuru, oshieru)　2. Wasuremono wa mada jimu-shitsu ni (　) imasen. (todoku)　3. Mainichi uchi ni (　) kara, 1-jikan gurai Nihongo o benkyō shimasu. (kaeru)　4. Yoku (　) kara (　) kudasai. (kangaeru, kimeru)　5. Kodomo ni (　) mae ni, kanai to yoku sōdan shimasu. (hanasu)　6. Nihon no uta o (　) koto ga dekimasu ka. (utau)

V. Answer the following questions.
1. Anata wa Nihon-go ga jōzu ni narimashita ka.　2. Anata wa mō kesa no shimbun o yomimashita ka.　3. Asa shokuji o suru mae ni ha o migakimasu ka, shokuji o shitekara ha o migakimasu ka.　4. Anata no sukina ryōri no tsukuri-kata o kantan ni setsumei shite kudasai. (Use . . . te kara, . . . mae ni.)

6. A PALE FACE

Opening Dialogue

Katō:　Kaoiro ga yoku arimasen ne. Kaze desu ka.

Chan:　Ee, ototoi isha ni itte kusuri o moratte kimashita ga, nakanaka yoku narimasen. Kesa wa netsu ga 38-do arimashita.

Katō:　Soreja, hayaku uchi ni kaette yasunda hō ga ii desu yo.

Chan:　Demo, kono purojekuto ga hajimatta bakari desu kara . . .

Katō:　Muri o shinai hō ga ii desu yo. Raishū wa motto isogashiku narimasu kara, ima no uchi ni naoshita hō ga ii desu yo.

Chan:　Soredewa mōshiwake arimasen ga, Suzuki-kun ka Kimura-kun ni ato o yoku tanonde kara, kaerimasu.

Katō:　Suzuki-kun niwa sakki betsu no yōji o tanomimashita kara, Kimura-kun no hō ga ii desu yo.

Chan:　Wakarimashita. Dewa, o-saki ni shitsurei shimasu.

Katō:　O-daiji ni.

Key Sentences —————————————————————————————

1. Sugu keisatsu ni denwa shita hō ga ii desu.
2. Ano mise e itte, tabako o katte kimasu.

EXERCISES —————————————————————————————

I. Review: Study the examples again and convert the verbs into the -nai form.
   A. Regular I: iku → ikanai; isogu → isoganai; nomu → nomanai; shinu → shinanai; asobu → asobanai; hanasu → hanasanai; matsu → matanai; narau → narawanai; naoru → naoranai; aru → nai
      1. oyogu 2. tsukuru 3. migaku 4. morau 5. otosu 6. motsu 7. sumu 8. kakaru 9. yobu 10. hirou 11. kesu 12. tsukau

   B. Regular II and Irregular: shimeru → shimenai; oriru → orinai; kuru → konai; suru → shinai
      1. hajimeru 2. dekiru 3. iru 4. kimeru 5. mottekuru 6. setsumei suru 7. denwa suru 8. wasureru

II. Make dialogues by changing the underlined parts as in the examples given.
   A. ex. A: <u>Takushī de ikimashō</u> ka.
         B: Iie, <u>chikatetsu de itta</u> hō ga ii desu yo.
            1. Suzuki-san ni kiku, Katō-san ni 2. gogo denwa suru, gozen-chū ni 3. ashita shorui o okuru, ima sugu

   B. ex. Q: <u>Iku mae ni denwa shita</u> hō ga ii desu ka.
         A: Ee, sono hō ga ii desu yo.
            1. neru mae ni kusuri o nomu 2. funabin de okuru 3. sutōbu o kesu 4. Tanaka-san ni shiraseru

   C. ex. Q: Dō shimashō ka.
         A: <u>Hayashi-san ni hanashita</u> hō ga ii desu.
            1. mado o shimeru 2. Tanaka-san ni iu 3. sugu dekakeru 4. basu de iku 5. Hayashi-san ni sōdan suru 6. (o)sake o mottekuru

   D. ex. Q: <u>Ima denwa shi</u>te mo ii desu ka.
         A: <u>Mō osoi desu</u> kara, <u>shinai</u> hō ga ii desu yo.
            1. tabako o suu, kenkō ni yoku nai desu 2. koko ni kuruma o tomeru, kōsaten ni chikai desu 3. sake o nomu, mada byōki ga naotte imasen 4. mō happyō suru, mada buchō ni hanashite imasen

   E. ex. Q: <u>Dare</u> ga ii desu ka.
         A: <u>Suzuki-kun</u> ka <u>Kimura-kun</u> ga ii desu.
            1. nani, Chūka ryōri, Furansu ryōri 2. itsu, getsu-yō, ka-yō 3. doko, Ginza, Shinjuku 4. ikura no, 1,500 en, 2,000 en no

   F. ex. Q: Dochira e.
         A: <u>Isha ni itte</u>, <u>kusuri o moratte</u> kimasu.
            1. hon-ya ni iku, shūkanshi o kau 2. shokudō e iku, shokuji o suru 3. uchi e kaeru, hiru-gohan o taberu 4. ginkō ni iku, o-kane o harau 5. yūbinkyoku e iku, tegami o dasu

Short Dialogues —————————————————————————————

1. A: O-kaze desu ka.
   B: Ee. Taishita koto wa arimasen ga, seki ga tomarimasen.
   A: Sore wa ikemasen ne.

2. A: O-kaze wa ikaga desuka.
   B: Okagesama de daibu yoku narimashita.
   A: Sorewa yokatta desu ne.

3. Suzuki: Moshi-moshi, Suzuki desu. Kore kara byōin ni yotte kara, kaisha ni ikimasu. Sumi-
masen ga, sukoshi osoku narimasu.
   Katō: Dōka shimashita ka.
   Suzuki: Ee, chotto ashi ni kega o shimashita.

Quiz

I. Read this lesson's Opening Dialogue and answer the following questions.
1. Chan-san wa dare ni kusuri o moraimashita ka. 2. Chan-san wa kesa nan-do netsu ga arimashita ka. 3. Isha ni itte kara, Chan-san no kaze wa sugu yoku narimashita ka. 4. Chan-
san wa kyō hayaku uchi ni kaerimasu ka.

II. Put the appropriate particles in the parentheses.
1. Ima no uchi (　) naoshita hō (　) ii desu yo. 2. Katō-san wa getsu-yōbi (　) ka-yōbi (　)
Nihon ni kaerimasu. 3. [Watashi wa] sakki Suzuki-kun (　) betsu (　) yōji o tanomimashita.
4. Kaze (　) naorimasen. Mōshiwake arimasen (　), uchi (　) kaette mo ii desu ka. 5. Dewa,
o-saki (　) shitsurei shimasu.

III. Complete the sentences with the appropriate form of the verbs indicated.
1. Jikan ga arimasen kara, (　) hō ga ii desu yo. (isogu) 2. Kono sakana wa furui desu kara,
(　) hō ga ii desu yo. (taberu) 3. Mada kaze ga (　) imasen kara, uchi de (　) mo iidesu ka.
(naoru, yasumu) 4. Hayaku kazoku ni (　) hō ga ii desu yo. (shiraseru) 5. Watanabe-san no
heya ni (　), taipu o (　) kimasu. (iku, tanomu) 6. Kyō wa michi ga (　) imasu kara,
kuruma de (　) hō ga ii desu yo. (komu, iku)

IV. Circle the correct words in the parentheses.
1. Watashi wa (amari, taitei) densha no naka de shimbun o yomimasu. 2. Takushī o matte
imasu ga, (nakanaka, yukkuri) kimasen. 3. (Hajimete, mazu) Hayashi-san ni shirasete (soredewa, sorekara) minna ni shirasete kudasai. 4. Suzuki-kun wa (sakki, mō sugu) kimashita.

V. Choose a sentence to make a suggestion appropriate to the situation described.
  A. Your friend is embarrassed about having left his bag on the train.
    1. Densha o orite, eki-in ni hanashite kimasu. 2. Eki no jimu-shitsu ni itte, eki-in ni
hanashita hō ga ii desu. 3. Densha ni notte, eki-in ni hanashita koto ga arimasu.
  B. Your friend, despite having a fever, is drinking sake.
    1. O-sake o takusan nonda hō ga ii desu yo. 2. Hayaku neta hō ga ii desu yo. 3. Sukoshi
o-sake ga nomitai desu.

7. MR. JOHNSON'S ARRIVAL

Opening Dialogue

Katō: Ashita wa Jonson-san ga Nihon ni kuru hi desu ne.

Suzuki: Ee, sō desu.

Katō: Dare ka Narita Kūkō made mukae ni itte kuremasen ka.

Suzuki: Watashi ga ikimasu. Jikan ga arimasu kara.

Katō: Kesa tanonda shigoto wa kyō-jū ni owarimasu ka.

Suzuki: Hai, dekimasu.

Katō: Ja, onegaishimasu. Tokorode, Jonson-san o shitte imasu ka.

Suzuki: Rondon no jimusho ni ita hito desu ne.

Katō: Ee.

Suzuki: Shashin de mita koto ga arimasu.

Katō: Narita Kūkō ni tsuku jikan wa 14-ji 50-pun desu. Hikōki wa hayaku tsuku koto mo arimasu kara, hayame ni chūshoku o sumasete shuppatsu shite kudasai.

Suzuki: Hai. Jonson-san no tomaru hoteru wa doko desu ka.
Katō: Watanabe-san ga shitte imasu kara, Watanabe-san ni kiite kudasai.
Suzuki: Hai.

Key Sentences

1. Sumisu-san wa ABC de hataraite iru bengoshi desu.
2. Kyūshū wa atatakai tokoro desu ga, fuyu wa yuki ga furu koto mo arimasu.

EXERCISES

I. Noun-modifying patterns: Memorize the following sentences.
   A. 1. Kore wa <u>ashita okuru</u> nimotsu desu.   2. Tanaka-san wa <u>asoko de hon o yonde iru</u> hito desu.   3. Kore wa <u>haha ga kaita</u> e desu.   4. <u>Raishū narau</u> ressun wa 8-ka desu.   5. <u>Kinō kita</u> hito wa Yamada-san desu.   6. <u>Watashi ga tomatta</u> hoteru wa subarashikatta desu.
   B. 1. <u>Ginkō ni iku</u> jikan ga arimasen.   2. <u>Shiranai</u> hito ga tazunete kimashita.   3. <u>Kitte o utte iru</u> tokoro o shitte imasu ka.   4. <u>Rondon kara kita</u> tomodachi ni aimashita.   5. <u>Kinō konakatta</u> hito wa te o agete kudasai.
   C. 1. Kare wa <u>atama ga ii</u> hito desu.   2. Are wa <u>chichi ga sukina</u> e desu.   3. <u>Kami ga nagai</u> hito wa Howaito-san desu.   4. <u>Furansu-go ga jōzuna</u> hito o shitte imasu ka.

II. Make dialogues by changing the underlined parts as in the examples given.
   A. *ex.* Q: Kore wa nan desu ka.
             A: <u>E o kaku</u> dōgu desu.
                 1. yude-tamago o kirimasu   2. toire o sōji shimasu   3. omoi nimotsu o hakobimasu   4. kēki o yakimasu
   B. *ex.* Q: Sumimasen, <u>Tōkyō e iku</u> basu wa dore desu ka.
             A: Ano eki no mae ni tomatte iru basu desu.
                 1. 10-ji ni demasu   2. Ginza o tōrimasu   3. Ōsaka kara kimashita   4. Ōsaka o 10-ji ni shuppatsu shimashita
   C. *ex.* Q: <u>Shimbun o utte iru</u> tokoro o shitte imasu ka.
             A: Sa, chotto wakarimasen.
                 1. tenisu ga dekimasu   2. Tanaka-san ga tsutomete imasu   3. yasukute oishii desu   4. oishikute amari takaku nai desu
   D. *ex.* Q: Mainichi isogashii desu ka.
             A: Ee, <u>tegami o kaku</u> jikan mo arimasen.
                 1. shimbun o yomimasu   2. kodomo to asobimasu   3. tomodachi to o-shaberi shimasu   4. fūfu-genka o shimasu
   E. *ex.* Q: <u>Pātī ni kita</u> hito wa dare desu ka.
             A: Kimura-san desu.
                 1. kyonen kekkon shimashita   2. kasa o wasuremashita   3. mada kite imasen   4. mada mōshikonde imasen   5. kaigi ni shusseki shimasen deshita
   F. *ex.* A: Ano hito wa dare desu ka.
             B: Dono hito desu ka.
             A: <u>Megane o kakete iru</u> hito desu.
             B: Aa, ano <u>megane o kakete iru</u> hito desu ka. Are wa Howaito-san desu.
                 1. seki o shite imasu   2. ima tachimashita   3. ōkii koe de waratte imasu   4. kami ga mijikai desu   5. se ga takai desu

III. Practice the following pattern by changing the underlined parts as in the example given.
   ex. <u>Dare</u> ka <u>kimashita ka.</u>
         1. nani, itte kudasai   2. doko, ikitai desu ne   3. itsu, asobi ni kite kudasai   4. dare, yobimashō ka

IV. Make dialogues by changing the underlined parts as in the example given.
    ex. Q: Itsumo <u>hikōki de ikimasu</u> ka.
        A: Ee, taitei <u>hikōki de ikimasu</u> ga, <u>Shinkansen de iku</u> koto mo arimasu.
            ' 1. jibun de nekutai o erabimasu, tsuma ga erabimasu   2. asa-gohan o tabemasu, tabe-masen   3. yakusoku no jikan o mamorimasu, tama ni osokunarimasu

Short Dialogues ───────────────────────────────

1. Kachō: Dare ka chotto te o kashite kudasai.
   Watanabe: Nan deshō ka.
   Kachō: '   Kono shiryō o katazukete kuremasen ka.
   Watanabe: Hai, wakarimashita.

2. A: Sūpā ni ikimasu ga, nani ka katte kimashō ka.
   B: Jūsu o katte kite kudasai.
   A: Donna jūsu ga ii desu ka.
   B: Amari amakunai no o onegaishimasu.

Quiz ──────────────────────────────────────

   I. Read this lesson's Opening Dialogue and answer the following questions.
     1. Dare ga Jonson-san o kūkō made mukae ni ikimasu ka.   2. Jonson-san wa doko no jimusho ni ita hito desu ka.   3. Katō-san wa Jonson-san no tomaru hoteru o shitte imasu ka.   4. Suzuki-san wa Jonson-san ni atta koto ga arimasu ka.

   II. Put the appropriate particles in the parentheses.
     1. Kore wa watashi ( ) kaita e desu.   2. Eki ( ) tsuku jikan wa nan-ji desu ka.   3. Watashi wa Jonson-san ( ) atta koto wa arimasen ga, shashin ( ) mita koto wa arimasu.   4. Hayaku shigoto ( ) sumasete, uchi ni kaerimasu.   5. Kūkō made kuruma ( ) mukae ( ) ikimasu.   6. Taitei hitori ( ) ryokō shimasu ga, tomodachi ( ) issho ni iku koto ( ) arimasu.

   III. Complete the sentences with the appropriate form of the verbs indicated.
     1. Supein-go ga ( ) hito wa dare desu ka. (dekimasu)   2. [Anata ga] Yamada-san ni ( ) hi wa itsu desu ka. (aimasu)   3. Kinō suraido o ( ) hito wa kyō mite kudasai. (mimasen deshita)   4. Eigo ga ( ) hito niwa Nihon-go de setsumei shimashō. (wakarimasen)   5. Kinō ( ) hito ni kono tegami o okutte kudasai. (kimasen deshita)   6. Kyō ( ) mono no naka de kore ga ichiban takakatta desu. (kaimashita)   7. Jonson-san ga ( ) hoteru o shitte imasu ka. (tomatte imasu)   8. Kore wa pan o ( ) dōgu desu. (yakimasu)   9. Kyō o-kane o ( ) hito wa kochira de ( ) kudasai. (haraimasu, haraimasu)   10. Kore wa tsuma ga ( ) nekutai desu. (erabimashita)

   IV. Look at the picture and answer the questions.
     1. Isu ni suwatte iru hito wa dare desu ka.   2. Megane o kakete iru hito wa dare desu ka.   3. Sētā o kite iru hito wa dare desu ka.   4. Kasa o motte iru hito wa dare desu ka.   5. Tatte iru hito wa dare desu ka.

   V. Answer the following questions.
     1. Anata ga sunde iru tokoro wa doko desu ka. Soko wa donna machi desu ka.   2. Anata no suki na ryōri wa nan desu ka.   3. Anata ga mita eiga no naka de nani ga ichiban omoshi-rokatta desu ka.   4. Ima made ryokō ni itta tokoro no naka de doko ga ichiban sub-arashikatta desu ka.

8. THE O-BON FESTIVAL

Opening Dialogue

Chan: 8-gatsu no 10-ka goro Kyōto e asobi ni ikitai to omoimasu ga, Shinkansen to hikōki to dochira ga benri desu ka.

Katō: Shinkansen no hō ga benri da to omoimasu yo. Demo Shinkansen no shitei-ken wa mō nai to omoimasu. Hikōki no kippu mo tabun urikire deshō.

Chan: Dōshite desu ka.

Katō: 8-gatsu no naka goro wa O-Bon de, kuni e kaeru hito ga ōzei imasu. 10-ka goro kara, kono kisei rasshu ga hajimarimasu kara, ryokō wa yameta hō ga ii desu yo.

Chan: Suzuki-kun mo 10-ka ni Kyōto no ie ni kaeru to kikimashita ga . . .

Katō: Ee, kare wa 1-kagetsu mae ni kippu o katta to itte imashita.

Chan: Sō desu ka. Ja, Kyōto made kuruma de donogurai kakarimasu ka.

Katō: 10-jikan ijō kakaru to omoimasu yo. Suzuki-kun wa kyonen wa kuruma de ikimashita ga, sugoi jūtai datta to itte imashita.

Chan: Nihon wa hito mo kuruma mo ōi desu kara ne. Rasshu no nai tokoro e ikitai desu nē.

Katō: Rasshu no nai tokoro ga arimasu yo.

Chan: Doko desu ka.

Katō: Doko da to omoimasu ka. O-Bon no koro no Tōkyō desu yo.

Chan: Naruhodo.

Key Sentences

1. Ashita wa suto desu kara, densha mo basu mo ugokanai to omoimasu.
2. Kimura-san wa Sapporo o shitte iru to itte imashita.
3. Ashita wa tabun ame deshō.

EXERCISES

Make dialogues by changing the underlined parts as in the examples given.

A. *ex.* Q: Atarashii purojekuto o dō omoimasu ka.
   A: Taihen da to omoimasu.
      1. muzukashii desu   2. omoshiroi desu   3. tsumaranai desu   4. taikutsu desu   5. risāchi ga hitsuyō desu   6. muzukashii shigoto desu

B. *ex.* Q: Tanaka-san wa kimasu ka.
   Aa: Hai, kuru to omoimasu.
   An: Iie, konai to omoimasu.
      1. kono shigoto wa ashita made ni dekimasu   2. nimotsu wa kyō-jū ni tsukimasu
      3. shushō wa kono nyūsu o mō shitte imasu   4. Tanaka-san wa kodomo ga arimasu

C. *ex.* Q: Tanaka-san wa mō kaerimashita ka.
   Aa: Ee, mo kaetta to omoimasu.
   An: Iie, mada kaette inai to omoimasu.
      1. shūkai wa mō hajimarimashita   2. daijin wa kono nyūsu o mō kikimashita   3. Tanaka-san wa o-kyaku-san ni mō aimashita   4. kenkyū shiryō wa mō matomarimashita

D. *ex.* Q: Natsuyasumi ni nani o shimasu ka.
   A: Hokkaidō e asobi ni ikitai to omoimasu.
      1. hon o takusan yomu   2. suiei o narau   3. niwa no teire o suru   4. Kyūshū no tomodachi o tazuneru

E. *ex.* Q: Ano hito no jimusho no aru tokoro o shitte imasu ka.
   A: Keisatsu no tonari da to omoimasu.

1. o-kuni, atatakai tokoro desu   2. sotsugyō shita daigaku, Nihon no daigaku dewa arimasen   3. shiken no kekka, amari yoku arimasen deshita   4. wakai koro no shigoto,
kangofu-san deshita

F. *ex.* Q: <u>Suzuki</u>-san wa nan to itte imashita ka.
 A: <u>Suzuki</u>-san wa <u>kinō wa doko nimo ikanakatta</u> to itte imashita.
  1. Rinda, sakura wa totemo kirei deshita   2. Buraun, ano myūjikaru wa amari omoshiroku arimasen deshita   3. Sumisu, ashita kaigi ni detakunai desu   4. Yamada, amari
supōtsu o suru jikan ga arimasen

G. *ex.* Q: <u>Ashita no tenki</u> wa dō deshō ka.
 A: Tabun <u>ame</u> deshō ne.
  1. ano mise, takai desu   2. ano shibai, omoshirokunai desu   3. nichi-yōbi no kōen,
nigiyaka desu   4. kore, tekitō ja nai desu   5. ashita no tenki, yuki ga furimasu   6. Tanaka-
san, kuru koto ga dekimasen   7. Chan-san no kaze, yoku narimashita

Short Dialogues

1. Buraun: Shinkansen no zaseki shitei-ken wa doko de utte imasu ka.
 Tsūkōnin: Asoko no midori no madoguchi de utte imasu.

 Buraun: Kyōto made otona 2-mai, kodomo 1-mai onegaishimasu.

2. A: 10-ji 30-pun-hatsu Nagano-iki no tokkyū wa nan-bansen kara demasu ka.
 B: 8-bansen desu.

Quiz

I. Read this lesson's Opening Dialogue and answer the following questions.
 1. Chan-san wa 8-gatsu no 10-ka goro doko e asobi ni ikitai to omotte imasu ka.   2. O-Bon
no koro wa dōshite hayaku hikōki ya Shinkansen no kippu ga urikire ni narimasu ka.
3. Suzuki-san wa kyonen kuruma de kuni e kaerimashita ka, Shinkansen de kaerimashita ka.
4. O-Bon no koro no Tōkyō niwa rasshu ga nai to dare ga iimashita ka.   5. Anata wa Chan-
san ga 8-gatsu 10-ka ni Kyōto e iku to omoimasu ka, ikanai to omoimasu ka.

II. Put the appropriate particles in the parentheses.
 1. 8-ban no basu wa Ginza ( ) tōru ( ) omoimasu.   2. Sumisu-san wa sono shigoto ( )
Ogawa-san ( ) tanonda ( ) itte imashita.   3. Netsu ga arimasu ( ), nodo mo itai desu
( ), kaze da ( ) omoimasu.   4. Kare mo 8-gatsu 10-ka ( ) Ōsaka ( ) uchi ( ) kaeru ( )
itte imashita.

III. Complete the questions so that they fit the answers. (Use a question word.)
 1. Suzuki-kun to Kimura-kun to ( ) ga wakai desu ka./Kimura-kun no hō ga wakai to
omoimasu.   2. Rinda-san wa ( ) Nihon ni kuru deshō ka./Tabun rainen kuru deshō.
3. Kare wa ( ) to itte imashita ka./Ashita wa tsugō ga warui to itte imashita.   4. Kono e o
( ) omoimasu ka./Nakanaka subarashii to omoimasu.   5. Anata wa ( ) ikimasen ka./ Atsui
desu shi, hito ga ōi desu shi, ikitaku arimasen.

IV. Complete the sentences with the appropriate form of the verbs indicated.
 1. Kare wa kinō taishikan e ( ) to omoimasu. (ikimasen deshita)   2. Suzuki-san wa ashita
( ) to itte imashita. (kimasen)   3. Katō-san wa ( ) to dare ga itte imashita ka. (genki
deshita)   4. Kare wa Jonson-san ni atta koto ga ( ) to itte imashita. (arimasen)   5. Kinō no
eiga wa ( ) to minna itte imashita (omoshirokunakatta desu)   6. Ano hito wa Buraun-san
no ( ) to omoimasu. (okusan dewa arimasen)   7. Ashita wa tabun ame ga ( ) deshō. (furi-
masen)   8. Kaigi wa mada ( ) to omoimasu. (owatte imasen)

V. Answer the following questions.
1. Ashita wa ii tenki deshō ka.   2. Anata wa itsu kara Nihon-go o naratte imasu ka.
3. Nihon-go no benkyō wa omoshiroi to omoimasu ka.   4. Anata wa natsu-yasumi ni dokoka ryokō ni ikimasu ka.

9. PREP SCHOOL

Opening Dialogue

Keiko:	Ara, Jonson-san.
Jonson:	A, Keiko-san. O-dekake desu ka.
Keiko:	Ee, korekara dekakenakereba narimasen.
Jonson:	Ima sugu desu ka.
Keiko:	Gomennasai. Kyō-jū ni yobikō no mōshikomi o shinakereba narimasen kara.
Jonson:	Yobikō?
Keiko:	Ee. Ichiban hairitakatta daigaku ni gōkaku dekimasen deshita kara, rainen mata shiken o ukemasu.
Jonson:	Sō desu ka. Ja, itterasshai.
Keiko:	Ittemairimasu.
Keiko:	Mōshikomi no shorui wa kore de ii desu ka. Kore, nyūgaku-kin to 3-kagetsu-bun no jugyō-ryō desu. Sorekara samā kōsu mo mōshikomitai to omoimasu ga, ato de yūbin de mōshikonde wa ikemasen ka.
Madoguchi no hito:	Yūbin demo ii desu yo. Shiharai mo wazawaza koko made konakute mo ii desu yo. Ginkō ni furikonde kudasai.
Keiko:	Genkin kakitome demo ii desu ka.
Madōguchi no hito:	Hai, dochira demo kekkō desu.

Key Sentences

1. Sugu dekakenakereba narimasen.
2. Ashita gakkō ni ikanakute mo ii desu.
3. Yūbin de okutte wa ikemasen ka.
4. Mōshikomi wa yūbin demo ii desu.

EXERCISES

I. Verbs: Review the examples and convert the verbs into the plain negative form.
  ex. Reg. I: hajimaru → hajimaranai
  Reg. II: iru → inai
  Irreg: kuru → konai; suru → shinai
  1. matomaru 2. kaeru (change) 3. tanomu 4. shiraseru 5. harau 6. dasu 7. tomaru
  8. yobu 9. deru 10. tazuneru 11. shuppatsu suru 12. furu 13. kiru (cut) 14. mukaeru
  15. yaku 16. sōji suru 17. yameru 18. katte kuru 19. warau 20. katazukeru 21. erabu
  22. mamoru 23. sotsugyō suru 24. kawaru 25. iru (need) 26. kasu 27. moratte kuru
II. Practice the following pattern by changing the underlined part as in the example given.
  ex. Anō chotto taishikan ni ikanakereba narimasen kara, o-sakini shitsurei shimasu.
  1. byōin e iku 2. 6-ji no tokkyū ni noru 3. biza o morai ni iku 4. ginkō de okane o orosu

III. Make dialogues by changing the underlined parts as in the examples given.
  A. *ex.* Q: Ima o-kane o harawanakereba narimasen ka.
    Aa: Hai, onegaishimasu.

An: Iie, <u>ima hara</u>wanakute mo ii desu.
1. watashi mo kuru   2. ashita made ni suru   3. ima mōshikomu   4. pasupōto o miseru   5. kyō-jū ni shiraseru

B. *ex.* Q: <u>Namae o kaka</u>nakute mo ii desu ka.
Aa: Hai, <u>kaka</u>nakute mo ii desu.
An: Sumimasen ga, <u>kaite</u> kudasai.
1. Sumisu-san o mukae ni iku   2. minasan ni setsumei suru   3. hisho ni shiraseru
4. kopī o tanomu

C. *ex.* <u>Byōin de tabako o sutte</u> wa ikemasen.
1. kurasu ni okureru   2. michi ni gomi o suteru   3. kōsaten ni kuruma o tomeru

D. *ex.* Q: <u>Kono heya o tsukatte</u> wa ikemasen ka.
Aa: Dōzo, <u>tsukatte</u> mo ii desu yo.
An: Sumimasen ga, <u>tsukawa</u>naide kudasai.
1. koko de tabako o suu   2. namae o happyō suru   3. kūrā o tsukeru   4. kuruma de kuru   5. niwa de shashin o toru

E. *ex.* Q: Ima <u>hanko</u> ga arimasen. <u>Sain</u> demo ii desu ka.
A: Hai, <u>sain</u> demo kekkō desu.
1. pen, empitsu   2. jikan, ato   3. hima, nichi-yōbi   4. genkin, kādo

Short Dialogues

1. Otoko no hito: Kangofu-san, o-sake o sukoshi nonde wa ikemasen ka.
   Kangofu: Mada dame desu yo. Mō sukoshi gaman shite kudasai.

2. Yamada: Tadaima.
   Watanabe: Okaeri nasai. Nakayama-san wa imashita ka.
   Yamada: Ee, atte shorui o watashite kimashita.

Quiz

I. Read this lesson's Opening Dialogue and answer the following questions.
1. Keiko-san wa ichiban hairitakatta daigaku ni gōkaku shimashita ka.   2. Keiko-san wa doko ni ikanakereba narimasen ka.   3. Keiko-san wa samā kōsu no mōshikomi ni mata yobikō made ikanakereba narimasen ka.   4. Samā kōsu no shiharai wa genkin kakitome demo ii desu ka.   5. Keiko-san wa samā kōsu no shiharai o ginkō ni furikomu deshō ka, genkin kakitome de okuru deshō ka.

II. Put the appropriate particles in the parentheses.
1. Tōfu o chiisaku kirimashita ga, kore (   ) ii desu ka.   2. Uchi (   ) musuko wa kotoshi daigaku (   ) gōkaku shimashita.   3. Empitsu (   ) kaite wa ikemasen ka./Pen (   ) onegai shimasu.   4. Yoku kangaete (   ), kimemasu.   5. Jugyō-ryō o ginkō (   ) furikomimasu.

III. Complete the questions so that they fit the answers.
1. (   ) made ni mōshikomanakereba narimasen ka./Raishū-chū ni mōshikonde kudasai.
2. (   ) harawanakereba narimasen ka./5,000-en desu.   3. (   ) taishikan e ikanakereba narimasen ka./Pasupōto ga hitsuyō desu kara.   4. Kōhī to kōcha to (   ) ga ii desu ka./ Dochira demo kekkō desu.   5. (   )-bun no jugyō-ryō desu ka./6-kagetsu-bun desu.

IV. Complete the sentences with the appropriate form of the verbs indicated.
1. Ashita no asa 5-ji ni (   ) nakereba narimasen. (okiru)   2. Shorui o (   ) wa ikemasen yo. (wasureru)   3. Kono hon o kyō-jū ni (   ) nakereba narimasen. (yomu)   4. Kanji de (   ) nakereba narimasen ka. (kaku)   5. Itsu made ni o-kane o (   ) nakereba narimasen ka. (harau)   6. Koko o (   ) mo ii desu ka. (katazukeru)/Mada tsukaimasu kara, (   ) nakute mo

ii desu. (katazukeru)   7. Koko wa chūsha kinshi desu kara, kuruma o (   ) wa ikemasen. (tomeru)

V. Answer the following questions.
1. Nihon ni iru gaikoku no hito wa minna Nihon-go o benkyō shinakereba narimasen ka.
2. Kōsaten ni kuruma o tomete mo ii desu ka.   3. Depāto dewa genkin de harawanakute mo ii desu ka.   4. Anata wa ashita nani o shinakereba narimasen ka.

10. LETTER FROM KYŪSHŪ

Tanaka Ichirō-sama
Gobusata shite imasu ga, o-genki desu ka.
Watashi wa ima kazoku to issho ni Kyūshū ni kite imasu. Kinō, mae kara ikitakatta Aso-san ni ikimashita. Subarashii nagame deshita.
Watashi-tachi ga tomatte iru ryokan no niwa de yūbe hotaru o mimashita. Mae ni Tōkyō no ryōtei de kago no naka no hotaru o mita koto wa arimasu ga, shizen no hotaru wa hajimete desu. Hotaru o minagara ryokan no shujin to hanashimashita. Shujin wa nōyaku no shiyō o yamete kara, kawa ga kirei ni natte, hotaru ga fueta to itte imashita.
Asatte, watashi-tachi wa koko o dete, Kumamoto shinai o kembutsu shita ato, Nagasaki e ikimasu. Nagasaki wa Edo jidai no Nihon no tatta hitotsu no bōeki-kō de, sono koro wa Nihon no naka de ichiban kokusai tekina machi datta to zasshi de yonda koto ga arimasu. Kanai wa Nihon no rekishi ni kyōmi ga arimasu kara, totemo tanoshimi ni shite imasu.
Minami Kyūshū nimo ikitai to omoimasu ga, raishū moku-yōbi ni Amerika honsha kara shachō ga kimasu kara, sore made ni Tōkyō ni kaeranakereba narimasen.
Oku-sama nimo dōzo yoroshiku o-tsutae kudasai.
7-gatsu 30-nichi

Jon Buraun

EXERCISES ──────────

Make dialogues by changing the underlined parts as in the example given.
ex. Q: Katō-san wa nani o shite imasu ka.
   A: Rajio o kikinagara shimbun o yonde imasu.
   1. kōhī o nomimasu, shigoto o shimasu   2. tabako o suimasu, tegami o kakimasu   3. hanashi o shimasu, basu o machimasu   4. iyahōn de ongaku o kikimasu, benkyō shimasu

Quiz ──────────

Read this lesson's letter and answer the following questions.
1. Buraun-san wa dare ni tegami o dashimashita ka.   2. Buraun-san wa hitori de ryokō o shite imasu ka.   3. Buraun-san ga mae kara ikitakatta tokoro wa doko desu ka.   4. Buraun-san wa Aso no ryokan de hajimete hotaru o mimashita ka.   5. Ryokan no shujin wa dōshite hotaru ga fueta to itte imashita ka.   6. Buraun-san wa doko o kembutsu shite kara Tōkyō ni kaerimasu ka.   7. Edo jidai no Nagasaki wa donna machi deshita ka.   8. Nihon no rekishi ni kyōmi ga aru hito wa dare desu ka.   9. Buraun-san wa dōshite raishū moku-yōbi made ni Tōkyō ni kaeranakereba narimasen ka.   10. Buraun-san wa minami Kyūshū nimo iku to omoimasu ka.

11. JOB INTERVIEW

Opening Dialogue

Hayashi: Nakamura-san wa ototoshi daigaku o sotsugyō shita n desu ka.

Nakamura: Hai. Sotsugyō shite kara shōsha ni tsutomete imashita.
Hayashi: Naze yameta n desu ka.
Nakamura: Watashi no semmon no shigoto ga dekimasen deshita kara, omoshirokunakatta n desu.
Hayashi: Dōshite kono kaisha o eranda n desu ka.
Nakamura: Kochira dewa kompyūtā o tsukau shigoto ga ōi to kiita kara desu. Watashi wa daigaku de kompyūtā saiensu o benkyō shite imashita. Kono kaisha dewa watashi no sukina shigoto ga dekiru to omotta n desu.
Hayashi: Kaisha ni haitte kara 1-kagetsu kenshū shinakereba naranai koto o shitte imasu ka.
Nakamura: Ee, shitte imasu.
Hayashi: Soreni gaikoku ni shutchō suru koto mo ōi desu yo.
Nakamura: Hai, daijōbu desu.
Hayashi: Sō desu ka. Dewa, kekka wa ato de renraku shimasu.

Key Sentences

1. Ashita kaigi ga arimasu kara, ima shiryō o kopī shite iru n desu.
2. Buraun-san ga Kyūshū e ryokō ni itta koto o shitte imasu ka.

EXERCISES

I. Practice the following patterns.
  A. *ex.* ikimasu → iku n desu/ikanai n desu/itta n desu/ikanakatta n desu
      1. oyogimasu 2. yomimasu 3. asobimasu 4. keshimasu 5. machimasu 6. aimasu
      7. iimasu 8. dekimasu 9. arimasu 10. imasu 11. sunde imasu 12. agemasu 13. mimasu
      14. kimasu 15. sōdan shimasu
  B. *ex.* yasui desu → yasui n desu/yasukunai n desu/yasukatta n desu/yasukunakatta n desu
      1. oishii desu 2. abunai desu 3. muzukashii desu 4. takai desu 5. tsumetai desu
      6. atama ga ii desu 7. tsugō ga warui desu 8. mizu ga hoshii desu 9. yasumitai desu
  C. *ex.* suki desu → sukina n desu/suki dewa nai n desu/suki datta n desu/suki dewa nakatta n desu
      1. jōzu desu 2. hima desu 3. benri desu 4. anzen desu 5. kaigi desu 6. shigoto desu 7. byōki desu 8. kenshū desu

II. Make dialogues by changing the underlined parts as in the examples given.
  A. *ex.* Q: Ashita gorufu ni ikimasen ka.
      A: Zannen desu ga, chotto ashita wa <u>isogashii</u> n desu.
        1. kaigi ga arimasu 2. byōin ni ikanakereba narimasen 3. tomodachi to au yakusoku o shimashita 4. kuni kara haha ga kite imasu 5. ashita kara shutchō desu 6. kanai ga byōki desu 7. gorufu wa amari suki dewa arimasen 8. chotto karada no guai ga yoku nai desu
  B. *ex.* Q: Kinō pātī ni kimasen deshita ne.
      A: Ee <u>isogashikatta</u> n desu.
        1. chotto yōji ga arimashita 2. shōtaijō o moraimasen deshita 3. kyū ni tsugō ga waruku narimashita 4. Pātī ga aru koto o shirimasen deshita 5. Kodomo ga byōki deshita
  C. *ex.* Q: <u>Ashita sutoraiki ga aru</u> koto o shitte imasu ka.
      A: Sō desu ka. Shirimasen deshita.
        1. Nakamura-san ga kon'yaku shimashita 2. ashita konakute mo ii desu 3. Jōnzu-san ga kochira ni kite imasu 4. Suzuki-san no okā-sama ga nakunarimashita
  D. *ex.* A: Itsu kara <u>jogingu</u> o hajimemashita ka.
      B: <u>Kekkon shite</u> kara hajimemashita.
      A: Dōshite yameta n desu ka.
      B: <u>Kega o shita</u> kara desu.
        1. piano, shōgakkō ni hairimasu, kyōmi ga nakunarimashita 2. eikaiwa, daigaku o

sotsugyō shimasu, isogashiku narimashita   3. yamanobori, kaisha ni hairimasu, kodomo ga umaremashita

Short Dialogues

1. Sumisu: Kono chikaku no chizu ga hoshii n desu ga, arimasuka.
   Hoteru no hito: Hai, dōzo.
   Sumisu: Dōmo.

2. Kyaku: Tokei o kaitai n desu ga, nan-kai desu ka.
   Depāto no ten'in: Tokei uriba wa 6-kai de gozaimasu.

3. Sumisu: Ōkii baggu desu ne.
   Buraun: Ee, tenisu no dōgu ga haitte iru n desu. Tenisu o hajimeta n desu yo.
   Sumisu: Sōdesu ka. Supōtsu wa karada ni ii desu ne.

4. Suzuki: Ashita uchi de bābekyū pātī o yaru n desu ga, kimasen ka.
   Kimura: Zannen desu ga, ashita wa chotto yakusoku ga aru n desu.
   Suzuki: Sō desu ka. Ja tsugi no kikai niwa zehi.

Quiz

I. Read this lesson's Opening Dialogue and answer the following questions.
   1. Nakamura-san wa itsu daigaku o sotsugyō shimashita ka.
   2. Nakamura-san wa naze mae ni tsutomete ita shōsha o yamemashita ka.
   3. Nakamura-san no semmon wa nan desu ka.
   4. Nakamura-san wa ABC dewa sukina shigoto ga dekiru to omotte imasu ka.
   5. Ikkagetsu kenshū shinakereba naranai koto o Nakamura-san wa shitte imashita ka.

II. Put the appropriate particles in the parentheses.
   1. Nakamura-san wa shōsha (　) tsutomete imashita. 2. Kare wa 1965-nen (　) daigaku (　) sotsugyō shimashita. 3. Kare ga bengoshi (　) natta koto (　) shitte imasu ka. 4. Kekka wa ato (　) renraku shimasu. 5. Dōshite kono kaisha (　) eranda n desu ka./Kochira dewa Nihon-go o tsukau shigoto (　) ōi (　) kiita (　) desu.

III. Complete the questions so that they fit the answers.
   1. (　) pātī ni konakatta n desu ka./Atama ga itakatta n desu. 2. (　) shita n desu ka./ Te ni kega o shita n desu. 3. Kono kompyūtā wa (　) tsukau n desu ka./Chotto fukuzatsu desu kara, Watanabe-san ni kiite kudasai. 4. (　) o mite iru n desu ka./Kyōto de totta shashin o mite iru n desu.

IV. Complete the sentences with the appropriate form of the words indicated.
   1. Suzuki-san wa imasen ka. Mō uchi ni (　) n desu ka./Ee, 30-pun gurai mae ni kaerimashita yo. (kaerimashita) 2. Ogawa-san ni (　) n desu ka./Ee, Ogawa-san wa kinō (　) n desu. (shirasemasen deshita, yasumi deshita) 3. Doko ni (　) n desu ka. Denwa ga arimashita yo./Dōmo sumimasen. Chotto kōhī o nomi ni itte imashita. (itte imashita) 4. Nani mo (　) n desu ka./Ee, (　) n desu. (tabemasen, tabetakunai desu) 5. Takushī de (　) n desu ka./Ee, jikan ga amari (　) n desu. (dekakemasu, arimasen) 6. Suzuki-san wa yasumi desu ka./Ee (　) n desu. (byōki desu) 7. Kinō anata ga (　) koto o kare nimo (　) kudasai. (iimashita, hanashimasu) 8. Kanji o (　) koto wa muzukashikunai desu. (oboemasu)

V. Choose a statement appropriate to the situations described.
   A. You hear a friend has quit his job and you ask him about it.
      1. Itsu kaisha o yameru n desu ka. 2. Kaisha o yamete wa ikemasen ka. 3. Hontō ni kaisha o yameta n desu ka.
   B. You see a friend doing something ridiculous.

1. Nani o shite iru n desu ka.   2. Nani o shinakereba narimasen ka.   3. Kare wa nan to itte imasuka.
C. You tell a friend that you didn't go to the party because of a headache.
1. Totemo atama ga itai n desu.   2. Kyū ni atama ga itaku natta n desu.   3. Atama ga itakatta to omoimasu.

12. HOTEL RESERVATIONS

Opening Dialogue

Yoyaku-gakari: Miyako Ryokan de gozaimasu.
Sumisu: Moshi moshi, raigetsu no yokka to itsuka ni yoyaku o onegaishitai n desu ga, heya wa aite imasu ka.
Yoyaku-gakari: Hai, gozaimasu. Nan-mei-sama desu ka.
Sumisu: Futari desu. Ikura desu ka.
Yoyaku-gakari: 1-paku 2-shoku-tsuki de, o-hitori 18,000 en de gozaimasu. Zeikin to sābisu-ryō wa betsu de gozaimasu.
Sumisu: Hai, ja, sore de onegaishimasu.
Yoyaku-gakari: O-namae to o-denwa-bangō o dōzo.
Sumisu: Sumisu to iimasu. Denwa-bangō wa Tōkyō 03-3405-3636 desu. Sochira wa Kyōto no eki kara chikai desu ka.
Yoyaku-gakari: Eki kara kuruma de 10-pun gurai desu. Eki made o-mukae ni ikimasu ga . . .
Sumisu: Ja, eki ni tsuita toki, denwa o shimasu kara, yoroshiku onegaishimasu.
Yoyaku-gakari: Hai, kashikomarimashita. Go-tōchaku wa nan-ji goro desu ka.
Sumisu: 4-ji goro desu.
Yoyaku-gakari: Hai, wakarimashita. 8-ji yori osoku naru baai wa, kanarazu go-renraku kudasai.
Sumisu: Hai. Sorede, ryōkin wa itsu haraimashō ka.
Yoyaku-gakari: Osoreirimasu ga, uchikin to shite, 18,000-en o-okuri kudasai.
Sumisu: Wakarimashita.

Key Sentences
1. Sumisu-san wa hon o yomu toki, megane o kakemasu.
2. Eki ni tsuita toki, denwa o shimasu.
3. Osoku naru baai wa renraku shimasu.
4. Watashi wa Sumisu to iimasu.

EXERCISES
I. Make dialogues by changing the underlined parts as in the examples given.
   A. ex. Q: Yoku sampo shimasu ka.
         A: Ee, asa suzushii toki, sampo shimasu.
            1. kono kusuri o nomu, atama ga itai   2. jogingu o suru, tenki ga yokute samuku nai
            3. kūrā o tsukau, totemo atsui   4. eiga o miru, himana
   B. ex. Q: Kodomo no toki doko ni sunde imashita ka.
         A: Ōsaka ni sunde imashita.
            1. kaigi, dono heya o tsukaimasuka, kono heya o   2. gakusei, doko o ryokō shima-shitaka, Yōroppa o   3. shiken, nani o motte ikimasuka, empitsu to keshigomu o
   C. ex. Q: Shokuji o hajimeru toki, nan to iimasu ka.
         A: "Itadakimasu." to iimasu.
            1. shokuji ga owarimashita, gochisōsama deshita   2. uchi o demasu, itte mairimasu
            3. uchi ni kaerimashita, tadaima   4. hajimete hito ni aimashita, hajimemashite

5. hito to wakaremasu, sayōnara   6. saki ni kaerimasu, o-saki ni shitsurei shimasu
7. hito ni nanika o tanomimasu, onegaishimasu   8. purezento o moraimashita, ari-gatō gozaimasu

II. Practice the following patterns by changing the underlined parts as in the examples given.
   A. *ex.* <u>Shimbun o yomu</u> toki, <u>megane o kakemasu</u>.
      1. kuni ni kaeru, omiyage o kaimasu   2. kaisha ni iku, chikatetsu o tsukaimasu   3. michi ga wakaranai, keikan ni kikimasu   4. daigaku o sotsugyō suru, rombun o kakimasu
   B. *ex.* <u>Eki ni tsuita</u> toki, <u>denwa shimasu</u>.
      1. tsukareta, Mōtsuaruto o kikimasu   2. sochira ni itta, kuwashiku setsumei shimasu
      3. moku-yōbi ni atta, issho ni shokuji o shimashō   4. nemuku natta, kōhī o nomimasu
   C. *ex.* <u>Doitsu ni sun de ita toki</u>, <u>kekkon shimashita</u>.
      1. kinō shokuji o shite ita, jishin ga arimashita   2. sensō ga owatta, Tōkyō ni imasen deshita   3. shachō ga shinda, o-sōshiki ni ōzei hito ga kimashita

III. Make dialogues by changing the underlined parts as in the examples given.
   A. *ex.* Q: Shūmatsu no ryokō wa dō shimashō ka.
         A: <u>Ame</u> no baai wa yamemashō.
            1. densha ga suto desu   2. Tanaka-san no tsugō ga warui desu   3. tenki ga yoku nai desu
   B. *ex.* Q: <u>Osoku naru</u> baai wa renraku shite kudasai.
         A: Hai, sō shimasu.
            1. okuremasu   2. kimasen   3. o-kane ga tarimasen   4. yotei ga kawarimashita
            5. byōki ni narimashita
   C. *ex.* Q: <u>Rose</u> wa Nihon-go de nan to iu n desu ka.
         A: <u>Bara</u> to iimasu.
            1. ball point pen, bōru pen   2. pants, zubon   3. contract, keiyaku

Short Dialogues ───────────────────────────────────

1. A: Himana toki wa nani o shimasu ka.
   B: Himana toki desu ka. Sō desu nē, ongaku o kiitari shite imasu.
2. Watanabe: Nihon no seikatsu ni naremashita ka.
   Jonson: Ee, sukoshi-zutsu.
   Watanabe: Komatta toki wa itsu demo itte kudasai.
3. Kimura: Ashita no supōtsu taikai no koto na n desu ga, ame ga futta toki wa dō shimasu ka.
   Suzuki: Asa 6-ji made ni yamanai baai wa chūshi desu.
   Kimra: Yoku wakaranai toki wa dō shimasu ka.
   Suzuki: Sono baai wa koko ni denwa o shite tashikamete kudasai.

Quiz ───────────────────────────────────

I. Read this lesson's Opening Dialogue and answer the following questions.
   1. Sumisu-san wa doko ni denwa o shimashita ka.   2. Ryokan no hito wa heya ga aite iru to iimashita ka.   3. Miyako Ryokan wa eki kara kuruma de nan-pun gurai kakarimasu ka.
   4. Sumisu-san wa 1-paku 2-shoku no ryōkin to nani o harawanakereba narimasen ka.
   5. Miyako Ryokan no baai wa tomaru mae ni uchikin o harawanakereba narimasen ka.

II. Put the appropriate particles in the parentheses.
   1. Ryōkin wa o-hitori 10,000-en ( ) gozaimasu.   2. Watashi wa Sumisu ( ) iimasu.   3. Eki ( ) tsuita toki, denwa o shimasu. Eki ( ) mukae ( ) kite kuremasen ka.   4. 6-ji ( ) osoku naru baai wa, kanarazu renraku shite kudasai.   5. 1-paku 2-shoku tsuki ( ) hitori 15,000 en kakarimasu ga, ii desu ka.   6. Kare wa A Daigaku no kyōju ( ) shite, Nihon ni kite imasu.
   7. Kaigi ( ) toki, o-cha o mottekite kudasai.

III. Complete the questions so that they fit the answers.

1. Rinda-san wa (   ) kita n desu ka./7-ji no nyūsu o kiite iru toki kimashita.   2. Kore wa Nihon-go de (   ) to iu n desu ka./Keshigomu to iimasu.   3. (   ) ryokan ni osoku naru to renraku shinakatta n desu ka./Denwa o suru jikan ga nakatta n desu.

IV. Complete the sentences with the appropriate form of the words indicated.

1. Kyonen Kyōto ni (   ) toki, kirei na kami no kasa o kaimashita. (ikimashita)   2. Uketsuke no hito ga (   ) baai wa denwa o shite kudasai. (imasen)   3. Asa (   ) toki, ame ga (   ) imashita. (okimashita, furimasu)   4. Ashita made ni (   ) baai wa, kyō-jū ni renraku o (   ) kudasai. (dekimasen, shimasu)   5. Musume ga (   ) toki, Sumisu-san kara supūn o moraimashita. (umareta)   6. Raishū kochira ni (   ) baai wa kanarazu (   ) kudasai. (kimasu, shirasemasu)   7. Kinō hiru-gohan o (   ) toki, kyū ni onaka ga (   ) narimashita. (tabete imashita, itai)   8. Jikan ga (   ) toki, sandoitchi o tabemasu. (arimasen)   9. (   ) toki, Igirisu o (   ) koto ga arimasu. (wakai, ryokō shimasu)   10. (   ) toki, hon o (   ) dari, kodomo to (   ) dari shite imasu. (hima, yomimasu, asobimasu)

V. Choose the most polite statement appropriate to the situation described.

A. You're at work and you answer the phone.
   1. ABC de gozaimasu.   2. ABC to iimasu.   3. ABC desu.
B. You tell a client you will show him around when it's convenient for him.
   1. Go-tsugō no ii toki, go-annai kudasai.   2. Jikan ga aru toki, annai shimasu yo.   3. Go-tsugō no ii toki, go-annai shimasu.
C. You call Katō's house and ask if he is at home.
   1. Katō-san ni go-renraku kudasai.   2. Katō-san wa irasshaimasu ka.   3. Katō-san wa imasuka.

13. A GIFT OF CHOCOLATE

Opening Dialogue

Chan: Jonson-san, kore, Watanabe-san kara Jonson-san e no purezento desu yo. Kinō Jonson-san ga inakatta node, boku ga azukarimashita. Kādo mo arimasu yo.

Jonson: Dōmo arigatō. Watanabe-san kara no okurimono, ureshii desu ne.

Chan: Nakami wa chokorēto deshō.

Jonson: Aketa n desu ka.

Chan: Kādo wa rabu retā kamo shiremasen yo.

Jonson: E, yonda n desu ka.

Chan: Hahaha . . . . Jitsuwa boku mo onaji mono o moratta n desu. Suzuki-kun mo moratta darō to omoimasu yo.

Jonson: E. Minna moratta n desu ka.

Chan: Giri-choko desu yo, giri-choko.

Jonson: Giri-choko tte nan desu ka.

Chan: Giri no chokorēto desu. Nihon no Barentain dē no shūkan desu. Shokuba demo yoku josei kara dansei no jōshi ya dōryō ni chokorēto o purezento shimasu.

Jonson: "Itsumo o-sewa ni natte imasu. Korekara mo yoroshiku. Mayumi" Yappari giri-choko deshita.

Chan: Zannen deshita.

Jonson: Demo, giri-choko o takusan moratta hito wa dō suru n deshō ka.

Chan: Tabun okusan ya gāru furendo ga taberu n deshō.

Jonson: Ja, yorokobu hito wa josei to kashi-ya desu ne.

Key Sentences ──

1. Yuki ga takusan futte iru kara, hikōki wa tobanai kamo shiremasen.
2. Suzuki-san wa Rinda-san o shiranai darō to omoimasu.
3. Hikōki ga tobanai node, ryokō ni iku koto ga dekimasen.

EXERCISES ──

I. Make dialogues by changing the underlined parts as in the examples given.
   A. *ex.* A: Kuruma ga takusan tomatte imasu ne.
      B: Sō desu ne. Jiko kamo shiremasen ne.
         1. tonari no uchi wa nigiyaka desu, pātī desu   2. Tanaka-san ga kite imasen, yasumi desu   3. samuku narimashita, ashita wa yuki desu   4. michi ga konde imasu, kuruma yori chikatetsu no hō ga hayai desu.
   B. *ex.* A: Tanaka-san wa jikan ga aru kamo shiremasen yo.
      B: Sō desu ka.
      A: Kyō wa hima da to itte imashita kara.
         1. rekishi ni kyōmi ga arimasu, Nara ya Kyōto ga suki desu   2. ryokō ni ikimashita, konshū wa yasumi desu   3. kyō kaisha ni kimasen, okusan ga byōki desu   4. minna to karaoke ni ikimasen deshita, karaoke wa kirai desu
   C. *ex.* A: Kaigi wa itsu desu ka.
      B: Ashita no gozen-chū darō to omoimasu yo.
         1. Tanaka-san, doko, 3-kai no kaigi-shitsu.   2. tantōsha, dare, Suzuki-san ka Sato-san   3. shiken, nan-ka kara nan-ka made, 1-ka kara 10-ka made   4. B-sha no atarashii pasokon, ikura gurai, 18-man-en gurai
   D. *ex.* A: Hokkaidō wa ima samui deshō ka.
      B: Ee, samui darō to omoimasu yo.
         1. kono kikai no hō ga benri desu   2. Yamada-san wa kaisha o yamemasu   3. chikatetsu wa mō suite imasu   4. Tanaka-san wa mō kaerimashita
   E. *ex.* Q: Tanaka-san wa kuru deshō ka.
      A*a*: Ee, tabun kuru darō to omoimasu.
      A*n*: Tabun, konai darō to omoimasu.
         1. atarashii hisho wa Supein-go ga wakarimasu   2. Sumisu-san wa watashi o shitte imasu   3. eki no chikaku no sūpā de o-sake o utte imasu   4. Sumisu-san wa Watababe-san kara giri-choko o moraimashita

II. Practice the following pattern by changing the underlined parts as in the example given.
   ex. Saifu o wasureta node tomodachi ni o-kane o karimashita.
      1. isogashii desu, dēto o kotowarimashita   2. yasetai desu, supōtsu kurabu ni hairimashita   3. benri desu, chikatetsu de kaisha ni ikimasu   4. kinō wa yasumi deshita, minna de haikingu ni ikimashita   5. raigetsu ryokō shimasu, hoteru no yoyaku o shimashita   6. basu mo takushī mo kimasen deshita, eki made arukimashita   7. muri o shimashita, byōki ni narimashita

III. Make dialogues by changing the underlined parts as in example given.
   ex. A: Kuruma de ikimasu ka.
      B: Iie, michi ga konde iru node ...
         1. zangyō shimasu, dēto ga arimasu   2. kēki o tabemasu, ima onaka ga ippai desu   3. gorufu o shimasu, suki ja nai desu   4. atarashii wāpuro o kaimashita, takakatta desu

IV. Practice the following dialogues.
   A. Q: Kore wa Watanabe-san kara moratta okurimono desu ka.
      A: Hai, Watanabe-san kara no okurimono desu.
   B. Q: Kore wa Tanaka-san ni dasu tegami desu ka.
      A: Hai, Tanaka-san e no tegami desu.

C. Q: Kore wa doko <u>de okita</u> mondai desu ka.
   A: Ōsaka shisha <u>de no</u> mondai desu.
D. Q: Kore wa dono kaisha <u>to shita</u> keiyaku desu ka.
   A: ABC <u>to no</u> keiyaku desu.

Short Dialogues

1. Tanaka: Anō, kore, tsumaranai mono desu ga . . .
   Katō: Yā, dōmo. Enryo naku itadakimasu.

2. A: Misoshiru tte nan desu ka.
   B: Nihon-jin ga yoku nomu sūpu desu.

3. Kimura: Tōkyō Denki no Tanaka-san to yakusoku ga arimasu node, kore de shitsurei shi-
           masu.
   Katō: Soreja, Tanaka-san ni yoroshiku itte kudasai.

Quiz

I. Read this lesson's Opening Dialogue and answer the following questions.
   1. Jonson-san ga moratta chokorēto wa dare kara no purezento desu ka.   2. Chan-san mo
   chokorēto to kādo o moraimashita ka.   3. Chan-san ga Jonson-san e no purezento o
   azukatta hi wa nan no hi desu ka.   4. Giri-choko o takusan moratta dansei wa hitori de
   zembu taberu darō to Chan-san wa iimashita ka.

II. Put the appropriate words in the parentheses.
   1. Gāru-furendo (   ) no purezento o kai ni ikimashita.   2. Tōkyō (   ) no seikatsu wa hontō
   ni tanoshikatta desu.   3. Rondon (   ) no nimotsu ga todokimashita.   4. Itsumo o-sewa (   )
   natte imasu. Kore (   ) mo dōzo yoroshiku.   5. Yobikō (   ) nan desu ka.

III. Complete the questions so that they fit the answers.
   1. Kinō (   ) konakatta n desu ka./Isogashikatta node, shitsurei shimashita.   2. (   ) shite iru
   n desu ka./Bengoshi ga konai node, matte iru n desu.   3. Atarashii buchō wa (   ) hito deshō
   ka./Atama ga yokute majimena hito darō to omoimasu yo.   4. Misoshiru tte (   ) desu
   ka./Miso no sūpu desu yo.

IV. Complete the sentences with the appropriate form of the words indicated.
   1. Kare ga (   ) node, anshin shimashita. (genki desu)   2. Kore wa (   ) darō to omoimasu.
   (Sumisu-san no mono dewa arimasen)   3. Tanaka-san wa (   ) kamo shiremasen yo. (byōki
   desu)   4. Kinō wa (   ) node (   ) darō to omoimasu yo. (matsuri deshita, nigiyaka deshita)
   5. Shujin wa tabun kasa o (   ) darō to omoimasu. (motte ikimasen deshita)   6. Kono
   chikatetsu wa Ginza o (   ) darō to omoimasu. (tōrimasen)   7.Shimbun wa isu no ue ni (   )
   kamo shiremasen. (okimashita)   8. Sugu atarashii seikatsu ni (   ) deshō. (naremasu)   9. Densha ga (   ) node, basu de kimashita. (ugokimasen deshita)   10. Chokorēto o moratta dansei
   wa (   ) darō to omoimasu yo. (yorokobimasu)

V. Choose a statement appropriate to the situation described.
   A. You tell your section chief you have to go to the hospital to see your father.
      1. Chichi ga byōki na node, byōin e iku kamo shiremasen.   2. Otō-san ga byōki na node,
      byōin e itte wa ikemasen ka.   3. Chichi ga byōki na node, byōin e ikanakereba naranai n
      desu ga . . .
   B. You want to know the meaning of the acronym UFO.
      1. Yūfō tte nan desu ka.   2. Yūfō to iimasu.   3. Yūfō wa nan to iimasu ka.
   C. You finish working and go out of the office, leaving your section chief behind.
      1. Gomen nasai, kaerimasu.   2. Enryo naku, sayōnara.   3. O-saki ni shitsurei shimasu.

14. THE REFEREE'S ROLE

Opening Dialogue

Sumisu: Wā, sugoi hito desu ne.

Tanaka: Sumō no shonichi wa itsumo man'in desu. Hito ga takusan ite, Rinda-san ya okusan ga yoku miemasen ne.

Sumisu: A, asoko ni imashita. Hora, sumō o minagara yakitori o tabete iru no ga miemasu yo.

Tanaka: Sā, watashi-tachi mo asoko e itte, bīru demo nominagara suwatte mimashō.

Sumisu: Ee, demo kono torikumi ga owaru made koko de ii desu. Urusakute anaunsu ga yoku kikoemasen ga, dohyō no ue ni iru no wa?

Tanaka: Fujinomine to Sakuraryū desu.

Sumisu: Hadena kimono o kite, dohyō no ue de ugokimawatte iru no wa dō iu hito desu ka.

Tanaka: Are wa gyōji desu.

Sumisu: Aa, jajji desu ne.

Tanaka: Ee, demo kuroi kimono o kite, dohyō no mawari ni suwatte iru no ga hontō no jajji desu. Ano hito-tachi wa rikishi no OB de, erai n desu yo.

Sumisu: Ja, gyōji wa jajji dewa nai n desu ka.

Tanaka: Ee, jitsuwa kettei-ken wa nai n desu.

Sumisu: Sō desu ka. Chotto nattoku dekimasen ne.

Tanaka: Demo hatsugen-ken wa arimasu yo.

Sumisu: Sore o kiite anshin shimashita.

Key Sentences

1. Sono hanashi o kiite, anshin shimashita.
2. Kimura-san wa aruite kaisha ni ikimasu.
3. Jonson-san o Narita Kūkō made mukae ni itta no wa Suzuki-san desu.
4. Hoteru no mado kara Fuji-san ga miemasu.

EXERCISES

I. Make dialogues by changing the underlined parts as in the example given.

   ex. Q: Dō shita n desu ka.

      A: Atsukute nomu koto ga dekinai n desu.

        1. omoi, hitori de mochimasu 2. kurai, yomimasu 3. fukuzatsu, setsumei shimasu 4. konde imasu, hairimasu 5. Hayashi-san ga imasen, sōdan shimasu

II. Practice the following patterns by changing the underlined parts as in the examples given.

   A. *ex.* Nyūsu o kiite anshin shimashita.

        1. haha kara tegami o moraimashita, anshin shimashita 2. yonaka ni denwa ga arimashita, odorokimashita 3. henji ga kimasen, komatte iru n desu 4. shiken ni ochimashita, gakkari shimashita

   B. *ex.* Hashitte isha o yobi ni ikimasita.

        1. suwaru, hanashimashō 2. isogu, shiryō o atsumete kudasai 3. denwa o suru, kikimasu 4. chizu o kaku, setsumei shimashita

III. Make dialogues by changing the underlined parts as in the examples given.

   A. *ex.* Q: Mainichi benkyō shite imasu ka.

      A: Ee, mainichi benkyō suru no wa taihen desu.

        1. yoru osoku made shigoto o shimasu, taihen 2. kodomo to asobimasu, tanoshii 3. shokuji o tsukurimasu, mendō 4. asa 5-ji ni okimasu, muzukashii

   B. *ex.* Q: Yoku, e o kakimasu ne.

      A: Ee, e o kaku no ga sukina n desu.

1. yama o arukimasu   2. jōdan o iimasu   3. ryokō o shimasu   4. eiga o mimasu

C. *ex.* Q: Nani o wasureta n desu ka.
  A: <u>Shukudai o mottekuru</u> no o wasureta n desu.
   1. denwa shimasu   2. o-kane o haraimasu   3. sekken o kaimasu   4. Tanaka-san ni renraku shimasu

D. *ex.* Q: <u>Kyō kuru</u> no wa <u>dare</u> desu ka.
  A: Ēto, <u>kyō kuru</u> no wa <u>Tanaka-san</u> desu.
   1. tomodachi ni aimasu, itsu, do-yōbi   2. pātī ni kimasen, dare, Sumisu-san   3. Kinō jiko ga arimashita, doko, Tōkyō Hoteru no chikaku   4. Supein-go ga jōzu desu, dare, Hayashi-san no atarashii hisho

E. *ex.* Q: O-taku kara <u>Fuji-san</u> ga miemasu ka.
  A: Tenki ga ii toki wa yoku miemasu.
   1. umi   2. Tōkyō tawā   3. tōku no yama

IV. Practice the following pattern by changing the underlined parts as in the example given.
 ex. <u>Kōen</u> de <u>kodomo-tachi ga asonde iru</u> no ga <u>miemasu</u>.
  1. pūru, Tanaka-san ga oyoide imasu, miemasu   2. sūpā no mae, Suzuki-san ga takushī o matte imsu, miemasu   3. dokoka, piano o hiite imasu, kikoemasu   4. tonari no heya, kodomo ga uta o utatte imasu, kikoemasu

V. Make dialogues by changing the underlined parts as in the examples given.
 A. *ex.* Q: <u>Hiru-gohan o tabenai</u> n desu ka.
  A*a*: Ee, <u>tabemasen</u>.
  A*n*: Iie, <u>tabemasu</u> yo.
   1. jikan ga arimasen   2. kesa no shimbun o yomimasen deshita   3. wasuremono o tori ni ikimasen deshita

 B. *ex.* Q: Kinō itsu made matte ita n desu ka.
  A: <u>Kaigi ga owaru</u> made matte imashita.
   1. kuraku narimasu   2. henji ga kimasu   3. shiryō ga todokimasu

Short Dialogues

1. Suzuki: Moshi moshi, moshi moshi, kikoemasu ka.
 Yamakawa: Moshi moshi, o-denwa ga tōi n desu ga, mō sukoshi ōkii koe de onegaishimasu.
 Suzuki: Kochira wa Suzuki desu ga, kikoemasu ka.
 Yamakawa: A, kikoemashita. Suzuki-san desu ne.

2. A: Shitsurei desu ga, Tanaka-san ja arimasen ka.
 B: Hai, Tanaka-desu ga . . . .

Quiz

I. Read this lesson's Opening Dialogue and answer the following questions.
 1. Rinda-san to Sumisu-san no okusan wa sumō o minagara nani o shite imasu ka.   2. Urusakute anaunsu ga yoku kikoenai to itta no wa dare desu ka.   3. Hadena kimono o kite dohyō no ue de ugokimawatte iru no wa dare desu ka.   4. Hontō no jajji wa doko ni imasu ka.

II. Put the appropriate particles in the parentheses.
 1. Tenki ( ) ii toki, Fuji-san ( ) miemasu.   2. Watashi wa tegami ( ) todoku ( ) o matte imashita.   3. Yoru osoku kuruma ( ) oto ( ) kikoemashita.   4. Kuroi kimono ( ) kite iru ( ) wa Tanaka-san no okusan desu.   5. Kore wa hontō ( ) hanashi desu. Jōdan dewa arimasen.

III. Complete the questions so that they fit the answers.
 1. Ano hito wa ( ) hito desu ka./Daitōryō no musuko de, yūmei na pianisuto desu.   2. ( ) made koko de matsu n desu ka./Kaigi ga owaru made matte ite kudasai.   3. ( ) o mite iru n

desu ka./Kēki o tsukutte iru no o mite iru n desu.   4. 3-gatsu 3-ka wa (   ) hi desu ka./ Onna no ko no o-matsuri no hi de, tomodachi o yonde pātī o shitari suru hi desu.

IV. Complete the sentences with the appropriate form of the words indicated.
1. Nyūsu o (   ), odorokimashita. (kikimasu)   2. Chikatetsu no naka de tēpu o (   ) nagara, Nihon-go o benkyō shite imasu. (kikimasu)   3. Asoko de (   ) no ga miemasu ka./(   ) te yoku miemasen. (tsuri o shite imasu, tōi desu)   4. Tegami o (   ) no o wasuremashita. (dashimasu)   5. Jikan ga (   ) te, iku koto ga dekimasen. (arimasen)   6. Shokuji ga (   ) made, terebi demo mimashō. (dekimasu)   7. Hanashi ga (   ) de yoku wakarimasen. (fukuzatsu desu)   8. Denwa o (   ) nagara (   ) nowa abunai desu. (shimasu, unten shimasu)

V. Circle the correct words in the parentheses.
1. Atsui desu ne. Bīru (ya, demo, goro) nomimasen ka./Ii desu ne.   2. 6-ji made ni (kanarazu, wazawaza, taitei) renraku shite kudasai.   3. Gōkaku suru no wa muzukashii to omotte imashita ga, (kanarazu, yappari, tabun) dame deshita.   4. Anata wa shiranakatta n desu ka./Ee, (zehi, soreni, jitsuwa) shiranakatta n desu.

VI. Answer the following questions.
1. Anata wa sumō o mita koto ga arimasu ka.   2. Anata no heya kara nani ga miemasu ka.   3. Yoru anata no heya ni iru toki, kuruma no oto ga kikoemasu ka.   4. Anata wa yama ni noboru no ga suki desu ka.   5. Shokuji o hajimeru toki, Nihon-go de nan to iimasu ka.

15. A FORGOTTEN UMBRELLA

Opening Dialogue

Buraun: Kinō supōtsu kurabu ni ittara Yamamoto-san ni aimashita.
Watanabe: Yamamoto-san? Ototoi koko ni kita Yamamoto-san desu ka.
Buraun: Ee, kare mo soko no kaiin da to itte imashita.
Watanabe: A sō sō, Yamamoto-san ga kasa o wasurete kaerimashita ga, dō shimashō ka.
Buraun: Watashi ga sono kasa o azukarimashō. Mata au kamo shiremasen kara. Kondo supōtsu kurabu e iku toki, motteikimasu.
Watanabe: Ja kore, onegaishimasu.
Buraun: Yamamoto-san ni attara watashimasu. Moshi awanakattara, uketsuke ni azukemasu.

Uketsuke: Ohayō gozaimasu.
Buraun: Ohayō gozaimasu. Yamamoto Tarō-san wa kyō kimasu ka.
Uketsuke: Kaiin no Yamamoto-sama desu ne. Kyō wa Yamamoto-sama wa yūgata 6-ji ni irasshaimasu.
Buraun: Sō desu ka. Kore, Yamamoto-san no kasa na n desu ga, 6-ji ni kuru nara, ima azukete mo ii desu ka.
Uketsuke: Hai, dōzo.
Buraun: Ja, kare ga kitara watashite kudasai.
Uketsuke: Hai, tashika ni.

Key Sentences
1. Kyōto made kuruma de ittara 10-jikan kakarimashita.
2. Moshi yotei ga wakatta ra shirasemasu.
3. Hikōki de iku nara hayaku kippu o katta hō ga ii desu yo.

EXERCISES ───────────────────────────────────

I. Practice the following patterns by changing the underlined parts as in the example given.

   ex. <u>Supōtsu kurabu ni ittara</u>, <u>mukashi no tomodachi ni aimashita</u>.

      1. kado o magarimashita, umi ga miemashita   2. tanjō-bi no puresento o akemashita, kawaii inu ga dete kimashita   3. undō shimashita, senaka ga itaku narimashita   4. asa okimashita, yuki ga futte imashita   5. uchi ni kaerimashita, tegami ga kiteimashita

II. Make diaogues by changing the underlined parts as in the examples given.

   A. *ex.* Q: Kaigi wa itsu hajimemasu ka.

         A: <u>10-ji ni nattara</u> sugu hajimemasu.

            1. shachō ga kimasu   2. zen'in ga soroimasu   3. chūshoku ga sumimasu   4. shiryō no kopī ga dekimasu

   B. *ex.* Q: <u>Hima</u> ga attara dō shimasu ka.

         A: <u>Hima</u> ga attara <u>Nihon-jū ryokō shitai</u> desu.

            1. o-kane, ōkii uchi o kaimasu   2. takusan o-kane, hambun kifu shimasu   3. kuruma, Hokkaidō o mawarimasu   4. o-kane to jikan, sekai-jū no tomodachi o tazunemasu

   C. *ex.* Q: <u>Michi ga wakaranai</u> kamo shiremasen yo.

         A: Moshi <u>wakaranakattara</u> <u>kōban de kikimasu</u>.

            1. o-kane ga tarimasen, tomodachi ni karimasu   2. kyō wa kaigi ga arimasen, hoka no shigoto o shimasu   3. basu ga hashitte imasen, takushī de kaerimashō

III. Practice the following pattern by changing the underlined parts as in the example given.

   ex. <u>Atsukatta</u> ra <u>mado o akete kudasai</u>.

      1. samui, hītā o tsukete mo ii desu   2. takai, kawanaide kudasai   3. tsugō ga warui, hoka no hi ni shimashō   4. kibun ga yokunai, yasunda hō ga iidesu yo   5. tsumaranai, yomanakute mo ii desu

IV. Make dialogues by changing the underlined parts as in the examples given.

   A. *ex.* Q: <u>Ame</u> dattara dō shimasu ka.

         A: <u>Ame</u> nara <u>yotei o kaemasu</u>.

            1. suto, ikimasen   2. Tanaka-san ga rusu, mata ato de denwa shimasu   3. kekka ga dame, mō ichido yarimasu   4. tsukaikata ga fukuzatsu, kau no o yamemasu

   B. *ex.* A: <u>Hiru-gohan o tabetai</u> n desu ga.

         B: <u>Hiru-gohan o taberu</u> nara <u>ano resutoran ga ii desu yo</u>.

            1. supōtsu kurabu ni hairimasu, ii kurabu o shōkai shimashō   2. umi ni ikimasu, watashi no kuruma o tsukatte mo ii desu yo   3. tēpurekōdā o kaimasu, chiisai hō ga benrida to omoimasu   4. Kyūshū ni ikimasu, ferī ga ii to omoimasu yo   5. Yōroppa o ryokō shimasu, 5-gatsu goro ga kireide ii desu yo.

Short Dialogues ───────────────────────────────────

1. A: Kono hen ni nimotsu o azukeru tokoro wa arimasen ka.
   B: Asoko ni koin rokkā ga arimasu. Moshi ippai nara, kaisatsuguchi no soba ni mo arimasu yo.

2. Howaito: Kaigi wa nakanaka owarimasen ne.
   Watanabe: 9-ji ni nattara owaru deshō.
   Howaito: Sō desu ka. Sonnani osoku naru nara osaki ni shitsurei shimasu.

3. A: Chūgoku-go no tsūyaku o sagashite iru n desu ga.
   B: Chūgoku-go kara Nihon-go e no tsūyaku desu ne.
   A: Ee, dare ka ii hito ga itara, zehi shōkai shite kudasai.

I. Read this lesson's Opening Dialogue and answer the following questions.

1. Buraun-san wa Yamamoto-san no wasureta kasa o dare kara azukarimashita ka. 2. Buraun-san wa doko de Yamamoto-san ni sono kasa o watashitai to omotte imasu ka. 3. Buraun-san wa supōtsu kurabu ni itta toki, Yamamoto-san ni au koto ga dekimashita ka. 4. Yamamoto-san wa kono supōtsu kurabu no kaiin desu ka.

II. Put the appropriate particles in the parentheses.

1. Buraun-san wa uketsuke no hito (　) nimotsu (　) azukemashita. 2. Kaiin (　) Yamamoto-sama wa kyō yūgata 6-ji (　) irasshaimasu. 3. Yamamoto-san ga kasa (　) wasurete kaerimashita./Ja, watashi (　) sono kasa (　) azukarimashō. Supōtsu kurabu (　) Yamamoto-san (　) attara, watashimasu. 4. Chūshoku (　) sundara, kippu (　) kai (　) itte kudasai.

III. Complete the questions so that they fit the answers.

1. Moshi Yamamoto-san ga konakattara, (　) shimashō ka./Tegami de shirasete kudasai. 2. (　) hikkosu n desu ka./Uchi ga dekitara, hikkoshimasu. 3. (　) ni shōtaijō o watashimashita ka./Hisho ni watashimashita. 4. (　) pātī ni ikanai n desu ka./Pātī wa taikutsu na node ikitakunai n desu.

IV. Complete the sentences with the appropriate form of the words indicated.

1. Wāpuro o (　) nara, ii mise o oshiemashō. (kaimasu) 2. Zen'in ga (　) tara, (　) kudasai. (soroimasu, hajimemasu) 3. Takushī ni (　) tara, kibun ga (　) narimashita. (norimasu, warui desu) 4. (　) nara, eiga o (　) ni ikimasen ka. (hima desu, mimasu) 5. Kono kaban wa tsukatte imasen./(　) nara, (　) hō ga ii desu yo. (tsukaimasen, sutemasu) 6. (　) tara, sukoshi (　) kudasai. (tsukaremasu, yasumimasu) 7. (　) tara, jūsu o (　) kudasai. (iso-gashikunai desu, katte kimasu) 8. Tsukuri-kata ga (　) nara, (　) no o yamemasu. (mendō desu, tsukurimasu) 9. Ashita (　) tara, dekakemasen. (ame desu) 10. Kyōto ni (　) nara, kono chizu o (　) mashō. (ikimasu, agemasu) 11. Nimotsu ga (　) node, (　) kudasai. (omoi desu, azukarimasu)

V. Answer the following questions.

1. Saifu o otoshitara, anata wa dō shimasu ka. 2. 1-kagetsu yasumi ga attara, nani o shimasu ka. 3. Tomodachi no gāru furendo/bōi furendo kara raburetā o morattara dō shimasu ka.

---

16. THE NEW SHOWROOM DESIGN

Opening Dialogue

Yamakawa: Moshi moshi, Hayashi-buchō desu ka. Kochira wa M sekkei jimusho no Yamakawa desu ga, go-irai no shōrūmu no sekkei ga dekiagarimashita.

Hayashi: Aa, sakki fakkusu de zumen o itadakimashita. Nakanaka iidesu ne.

Yamakawa: Nanika mondai wa arimasen ka. Raishū kara kōji o hajimereba, raigetsu-chū ni deki-agarimasu.

Hayashi: Sō desu nē.

Yamakawa: Moshi mondai ga nakereba sassoku hajimetai to omoimasu ga . . .

Hayashi: Nemmatsu ni naru to gyōsha mo isogashiku narimasu kara ne.

Yamakawa: Ee. Hayakereba hayai hodo iito omou n desu ga . . .

Hayashi: Sumimasen ga, hajimeru mae ni chotto sōdan shitai koto ga aru n desu ga . . .

Yamakawa: Wakarimashita. Sochira no go-tsugō ga yokereba, korekara ukagaimasu.

Hayashi: Dekireba sō shite kudasai. 6-ji ni naru to omote no iriguchi wa shimarimasu. Hantai-gawa ni mawaru to uraguchi ga arimasu kara, soko kara haitte kudasai.

Yamakawa: Wakarimashita.

Hayashi: Uraguchi wa 10-ji made aite imasu. Ja, yoroshiku onegaishimasu.

Key Sentences ————————————————————————————————

1. A: Bīru wa arimasu ka.
   B: Iie, arimasen ga, saka-ya ni denwa-sureba sugu mottekimasu.
2. Haru ni naru to sakura no hana ga sakimasu.
3. Sakana wa atarashikereba atarashii hodo ii desu.

EXERCISES ————————————————————————————————

I. Verbs: Study the examples, convert into the conditional forms, and memorize.
   ex. iku → ikeba, ikanakereba; taberu → tabereba, tabenakereba; kuru → kureba, ko-
   nakereba; suru → sureba, shinakereba
   1. arau 2. tatsu 3. uru 4. tanomu 5. tsukau 6. aruku 7. dekiru 8. oriru 9. tsutomeru 10. shiraseru 11. motte kuru 12. denwa suru

II. Practice the following patterns by changing the underlined parts as in the example given.
   ex. Uchi kara eki made arukeba 30-pun kakarimasu.
   1. megane o kakemasu, yoku miemasu 2. yukkuri hanashimasu, wakarimasu 3. eki ni
   tsuku jikan ga wakarimasu, mukae ni ikimasu 4. shitsumon ga arimasen, kore de owarimasu 5. hakkiri iimasen, wakarimasen 6. kaiin ni narimasen, kono pūru o riyō suru
   koto ga dekimasen

III. Adjectives: Study the examples, convert into the conditional forms, and memorize.
   ex. atsui → atsukereba, atsukunakereba
   1. warui 2. omoshiroi 3. katai 4. omoi 5. mezurashii 6. sukunai 7. tsugō ga ii 8. atama
   ga itai 9. hanashitai

IV. Practice the following patterns by changing the underlined parts as in the examples given.
   A. *ex.* Yasukereba kaimasu ga, takakereba kaimasen.
   1. atarashii, furui 2. oishii, mazui 3. ii, warui 4. omoshiroi, tsumaranai
   B. *ex.* Tsugō ga warukereba denwa o kudasai.
   1. omoshiroi, watashi mo mitai to omoimasu 2. isogashii, hoka no hito ni tanomimasu 3. muzukashii, shinakutemo ii desu yo 4. isogashikunai, issho ni eiga ni ikimasen ka 5. ikitaku nai, ikanakute mo ii desu

V. Make dialogues by changing the underlined parts as in the examples given.
   A. *ex.* A: Supōtsu kurabu ni hairimasen ka.
   B: Eki ni chikakereba hairitai to omoimasu.
   1. takaku nai desu 2. pūru ga arimasu 3. ii kōchi ga imasu 4. konde imasen
   5. gorufu no renshū ga dekimasu 6. asa hayaku kara aite imasu
   B. *ex.* Tanaka fujin: Anata mo furawā shō ni ikimasu ka.
   Sumisu fujin: Hima ga areba ikimasu.
   1. jikan ga arimasu 2. Eigo no setsumei ga arimasu 3. bebīshittā ga mitsukarimasu
   4. sono hi ni hokano yotei ga arimasen 5. tenki ga warukunai desu 6. otto no tsugō
   ga iidesu

VI. Make dialogues by changing the underlined parts as in the examples given.
   A. *ex.* A: Shigoto wa hayakereba hayai hodo ii desu ne.
   B: Ee, watashi mo sō omoimasu.
   1. yachin, yasui 2. kyūryō, ōi 3. zeikin, sukunai 4. yasumi, nagai
   B. *ex.* Q: Sonna ni kaitai n desu ka.
   A: Ee, mireba miru hodo hoshiku narimasu.
   1. tenisu ga suki, yaru, omoshiroi 2. kekkon shitai, au, suki 3. muzukashii, kan-
   gaeru, wakaranai

VII. Practice the following patterns by changing the underlined parts as in the example given.
   ex. Massugu iku to hidari-gawa ni posuto ga arimasu.

1. o-sake o nomimasu, tanoshiku narimasu   2. kaisatsu-guchi o demasu, me no mae ni sūpā ga arimasu   3. Satō-san wa kaisha ni tsukimasu, mazu kōhī o nomimasu   4. tabako o takusan suimasu, gan ni narimasu yo   5. yasumimasen, byōki ni narimasu yo.

VIII. Make dialogues by changing the underlined parts as in the example given.
ex. Q: Dō suru to aku n desu ka.
    A: Botan o osu to akimasu.
        1. jūsu ga dete kimasu, o-kane o iremasu   2. denki ga kiemasu, doa o shimemasu   3. mado ga akimasu, rebā o hikimasu   4. rajio no oto ga ōkiku narimasu, kore o mawashimasu

Short Dialogue

A: Taihen. Mō 10-ji han desu ka. Hikōki no jikan ni maniawanai kamo shiremasen.
B: Kuruma de kūkō made okurimashō. Isogeba maniaimasu yo.
A: Ja, go-meiwakude nakereba onegaishimasu.

Quiz

I. Read this lesson's Opening Dialogue and answer the following questions.
1. Yamakawa-san wa Hayashi-san ni fakkusu de nani o okurimashita ka.   2. Yamakawa-san wa raishū kara kōji o hajimereba itsu dekiagaru to iimashita ka.   3. Hayashi-san no kaisha ni nan-ji made ni ikeba, omote no iriguchi kara hairu koto ga dekimasu ka.   4. ABC no uraguchi wa nan-ji ni naru to shimarimasu ka.

II. Put the appropriate words or word parts in the parentheses.
1. Nani (　) nomimono wa arimasen ka.   2. Itsu made (　) harawanakereba narimasen ka./Hayakere (　) hayai hodo ii darō (　) omoimasu.   3. Kono mise wa hiru kara yoru 12-ji (　) aite imasu.   4. Atarashii jimusho (　) sekkei ga dekiagarimashita node, fakkusu (　) okurimasu.

III. Complete the questions so that they fit the answers.
1. Sakura no hana wa (　) sakimasu ka./4-gatsu ni naru to sakimasu.   2. (　) ka aite iru heya wa nai deshō ka./Kaigi-shitsu ga aite imasu yo.   3. Yamada-san ga kaita e wa (　) deshita ka./Nakanaka yokatta desu yo.

IV. Convert the following verbs and adjectives into their -ba/-kereba form.
1. au 2. kaku 3. shimaru 4. furu 5. mieru 6. maniau 7. okureru 8. kekkon suru 9. mottekuru 10. nai 11. mezurashii 12. ii

V. Complete the sentences with the appropriate form of the words indicated.
1. Yoku (　) ba, genki ni (　) deshō. (yasumimasu, narimasu) 2. Tōkyō tawā ni (　) ba, umi ga (　) deshō. (noborimasu, miemasu) 3. Tsugi no kado o migi ni (　) to, hana-ya ga arimasu. (magarimasu) 4. O-sake o (　) to, (　) narimasu. (nomimasu, tanoshii desu) 5. Go-tsugō ga (　) ba, gogo (　) tai to omoimasu. (ii desu, ukagaimasu) 6. (　) ba, (　) narimasen. (renshū shimasen, jōzu desu) 7. Botan o (　) to doa ga shimarimasu. (oshimasu) 8. (　) ba, motto (　) mashō. (hoshii desu, mottekimasu) 9. Denwa de (　) ba, (　) to omoimasu. (tanomimasu, mottekimasu) 10. (　) ba, (　) hodo wakaranaku narimasu. (kangaemasu, kangaemasu)

VI. Circle the correct words in the parentheses.
1. Itsu shorui o azuketa n desuka./Kinō (hakkiri, tashikani, nakanaka) uketsuke ni azukemashita.   2. Nan-ji goro ukagaimashō ka./Gozen-chū wa isogashii node, (dekireba, nakanaka, sakki) gogo 2-ji goro kite kuremasen ka.   3. Jikan ga nai node, (sakki, tashika ni, sassoku) hajimete kudasai.

17. BROWN'S DIARY

12-gatsu 31-nichi (sui) hare nochi kumori

Kyō wa ō-misoka da. Tonari no Ōno-san no uchi dewa, asa kara kazoku zen'in de sōji o shite ita. Minna de hei ya kuruma ya, soshite inu made aratte ita.

Gogo wa Nihon-go de Nengajō o kaita ga, ji ga heta da kara yominikui darō. Yūgata, Tanaka-san ikka to soba o tabe ni itta.

Yoru wa fudan wa amari minai terebi o mita. Channeru o tsugitsugi ni kaeru to, sawagashii shō ya samurai no jidai-geki o yatte ita. 3-channeru dewa Bētōben no Dai-ku o ensō shite ita. Senjitsu, Nakamura-san ga "Maitoshi, 12-gatsu ni naru to, Nihon kakuchi de Dai-ku o ensō suru n desu yo," to itte ita ga, omoshiroi kuni da.

1-gatsu tsuitachi (moku) hare

Nihon de shinnen o mukaeta. Machi wa hito mo kuruma mo sukunakute, taihen shizuka da. Kōjō mo kaisha mo yasumi na node, itsumo wa yogorete iru Tōkyō no sora ga, kyō wa kirei de kimochi ga ii. Kinjo no mise mo sūpā mo minna yasumi datta. Ano rasshu awā no sararīman ya gakusei wa doko ni itta no darō ka.

Nihon-jin no dōryō ya tomodachi kara nengajō ga todoita. Gyōsha kara mo kita. Insatsu no mono ga ōi ga, fude de kaita mono mo aru. Yahari utsukushii. Moratta nengajō wa hotondo zembu kuji-tsuki de aru.

Key Sentences

1. Kinō wa atsukatta kara, tomodachi to oyogi ni itta.
2. Hako o akeru to, naka wa kara datta.

EXERCISES

I. Practice the following patterns by changing the verbs and adjectives as in the examples given.

A. *ex.* Watashi wa Kyōto e <u>ikimasu</u>. → Watashi wa Kyōto e iku./Watashi wa Kyōto e ikanai./Watashi wa Kyōto e itta./Watashi wa Kyōto e ikanakatta.

   1. Sumisu-san to dansu o shimasu 2. Tanaka-san wa 10-ji ni kimasu 3. Jonson-san ni aimasu 4. tomodachi to eiga o mimasu 5. koko ni kagi ga arimasu

B. *ex.* Tanaka-san wa <u>isogashii desu</u>. → Tanaka-san wa isogashii./Tanaka-san wa isogashiku nai./Tanaka-san wa isogashikatta./Tanaka-san wa isogashiku nakatta.

   1. benkyō wa tanoshii desu 2. kuruma ga sukunai desu 3. atama ga ii desu 4. ano resutoran wa mazui desu 5. tsugō ga warui desu

C. *ex.* Sumisu-san wa <u>genki desu</u>. → Sumisu-san wa genki da./Sumisu-san wa genki dewa nai./Sumisu-san wa genki datta./Sumisu-san wa genki dewa nakatta.

   1. kono hoteru wa shizuka desu 2. Sumisu-san wa bīru ga suki desu 3. Sumisu-san wa ryōri ga jōzu desu 4. depāto wa yasumi desu 5. Yamamoto-san wa pairotto desu

D. *ex.* Kinō gakkō o <u>yasunda</u>. → Kinō gakko o yasumimashita.

   1. ashita zeimusho ni ikanakereba naranai 2. 6-ji ni uchi ni kaeru koto ga dekinai 3. tsuki ni itta koto ga nai 4. taikin o hirotta koto ga aru 5. tenisu o shitari tsuri o shitari shita 6. Tanaka-san wa iku darō 7. hayaku yasunda hō ga ii 8. Tanaka-san wa suraido o mite ita 9. ashita wa yuki kamo shirenai 10. mada Jonson-san ni atte inai

II. Make dialogues by changing the underlined parts as in examples given.

A. *ex.* Q: <u>Ano hito no hanashi-kata</u> wa dō desu ka.

   A: <u>Hayakute</u> <u>kikinikui</u> desu.

   1. kono shimbun, ji ga chiisai, yomu 2. kono tēpu, oto ga warui, kiku 3. nattō, kusai, taberu 4. kono kusuri, nigai, nomu

B. *ex.* Q: <u>Sono kutsu</u> wa ikaga desu ka.

    A: <u>Hakiyasukute</u> ki ni itte imasu.

        1. sono pen, kaku   2. kono jisho, hiku   3. sono sūtsu, kiru   4. atarashii wāpuro, tsukau

III. Practice the following patterns by changing the underlined parts as in the example given.

    ex. <u>Heya ni hairu</u> to <u>denwa ga natte imashita</u>.

        1. mado o akemashita, suzushii kaze ga haitte kimashita   2. soto ni demashita, ame ga futte imashita   3. uchi ni kaerimashita, tomodachi ga matte imashita   4. kinko o akemashita, naka wa kara deshita

Short Dialogues ───────────────────────────────────────

1. Otoko A: Mō ano eiga mita?
   Otoko B: Uun, mada. Kimi wa?
   Otoko A: Un, mō mita.
   Otoko B: Dō datta?
   Otoko A: Ammari omoshiroku nakatta.

2. Onna: Mō sugu O-shōgatsu ne. Shigoto wa itsu made?
   Otoko: 12-gatsu 28-nichi made. Nemmatsu wa isogashikute iyana n da.
   Onna: O-shōgatsu wa dokka ni iku?
   Otoko: Uun, doko nimo. Shōgatsu wa nombiri shitai ne.

Quiz ──

  I. Read this lesson's opening passage and answer the following questions.

    1. Buraun-san wa ō-misoka no yūgata dare to nani o tabe ni ikimashita ka. 2. 12-gatsu niwa Nihon kakuchi de Bētōben no Dai 9 o ensō suru to Buraun-san ni hanashita no wa dare desu ka. 3. O-shōgatsu ni Buraun-san no kinjo no mise wa aite imashita ka. 4. Buraun-san wa dare kara Nengajō o moraimashita ka. 5. Buraun-san wa fude de kaita Nengajō o utsukushii to omotte imasu ka.

  II. Complete the questions so that they fit the answers.

    1. ( ) ni dekakeru?/9-ji ni deru. 2. Kinō no eiga wa ( ) datta?/Ammari omoshiroku nakatta. 3. ( ) ni sumitai?/Anzenna tokoro ga ii. 4. Kare wa ( ) kuru?/Ashita kuru darō. 5. ( ) to isshoni iku?/Hitori de iku.

  III. Complete the sentences with the appropriate form of the words indicated.

    1. Kono niku wa ( ), ( ) nikui. (katai, taberu) 2. Kare no setsumei wa ( ), ( ) nikui. (fukuzatsu, wakaru) 3. Kono kikai wa ( ), ( ) yasui. (benri, tsukau) 4. Kotoshi wa ( ), nengajō o zenzen ( ) koto ga dekinakatta. (isogashii, kaku) 5. Heya ga ( ) kimochi ga ii. (kirei)

  IV. Answer the following questions.

    1. Anata no kuni dewa Ō-misoka ya O-shōgatsu ni nani o shimasu ka. 2. O-shōgatsu no yasumi wa nan-nichi made desu ka. 3. Anata no sunde iru machi dewa Kurisumasu to O-shōgatsu to dochira ga nigiyaka desu ka.

  V. Nihon-go de nikki o kaite kudasai.

18. BIRTHDAY FLOWERS

Opening Dialogue

Jonson: Suzuki-san, chotto.
Suzuki: Nan deshō.
Jonson: Nihon no shūkan o shiranai node oshiete kudasaimasen ka. Tomodachi no tanjōbi ni hana o ageyō to omou n desu ga, okashikunai desu ka.
Suzuki: Onna no hito desu ka.
Jonson: Ee, demo tokubetsu no tomodachi dewa nai n desu ga . . .
Suzuki: Okashiku nai desu yo. Daijōbu desu. Dēto desu ka. Ii desu ne.
Jonson: Uun, mā.

Jonson: Tomodachi ni hana o okurō to omou n desu ga, onegai dekimasu ka.
Hanaya: Hai, o-todoke desu ne. Dekimasu. Nan-nichi no o-todoke deshō ka.
Jonson: Ashita todokete kudasai.
Hanaya: Kashikomarimashita.
Jonson: Kono bara wa ikura desu ka.
Hanaya: 1-pon 250 en desu.
Jonson: Ja, kore o 20-pon onegaishimasu. Tanjōbi no purezento ni suru tsumori desu kara, kono kādo o tsukete, todokete kuremasen ka.

> Tanaka Keiko sama
> O-tanjōbi omedetō gozaimasu.
> Maikeru

Hanaya: Hai. O-todoke-saki wa dochira desu ka.
Jonson: Yokohama desu.
Hanaya: Sōryō ga 500-en kakarimasu ga, yoroshii desu ka.
Jonson: Ee. Ja, onegaishimasu.

Key Sentences

1. Mainichi Nihon-go o benkyō shiyō to omoimasu.
2. Ashita haretara, tenisu o suru tsumori desu.

EXERCISES

I. Verbs: Study the examples, convert into the volitional form, and memorize.
   ex. kaku → kakō, iu → iō, taberu → tabeyō, okiru → okiyō, kuru → koyō, suru → shiyō
     1. kaeru (return) 2. oyogu 3. yasumu 4. oboeru 5. azukeru 6. miru 7. kariru 8. katte kuru 9. ryōri suru

II. Make dialogues by changing the underlined parts as in the example given.
   *ex.*Q: <u>Kyō Tanaka-san ni ai</u>masu ka.
     A: Ee, <u>aō</u> to omoimasu.
       1. tabako o yameru 2. shachō ni sōdan suru 3. tomodachi ni kodomo o azukeru 4. hikōki de ikimasu

III. Practice the following patterns by changing the underlined parts as in the example given.
   ex. <u>Kono purojekuto ga owattara natsu-yasumi o torō</u> to omoimasu.
     1. raishū tenki ga yokereba Fuji-san ni noboru 2. kodomo ga dekitara shigoto o kaeru 3. hima ga dekita toki kono hon o yomu 4. daigaku no nyūgaku-shiken ni shippai shita baai wa mō 1-nen gambaru

IV. Make dialogues by changing the underlined parts as in the examples given.
A. *ex.* Q: Kaisha o yamete nani o suru n desu ka.
   A: <u>Hitori de shigoto o hajimeru</u> tsumori desu.
      1. daigaku ni haitte mō ichido benkyō shimasu   2. kuni ni kaette shōrai no koto o kangaemasu   3. dezainā ni natte jibun no mise o mochimasu   4. motto kyūryō no ii shigoto o sagashimasu
B. *ex.* Q: <u>Kekkon shinai</u> n desu ka.
   A: Ee, <u>kekkon shinai</u> tsumori desu.
      1. mō tabako o suimasen   2. dare nimo misemasen   3. kamera o motteikimasen 4. kodomo o tsurete ikimasen
C. *ex.* Q: Sumimasen ga, <u>shio o totte</u> kudasaimasen ka.
   A: Hai.
      1. sono kamera o miseru   2. koko de matte iru   3. kūrā o kesu   4. isu o hakobu no o tetsudau

Short Dialogues

1. Kachō: Kaeri ni dō? Ippai nomō.
   Ogawa: Kyō wa kanai ga kaze o hiite iru node ...
   Kachō: Chotto nara ii darō.
   Ogawa: Ie, yappari dame na n desu.
   Kachō: Sō ka. Ja, akirameyō.

2. Katō: Kotoshi no Nihon-go supīchi kontesuto ni demasu ka.
   Buraun: Ee, sono tsumori desu ga, jūbun jumbi ga dekinakereba, rainen ni suru kamo shiremasen.

Quiz

I. Read this lesson's Opening Dialogue and answer the following questions.
   1. Jonson-san wa onna no tomodachi e no purezento ni tsuite dōshite Suzuki-san ni sōdan shimashita ka.   2. Jonson-san wa dare ni purezento o okurō to omotte imasu ka.   3. Jonson-san ga katta bara wa 20-pon de ikura desu ka.   4. Keiko-san wa doko ni sunde imasu ka.

II. Convert the following verbs into their volitional form.
   1. hanasu   2. todokeru   3. au   4. yameru   5. tsukuru   6. aruku   7. wakareru   8. harau 9. shitsumon suru 10. matsu 11. dēto suru 12. mottekuru

III. Complete the sentences with the appropriate form of the verbs indicated.
   1. Nani o (   ) iru n desu ka. /Tana no ue no hako o (   ) to omou n desu ga, te ga (   ) n desu. (shimasu, torimasu, todokimasen)   2. Donna wāpuro o (   ) tsumori desu ka. /Chiisakute, tsukaiyasui wāpuro o (   ) to omou n desu ga, dore ga ii deshō ka. (kaimasu, kaimasu)   3. Ima kara yūbinkyoku e (   ) to omou n desu ga, nani ka yōji ga arimasen ka. /Sumimasen ga, kono tegami o (   ) kudasaimasen ka. (itte kimasu, dashimasu)   4. Hontō ni kare to (   ) n desu ka. /Ee, mō (   ) tsumori desu. (   ) ba, mata kenka shimasu kara. (wakaremashita, aimasen, aimasu)   5. Nihongo no benkyō o (   ) to omou n desu ga, dokoka ii gakkō o (   ) kudasai masen ka. (hajimemasu, oshiemasu)

IV. Choose a sentence appropriate to the situation described.
   A. Congratulate a friend for passing his examination.
      1. Gōkaku suru deshō.   2. Gōkaku omedetō gozaimasu.   3. Gōkaku shimashita.
   B. You want to ask your section chief if it's all right to call him very late tomorrow evening.
      1. Ashita no ban osoku o-denwa kudasaimasen ka.   2. Ashita no ban osoku kaette kara denwa suru.   3. Ashita no ban osoku denwa o shite mo yoroshii desu ka.
   C. On the phone you ask the wife of an acquaintance of yours what time he will get home.

1. Go-shujin wa nan-ji goro kaerimashita ka.   2. Go-shujin wa nan-ji goro o-kaeri deshō ka.
3. Shujin wa nan-ji goro kaeru tsumori desu ka.
D. You answer a question by saying you really do intend to quit your job.
1 Hai, hontō ni yameru tsumori desu.   2. Hai, tabun yameta to omoimasu.   3. Hai, tabun yameru darō to omoimasu.

V. Answer the following questions.
1. Anata wa ashita nani o shiyō to omoimasu ka.   2. Nihon-go no benkyō ga owattara, Nihon no kaisha de hataraku tsumori desu ka.   3. Anata wa sekai-jū o ryokō shitai to omoimasu ka.
4. Anata no raishū no yotei o hanashite kudasai.

19. THE PUBLIC LIBRARY

Opening Dialogue

Chan: Are wa nan desu ka.
Daisuke: Toshokan desu.
Chan: Dare demo riyō dekimasu ka.
Daisuke: Ee, mochiron desu. Dare demo hairemasu yo. Asoko wa jibun de hon o te ni totte miraremasu kara, totemo riyō shiyasui desu yo.
Chan: Sore wa ii desu ne. Boku wa kādo o mite erabu no wa nigate na n desu.
Daisuke: Demo, Chan-san wa kanji ga yomeru deshō.
Chan: Ee, imi wa wakarimasu. Demo, boku wa jibun de hon o minagara eraberu toshokan ga sukina n desu.
Daisuke: Chotto fubenna tokoro ni aru kedo, hiroi shi shizuka da shi, ii desu yo.
Chan: Hon o karitari kopī shitari suru koto mo dekimasu ka?
Daisuke: Ee, tetsuzuki o sureba kariraremasu. Boku mo ima 2-satsu karite imasu.
Chan: Shimbun ya zasshi mo kariraremasu ka?
Daisuke: Iie, hon shika kariraremasen. Demo shimbun ya zasshi wa kopī o tanomemasu. 2, 3-pun de ikemasu kara, korekara issho ni ikimasen ka.

Key Sentences ───────────────────────────

1. Buraun-san wa Nihon-go ga hanasemasu.
2. Tetsuzuki o sureba, dare demo hon ga kariraremasu.
3. Watanabe-san wa yasai shika tabemasen.

EXERCISES ───────────────────────────

I. Verbs:Study the examples, convert into the potential forms, and memorize.
   ex. kaku → kakeru, kakenai; iru → irareru, irarenai; kuru → korareru, korarenai; kau → kaeru, kaenai; oboeru → oboerareru, oboerarenai; suru → dekiru, dekinai
   1. kiku 2. tobu 3. arau 4. hairu 5. oshieru 6. okiru 7. tsutomeru 8. mottekuru
   9. renshū suru

II. Make dialogues by changing the underlined parts as in the examples given.
   A. *ex.* Q: Gaikoku-go de uta ga/o utaemasu ka.
          A: Hai, utamemasu.
             1. kono kanji o yomu 2. ashita asa 7-ji ni dekakeru 3. gaikoku-jin no namae o sugu oboeru 4. Nihon-go de setsumei suru
   B. *ex.* Q: Eki mae ni kuruma ga/o tomeraremasu ka.
          A: Iie, tomeraremasen.

1. sugu shiryō o atsumeru   2. ano hito no hanashi o shinjiru   3. kono denwa de kokusai-denwa o kakeru   4. 100-mētoru o 10-byō de hashiru

C. *ex.* Q: <u>Hiragana</u> mo <u>kanji</u> mo <u>kake</u>masu ka.
  A: <u>Hiragana</u> wa <u>kake</u>masu ga, <u>kanji</u> wa <u>kake</u>masen.
   1. jitensha, ōtobai, noru   2. sakana, niku, taberu   3. Tanaka-san, Yamamoto-san, kuru   4. tenisu, gorufu, suru

D. *ex.* Q: <u>Nan-ji goro kaere</u>masu ka.
  A: <u>8-ji made ni kaereru</u> to omoimasu.
   1. dare ga naosu, Tanaka-san ga naosu   2. dare ni azukeru, dare nimo azukenai
   3. itsu Tanaka-san ni au, raishū no moku-yōbi ni au   4. doko de kariru, toshokan de kariru   5. nan-mētoru oyogu, 10-metoru mo oyoganai

E. *ex.* Q: <u>Nihon de Igirisu no shimbun ga kae</u>masu ka.
  A: <u>Hoteru ni ikeba kae</u>masu.
   1. Nihon-go no shimbun o yomu, jisho o tsukau   2. konpyūtā o tsukau, setsumei o yomu   3. ashita pātī ni iku, shigoto ga nai   4. kono kaiwa o oboeru, mō sukoshi mijikai

F. *ex.* Q: <u>Tetsuzuki</u> wa <u>itsu</u> ga ii desu ka.
  A: <u>Konshū-chū nara itsu</u> demo ii desu.
   1. ryōri, nani, butaniku de nakereba   2.tomaru tokoro, doko, benri na tokoro dattara
   3. atsumaru jikan, nanji, heijitsu no yūgata nara   4. uketsuke o tetsudau hito, dare, Eigo ga dekireba

G. *ex.* Q: <u>O-ko-san wa nan-nin imasu</u> ka.
  A: <u>Hitori</u> shika imasen.
   1. ima okane o takusan motte iru, 500-en   2. yoku renshū dekita, 1-jikan   3. nan demo taberu, yasai   4. ano toshokan wa dare demo riyō dekiru, 15-sai ijō no hito

Short Dialogue

A: Kaigi no uketsuke ga hitori tarinai n desu ga, asatte tetsudai ni korareru hito wa inai deshō ka.
B: Watashi de yokereba o-tetsudai shimasu.
A: Tasukari masu. Zehi onegai shimasu.

Quiz

I. Read this lesson's Opening Dialogue and answer the following questions.
 1. Chan-san wa donna toshokan ga suki desu ka.   2. Kono toshokan wa hirokute shizuka desu ka.   3. Hon o karitai hito wa dō sureba kariraremasu ka.   4. Toshokan dewa shimbun ya zasshi mo kariraremasu ka.

II. Put the appropriate words in the parentheses.
 1. Kaiin shika sono supōtsu kurabu o riyō dekimasen ka./Iie, dare (　) riyō dekimasu.
 2. Kono heya wa hiroi (　) kireida (　), kimochi ga ii.   3. Kono hana wa Jonson-san kara Keiko-san (　) no purezento desu.   4. Koko (　) Ginza (　) donogurai kakarimasu ka./15-fun (　) ikemasu yo.   5. Yūbe wa 1-jikan (　) benkyō shimasen deshita. 6. Samui kedo kūki ga warui (　), mado (　) akemashō.

III. Without changing the level of politeness, convert the following verbs into the potential form.
 1. machimasu 2. kakimasen 3. hanashimasu 4. yakusoku shimasen 5. iimasen 6. erabimasu 7. utau 8. awanai 9. wasurenai 10. kiru (wear) 11. mottekuru 12. yasumanai

IV. Complete the questions so that they fit the answers.
 1. (　) oyogemasu ka./100-mētoru gurai oyogemasu.   2. Tsugi no kaigi wa (　) ga ii desu ka./Itsu demo kekkō desu.   3. (　) ni ikeba kaemasu ka./Depāto de utte imasu yo.   4. (　) kyō wa hayaku kaeru n desu ka./Tsuma no tanjōbi na node, hayaku kaerimasu.

V. Complete the sentences with the potential form of the verbs indicated.
1. Koko wa chūsha kinshi na node, kuruma wa ( ). (tomemasen)   2. Sukī ni itte kega o shita node ( ). (arukimasen)   3. 1-nen ni nan-nichi kaisha o ( ) ka. (yasumimasu) 4. Rainen ( ) ka. (sotsugyō shimasu)   5. Ima sugu ( ) ka. (dekakemasu)   6. Howaito-san wa misoshiru ga ( ) ka? (tsukurimasu)   7. Uketsuke ni aru denwa wa ( ) ka. (tsukaimasu) 8. Doko ni ikeba oishii sushi ga ( ) ka. (tabemasu)   9. Shiken ni gōkaku shinakere ba, kono daigaku ni ( ). (hairimasen)   10. Terebi de Nihon no furui eiga ga ( ). (mimasu)

VI. Answer the following questions.
1. Anata wa Furansu-go ga hanasemasu ka.   2. Anata wa kanji ga ikutsu gurai yomemasu ka.   3. Anata wa yūbe yoku neraremashita ka.   4. Anata wa Nihon-go no jisho ga hikemasu ka.   5. Anata wa Nihon-go de tegami ga kakemasu ka.

20. CHERRY BLOSSOMS

Sakura zensen to iu kotoba o kiita koto ga arimasu ka.

Nihon no haru o daihyō suru hana wa nan to itte mo sakura deshō. Hito-bito wa haru ga chikazuku to, sakura no saku hi o yosoku shitari, tomodachi to o-hanami ni iku hi o yakusoku shi-tari shimasu.

Tokorode, Nihon wa minami kara kita e nagaku nobite iru shima-guni desu. Kyūshū, Shikoku, Honshū, Hokkaidō dewa, zuibun kion no sa ga arimasu kara, sakura no saku hi mo sukoshi-zutsu kotonatte imasu. Kyūshū no nambu dewa, 3-gatsu no sue goro sakimasu ga, Hokkaidō dewa 5-gatsu no hajime goro sakimasu. Kono yō ni yaku 40-nichi mo kakatte, Nihon rettō o minami kara kita e hana ga saite iku yōsu o sen de arawashita mono ga sakura zensen desu.

Sakura zensen no hoka ni ume zensen ya tsutsuji zensen nado no hana zensen mo arimasu. Ume wa sakura yori zutto hayaku Kyūshū o shuppatsu shimasu ga, Hokkaidō ni tsuku no wa daitai sakura to onaji koro desu. Desukara, 5-gatsu no jōjun kara chūjun ni kakete Hokkaidō e ryokō sureba, ichido ni haru no hana ga mirareru no desu. Kore to wa hantai ni, aki ni naru to, kōyō zensen wa yama no ki-gi o aka ya kiiro ni somenagara, kita kara minami e susunde ikimasu.

Hito-bito wa haru niwa o-hanami, aki niwa momiji-gari nado o shite, kisetsu o tanoshimimasu.

Quiz

I. Read this lesson's opening passage and answer the following questions.
1. Nihon no haru o daihyō suru hana wa sakura desu ka, tsutsuji desu ka.   2. Nihon-jin wa haru ni naru to yoku nani o shimasu ka.   3. Kyūshū no nambu dewa itsugoro sakura ga saki-masu ka.   4. Kyūshū dewa sakura to ume to dochira ga saki ni sakimasu ka.   5. Hokkaidō dewa itsugoro ume ga sakimasu ka.   6. Sakura zensen to iu no wa nan desu ka.   7. Kōyō zensen mo minami kara kita e susumimasu ka.

II. Anata no kuni no kisetsu ni tsuite kaite kudasai.

二十課　桜　前　線

　桜前線という言葉を聞いたことがありますか。
日本の春を代表する花は何といっても桜でしょう。人々は春が
近づくと、桜の咲く日を予測したり、友達とお花見に行く日を約
束したりします。
　ところで、日本は南から北へ長く延びている島国です。九州、
四国、本州、北海道ではずいぶん気温の差がありますから、桜の
咲く日も少しずつ異なっています。九州の南部では、三月の末ご
ろ咲きますが、北海道では五月の始めごろ咲きます。このように
約四十日もかかって、日本列島を南から北へ花が咲いていく様子
を線で表したものが桜前線です。
　桜前線のほかに梅前線やつつじ前線などの花前線もあります。
梅は桜よりずっと早く九州を出発しますが、北海道に着くのはだ
いたい桜と同じころです。ですから、五月の上旬から中旬にかけ
て北海道へ旅行すれば、一度に春の花が見られるのです。これと
は反対に、秋になると、紅葉前線は山の木々を赤や黄色に染めな
がら、北から南へ進んでいきます。
　人々は春にはお花見、秋には紅葉狩りなどをして、季節を楽し
みます。

271

ジョンソン　うん、まあ。

ジョンソン　友達に花を送ろうと思うんですが、お願いできます
　　　　　　か。

花　　屋　はい。お届けですね。できます。何日のお届けでし
　　　　　　ょうか。

ジョンソン　あした届けてください。

花　　屋　かしこまりました。

ジョンソン　このばらはいくらですか。

花　　屋　一本二百五十円です。

ジョンソン　じゃ、これを二十本お願いします。誕生日のプレゼ
　　　　　　ントにするつもりですから、このカードをつけて届
　　　　　　けてくれませんか。

花　　屋　はい。お届け先はどちらですか。

ジョンソン　横浜です。

花　　屋　送料が五百円かかりますが、よろしいですか。

ジョンソン　ええ。じゃ、お願いします。

十九課　図　書　館

チャン　　あれは何ですか。

大　介　　図書館です。

チャン　　だれでも利用できますか。

大　介　　ええ、もちろんです。だれでも入れますよ。あそこ
　　　　　　は自分で本を取って見られますから、とても利
　　　　　　用しやすいですよ。

チャン　　それは、いいですね。僕はカードを見て選ぶのは苦
　　　　　　手なんです。

大　介　　でもチャンさんは漢字が読めるでしょう。

チャン　　ええ、意味は分かります。でも僕は自分で本を見な
　　　　　　がら選べる図書館が好きなんです。

大　介　　ちょっと不便な所にあるけど、広いし静かだし、い
　　　　　　いですよ。

チャン　　本を借りたりコピーしたりすることもできますか。

大　介　　ええ。手続きをすれば借りられます。僕も今二冊借
　　　　　　りています。

チャン　　新聞や雑誌も借りられますか。

大　介　　いいえ、本しか借りられません。でも、新聞や雑誌
　　　　　　はコピーを頼めます。二、三分で行けますから、こ
　　　　　　れから一緒に行きませんか。

林　できれば、そうしてください。六時になると表の入口は閉まります。反対側に回ると裏口がありますから、そこから入ってください。

山川　わかりました。

林　裏口は十時まで開いています。じゃ、よろしくお願いします。

十七課　大みそかとお正月

十二月三十一日（水）晴れのち曇り

今日は大みそかだ。隣の大野さんのうちでは、朝から家族全員で掃除をしていた。みんなで塀や車や、そして犬まで洗っていた。

午後は日本語で年賀状を書いたが、字が下手だから読みにくいだろう。夕方、田中さん一家とそばを食べに行った。

夜はふだんはあまり見ないテレビを見た。チャンネルを次々に変えると、騒がしいショーや侍の時代劇をやっていた。三チャンネルではベートーベンの『第九』を演奏していた。先日、中村さんが「毎年、十二月になると日本各地で『第九』を演奏するんですよ」と言っていたが、おもしろい国だ。

一月一日（木）晴れ

日本で新年を迎えた。町は人も車も少なくて、たいへん静かだ。工場も会社も休みなので、いつもは汚れている東京の空が、今日はきれいで気持ちがいい。近所の店もスーパーもみんな休みだった。あのラッシュアワーのサラリーマンや学生はどこに行ったのだろうか。

日本人の同僚や友達から年賀状が届いた。業者からも来た。印刷のものが多いが、筆で書いたものもある。やはり美しい。もらった年賀状はほとんど全部くじ付きである。

十八課　花を送る

ジョンソン　鈴木さん、ちょっと。

鈴木　何でしょう。

ジョンソン　日本の習慣を知らないので教えてくださいませんか。友達の誕生日に花をあげようと思うんですが、おかしくないですか。

鈴木　女の人ですか。

ジョンソン　ええ、でも特別の友達ではないんですが・・・。

鈴木　おかしくないですよ。大丈夫です。デートですか。

ジョンソン　いいですねえ。

十五課　預かりもの

ブラウン　きのうスポーツクラブに行ったら山本さんに会いました。

渡辺　山本さん？　おとといここに来た山本さんですか。

ブラウン　ええ、彼もそこの会員だと言っていました。

渡辺　あっ、そうそう、山本さんが傘を忘れて帰りましたが、どうしましょうか。

ブラウン　私がその傘を預かりましょう。また会うかもしれませんから。今度スポーツクラブへ行く時、持っていきます。

渡辺　じゃ、これ、お願いします。

ブラウン　山本さんに会ったら渡します。もし会わなかったら受付に預けます。

受付　おはようございます。

ブラウン　おはようございます。山本太郎さんは今日来ますか。

受付　会員の山本様ですね。今日は山本様は夕方六時にいらっしゃいます。

ブラウン　そうですか。これ、山本さんの傘なんですが、六時に来るなら、今預けてもいいですか。

受付　はい、どうぞ。

ブラウン　じゃ、彼が来たら渡してください。

受付　はい、確かに。

十六課　早ければ早いほどいいです

山川　もしもし、林部長ですか。こちらは、M設計事務所の山川ですが、ご依頼のショールームの設計ができあがりました。

林　ああ、さっきファックスで図面をいただきました。

山川　何か問題はありませんか。来週から工事を始めれば、来月中にできあがります。

林　そうですね。

山川　もし問題がなければ、早速始めたいと思いますが・・・。

林　年末になると業者も忙しくなりますからね。

山川　ええ。早ければ早いほどいいと思うんですが・・・。

林　すみませんが、始める前にちょっと相談したいことがあるんですが・・・。

山川　わかりました。そちらのご都合がよければ、これから伺います。

チャン　義理のチョコレートです。日本のバレンタインデー
　　　　の習慣です。職場でもよく女性から男性の上司や同
　　　　僚にチョコレートをプレゼントします。

ジョンソン　「いつもお世話になっています。これからもよろし
　　　　く。まゆみ」

チャン　やっぱりギリチョコでした。

ジョンソン　残念でした。

チャン　でも、ギリチョコをたくさんもらった人はどうする
　　　　んでしょうか。

ジョンソン　たぶん奥さんやガールフレンドが食べるんでしょ
　　　　う。

チャン　じゃ、喜ぶ人は女性と菓子屋ですね。

十四課　行司の権限

スミス　わあ、すごい人ですね。

田中　相撲の初日はいつも満員です。人がたくさんいて、
　　　　リンダさんや奥さんがよく見えませんね。

スミス　あ、あそこにいました。ほら、相撲を見ながら焼き
　　　　鳥を食べているのが見えますよ。

田中　さあ、私たちもあそこへ行って、ビールでも飲みな
　　　　がら座って見ましょう。

スミス　ええ、でもこの取り組みが終わるまでここでいいで
　　　　す。うるさくてアナウンスがよく聞こえませんが、
　　　　土俵の上にいるのは？

田中　富士の嶺と桜龍です。

スミス　派手な着物を着て、土俵の上で動き回っているのは
　　　　どういう人ですか。

田中　あれは行司です。

スミス　ああ、ジャッジですね。

田中　ええ、でも黒い着物を着て、土俵の周りに座ってい
　　　　るのが本当のジャッジです。あの人たちは力士の○
　　　　Bで、偉いんですよ。

スミス　じゃ、行司はジャッジではないんですか。

田中　ええ、実は決定権はないんです。

スミス　そうですか。ちょっと納得できませんね。

田中　でも発言権はありますよ。

スミス　それを聞いて安心しました。

275

十二課　旅館の予約

予約係り　みやこ旅館でございます。

スミス　もしもし、来月の四日と五日に予約をお願いしたいんですが、部屋は空いていますか。

予約係り　はい、ございます。何名様ですか。

スミス　二人です。いくらですか。

予約係り　一泊二食付きで、お一人一万八千円でございます。税金とサービス料は別でございます。

スミス　はい、じゃ、それでお願いします。

予約係り　お名前とお電話番号をどうぞ。

スミス　スミスと言います。電話番号は東京〇三ー三四〇五ー三六三六です。そちらは京都の駅から近いですか。

予約係り　駅から車で十分ぐらいです。駅までお迎えに行きますが・・・。

スミス　じゃ、駅に着いた時、電話をしますから、よろしくお願いします。

予約係り　はい、かしこまりました。ご到着は何時ごろですか。

スミス　四時ごろです。

予約係り　はい、わかりました。八時より遅くなる場合は、必ずご連絡ください。

スミス　はい。それで、料金はいつ払いましょうか。

予約係り　恐れ入りますが、内金として一万八千円お送りください。

スミス　わかりました。

十三課　ギリチョコって何ですか

チャン　ジョンソンさん、これ、渡辺さんからジョンソンさんへのプレゼントですよ。きのうジョンソンさんがいなかったので、僕が預かりました。カードもありますよ。

ジョンソン　どうもありがとう。渡辺さんからの贈り物、うれしいですね。

チャン　中身はチョコレートでしょう。

ジョンソン　開けたんですか。

チャン　カードはラブレターかもしれませんよ。

ジョンソン　えっ、読んだんですか。

チャン　ははは・・・。じつは僕も同じものをもらったんです。鈴木君ももらっただろうと思いますよ。

ジョンソン　えっ？　みんなもらったんですか。

チャン　ギリチョコですよ、ギリチョコ。

ジョンソン　ギリチョコって何ですか。

276

田中一郎様

ごぶさたしていますが、お元気ですか。

私は今、家族と一緒に九州に来ています。きのう、前から行きたかった阿蘇山に行きました。すばらしい眺めでした。

私たちが泊まっている旅館の庭で夕べほたるを見ました。前に、東京の料亭でかごの中のほたるを見たことはありますが、自然のほたるは初めてです。ほたるを見ながら旅館の主人と話しました。主人は農薬の使用をやめてから、川がきれいになって、ほたるが増えたと言っていました。

あさって、私たちはここを出て、熊本市内を見物した後、長崎へ行きます。長崎は江戸時代の日本のたった一つの貿易港で、そのころは日本の中で一番国際的な町だったと雑誌で読んだことがあります。家内は日本の歴史に興味がありますから、とても楽しみにしています。

南九州にも行きたいと思いますが、来週木曜日にアメリカ本社から社長が来ますから、それまでに東京に帰らなければなりません。

奥様にもどうぞよろしくお伝えください。

七月三十日

ジョン・ブラウン

十一課　面接

林　中村さんはおととし大学を卒業したんですか。

中村　はい。卒業してから商社に勤めていました。

林　なぜ辞めたんですか。

中村　私の専門の仕事ができませんでしたから、おもしろくなかったんです。

林　どうしてこの会社を選んだんですか。

中村　こちらではコンピューターを使う仕事が多いと聞いたからです。私は大学でコンピューターサイエンスを勉強していました。この会社では私の好きな仕事ができると思ったんです。

林　会社に入ってから一か月研修しなければならないことを知っていますか。

中村　ええ、知っています。

林　それに外国に出張することも多いですよ。

中村　はい、大丈夫です。

林　そうですか。では結果は後で連絡します。

加藤　ラッシュのない所がありますよ。

チャン　どこですか。

加藤　どこだと思いますか。お盆のころの東京ですよ。

チャン　なるほど。

九課　予備校

けい子　あら、ジョンソンさん。

ジョンソン　あ、けい子さん、お出かけですか。

けい子　ええ、これから出かけなければなりません。

ジョンソン　今すぐですか。

けい子　ごめんなさい。今日中に予備校の申し込みをしなければなりませんから。

ジョンソン　予備校？

けい子　ええ。一番入りたかった大学に合格できませんでしたから、来年また試験を受けます。

ジョンソン　そうですか。じゃ、行ってらっしゃい。

けい子　行ってまいります。

けい子　申し込みの書類はこれでいいですか。これ、入学金と三か月分の授業料です。それからサマーコースも申し込みたいと思いますが、後で郵便で申し込んではいけませんか。

窓口の人　郵便でもいいですよ。支払いもわざわざここまで来なくてもいいですよ。銀行に振り込んでください。

けい子　現金書留でもいいですか。

窓口の人　はい、どちらでも結構です。

七課　空港へ迎えに行く

加藤　あしたはジョンソンさんが日本に来る日ですね。

鈴木　ええ、そうです。

鈴木　だれか成田空港まで迎えに行ってくれませんか。

鈴木　私が行きます。時間がありますから。

加藤　今朝頼んだ仕事は今日中に終わりますか。

鈴木　はい、できます。

加藤　じゃ、お願いします。ところで、ジョンソンさんを
　　　知っていますか。

鈴木　ロンドンの事務所にいた人ですね。

加藤　ええ。

鈴木　写真で見たことがあります。

加藤　成田空港に着く時間は十四時五十分です。飛行機は
　　　早く着くこともありますから、早めに昼食を済ませ
　　　て出発してください。

鈴木　はい。ジョンソンさんの泊まるホテルはどこですか。

加藤　渡辺さんが知っていますから、渡辺さんに聞いてく
　　　ださい。

鈴木　はい。

八課　お盆

チャン　八月の十日ごろ京都へ遊びに行きたいと思います
　　　が、新幹線と飛行機とどちらが便利ですか。

加藤　新幹線のほうが便利だと思いますよ。でも新幹線の
　　　指定券はもうないと思います。飛行機の切符もたぶ
　　　ん売り切れでしょう。

チャン　どうしてですか。

加藤　八月の中ごろはお盆で、国へ帰る人が大勢います。
　　　十日ごろから、この帰省ラッシュが始まりますから、
　　　旅行はやめたほうがいいですよ。

チャン　鈴木君も十日に京都の家に帰ると聞きました
　　　が・・・。

加藤　ええ、彼は一か月前に切符を買ったと言っていまし
　　　た。

チャン　そうですか。じゃ、京都まで車でどのぐらいかかり
　　　ますか。

加藤　十時間以上かかると思いますよ。鈴木君は去年は車
　　　で行きましたが、すごい渋滞だったと言っていまし
　　　た。

チャン　日本は人も車も多いですからね。ラッシュのない所
　　　へ行きたいですねえ。

五課　新しいワープロ

林　　ワープロのカタログがたくさんありますね。

チャン　ええ、きのうセールスの人がくれました。うちの課のワープロが古くなりましたから、新しいのに変えたいです。

林　　ほう、どれにしますか。

チャン　A社の45Sが安くなりましたが、まだ決めていません。

林　　ところで、システム部の小川さんに話しましたか。

チャン　いいえ、まだ話していません。

林　　ちょっとまずいですね。まず小川さんと相談してから決めてください。

チャン　わかりました。

鈴木　あ、新しいワープロが来ましたね。

チャン　ええ。これは使い方が簡単ですし、画面も大きいですし、いいですよ。

鈴木　ぼくもこんなワープロがほしいなあ。

六課　早退

加藤　顔色がよくありませんね。風邪ですか。

チャン　ええ、おととい医者に行って薬をもらってきましたが、なかなかよくなりません。今朝は熱が三十八度ありました。

加藤　それじゃ、早くうちに帰って休んだほうがいいですよ。

チャン　でも、このプロジェクトが始まったばかりですから・・・。

加藤　無理をしないほうがいいですよ。来週はもっと忙しくなりますから、今のうちに治したほうがいいですよ。

チャン　それでは申し訳ありませんが、鈴木君か木村君に後をよく頼んでから、帰ります。

加藤　鈴木君にはさっき別の用事を頼みましたから、木村君のほうがいいですよ。

チャン　わかりました。では、お先に失礼します。

加藤　お大事に。

280

三課　スポーツクラブで

ブラウン　あのう、ちょっとお願いします。こちらのスポーツクラブに申し込みをする前に、中を見ることができますか。

クラブの人　はい。失礼ですが、どちら様でしょうか。

ブラウン　ブラウンです。

クラブの人　ブラウン様ですか。では、ご案内しましょう。

ブラウン　とても広くてきれいな所ですね。

クラブの人　こちらのテニスコートにはコーチがいますから、コーチに習うこともできます。こちらは温水プールで、一年中泳ぐことができます。

ブラウン　こちらではみんないろいろなマシーンを使っていますね。

クラブの人　ええ。どれでもお好きなものを使うことができますが、始める前にインストラクターにご相談ください。

ブラウン　ええ、そうします。

クラブの人　いかがでしたか。

ブラウン　とても気に入りました。申込書がありますか。

クラブの人　はい。こちらにお名前とご住所をお書きください。

四課　出　張

木　村　ブラウンさん、出張ですか。

ブラウン　ええ、あしたから札幌支店に出張です。木村さんは北海道に行ったことがありますか。

木　村　ええ、学生のころ一度北海道へ旅行に行ったことがあります。車で北海道を回りました。

ブラウン　札幌はどんな所ですか。

木　村　札幌の町はにぎやかで、なかなかおもしろいですよ。ブラウンさんは初めてですか。

ブラウン　ええ、写真を見たことはありますが、行ったことはありません。

木　村　一人で出張ですか。

ブラウン　加藤さんも一緒です。二人で札幌市内の取引先を回ったり、銀行にあいさつに行ったりします。

木　村　加藤さんは住んでいたことがありますから、札幌をよく知っていますよ。

ブラウン　そうですか。安心しました。

一課　通勤ラッシュ

チャン　今朝初めて電車で会社に来ました。とても込んでいました。すごかったですよ。

スミス　でも電車のほうが車より速いですよ。道が込んでいますから。

チャン　スミスさんは毎日何で会社に来ますか。

スミス　私は行きも帰りも地下鉄です。東京の交通機関の中で地下鉄が一番便利ですよ。

チャン　地下鉄は朝も夕方も込んでいますか。

スミス　ええ。でも朝のほうが夕方より込んでいます。朝の八時半ごろがピークですから、私は毎朝七時にうちを出ます。

チャン　その時間はすいていますか。

スミス　ええ、七時ごろは八時ごろよりすいています。私は毎朝地下鉄の中で日本語を勉強しています。

チャン　そうですか。

二課　忘れ物

チャン　すみません。

駅員　はい、何でしょうか。

チャン　忘れ物をしました。

駅員　どの電車ですか。

チャン　二十分ぐらい前の電車で、後ろから二番目の車両です。

駅員　何を忘れましたか。

チャン　黒くて大きい紙の袋です。

駅員　中身は何ですか。詳しく説明してください。

チャン　マフラーとセーターです。マフラーはウールで、黒と白のしまの模様です。セーターは赤くて、胸に馬の模様があります。

駅員　今東京駅に電話をかけて聞きますから、ちょっと待ってください。

チャン　すみません。

駅員　ありました。東京駅の事務室に届いていますから、今日中に取りに行ってください。

282

KODANSHA INTERNATIONAL DICTIONARIES

Easy-to-use dictionaries designed for non-native learners of Japanese.

ふりがな和英辞典
KODANSHA'S FURIGANA
JAPANESE-ENGLISH DICTIONARY
The essential dictionary for all students of Japanese.
  • Furigana readings added to all Kanji   • Comprehensive 16,000-word basic vocabulary
Vinyl binding, 592 pages, ISBN 4-7700-1983-1

ふりがな英和辞典
KODANSHA'S FURIGANA
ENGLISH-JAPANESE DICTIONARY
The essential dictionary for all students of Japanese.
  • Furigana readings added to all Kanji   • Comprehensive 14,000-word basic vocabulary
Vinyl binding, 728 pages, ISBN 4-7700-2055-4

ポケット版　ローマ字和英辞典
KODANSHA'S POCKET ROMANIZED
JAPANESE-ENGLISH DICTIONARY
Easy-to-use and convenient, an ideal pocket reference for beginning and intermediate students, travelers, and business people.
  • 10,000-word vocabulary.   • Numerous example sentences.
Paperback, 480 pages, ISBN 4-7700-1800-2

ローマ字和英辞典
KODANSHA'S ROMANIZED JAPANESE-ENGLISH DICTIONARY
A portable reference written for beginning and intermediate students of Japanese.
  • 16,000-word vocabulary.   • No knowledge of *kanji* necessary.
Vinyl binding, 688 pages, ISBN 4-7700-1603-4

ポケット版　教育漢英熟語辞典
KODANSHA'S POCKET KANJI GUIDE
A handy, pocket-sized character dictionary designed for ease of use.
  • 1,006 *shin-kyoiku kanji*.   • 10,000 common compounds.
  • Stroke order for individual characters.
Paperback, 576 pages, ISBN 4-7700-1801-0

常用漢英熟語辞典
KODANSHA'S COMPACT KANJI GUIDE
A functional character dictionary that is both compact and comprehensive.
  • 1,945 essential *joyo kanji*.   • 20,000 common compounds.
  • Three indexes for finding *kanji*.
Vinyl binding, 928 pages, ISBN 4-7700-1553-4

日本語学習使い分け辞典
EFFECTIVE JAPANESE USAGE GUIDE
A concise, bilingual dictionary which clarifies the usage of frequently confused Japanese words and phrases.
  • Explanations of 708 synonymous terms.   • Numerous example sentences.
Paperback, 768 pages, ISBN 4-7700-1919-X

Japanese Language Learning Materials from Kodansha International

NHKラジオ日本「やさしい日本語」 全4巻
LET'S LEARN JAPANESE   *Nobuko Mizutani, Ph.D.*
Basic Conversation Skills

A four-volume series of easy lessons in practical conversational Japanese from NHK's popular Radio Japan language program. Audio cassettes of the broadcasts are also available for individual or classroom study.

Volume I:	Text	paperback, 136 pages	ISBN 4-7700-1711-1
	Tapes	three audio cassettes, 195 mins.	ISBN 4-7700-1741-3
Volume II:	Text	paperback, 136 pages	ISBN 4-7700-1784-7
	Tapes	three audio cassettes, 195 mins.	ISBN 4-7700-1785-5
Volume III:	Text	paperback, 136 pages	ISBN 4-7700-1786-3
	Tapes	three audio cassettes, 195 mins.	ISBN 4-7700-1787-1
Volume IV:	Text	paperback, 152 pages	ISBN 4-7700-1788-X
	Tapes	three audio cassettes, 195 mins.	ISBN 4-7700-1789-8

ハンディ・ジャパニーズ
HANDY JAPANESE!   *Tom Gally*
Surviving with the Basics

Teaches enough language skills to communicate in everyday situations. Ideal for travelers, business people, and beginning students.

Paperback with audio cassette, 160 pages, ISBN 4-7700-1748-0

日本語で歌おう！
SING JAPANESE!   *Peter Tse*
The Fun Approach to Studying Japanese

Learn to croon popular Japanese standards with this innovative guide to the world of *karaoke*. Includes a 60-min. prerecorded cassette with twelve songs. For beginners and intermediate students.

Paperback with audio cassette, 168 pages, ISBN 4-7700-1866-5

モジュール学習　コミック日本語講座
DO-IT-YOURSELF JAPANESE THROUGH COMICS
Kazuhiko Nagatomo, Miho Steinberg

Twelve manga-illustrated modules cover all the main elements of basic Japanese. Companion cassette tape available separately.

Text; paperback, 112 pages, ISBN 4-7700-1935-1 / Tape; 40-minute cassette tape, ISBN 4-7700-1930-0

新聞の経済面を読む
READING JAPANESE FINANCIAL NEWSPAPERS
Association for Japanese-Language Teaching

An innovative and comprehensive textbook for business people who need direct access to the financial pages of Japanese newspapers.

Paperback, 388 pages, ISBN 0-87011-956-7

敬語読本
MINIMUM ESSENTIAL POLITENESS   *Agnes M. Niyekawa*
A Guide to the Japanese Honorific Language

Explains how to use polite and honorific Japanese, emphasizing how to avoid unintentional rudeness. Indispensable for business and everyday conversation.

Paperback, 168 pages, ISBN 4-7700-1624-7

Innovative Workbooks for Learning Japanese Kana & Kanji.

ひらがながんばって！
HIRAGANA GAMBATTE! *Deleece Batt*
An entertaining and effective illustrated workbook for younger learners. Clever mnemonic devices make learning the *hiragana* syllabary fun and easy.
Paperback, 112 pages, ISBN 4-7700-1797-9

カタカナがんばって！
KATAKANA GAMBATTE! *Deleece Batt*
This new, interactive workbook teaches *katakana* with *manga*-style art and nearly 100 mini-articles on Japanese society and culture.
Paperback, 112 pages, ISBN 4-7700-1881-9

ひらがな
LET'S LEARN HIRAGANA *Yasuko Kosaka Mitamura*
A well-tested, step-by-step program for individual study of the *hiragana* syllabary.
Paperback, 72 pages, ISBN 0-87011-709-2

カタカナ
LET'S LEARN KATAKANA *Yasuko Kosaka Mitamura*
The companion volume for learning the *katakana* syllabary used for foreign words and new terms.
Paperback, 88 pages, ISBN 0-87011-719-X

速習かなワークブック
KANA FOR BUSY PEOPLE *Association for Japanese-Language Teaching*
Through simultaneous use of the eyes, ears and hands, this text and audio cassette tape makes learning *kana* easier for adult beginners.
Paperback with audio cassette, 80 pages, ISBN 4-7700-1616-6

はじめての漢字ブック
KANJI FROM THE START *Martin Lam and Kaoru Shimizu*
A basic-level reader which teaches *kanji* reading and writing skills in 12 graded lessons. Includes a grammar glossary and index, and Japanese-English and English-Japanese word lists.
Paperback, 372 pages, ISBN 4-7700-1936-X

常用漢字完全ガイド
THE COMPLETE GUIDE TO EVERYDAY KANJI
Yaeko S. Habein and Gerald B. Mathias
An exhaustive guide to the 1,945 most frequently used Sino-Japanese characters in the Japanese language.
Paperback, 344 pages, ISBN 4-7700-1509-7

KODANSHA NIHONGO FOLKTALES SERIES
やさしい日本語教室シリーズ

Hiroko C. Quackenbush, Series Editor
An innovative series of colorfully illustrated readers for practicing the *hiragana* syllabary. Each story is presented in Japanese, and includes an English translation and notes on usage and culture.

ANIMAL FABLES　イソップどうわ
A series of traditional European folk tales told in Japanese offer a fun way to master *hiragana*.
Paperback, 32 pages, ISBN 4-7700-1794-4

CINDERELLA　シンデレラ
The familiar story of Cinderella is told in Japanese for those not so familiar with *hiragana*.
Paperback, 32 pages, ISBN 4-7700-1796-0

THE GRATEFUL CRANE　つるのおんがえし
A beautiful young girl brings a series of miracles to a poor farmer and his wife.
Paperback, 32 pages, ISBN 4-7700-1761-8

MOMOTARO, THE PEACH BOY　ももたろう
An old couple find an amazing baby boy in a giant peach.
Paperback, 32 pages, ISBN 4-7700-1760-X

THE RUNAWAY RICEBALL　おむすびころりん
A kindly old farmer finds a kingdom of mice and it leads to adventure.
Paperback, 32 pages, ISBN 4-7700-1762-6

THE STORY OF SNOW WHITE　しらゆきひめ
A familiar fairy tale told in Japanese for those not so familiar with *hiragana*.
Paperback, 32 pages, ISBN 4-7700-1795-2

The best-selling language course is now even better!

改訂版　コミュニケーションのための日本語　全3巻

JAPANESE FOR BUSY PEOPLE　Revised Edition

Association for Japanese-Language Teaching (AJALT)

The leading textbook for conversational Japanese has been improved to make
it easier than ever to teach and learn to speak Japanese.

- Transition to advancing levels is more gradual.
- English-Japanese glossary added to each volume.
- Short *kanji* lessons introduced in Volume I.
- Clearer explanations of grammar.
- Shorter, easy-to-memorize dialogues.

Volume I

Teaches the basics for communication and provides a foundation for further study.

- Additional appendices for grammar usage.

Text	paperback, 232 pages	ISBN 4-7700-1882-7
Text / Kana Version	paperback, 256 pages	ISBN 4-7700-1987-4
Tapes	three cassette tapes (total 120 min.)	ISBN 4-7700-1883-5
Compact Discs	two CD's (total 120 min.)	ISBN 4-7700-1909-2
Workbook	paperback, 184 pages	ISBN 4-7700-1907-6
Workbook Tapes	two cassette tapes (total 100 min.)	ISBN 4-7700-1908-4
Japanese Teacher's Manual	paperback, 160 pages	ISBN 4-7700-1906-8

Volume II & Volume III

Teaches the basic language skills necessary to function in a professional environment.

- Original Volume II has been divided into two separate volumes.
- New, larger type size is easier to read

Volume II

Text	paperback, 288 pages	ISBN 4-7700-1884-3
Tapes	three cassette tapes (total 200 min.)	ISBN 4-7700-1885-1

Volume III

Text	paperback, 248 pages	ISBN 4-7700-1886-X
Tapes	three cassette tapes (total 200 min.)	ISBN 4-7700-1887-8

KANJI in order of introduction

11 百	12 千	13 万	14 日	15 月	16 火	17 水	18 木	19 金	20 土	JI
30 車	31 分	32 前	33 大	34 東	35 京	36 駅	37 話	3	38 見	
50 内	51 銀	52 知	5	53 課	54 古	55 新	56 安	57 部	6	
69 出	70 発	8	71 都	72 思	73 家	74 聞	75 言	9	76 子	
11	88 村	89 商	90 多	91 好	92 外	93 国	12	94 屋	95 何	
106 飲	107 終	108 上	109 動	110 黒	111 心	15	112 員	113 帰	114 持	
125 午	126 書	127 先	128 毎	129 少	130 生	18	131 友	132 花	133 送	
144 春	145 南	146 北	147 秋	148 々	JBP III	Lesson 1	149 始	150 若	151 物	
4	162 高	163 有	164 作	165 品	166 買	167 使	5	168 務	169 遠	
180 運	181 道	182 切	183 計	184 画	8	185 建	186 集	187 小	188 米	
199 活	200 利	11	201 返	202 様	203 最	204 目	205 場	206 理	12	
217 遅	218 束	219 進	220 配	221 急	15	222 働	223 関	224 係	225 世	
18	236 段	237 符	238 歌	239 不	240 音	19	241 売	242 反	243 感	